MUSICIAN

MUSICIAN

A HOLLYWOOD JOURNAL

*Of wives, women, writers,
lawyers, directors, producers
and music*

by Lyn Murray

Introduction by Norman Corwin

Lyle Stuart Inc. Secaucus, New Jersey

Published by Lyle Stuart Inc.
120 Enterprise Ave., Secaucus, N.J. 07094
In Canada: Musson Book Company
a division of General Publishing Co. Limited
Don Mills, Ontario

Library of Congress Cataloging-in-Publication Data

Murray, Lyn, 1909–
  Musician : a Hollywood journal.

  Includes index.
  1. Murray, Lyn, 1909–   . 2. Composers—United
States—Biography. 3. Hollywood (Los Angeles, Calif.)
I. Title.
M1410.M965A3   1987   780'.92'4 [B]   86-30030
ISBN 0-8184-0432-9

For Joyce and Ann

Introduction

Lyn Murray's journals, which start when he was 37, were written for himself and a few friends. They chronicle a career in media music, set against a canvas crowded with people and events acutely observed.

When I first read examples of his writing many years ago, I was taken by the briskness and energy of his style, and urged him to think of eventual publication. He ignored the suggestion and went on composing and conducting scores, marrying and divorcing women, coping with shamans and bushmen in the jungles of showbiz, selectively loathing lawyers, and sporadically making entries in his register with no thought of getting them into print. Every five or ten years I would see another batch of pages, and I kept harping on him to do something about it. He finally got tired of being pestered, and let his manuscript be seen outside his circle of cronies.

Though Murray is completely unschooled as a writer, his letters and journals are fresh, lively, trenchant, searchingly honest, witty, and sometimes wicked in the admiring sense with which one says a pitcher has a wicked fast ball. His account is one that could only happen here. It is made in America, along an axis of Broadway and Hollywood, notwithstanding excursions to London, Paris, Rome, Panama, Samoa and other ports of call.

Every journal is a self-portrait, but this one is also a mural of the times, a diorama of broadcast and film activity seen mostly through staves of music, a mingling of entities and nonentities, a ferment of professional, political, literary, and even religious ingredients.

As the journal opens in 1947, Murray and the second of his four wives, Florence Baker, are about to get divorced. Explanatory comments made during transcription of the text by Murray himself in 1985-86, are enclosed in brackets. The rest is just as it came out of his day book.

NORMAN CORWIN
1986

MUSICIAN

1947

Tuesday February 18

I left Florence.

Hotel rooms are hard to come by and stays are usually limited to one week. Robert Emmett Dolan, an old friend who is composing and conducting music for films at Paramount, got me a cell at the Brentwood Country Club and blarneyed them into letting me stay for a month while I combed the beaches of Malibu for an apartment.

Wednesday March 19

Moved into a tiny apartment on the top floor of a small three-story house at 20832 Pacific Coast Highway owned by Ben and Jean Hughey. Mrs. Hughey is a smart business lady. I am paying $250 a month for an apartment listed at $80 by the Office of Price Administration, a wartime bureaucracy set up to control rents, among other things. The middle apartment is leased to an elegant couple named Kenaston. She was Billie Dove. The lower one—the least desirable because it is separated from a rather aromatic cesspool by only a thin, wooden wall—was empty until I persuaded Gene Lanham to rent it for the summer. (Gene runs the Hit Paraders chorus for me.)

To anyone facing divorce I recommend taking one of Jean Hughey's flats at the beach. One does not lack for company.

Friends rally round to help you decompress, but when you would give your arm for a little privacy, they still keep coming. Sign on a neighbor's house: "Dear friends, we love you but for God's sake CALL before you come down." I thought of putting one up when I met Maria Van Slyke. She is a lady who works in the press relations division of Universal-International, in the New York office, and is here for a week. She is bright, New Yorkey, well-dressed and we lit up like a pair of magnesium flares and in no time were much closer than the Hylton Sisters.

Saturday April 5

Maria is back from New York and we went to the Santa Barbara Biltmore for a little privacy. I am sorry to say that the passion cooled somewhat when the subject of marriage came up. I guess I'm not quite ready for another, although divorce proceedings are under way.

Sunday May 11

Lunched with Bill Schneider at the Beverly Hills Hotel. He's an old pal who works for Donahue & Coe, an advertising agency, and spends his weekends painting. Big talk of compromise of talents. His argument, and I like it: Here we are working for advertisers or networks, buying nice things and living well—and why not? He's 43, I'm 37, and we are slick and good at our jobs and are not really blunted by them. We should now devote one-third of our time to doing what we want. Dig inside your talent and bring up what is there; even if it's no good it doesn't matter. Mozart died at 36. Suppose you are 40 and are to die at 60; knowing what you know at 40 and having 20 years ahead to say it in is not bad. Bill is keeping a journal. Wants to put down how we manage in this business, now that the world is falling apart. He feels he should get some advertising stuff down on paper to answer *The Hucksters* and other books that blackwash his business. On another subject he says the true artist—the one who fights our society, our mores—usually turns bitter. I didn't quite agree with this one.

Saturday May 31

"Sound Off" continues but tonight is my last "Hit Parade." It is going on but I am going off. I started on it in 1938 so I have no complaints.

Saturday June 14

I have been engaged to write music for a radio version of "Philip Marlowe" starring Van Heflin.

Saturday July 26

Mark Warnow, the conductor of "Hit Parade" and "Sound Off," has had a heart attack and I am to conduct both shows until he recovers.

Tuesday August 19

George Zachary, an old director friend in New York, called and offered me "The Ford Theatre," a series of one-hour dramatic shows scheduled to start late in September.

Guy Rennie, an old friend from my Philadelphia days when we both worked on radio station WCAU, introduced me to a lithe and lissome red-headed manic nymph named Nina Bundy.

I accepted the Ford Theatre and Miss Bundy, who is tall, clean, freckled, has a Southern accent and believes in love every hour on the hour, which is fine for a while but can interfere with work.

Wednesday September 3

To New York. Checked into a large suite at the Wyndham Hotel. $14 a day.

Thursday September 4

Jumped out of bed, threw up a window, looked out at the roofs, listened to the noise of the traffic and the big ships blowing in the

North River and felt good. Called Lou Shoobe, my contractor at CBS, to start putting an orchestra together, alerted Lou Robbins, the librarian, and a pair of copyists, called Deems Taylor, Carl Van Doren, Dan Golenpaul, Burl Ives, Dave Terry, Mike Ellis and some other friends, ordered a portable Estey organ delivered to the hotel and arranged to get together with George Zachary, director, and Howard Teichmann, writer. I definitely feel more alive in New York.

Friday September 5

Zachary gave me two scripts, "Ah, Wilderness," to be ready to preview in nine days, and script #2, a version of the Preston Sturges film *The Great McGinty*.

Sunday September 14

"Ah, Wilderness" previewed on schedule and was well received. Howard Lindsay is the host and Kenneth Banghart the spokesman for Ford.

Thursday September 18

Popped up to Boston to see Alfred and Helen McIntyre. Alfred is president of Little, Brown and I had formed a friendship with him and Helen when *Panama Hattie* played Boston in 1940. He seems partial to raffish show biz characters. I stayed in their house at 13 Louisburg Square. On my night table was the manuscript of *B.F.'s Daughter* by J. P. Marquand, whom Alfred edits. He had done his work on the first 50 pages, transposing clauses, changing or eliminating adjectives to such effect that when I got to the unedited pages it all seemed to bog down. The prose seemed lumpy and difficult to read. When I left they asked me to come up for Christmas.

Monday September 22

I can't see myself paying $14 a day to a hotel, but apartments are extremely scarce. Mike Ellis, whom I had met when he was stage manager of *Finian's Rainbow,* found me one. He charmed Norman Pincus, owner of the Alvin Theatre and lots of apartment buildings, into renting me a one-room apartment on the sixth floor of a building at 2 East 60th Street. Sparsely furnished, no rug on the floor, no telephone, an operatic soprano next door and a walk up the five flights. The telephone was difficult but I got one eventually.

Saturday October 4

Miss Nina arrived from Jacksonville, her home town, sprang into action with the charge-a-plate and bought a rug, a table, some lamps and a Simmons Hide-a-Bed. "Ford" opens tomorrow. I had my usual dreams. Concert. We are about to play the Grieg A minor Piano Concerto. The pianist nods—he's ready. I've forgotten the piece. I say, "You start, I'll follow." Another: I am late for a broadcast, get into a cab and say, "NBC. Quick." The driver is slow, talkative, makes wrong turns. When we get there the show has been on for five minutes. #3. I ascend to a small platform at the top of a circus tent. I sit on a piano wire swing and conduct the orchestra from this perch. The musicians are on the tanbark and look like ants.

Sunday October 5

All went well with "Ah, Wilderness" and fortunately I have finished the score for next week. It took 31 writing hours spread over five days at about six hours a day.

Wednesday October 15

The House Committee on Un-American Activities has begun hearings on Communist infiltration into the arts in general and the motion picture industry in particular. I listened to the radio as the committee browbeat a bewildered Bertolt Brecht, and I wrote a letter of protest to President Truman ending with the statement: "I am not a Communist." Tonight to a meeting at Paul Draper's apartment to discuss the subpoenas issued to nineteen "un-friendly" Hollywood personalities.

Wednesday October 22

Attended another meeting at Draper's home. This resulted in
the formation of the "Freedom From Fear Committee," promptly
labeled a Communist front by the Committee on Un-American
Activities. In a taxicab one night Howard Lindsay, the host on the
Ford program who by now had become a friend, made strong
arguments against people in show business joining in political
protest. He felt that the anti-communist crusade was only beginning; any entertainer taking a sympathetic position in public was
asking for trouble. In the case of the Hollywood 19, I argued, I
would rather be with Orson Welles, Thomas Mann, Arthur Rubin-
stein, Norman Corwin, Humphrey Bogart, Lewis Milestone and
Gregory Peck than with Duke Wayne, Sam Wood, Adolph Menjou
and Walt Disney.

During the war Pete Seeger, a private in the army, started
"People's Songs." He was about to leave for the Pacific theatre
where he intended to collect and publish songs sung by the GIs.
Along with Leonard Bernstein, Aaron Copland, Artie Shaw, Burl
Ives, Yip Harburg, Lena Horne and other subversives I contributed $100. I was musical director then of the "March of Time."
When crude mimeographed sheets, bearing melodies and words,
began to arrive from faraway places, we performed the few songs fit
for public consumption on the show.

Wednesday November 19

I went to see how my chorus was doing in *Finian's Rainbow*, now
in the 10th month of its run. It had become sloppy and on Friday (21)
I held a rehearsal to bring them back to a semblance of their earlier
excellence. They had grievances. They were paid $65 for eight
performances. Lee Sabinson, the producer, had promised a $10 raise
if the show became a hit. It had not been forthcoming and I promised
to see what I could do.

Big snowfall, traffic non-existent except for an occasional horse-
drawn sleigh.

A sour note has sounded. I was devoting a great deal of time to
the Ford show and one night quite late, when I was busy scoring,
Nina went for a walk in the snow. She was excited by it. She was

gone a long time: three hours, from eleven until two. When she came home she told of an experience which provoked our first New York row. She had been walking in Central Park, jumping up every now and then to touch the bough of a tree, flicking off the snow. A man saw her, came over and said, "Anyone who can do that has the kind of spirit that appeals to me. Come and have a drink." They went to Reubens and talked for two hours. He was a picture director scouting locations in New York for a week or so and would she go to a play with him sometime? Nina explained about me. She thought I would not object but asked him to come up and meet me. He thought that perhaps I would object and would rather not come up until Nina had told me about him. I said I thought she was crazy to allow a man to pick her up at midnight in Central Park. Didn't she know by now that men have only one thing on their minds? I think she was really shocked that I thought this man might have such designs on her. Such cynical talk was spoiling a beautiful thing and my attitude came from having been married to a promiscuous woman—Carol. Sex is up to the woman. If the man makes a pass and is repulsed firmly you can still be friends. To bolster this argument she quoted her relationship with a Jacksonville business man named Lou Feldman who took her on weekends to Tampa and never suggested sex. (Compared to Nina, who likes to do it every hour on the hour, Carol was a virgin, and as far as Lou Feldman was concerned they probably didn't discuss it, they just did it). When she added a bit of dubious Southern philosophy—If you aren't getting enough lovin' at home it's okay to get it on the outside—I hid her pessary. This blew over as I tried to pay more attention to her and less to my life work.

December

The night of the great blizzard of 1947 we went to a party at Bil Baird's marionette loft in the West Seventies. I played the one string bass while Baird danced and Burl Ives drank seven quarts of beer from the bottle. Julio Diego, the scene painter-soldier-actor-fashion illustrator, was there with his wife Gypsy Rose Lee who made a pass at Nina. Diego, accompanied by Baird on the trombone, sang a song about a chicken from Madrid with the smallpox.

Spent a delightful Christmas with the McIntyres in Boston. The house on Louisburg Square was festive. 110 candles in holly wreaths in the windows were lit each night at dusk and extinguished at bedtime. I warmed my bottom before the crackling logs like an Oxford don and got light-headed on Alfred's perfect martinis. Talking about the Friday afternoon concerts of the Boston Symphony Orchestra, Helen said, "One does tire, eventually, of looking at Dr. Koussevitzky's back." Alfred took me to lunch at the Atheneum Club. Walking across the Common, Alfred pointed out where Mencken had got himself arrested for selling a banned issue of the *American Mercury.*

New Year's Eve to a party at Ann and Dan Golenpaul's where I played the piano for Dorothy Stickney and gave Larry Adler 50 cents I had owed him since 1930.

That year, in Philadelphia, I met Joey Martin, a recent graduate of Borrah Minnevitch's Harmonica Rascals. Martin was an excellent dancer and a harmonica virtuoso. We put a vaudeville act together and went to New York where, not being quite ready for the big time, we slowly starved. One night, standing on the sidewalk in front of the Palace, we noticed that Larry Adler (the other harmonica virtuoso) was headlining a Publix unit at the Paramount. Joey said, "Hey, he's a friend of mine. Let's go see him." We talked our way past the stage doorman, took the elevator up to Adler's dressing room, where Joey introduced me, told him how well we were doing, and hit him for fifty cents. We spent it on two plates of spaghetti with meatballs, rolls and coffee.

In spite of all these seasonable carryings on I was happily turning out a score a week for "Ford".

1948

January, February

Our routine on Sunday, the day of the show, is very pleasant. At eleven o'clock George Wright, who plays piano and organ in the orchestra, rings our bell and we proceed down Fifth Avenue to the Sherry Netherland Hotel for breakfast. Full skirts are in right now, and sometimes George, who is very gay and full of high spirits, drops behind Nina, lifts her skirt, puts his head under it and pretends he is an old-fashioned photographer. The faithful, on their way to or from St. Patrick's, pay no attention. We have a gin fizz and our breakfast and segue to NBC for the rehearsal. I always record the cues and listen to them, with a few members of the orchestra, in the break before the dress rehearsal. One morning the Sherry Netherland restaurant was taken over for a briss, and we had to settle for Longchamps, which we are not fond of, but Stokowski and Gloria Vanderbilt were there. The maestro had them turn off the Muzak.

March

The city is emerging from the grip of winter and something has gone wrong with my right eye. Dr. Britten Payne (ominous name) says I have to go into Doctors' Hospital right away. First, however, I went home and called Howard Barlow to see if he could conduct the next show. He was available. Then I engaged my friend Maurice Gardner to compose the music and checked into the hospital on Gracie Square.

The next morning Dr. Payne had a colleague in for consultation. He shook my hand, said he was glad to meet me, looked in my eye, said, "Operate," and sent me a bill for $100.

My salary on "The Ford Theatre" is $1,000 a week. I paid Mr. Barlow $500 to conduct and Gardner $335 to compose and orchestrate leaving a net of $165. I called William Morris, my agents, and asked them to waive their commission while I was off the show. They compromised and just commissioned the $165. That's $16.50 for William Morris, folks.

I recovered rapidly from the operation, suffering only one minor setback when I got Dr. Payne's bill for $1,500. Incidentally, when I left the hospital I gave my nurse a bottle of champagne and Nina didn't speak to me for a week.

"The Ford Theatre," in spite of presenting beautifully written and directed dramas each week, gets the kind of ratings that cause account executives to blow their brains out. We tried things like doing capsule versions of musicals—George Gershwin's *Girl Crazy* and Oscar Hammerstein's *Carmen Jones*, but nothing helped. A radio version of a play doctor was called in and he diagnosed the trouble right away. He said, "What this show needs is more Betty Grable's legs."

During these last weeks of the Ford show, lawyers in Los Angeles were working out the details of the divorce from Florence. It was decided that she would get 25% of my gross, less agent's commissions, until the children reached the age of 21, at which time that figure would be cut in half. In the event that Florence remarried, her 12.5% would cease. [1986. She has not remarried yet, 38 years later, and is still collecting.]

Towards the end of the run of "The Ford Theatre," Nina's sister Dody joined us. I bought a second-hand Buick Roadmaster, then flew back to California to prepare for "The Hallmark Playhouse," leaving Nina and Dody to drive the car out.

June

Gene Lanham, who took over "Sound Off" when I left to do "Ford," lives in a big house at 23936 Old Malibu Road. There is a small guest house behind it. I rented the guest house and when the ladies arrived from New York, Nina moved in with me. It is another one-room ménage. Dody came down and stayed with us rather often and I found the situation not conducive to writing music. There were blowups about this. Nina was not happy with the arrangement either and we moved into the house I had earlier occupied with Florence and the children at 3257 Blair Drive.

We had the feeling we were starting afresh. We enjoyed the house. Nina, good at it, scrimped, saved, stole and cut corners to get it furnished the way she wanted it. Example: I had a platinum evening watch Carol had given me. I remember it cost $400. Because I almost never wore it Nina wanted me to sell it. She had her eye on a table she wanted to buy. I refused. The table arrived; a lovely round dining room table with its legs cut off to make a big coffee table. My platinum watch was missing. She had sold it for $150. I was mad, not that it did any good. During this time I tried to settle our arguments by trying something new for me—giving in. Nevertheless, during arguments Nina argued she was the one who gave most—that I gave very little. She may have been right;

work came first with me always. The making up was good and
always ended in sex and weeks would go by in complete happiness.

July

"The Hallmark Playhouse" opened. It is directed by Dee
Englebach for Foote, Cone & Belding. The host is James Hilton,
who wrote *Random Harvest, Goodbye, Mr. Chips* and *Lost Horizon*.
The format is similar to "Ford" except instead of presenting Betty
Grable's legs we propose to offer whole stars like Deborah Kerr,
Elizabeth Taylor and the like.

Jimmy Hilton lives frugally considering his wealth, and has no
illusions about Hollywood. He is open, honest and a joy to be with.
Adele Barriclaw, his secretary, lives with him, loves him, takes care
of him and vice versa. The show is done in the Huntington
Hartford Theatre across from the Brown Derby. Our group has
fallen into the habit of a ritual dinner in the Derby every Thursday
after the show.

October

All radio contracts can be cancelled or renewed every thirteen
weeks. Causes a lot of sweaty palms near the end of a cycle. We
have been renewed for another thirteen weeks but the ratings are
good enough for us to feel relatively secure for the season.

Hallmark is hard work—a lot of music every week—but it goes
well. I wish I could say the same about things at home. All is
definitely not well. While we were at the beach there was another
experience similar to the one in Central Park. A man had pulled up
beside her at a red light and asked if she were "so and so." "So and
so" was a girl Nina knew and, struck by the coincidence, she went
to a drive-in for coffee with the man. He asked her to come and
have dinner with him but, she said, she refused. However, she did
meet him the next night and after dinner the man invited her to
come to his apartment, which she said she refused to do. The guy
said if she didn't come up to his apartment he would call and tell
me "the whole story." In reconstructing this later I remember she
was quite disturbed when she got home that night although she
didn't say why. The next day she told me the above version.

Sometimes I think I retain the innocence I was born with, but to me this story was as full of holes as a colander. I told her she was foolish, that you can't go around letting men pick you up. One Thursday after Hallmark, when we were having dinner with Hilton, I told him the story and he joined me in insisting that she exercise some discretion in this sort of thing, especially in California where there are rapes and murders every day.

You thought this was going to be a musician's diary? It's a soap opera.

1949

January

Hallmark goes well. We have made friends with some neighbors. This hill seems to be populated by musicians. Next door lives a bassoon who is a hermit. We never see him. Next door to him lives an oboe from the Columbia Pictures studio orchestra. His name is Harry Schuchman and his wife is Helen. We see a lot of them.

March

Almost a year to the day after the first attack, I am having another flare-up of my eye problem. One of the symptoms is photophobia. You can't stand light. I called Dr. Albaugh and he said to get down to St. Vincent's Hospital right away. I asked Nina to drive me and she said she had something else planned. I don't understand this characteristic in some women. When the man becomes incapacitated they lash out.

Thursday May 12

Tonight on Hallmark a great Thurber story called "You Could Look It Up," with William Frawley. Tonight George Corey and

Betsy Beaton joined Jimmy Hilton, Adele, Nina and me for the after-show dinner at the Derby. Much talk analyzing director Englebach's neurotic drives. Today he was pounding as hard as I've ever seen him. Corey said they take Englebach out of his strait-jacket every Thursday to do the show. One thing I've noticed lately—whenever radio and picture people gather, they analyze. You rarely spend an evening without dissecting some poor son of a bitch or other. Of course, all of us doing the talking are normal.

Some UN people visited the show. One from the Hague, another from Sweden. They were impressed with our timing. No matter how good or how bad American radio shows are, they start and end when the clock is straight up. The Hague man said he liked the music.

Friday May 13

A good day for lunch with Dean Petty and Coulter. Coulter is my business manager, Petty is the lawyer who handled the divorce from my second wife, Florence.

Saturday May 14

Tonight to the Coreys. Present a Mr. and Mrs. Parton and Jim and Barbara Poe. Parton works for TIME and seems cut from Luce's bolt—bright, businesslike and Timey. Poe is a grandnephew or something and is a nice, rather sulky-looking man. After the group left, the Coreys started on the Hollywood pastime—dissecting.

Barbara Poe, daughter of a wealthy New York lawyer, educated in France, saw her parents in summer at Rome, etc., and grew up surrounded by art. She looks like a Julien Levy, nice wide mouth and flat shoes. Here she has worked for the Museum but lately has cut down her activity in its behalf because she doesn't like the director. She and Jim have the usual 1949 troubles. He's being analyzed, her hostility takes the form of urging him to work. Her family bothers him by sending them gifts of cars and things.

Sunday May 15

Lud Gluskin, my friend who runs the music department at CBS, has given me a half-hour comedy to do called "Life With Luigi," a creation of Cy Howard who gave the world "My Friend Irma." Luigi is played by a very good actor, J. Carroll Naish, who has got to be doing it for the money. There are two amusing things to tell about this program. By far the funniest is my salary—$150, to be reduced to $125 during the summer when apparently nobody listens. The other is when I met Cy Howard to get instructions. He said, "I don't want the kind of music where two faggots in New York sit up and say, 'Ah, the oboes!'" We did the first one tonight. Good. Evelyn Keyes was in the audience.

Stopped in to see Joe Losey on the way home. After dinner I played "The Long Name None Can Spell," one of Norman Corwin's wartime radio programs. The power of this work years after the end of the war is disturbing. We are so far from the indignation of this piece. The philistines are drowning Corwin's voice now.

Thursday May 19

Hallmark, "Enchanted Cottage" with Richard Widmark, very good.

May 27

To Martin and Josie Gang's after Hallmark. Martin Gang is Hilton's, and everybody else's, lawyer.

Tuesday June 7

Thursday was the last Hallmark of the season: "I Like It Here," with Paul Lukas.

During the rehearsal I had a note to call Sinatra. Got around to it Friday morning. He is going to do a five-a-weeker with Dorothy Kirsten for Lucky Strike. MCA is going to work out a deal for me to conduct the shows.

Monday, dentist at 11:30. When I got there a message to call Englebach. Big bombshell. He's been fired from Hallmark. Bill Gay is going to direct next season.

Saturday June 11

At St. Vincent's Hospital. The eye again. (Iritis is a recurring problem.) I expect to get out tomorrow. So it shouldn't be a total loss, had the wart on my behind removed this a.m.

Saturday June 25

Got home from the hospital Tuesday. The eye backed up and required drastic measures. I am taking it easy until it functions again. Jeff Alexander did "Luigi" the last two Sundays. I do it tomorrow.

Sunday July 24

Discussions have led Nina to believe analysis will enable her to find herself. We have the old apartment at the beach for two weeks.

Last night I dreamed I was boating with Bill Gay. The rowboat foundered and we both sank interminably. I fought to the surface.

I have started writing at the beach. For Jane Heinemann, who works for a local sheet, I did the story of Fred Allen interviewing a trained eagle. The great bird flew up to the top of a stage flat, turned his back on the audience and dropped a criticism.

I like putting words on paper, and am absorbing information on plotting and construction as fast as possible. I will devote a year to exercising in this fashion in the hope that what talent I may have for writing will cristalize. I'll have to learn to spell first, though.

Wednesday August 3

I have just finished a ten-day course of medication to kill a parasite discovered in my lower intestinal tract. The tests made by Dr. Brigham Bergstrom disclosed presence of undulant fever which Dr. Albaugh, the eye man, says will have been cured by the neomycin I took in the hospital. Also I have anemia.

Last night I had a recurring dream. About the fourth time this year. I am in a plane. There is no partition between the pilot's compartment and the passenger space. The plane loses altitude gradually but with no alarm. Then we fly carefully through a stand of big trees and land safely.

We got back from the beach last Sunday, July 31. We had a very happy time there but Nina embarked on a two-day course of criticism of me mostly voiced in the car. Out of 45 or so remarks addressed to me, about 40 of them were critical. I think the car bolsters her ego. If I go through a red light or make a wrong turn the criticism it draws must assure her she is superior at least in the matter of driving. They were all little things, but they added up to much discomfort. Dody, Nina's older sister, is here with us and possibly it is necessary for N to demonstrate superiority before her. Dody lives in Jacksonville, Florida, and is married to a man named Doc who owns a laundry. He goes to bed a 8 p.m. and rises at 4 a.m. Dody teaches at a Methodist Sunday school and is having an affair with the minister. They meet in a motel, go over the next Sunday's lesson, then attend to what they're there for.

Friday August 5

The Coreys, the Mohrs, the Englebachs, Harry Schuchman and Marie Windsor to dinner. Argument mostly on religion. Judaism: an eye for an eye, a tooth for a tooth because Jews were a minority in pagan lands and had to evolve this religion of survival. The Jew must make his place in the present world, the hereafter matters not. The Christian says eschew material things (this is not to say he practices that), turn the other cheek, bear your troubles, for you will be rewarded in Heaven.

Saturday August 20

Started on the Joan Davis show, Dick Mack director, last Monday. The only bad thing about these shows is you have to sign a five-year contract. CBS says take it or leave it. We did an audition with Humphrey Bogart last Wednesday. Englebach directed. It went fine. Jeff Alexander got the Sinatra five-a-week show and I am glad.

Dream last night. Arthur Q. Bryan, another guy, and I are sitting in an apartment with Elizabeth Taylor. We have to go to the bathroom so we go into the hall. There are two doors. Out of one comes a large, burly, white-clad nurse so we assume that's the ladies' room and go in the other door which turns out to be the men's. Arthur takes out his thing which immediately curves down to the floor and up again. This makes it about six feet long. I don't know what the hell that means. And I don't particularly want anybody to tell me.

Sunday August 21

Went down to the "Luigi" rehearsal this morning at eleven. Had the usual trouble getting through the Methodists on Gower Street and had a little problem parking because of several thousand aircraft workers meeting across the street in the Legion Stadium to decide whether to accept or reject management offers. Driving home through the Cahuenga Pass after the show all the aircraft guys were driving home, too. Thousands of them. I thought all these men are going home to their families probably very relieved that they don't have to strike to get whatever they think is a fair shake from the aircraft industry. Labor is a giant but it is a giant of guys with families. I thought of all the women and children waiting at home, probably scared to death, to hear what the union had decided. You can't convince me that labor is anxious to hang around the house for a few weeks in order to make a point. I had the feeling that this and any other union has enough sane and steady members to balance the few hotheads who behave irresponsibly.

Went to the Ackermans last night for cocktails. Lucille Ball, Eve Arden, Hans Conreid and wife, etc. The Ackermans live in Leland Hayward's house up Coldwater Canyon. Every time we spend some time with Ackerman I get a stronger impression that he is an excellent executive in a business which deals with talent. He has the courage to be a top guy.

Wednesday August 24

Victor Bay, once a violinist and conductor at CBS, comes to my house each week to teach a group of composers and arrangers how to analyze scores. Last night before he began the lesson he told a fascinating story.

Many years ago he was romancing a rich girl who lived with her parents in Pomfret, Connecticut. After a time she took him home to meet them. For a weekend. They got there Friday and a maid told Victor to dress for dinner. He didn't have a dinner jacket with him so he wore a dark suit. All the rest of the men were dressed. Since this was apparently a formal household the next morning Victor put on a suit and a tie; everybody else was wearing sweaters and slacks. That night he put on his dark suit and once again the men were dressed. Next day, since in the daytime the people were informal, Victor put on a sweater and slacks. Everybody else had ties on. Sunday night for dinner he put on his dark suit again and everybody was informal. They liked him, however, and the affair went along normally and ran itself out normally. Now, many years later, he saw in a newspaper that the girl (née Renée Perkins), who had married a professor at a Mississippi university, had strangled their two children and had poisoned herself. She survived, and was put in jail and released after a year when counsel were able to prove temporary insanity. She divorced her husband and is now working as a translator at the United Nations.

Corwin has wired me to come East to do the first of his projected series for the UN. I thought about it, asked permission to miss the first Hallmark and the second Joan Davis (it's commercial now—sponsored by Roi Tan cigars) then begged off. It would be too tough to get the stuff out for the second Hallmark, which is "Anna and the King of Siam." One amusing thing happened in connection with this. I phoned Western Union to wire Corwin my answer and got on the phone a girl who'll go far in that company. I said, "I want to send a telegram to Norman Corwin, United Nations, Lake Success—" She cut in and said, "Wait a minute." She looked up Lake Success, couldn't find it in the Western Union lists and said, "We don't seem to have a station at Lake Success. What state did you say?" I said, "It's in New York just outside of Manhattan, on Long Island." She said, "Do they have a phone?" I said, "They must have a few. It is where the representatives of 135 nations are meeting." She said, "I can't find it listed and if they don't have a phone there will be a 35-cent delivery charge."

Saturday September 10

This past week was the week of openings: Thursday Hallmark, Friday Joan Davis, and Disney called about "Cinderella." I must put all the ramifications of that deal down before I turn in tonight—that is if I can survive this hangover.

Went to a cocktail party given by Joan Davis at the Beverly Hills Hotel. It was very pleasant and lasted till about 4 a.m. I was quite drunk. I remember we all took our shoes off and sang every Rodgers & Hart song we could remember—that is, Mitzi Green and Keith Brown did the singing and Billy Gould and I did the playing.

I got home around five. Loaded. Nina woke up and said, "Don't touch me." Silent treatment next morning. The only thing that seems odd to me about this is that she talks quite gaily to her pals on the telephone and sings in the kitchen and the shower as though she were quite happy. She never did this before. I have made two or three overtures, all firmly repulsed, and I can't figure out what I did. The usual answer, "If you don't know, I'm not going to tell you."

Sunday October 2

Friday night, big party. The Becketts, Ackermans, Alexanders, Schuchmans and Dave Raksin. Beckett talking about the new Medical Center he is building at UCLA. He says in ten years he and his associates will have built $100,000,000 worth of buildings. That is, if the research scientists haven't cracked the air atom by then. Talk of flying saucers being real and manned, and measuring 25 miles in diameter. Last night, Saturday, to Betty Smith's. Very nice party. Met some new people. Notably a woman named Agnes Christine Johnson Daisy. Writes, or wrote, the Andy Hardy series for Metro and is a kind of Philadelphia-ish matron with two or three grown children. Told a funny story about how at the Uplifters Club someone had put a set of upper dentures into one of the guest's coffee. They appeared at the bottom of the cup as the guy drained the coffee. When he had his second cup he was mad because they were not at the bottom of his cup this time.

Mme. Daisy advanced the theory that since men envy women their reproductive capacity, a woman should give more to a marriage—say 75% more than the man. Reverse of Freud's penis envy. Hugo Butler and his wife Jean were there. She is the daughter of the woman who wrote the play the Andy Hardy series is based on. Butler and I had an argument about the effectiveness of Paul Robeson's current tour. Butler thinks Robeson's militancy is right and not at all harmful to the Negro fight for equality.

Today is the first Sunday I have had off in ages. The only good thing I can say about it is that within me I feel urges to compose something more or less serious now that I don't have to go down to the studio to do "Luigi." Jesus, what you do for money.

Heard Benny Herrmann playing Vernon Duke's "Ode to the Milky Way" with the CBS symphony today. Jim Fassett had Duke on in the intermission. Talked about how "Milky Way" came to be written. Duke said he was on a freighter going from Trinidad to Jamaica, looked at the sky and wrote the piece. When Leonard Bernstein played it at City Center at a Veterans concert, Duke changed the freighter to a Coast Guard vessel. He served in the Coast Guard during the war. Wrote to Beany asking him to stay with me when he comes. [Bernard Herrmann.]

Saturday October 29

Nina has been in Jacksonville and New York since the 9th. We are thinking it over. I did not write her for a week and then the letter I did write, including the check, was sent regular mail to J'ville and she didn't get it for almost two weeks. She was rather mad and I don't blame her. Meantime Mike Ellis, one of the stage managers on *Finian's Rainbow*, now a producer of plays, and Paton Price have spent ten days with me here. Mike was out here to look for a steady job after three years of intermittent activity. He produced *The Play's the Thing* last year with Louis Calhern, has a musical and a new Molnar play almost ready but has fallen in love with a 34-year-old English actress named Valerie White. Being of the theatre she yearns for some sense of financial security and is fending him off because he is a Young Man Interested in the Theatre and until a Young Man Interested in the Theatre gets a hit he is likely to be fairly broke. Paton is raising money to build the New Theatre in Hartford, Conn., designed by Frank Lloyd Wright, and is consumed with this dream.

It is good to know someone who is possessed by a dream. I feel that most of us making a living in radio are 50% cynical and if we are not we're fools. Paton, 33, was trained as an actor and director, taught at the American Academy, is painfully thin and has ears that stick out. He had a little plastic surgery performed so they don't stick out quite so much now, but they stick out. He has a theory about friendship: When the relationship stops being current and alive, neither has an obligation to the other. I think he invented this because Kirk Douglas is one of the people who initiated the New Theatre idea but since then has made a big success in the movies—referring to himself as a "$2,000,000 property"—and is no longer so interested in the project.

Finian's Rainbow was in town during Mike and Paton's visit. One of my theatre choruses is in it. I went to see it and was very pleasantly surprised at the cleanliness of the choral work. There are some conscientious people in the group and the pianist in the orchestra takes pride in keeping them on their toes.

Jim Fassett, CBS VP in charge of cultural matters, interviewed Mary Garden in the intermission on last Sunday's CBS Symphony program. She sounds like a tremendously commercial character (she'll sing anything, anywhere—provided the price is right) and Fassett was so affected by the august presence that at one point he committed a choice spoonerism. He asked the great prima donna for her impressions of her first performance in "Meleas and Pelisande."

Mike and Paton and I had some college-type bull sessions here analyzing each other and talking about the problems of art, women and careers. Mike has a unique talent. He lays every dame in show business and, unlike the rest of us, stays friends with them. Miriam Hopkins calls him and writes to him, Erin O'Brien Moore the same. He had two girls from *Finian's* here on separate nights.

Paton ran into Fred Clark, the actor who was so good in *Ride the Pink Horse*, playing a character with a hearing aid, in the Roosevelt bar. When Clark left, Paton picked up a girl with rolled stockings and was in her bed in 30 minutes. A non pro, he says. She has been calling here but Paton reasons that he was drunk when he gave her the number and to hell with it.

Oliver Wallace, the head of music at Disney, invited me to work on two sequences for *Alice in Wonderland*. I found the routine at Disney, when they construct a sequence, fascinating. The musician sits with the writers and artists before an elaborate storyboard. Mr.

Disney was in London making *Treasure Island*, but his presence in the room was palpable. Everyone criticizes and tears apart each frame, playing the absent devil's advocate, making sure the uncluttered storyline moves cleanly and inevitably, so that it might be understood by, and possibly *move*, your average four-year-old moron. These artists and writers were sweating to get into the boss's head, trying to anticipate and forestall his every question and objection. I put some music together and one day, on Mr. Disney's return, we all met in the same room before the same storyboard. Walt (everybody called him Walt) asked questions like, "Why do you have her do that particular move that way?" No one spoke. I broke the silence and explained our thinking. After the meeting one of the regulars said to me, "Those are rhetorical questions Walt asks. You don't answer them. He does." I was fired the day after that meeting. Still, it was fascinating, and the Disney people are nice, and shame me by being creative at eight-thirty a.m.

Sunday October 30

Just had breakfast at the Schuchmans and heard the story of the christening of Sinatra's youngest daughter Tina. The S's were living at Toluca Lake and were under the jurisdiction of the big Valley Catholic church, St. Charles. Frank didn't want the baby christened at all, but Nancy prevailed. They asked Morris Stoloff and his wife to be the godparents. There was a snag, explained to Nancy by a priest. The godparents had to be Catholic.

On the day of the christening a party made up of Nancy, her sister Julie (an excommunicated Catholic), Anthony, a relative by marriage, the Stoloffs, the Schuchmans and Don McGuire, a Jewish actor friend of the Sinatras, arrived at the church and went into the sacristy with the baby. The priest came in and said, "Where are the Catholic godparents?" Nancy's sister Julie and friend Anthony stepped forward. After the ritual Julie accepted the baby, turned to Mrs. Stoloff and said, ignoring the priest, "Here is your godchild."

Frank sold the Toluca Lake house, moved to Holmby Hills and forbade Nancy to enter any of his children in Catholic schools. "They'll go to a public school" said Frank, "like other kids."

Tuesday November 1

Nina has a number of complaints about me. I am not demonstrative enough—that is, I don't kiss her and say, "I love you" enough. I spend a lot of time at work here in the house and to this there is no objection, but when I am finished, Nina gets griped when I read. This argument is that work consumes so much time that what is left is little enough to devote to her. I don't pay enough attention to her at parties. I kiss other women hello, like Adele, Hilton's lady, Rita, Jerry Mohr's wife and a few others who are close friends, and Nina objects to this. She has complained that she does not like my lovemaking when I have been drinking. Also she has complained that when making love sometimes I will retune the radio. This revolts her because lovemaking is a spiritual and sacred thing with her and if I really loved her I wouldn't notice when the radio had switched to something I can't bear. If I finish work at one of the studios early and Nina finds out, she worries about me if I don't come straight home. An incident happened on one of the days I was recording at Disney's. We finished early, I heard the playbacks and drove to Fred Stark's house (the delightful old German Disney librarian) and had a cocktail and examined the little door he had cut in his kitchen to allow his animals in and out. One of the singers told Nina we had finished at 3 or 4 o'clock and Nina was angry because I had not called to let her know I would not be right home. During last summer when Nina was working at the May Company she found it hard to understand that sometimes it was inconvenient for me to come to the May Company and pick her up at 5 o'clock. I believe Nina thought this indicated I didn't love her. We compromised by my buying a small car for her use.

When I met Nina I was very lonely, having left Florence about four months before. The mystery of what I was looking for in a woman was unresolved after Carol (my first wife) and Florence. I had married Florence because she added up to the exact opposite of Carol. It wasn't long before I realized we were not compatible sexually, although she gave me two children, and our houses and apartments were a nightmare of disorganization, badly run and dirty. One of the first things that impressed me about Nina was the way she kept her little apartment and her clothes, and how clean everything, including Nina, was. Since I had been sexually virtually unused for some years (except for an occasional ballet dancer, singer and once, God forgive me, a black maid), our sex was wonderful and frequent. In the first six weeks I found out from Nina she had been married twice. The first time to a man who, if he wasn't a homo, was sexually inadequate. They separated almost immediately. The next was a boy in the service due to go overseas. Nina decided to have a baby by him, fully understanding he might not return. He shipped out and after about four months Nina lost the baby. Even I knew Nina was not constructed for child-bearing. (I remember sitting on a beach at Nassau with Mortimer Rodgers, almost as well-known a gynecologist as his brother Dick is a composer, watching Carol coming out of the water and Morty saying, "I would hate to have to deliver her.") After losing the baby, Nina had an affair with a man named Bill Bundy, skipper of a small Navy ship running in and out of Jacksonville. The sex was good. Nina said she had become proficient partly as a result of an experience with a very knowledgeable Army lad in the Canal Zone and possibly because she had been active in high school in spite of strict and unenlightened parents. (I am not sure what she meant by "unenlightened" since she is one of 13 children. Maybe they didn't know what was doing it.) Nina came to California to join Bundy who had apparently been transferred, but the affair gradually petered out. (That's what happens to affairs.) She said he was an anti-Semite and that was one reason it came to an end. Anyhow, she had a long affair next with a man named Joe Silvers, an orthodox Jew, and I suspect Bundy and Silvers overlapped. Joe loved Nina very much and I know she loved him. Not many days passed during our time together that Joe was not mentioned and, comparatively, he always had the edge. He was in retrospect more demonstrative than I, leading Nina to the conclusion that Jews make more satisfactory lovers than gentiles. The trouble was Joe had a wife and children, and in the end they won. It may be of interest to note that Nina took Bundy as her surname. She was née Higgins.

At the end of our first six weeks Nina had come to the conclusion that I was taking her too much for granted—"a piece of furniture" was the expression she used—and had about decided to end the relationship. That night there was a big party down at the beach in Gene Lanham's apartment. Lanham is a friend and a member of my chorus. Sitting at the bar was a man named Dick Stickney, and before long I noticed big vibrations between him and Nina. I learned from Pixie Rousseau, wife of Bill Rousseau, a Young & Rubicam producer, that Stickney had asked her what our arrangement was. She apparently told him something I had told her recently, that I enjoyed Nina but wasn't sure I loved her. Stickney made his move. A few days later I called Nina for a date and she said she was busy and couldn't see me. I drove into town and waited outside her apartment until she and Dick returned from an evening of dancing. (I don't dance, so he was ahead right there, although he doesn't sound especially Jewish.) When they went in, I went in too. Seeing them together upset me. I left, and on the way home phoned her from a gas station and announced that since she apparently preferred Stickney I would not expect her at the beach that weekend. This had been a standing thing with us. She said that he had left. I went on down to the beach and telephoned again and she said perhaps it would be a good idea if I drove in and we discussed the situation. Next day we had a long talk. I said that since Stickney's competition upset me so much, perhaps I loved her, and maybe we should work out a more permanent arrangement.

No man is a match for female strategy. Nina quit her job and moved into my apartment at the beach. There was nothing but happiness for the rest of the summer; there were no rows and we were very much in love. I had no reservations about it.

Our relationship is based on two things: First sex, terribly important to Nina, so important she has said if she didn't get enough at home she would go outside for it, and I suspect she has. Sex with her is sacred and totally humorless. No fun allowed. The other thing is the house, which is immaculate, well run and very comfortable.

Aside from these two things we have very little conversation, very little fun, almost no cultural pursuits, no exchange of ideas, no discussion of what's going on in the world or an alliance of interests. When we have time to go to the movies she chooses escapist films, nothing serious or what she considers morbid. She never initiates a proposal to go to a play or a concert. Perhaps the fact we are a little strapped for money deters her, but if there was any desire we would find ways and means.

During the past three weeks Nina has been away I have been

thinking all this out and have come to the conclusion that without sex we would have nothing.

1950

Monday February 27

Last Tuesday Nina moved to her own apartment. It was quite amicable considering that our being together was something Nina seemed to want very much. After an initial depression I felt relieved. Saturday I asked her to spend the night. She agreed, and after I finished the Christopher London score (radio show with Glenn Ford—22 cues, count 'em), we went to bed and made some terrific stuff. Then Nina said, "Can you tell me anything?" "Like what?" says I, so she got out of bed and went home.

Saturday July 29

Dreamed I bought a house from Ann Sothern. Nina and I in bed there. Ann and her mother come through. They are still living there—it is a dream overlap. There is some talk and then I start to have a do with Nina who informs me she is a virgin and has the curse.

Everyone I know is in money trouble. Taxes are going up and fees are going down in the disappearing radio business. I am barely able to keep my head above water even with Hallmark, one of the last well paying radio jobs. A kind word here for William Morris. They made me an interest-free loan of $1,000. I am about to do an audition with Joan Davis for television. CBS is producing it and Dick Mack, who produced and wrote her radio program, has been aced out. The money they want to pay is even less than the radio fee—less by $50. I thought TV was where the money was, but not in California.

October

We have two new sets of neighbors on Blair Drive. Harry and Trudy Katz, who bought Peggy Lee and Dave Barbour's house, and Lolly and Jarvis Quayle (or Quail). Jarvis and Lolly are très Republican, he has a woman on the side (Hope said once, "Is that a new way?") and enough on Lolly so she does no bitching except to lady friends. The reason I know all this is because Nina has become very thick with Lolly who looks like a very chic pouter pigeon. They share the same passion for small talk. Jarvis is boring when he is being Republican but I like him nevertheless. Van Cleave, one of the great arrangers, is a dyed-in-the-wool Republican and I love him.

Harry and Trudy Katz. He is a retired business man. She was once married to a son of Rumshinsky's. (Rumshinsky was the prolific composer of Yiddish musicals in the great days of Yiddish Theatre in New York.)

Feeling rather outgoing today, and to avoid starting work, I went next door to have a cup of coffee with Trudy. Must be something about me in this mood. She told me a lot about herself. During her ten-year marriage to Rumshinsky he seldom came home and she finally divorced him. She got a job in a department store and worked up to Buyer. She went out with a lot of men and every time they made a pass she thought to herself, "I left better than you." After a while she stopped playing the field and spent her evenings either working or attending lecture courses. She got her masters at Columbia and was working up to going for a doctorate when she got deflected.

She met a third-generation Harvard chap named Jack Pollack who manufactured a fine line of cosmetics. After six months she decided she didn't like the physical part of their relationship and they began to see less of each other. One afternoon he took her somewhere and she said she had to be home by 5:30, she was going to have dinner with her mother. He dropped her off at her apartment and half an hour later saw her leaving with another man. He called her the next day and complained of her shabby treatment. She felt sorry because he was a decent man and she respected him. She went her way for a while then one day sat down and wrote him a nice letter putting into words her feelings about him and why she had not thought marriage would work for them. Two days later she saw his picture in the paper. He was dead of a heart attack. She wondered if he got her letter. The man's lawyer called—he had introduced them—and asked to see her. He told her that one day in the hospital, when her friend was resting easy, he had the nurse read all the cards and letters he had received, including her's. When they discovered him dead a day or two later her letter was under his pillow.

Thursday November 2

Party at 3257 Blair Drive. Hiltons, Gays, Ballins. At the end of the party I saw everyone to their cars. Jimmy insisted on driving Adele's new Chevrolet. He got in and couldn't find where to put the key. "Put it in for me, Adele," said he plaintively. Then he couldn't find the starter. Adele is not too familiar with the car yet and while she was looking for the starter Jimmy asked, "Have we started yet?"

Sunday December 3

The score for this week's Hallmark play, "Theodore Roosevelt," is finished. I have been remiss about this journal. To fill in some spots during the last months I did a picture for an independent producer named Irving Allen. Sid Kuller did the lyrics. A remarkable fellow, Kuller. He is married to a Mormon and has two children; makes his living writing material for comics, mostly Billy Gray, Danny Thomas, Lessy & Moore, Billy Eckstine, Dan Dailey.

This Irving Allen thing is a western, a pot-boiler so he can make some quick money. His pregnant wife Nita seems to worry more about money than Irving does, but they do own a Renoir. Allen lacks what Hilton calls "superficial charm" and has to denigrate whatever he is working on. Everything has to be a piece of drek.

Tuesday December 19

Met James Caesar Petrillo today at the Ambassador Hotel, the poshie on Wilshire. The meeting was to present arguments why arrangers should retain rights to their work and get paid for its re-use.

Petrillo is a short man with eyes that say he loves a fight. Broad shoulders tapering to narrow hips. A sort of dowager figure without the tits. Blue suit, pearl gray hat sitting squarely on his head. He has a Durante accent and mentions money a lot. He said, "I made mistake and gave the chambermaid too much money for two days. She brought me 45 towels." Somebody said, "Can I carry your suitcase, Jimmy?" He said, "No. It's light. You know what's in there? Towels and $10 bills." Later when someone offered to carry his topcoat he said, "No. It's full of money. Why do I have to fly?" he asked, changing the subject. "I get on the plane and I sit down and some woman says, 'Are you Mr. Petrillo?' and I say 'No, I ain't Petrillo' and she says, 'You certainly look like him' and I say 'Alright, I'm Petrillo' and she says, 'I got a girl plays pianna' and we're off."

When you shake hands with him he offers his little finger. He has a phobia. You link little fingers with him and that's it.

He was getting ready to fly back to New York. We were walking up the path from his bungalow to the hotel proper. Phil Fischer, radio representative of Local 47, was describing some of the in-fighting going on in connection with the approaching union election. He said, "We told the truth in our brochure." Petrillo said, "'At's where you made your first mistake." Crossing the patio I said to him, "I wish the coming negotiations were to be televised. You would win anything you wanted." (Bearing in mind the appearance he made before a senate investigating committee some years ago. He was masterful and humorous. That is one of his great gifts—leavening serious matters with humor.) "Yes," he said, assuming a pose and waving his fist in the air, "If we was on the television I'd give 'em hell."

Saturday December 23

Rehearsing for "A Christmas Carol" at KHJ with Lionel Barrymore, Dick Mack directing. Mr. Barrymore asked us all if we knew Cecil the Seasick Serpent, a character on "Beanie," a children's show. He was proud of a Christmas card he had from Cecil. He said, "I don't know him but he sent me a card."

In the lines about Christmas being a humbug Mr. B's reading of the word "bah" was so expressive Mack said he had been trying for 30 years to write that word the way Barrymore said it. Mr. B said,

"I mean it when I say that word. What is Christmas? Christmas is what you don't get your option picked up two weeks before, or it is when you go on layoff or just plain get fired."

Mr. Barrymore is a composer. He is proud that the Philadelphia orchestra recently played one of his pieces. He told a story about Wagner going to Venice for a performance of one of his operas. Verdi attended, and because Wagner was then very old he resolved to go and see him. He put it off for a few days and then gondola'd over. Someone said he could not see the maestro. Verdi handed the person his card. You still can't see him. Why? He died half an hour ago.

Thursday December 28

Lunch at Lucey's with Irving Allen and Sid Kuller. Allen had finished a picture called *New Mexico*—shot in Arizona. Irving Reis directed it. Allen did the second unit stuff himself. Reis told me that when they ran the dailies there was footage from the second unit that had nothing to do with *New Mexico*. Allen was shooting another picture on United Artists' money. The lunch was to discuss a story Sid was to concoct to fit this footage.

When the script was finished I sat in on a meeting as Kuller and Allen argued about the cast. Allen had a foot buzzer under his desk. Whenever Kuller suggested an expensive actor Allen pressed his buzzer and picked up the phone. During the meeting he talked to Louis B. Mayer, Darryl F. Zanuck, Y. Frank Freeman and Ernest Hemingway. And once, for my benefit, Jan Sibelius. In the pauses Allen vetoed Kuller's suggestions saying, "This part can be played by a $1,000 actor. The guy you want gets $2,000. Look," he said, "why don't you just write the words and leave the casting to me?" Kuller said, "I want to be sure you get the right people to *say* the words." Allen said, "You wanna produce the goddam picture?" and Kuller replied, "I don't work that cheap."

Friday December 29

After dinner at Irving Allen's, Lud Gluskin told Allen he was going to sue Monogram Pictures. Lud's writers (Lud doesn't write) had supplied a score for one of Irving's pictures for that little quickie studio, and it was being released for television. Monogram settled for $500. Prompts me to wonder what ails the composers signing over their rights to Lud? I guess it's a case of either you do or someone else does the music.

1951

Tuesday January 16

Dinner at Cissie Collins's with Benny Herrmann and Vernon Duke. (Cissie lives with Tony Collins, the English composer and conductor. They never married but she is always referred to as Collins.) Duke collects books. Wants to live in Paris. He is here finishing two shows and may do a picture. Benny in the middle of dubbing *Mad With Much Heart* (later changed to *On Dangerous Ground*). Full of anger because in a big chase scene where eight horns are wailing, dogs chasing Ida Lupino drown out the horns. He told Constantin Bakaleinikoff (head of music: RKO) that if the dogs covered up the horns he would withdraw the whole score from the picture. A producer said, "But you've been paid." Benny said, "I haven't cashed the checks." He complains that no one comments on the music. The dubbers just go about their job mixing dialog, sound effects and music and have no interest in anything esthetic. Between the loss of the CBS Symphony and this current experience at RKO, Benny sounds ready to give up music.

Drove Vernon to his brother's house, with Benny, and we argued about the state of symphony orchestras and the practice of conductors buying themselves concerts in Paris. Somebody said Franz Waxman did this and when only 12 people showed up for the first concert he cancelled the second. Benny against buying yourself a concert. Vernon argued that France has a list of good conductors barely making a living so why should France import and pay Americans to give concerts? However he thinks Benny should spend $5,000 and give two sensational concerts of modern music there. Thinks it would lead to a job here.

Benny annoyed with Chicago for hiring Kubelik. "He's a Czech nazi" says Benny. Talked about Johnny Green. All agreed he has "gone over to the philistines." Johnny has referred to Benny as "one of the garret brigade." And Benny getting $18,000 a picture.

I am using Elgar's "Cockaigne Overture" as the basis for the Hallmark score this week. Only the second time I have done this—the first was "Appassionata." Fun and a good way to learn a piece.

Saturday February 3

Met Sid at the studio after the day's shooting on Irving Allen's epic, now called *Slaughter Trail*. Went to the Players for dinner, a restaurant on the Strip owned by Preston Sturges with a small theatre upstairs. While we were having dinner we heard declamatory noises from above. Went up and watched Sturges rehearsing his version of Chekhov's *The Boor,* one of six one-act plays he's going to present over the summer. There were three actors working. Ben Astar, Fritz Ruehe and a Russian woman whose name I didn't get. Sturges was dressed in an old suede jacket and baggy pants. He has plenty of gray hair and drinks a lot. Waiters were rushing him grog all through the reading. He is incandescent and waves his arms about a good deal when giving directions, clapping his hand to his brow and exclaiming. "That's the fortieth time I've told you . . . " etc. Sturges said he was 52.

In one of the intermissions the actor Fritz Ruehe, who looks a caricature of what a musician is supposed to look like—frizzy hair out at the sides, the front part of his cranium very bald—came over and hearing I was a musician said he had a musical hobby. "I whistle," he said, "the flute parts from Mozart." I said, "But the flute has such a great range and the human whistle such a limited one." He looked at me sadly and said, "Ah, that is my trouble."

I inquired about the bathroom and Sturges, the perfect host, went with me. We unbuttoned and relieved ourselves in adjoining urinals. He asked if I could get the quality of the piece from such a rough reading and I assured him I thought it excellent. And it was. I told him I had admired his work for many years and had seen a lot of his pictures over and over and that I thought he was a great man.

He ran out of the can either thinking I was a phony looking for something or maybe he was just embarrassed.

Tuesday February 6

Had dinner with the Corwins and afterwards went with Katie (Norman had to work) to the Cobbs. Lee J. Cobb (don't forget the J.) and his wife Helen, ex actress, live in Beverly Hills. Present were a doctor and wife and the consul of Israel and wife.

Katie has one of her projects on. This one is collecting recipes of celebrities for a cook book Paul Denis is getting together. The one she had picked out for me is called "Andante Canapé," a cream cheese and mushroom thing. She has a questionnaire with space for your comments on eating at the bottom. One such comment, I suspect written by Norman, says, "I consider eating one of the five major indoor sports and recommend it to all." Katie had a dish called "Apricot Piquante" picked out for Lee, but he thought it did not quite fit him.

The consul, Ruven Dafne, was most interesting. He and his English wife are about to return to Israel where they will work on a collective farm. The Israeli Philharmonic is touring the U.S. now, Koussevitzky and Bernstein sharing the podium, and I asked him why they hadn't sent an Israeli conductor. He said our State Department had arranged the tour and had not thought an Israeli conductor would draw. The consul's wife asked Lee if he would go to Israel and play *Death of a Salesman* there. She said he needn't worry about the language, she was a very talented woman and one of her greatest talents was teaching Hebrew in a hurry.

When we were leaving she couldn't see the flagstones across the lawn and said to me, "Extend an arm." All her statements were very definite. Later, when I told this to Norman, he said, "This is the kind of woman who, when she is ready, says to her husband, 'Extend your thing.'"

The doctor, who exuded a sense of well-being (don't these guys ever have any financial problems?) told a story. One by de Maupassant he had read in high school. Two brothers, fishermen, are out one day. As they turn the winch on to haul in the day's catch one of the brothers catches his arm in it. Not wanting to lose the catch the other brother lets the arm get mangled. As it goes into the winch the hurt man hollers, "Merde!" This was translated in the high school edition to "Oh, dear!" which reminded Cobb that when they were doing *Volpone* in Pasadena in which an actor runs across the stage crying "Rape! Rape!" it was toned down for Pasadenans to "Skulduggery! Skulduggery!"

Thursday February 8

Sid, Bobby Justman (Justman père, a lettuce farmer, owns a studio in Hollywood where Sid is making a film) and I to dinner before the Ellington concert at the Capri, an Italian restaurant owned by Eddie Rio. He is the AGVA (American Guild of Variety Artists) rep here. At lunch today the three of us were discussing forming a company with Joe Justman, Bobby's pa, and Sid warned Bobby he would have to learn to make deals with people. Tonight we pull into the parking lot next to the Capri. The fee is 35 cents. We could only muster 30 cents between us, so Sid told Bobby to make a deal with the parking lot lady. He did. She settled for the 30 cents.

The concert is at the Shrine Auditorium. It starts without Duke. He ambles on after a few numbers. We go back to see him in the intermission. He explains he was delayed by a delightful lady interviewing him for a newspaper. He is the most charming man you have ever met. Sid an I want him for a sequence of something we are writing called *Seven Lively Artists*. Sid said to Ellington, "This is for money." Ellington said, "There's so much more adventure in insecurity."

In the second half Ellington introduced one of the numbers as being about the most overindulged form of overindulgence.

Al Hibbler, the blind singer, has got to be one of the most biting of satirists. His biggest number tonight was, "I Think That I Shall Never See a Poem Lovely as a Tree." He has a vocal trick that is highly satirical. He slides down to a very bassy note when he wants to sneer at something. He usually does this on the word "love."

Friday February 9

I had a blowup with Irving Allen. We disagreed on an artistic point concerning the Main Title of *Slaughter Trail* and he an-

nounced that my opinion, and Sid's, did not count and the decision
had been made. He gave in the next day but I decided to hell with it,
I would withdraw. Then he got tricky about the deal. He had agreed
to pay $1,250 cash and a percentage. He maintained that the cash
payment was it—no percentage. There are three songs in the picture
which we have pre-recorded with Terry Gilkyson and Terrea Lee, and
a sort of ballad done by a chorus that goes through the whole picture.
But I am withdrawing from the underscore and we ain't speaking.

Jimmy Hilton lent me a copy of Arnold Bennett's *Journal* and I
am fascinated. He kept a record of the number of words he wrote each
day. In one year he wrote 280,000 words. He lived in Paris where the
atmosphere was more to his liking than London. One thing that
struck me was that when he was writing he read a great deal,
charging his batteries I guess. Works the same in music. I listen to a
few minutes of something, anything, before starting to work and it
gets you going. Bennett wrote a lot of plays—one in three weeks. Like
Coward.

Last Friday I recorded with Bing again (at Decca). One of the
sides I am quite happy with: "We All Have A Song In Our Hearts."
I can arrange this kind of song well. I had an oboe solo in the
instrumental part and as it went by Bing was imitating a trombone.
Only later did it strike me he would have preferred a trombone on
the phrase. Incidentally on these sessions you show up, start
rehearsing the orchestra and all of a sudden Bing is there at the
mike ready to go.

Last night we did "Cinderella" on Hallmark with Judy Garland.
(Written by Lawrence and Lee.) She did one song. In the setup I
was about three feet from her and the chills ran up me when she
sang; the orchestra felt it too. The score and the program were very
successful. Country Washburn, the famous bass player, sent me a
wire on it. I called the children to be sure they listened. Joyce
asked me afterward what Judy wore and what color her hair was.

Lunch today with Hugo Friedhofer who is on a diet and looks
eight years younger. He said he almost had diabetes. There was an
ugly rumor that he had broken down because his wife ran off with
another woman.. I asked him if his domestic situation was alright
and he said no trouble at all. He is building a studio at the bottom
of his garden. Now when he works he is in the middle of the house
and he feels it is unfair to his wife. I understand this. I work that
way and it is difficult.

I am going to record with Harry Babbitt this coming Tuesday at Coral. As usual the material is ghastly but it is a little money and needed, of course.

I feel I have been successful in my work lately. The orchestration has improved greatly. I seem to have a sense of power with the orchestra now and I think it will continue to improve. It is a good feeling. I have discovered that scarceness of the basic material is good. Few materials and good working out. The less parts going on in the orchestra the better.

Corwin dips into these notebooks occasionally and says they should be published. He himself keeps a journal. [Corwin says that this is not true, except for a log of a trip he made around the world for CBS.] In this diary I was struck by the number of entries concerning the state of his health. Mixed in with the interesting things he saw in dozens of countries, are notes of colds and other malaise. I think he cancelled an appointment with Prokofiev because he had a cold. [A vehement note from Corwin: "COLD? I had a strep throat and a fever of 104!"]

We were neighbors at Sneden's Landing in the summer of 1941, the summer he was writing, directing and producing "26 by Corwin." His medicine chest was full of tonics, balms, salts, gargles and bandaids and once, when I came across an unguent obtainable only from Germany, he borrowed it and I never saw it again. [Another note from Corwin (we believe in equal time here): "There were six small crystals, hardly enough for a lame humming bird, and I used them up. Serves you right anyway for buying an unguent from Germany!"]

Sunday February 11

To Borego Springs with Jimmy and Adele. Returned Tuesday and Nina was back from her trip to Jacksonville. The situation.

Saturday February 17

Moved into Jimmy's back apartment until we decide what to do. (While Jimmy lives in Long Beach he still keeps two apartments on La Cienega below Sunset. $60 a month each. When his ex-wife comes out she stays in one of them. And I suppose when friends have such problems as I am having he volunteers the breathing space).

Sunday February 18

Went to the Hollywood Ranch Market for some supplies. Saw a man wearing Levis with a gold watch chain looping into his side pocket. Saw an Italian woman of 50, her daughter about 30 and the daughter's son, aged 4. Only the child had a chubby, healthy American face. The women were bloodless and marked by suffering. Hopeless feeling. The child was wearing an overseas cap with two bars. Perhaps the father had been killed?

Sid has accepted a commission for us to write a song for the 17th Annual Police Show. This is a big do here in L.A. No money but we get badges. Sid says these come in handy for traffic violations and, said he, it pays to be on the side of the police when fascism comes in.

Dinner with Sid at the Capri—we had spent the afternoon writing a piece for the opening of the Jewish Chautauqua Society. Afterwards we walked on Hollywood Boulevard, stopping at the Pickwick bookshop. In the rack of bargains I saw Martha Keller's *Brady's Bend* for 19 cents and bought it for Sid. These are the lustiest, bustiest American poems ever. I met Martha at a dinner party at John and Ada Lewis's in Philadelphia when we were there opening *Finian's Rainbow.* We gobbled our dinner and I took her over to see the second act. Her husband teaches chemistry somewhere. I was very much taken with her. She said she wrote the poems in bed, in her head, and if she couldn't remember them in the morning they weren't worth writing down.

I made coffee in Jimmy's percolator and it was horrible. The second day it was even worse. But I find I recover from the first cup in about ten minutes and have another.

Two priceless things in Arnold Bennett. Pavlova dancing the Dying Swan. Two silent Englishmen. A feather falls off her costume. "Moulting," says one of the Englishmen. The other was a description of a man. Bennett says, "His socks were behind the times and he rouged his nostrils."

Wednesday February 21

Tonight was the ASCAP dinner. Talked to George Duning who has been nominated for an Academy Award for his score for *No Sad Songs for Me*. I wasn't mad about it. Story of a vicious, house-ridden woman which the music treated like a comedy. Saw Allie Wrubel who kindly invited me to spend a weekend or a week at his home in Twentynine Palms. While we were talking a small man who looked like an unemployed accountant came up and Allie introduced me. "This is Herb Magidson, one of our finer talents. He wrote 'Silent Night, Holy Night' and 'Jingle Bells'." Magidson said, "Oh, I wrote more than three."

Sat with David Raksin, Sid Kuller and Lee Wainer. David has just finished William Wyler's *Carrie*. Apparently had lots of trouble. Wyler wanted a romantic Main Title which David did against his will. At the preview Wyler didn't like it.

Franz Waxman had trouble with George Stevens on *An American Tragedy*, finally refusing to make all the changes requested. Stevens called in Daniele Amfitheatrof and Victor Young to make the changes. Waxman asked for his name to be taken off the film. Met Harry Warren on the way out. He looks like a Fuller brush salesman yet has written some of the most beautiful pop songs. A very gifted man.

In the men's room someone was being sick. Every time I go to the men's room in a hotel or a night club someone is being sick.

Sid and I went to the Wilshire Temple where they were having an evening of entertainment. After this we went to Billy Gray's. The green room jumping as usual. Rich stuff. Frank Fontaine, one of the new young comics who will happen this year, seems very smart and is quite a salesman. Max Gold, one of the owners of the club, an immense, gross man, arguing with Sid said, "Put your money where your mouth is and we can go to betting." All kinds of comedians, working and not working, go through this room. All ask Sid to write material for them. Frank Fontaine said he was going to do a television show and would have a writing budget of $5,000. We knew bullshit when we heard it. It's a CBS show.

I turned down a request from Decca to record Monday with Terry Gilkyson and the Weavers. I need a rest from notes for a few days.

Thursday February 22

"Valley Forge" with Van Heflin on Hallmark. Drinks with Van afterwards in Mike Lyman's next door to the Huntington Hartford Theatre where we do the show. He was talking about playing Chicago in *Philadelphia Story* with Hepburn. Clifton Webb was there in *Blithe Spirit,* Tallulah Bankhead in *The Little Foxes* and Noel Coward was in town drumming up some business for Bundles for Britain. Clifton gave an after theatre party. Van took Hepburn and sat open mouthed listening to the fine, bitchy talk while Tallulah got drunk and obstreperous. At one point she got to her feet and proposed a toast to the King. Coward said, "But I hardly know him." Tallulah impaled him and snarled, "You are a low English fag," and when Hepburn remonstrated, called that great lady "a tight-assed New England bitch." Clifton cried, "Tallulah! LEAVE!" whereupon Tallulah apologized. After a little more conversation Hepburn offered to take her home. They left, leaving Van in what he thought was a spot. When he said he ought to go, Coward said "I'll drop you off." Van demurred, then thought, "If I sit him out I'll be left with Clifton," so he left with Noel who was staying at the same hotel. Noel asked him up for a nightcap and Van declined, embarrassed. Noel said, "Please don't worry, my dear, you are not my type at all." Van went up with him and Noel talked for three hours about Van's performance in *Philadelphia Story,* analyzing it scene by scene and offering valuable suggestions and advice on how to fix it.

Saw a wonderful TV show called "Stud's Place." Called ABC today to find out who the people were. They knew very little. It was written by Charles Andrews and has a cast of four men and a woman. She is a waitress in the joint—Beverly Younger. Terrific. Studs is Studs; I will find out who he is sometime.

Friday February 23

Dr. Bergstrom's for checkup. Prelim tests OK. Next week the stomach. Lunch with Jimmy Hilliard talking about future plans for Coral Records. Sounds encouraging. Christmas stuff, childrens stuff, ballads. To Foote, Cone & Belding where Ed Cashman was sitting in the hall. He entertained me, as he used to do so often in New York, with stories of George Washington Hill (pres of American

Tobacco Company). A typical memo from Mr. Hill about the guitar notes in a singing commercial started him off. Ed was an account executive on the Lucky Strike account. A precarious position. He said, "If you look under your seat pad you see the face of your successor."

Saturday February 24

Drove to the beach and rented Jean Hughey's apartment for 3 months at $125.00 a month plus utilities. Drove back through Laurel Canyon and stopped to see Joe Losey. Louise there fixing dinner. Expecting the Roland Kibbees. She told me that Joe was still not working and that their son Mike, 18, had been arrested for stripping a car on Mulholland Drive. He got a year on probation.

On the way to the beach I drove alongside Irving Reis. We parked and talked. He told me the story of *New Mexico,* the film he directed for Irving Allen. He had made his deal with Joe Justman, Irving's partner. Terms $15,000 cash before beginning shooting, so much deferred, and 5 percent of the net profits. Justman had trouble raising the $15,000. Irving Reis went to him and said, "Write out a receipt for the $15,000 and I'll sign it." Joe's eyes filled but pointed out that Irving could not live on nothing while they were making the picture so he would give him $5,000 and the $10,000 would be a loan. A few days later Reis got a formal contract from Justal Productions (Justman and Allen's company) stating that the cash payment would be $5,000, the rest deferred. Reis said he couldn't sign such a contract since that made him a $5,000 director. His idea was to lend Joe money to help him over a rough spot, not to have in writing that he was working for $5,000. Joe persuaded him to sign it arguing that the corporate setup etc., etc., etc. Reis signed and Irving Allen then used the contract to show others what a good business man he was, how hard a bargain he could drive.

Dinner with Norman Corwin and Katie at the Rigoletto. Norman is reading a page of the dictionary every day. I mentioned that this was a fair enough item for me to put in my journal. He then told me one that is much better. He published a book called *Untitled* containing that radio play and others. There was a quote from me in the book in which I said something derogatory about commercial radio. Norman recalled the first printing of the book, 2,600 copies, and destroyed them. Cost him $2,600. He thought that the remark would hurt me in commercial radio.

Thursday March 1

Been in bed all week with flu, or the virus, enjoying such a vogue here. (In England much worse.) Patched up the music for *"Monsieur Beaucaire,"* Douglas Fairbanks, Jr. Turned out all right but Fairbanks is quite a square. I remember his appearance on Campbell Playhouse in New York when throughout the rehearsal he read TIME, Zachary having to call him through the talkback every time he had a cue. He missed the callback Thursday afternoon. Said he was sitting in his office and his watch stopped. He is active in British relief, is a big Anglophile. He got the CBE you know.

Jane Heinemann was in and told of her brother Gus Hill who was put in jail for passing bad checks. The day he left the jail he got the sheriff to cash a check for him. It bounced.

Sid called me while I was lunching at the Derby. They were going to run the picture and he wanted me to come. They want some more music. I ducked it. I don't want to sit in a projection room with Irving Allen. Sid said Allen wanted to talk to me and I said I didn't want to talk to *him.* Sid really presses. He put Allen on and I hung up. Later Sid tried to get me to demonstrate the score of *Seven Lively Artists* for a man from Chicago and I begged off on account of the flu. He pressed and pressed. I guess he is used to overpowering people.

Friday March 2

Moved into Jean Hughey's house at 20758 Pacific Coast Highway. Very charming, sits right on the beach.

Joe Losey is going to do a picture for Horizon Pictures, a company owned and operated by Sam Spiegel and John Huston. He has asked for me to do the score. Spiegel is reluctant because I have never done a film. Losey, Corwin and I mounted a campaign. The three of us and Spiegel met at La Rue for dinner to discuss it.

Spiegel, a charming, urbane gourmet, refused to talk business over food, and after dinner we adjourned to his mansion in Beverly Hills where we met John Huston.

Off in a corner Spiegel said he was afraid I would take too long to record the music. I said that when the picture was shot and cut, and when we decided how much music was needed I would go to any composer he named—Rozsa, Waxman, Raksin, Newman or anybody—ask them how long it should take to record the music and if I, in my inexperience, took longer I would pay for the overtime myself. He said, "There is only $5,000 in the budget for the composer." I said, "I'll take it."

He went into an aria about the budget—$600,000—based on a theme unfamiliar to me. Deferment. Deferment, I learned, is when an actor or a composer does his chores for no money up front, deferring his salary until the picture has earned back its cost. For example he said Van Heflin was doing the film for $75,000— deferred. I agreed to defer my $5,000 and indemnify him against overtime. Finally he agreed.

The shooting schedule of *The Prowler* began with some night shots outside a motel in Barstow where Heflin had taken Evelyn Keyes after murdering her husband. Nina and I drove to Las Vegas where we were married, then proceeded to Barstow to watch the filming. We spent the night in Barstow. Next day the company moved to Calico, a ghost town, to shoot the last scene in the picture. Van Heflin is trapped by forces of law and order in a draw behind the town. He climbs to the top of a 100-foot-high slag pile, cut to a kneeling pursuer squinting through the sights of his rifle, he fires and Heflin, frozen in the moment of death, pitches and rolls down the dusty mound. Zoom in on his lifeless eyes staring at the sky. I can hear the music now.

Later at supper Nina told me Sam was quite taken with her and had made what can only be described as an indecent proposal. I said, "I hope, under the circumstances, you asked him for a deferment."

There was a lot of so-called "source music" in the film. Keyes is married to a middle-aged disk jockey. For the first third of the film Keyes hangs around the house listening to her husband's program. Heflin, the cop on the beat, moves in and they begin having an affair while the radio plays incessantly in the background. I wrote 14 tunes of varying types and recorded them in a three-hour session at the RCA Victor studio on Sycamore. The less said about the sound on that stage the better. The rest of the score was written for an orchestra of 40 players and recorded at Goldwyn. (I insisted.) Of the 29 minutes recorded with this orchestra 23 were used in the picture. The story of the missing six minutes is a classic illustration of the function of music in films.

After the murder of her husband Heflin takes Keyes to the motel in Barstow where she reveals she is pregnant. Heflin testified at the trial that he had answered a prowler call and shot the husband whom he mistook for the prowler. He also testified he had not met Keyes before that night. If she had the baby the case could be re-opened and proof presented that Heflin *had* known Keyes before the murder. In a long, ugly scene Heflin demands that she abort. Sam wanted music. We didn't on the grounds that *any* music would soften the scene. The usual compromise was reached. I would write the music and we would see in the dubbing who was right. Losey and I conferred. I wrote a six-minute piece that underscored a childless woman's yearning for fulfillment and threw the whole scene out of kilter.

There is an amusing sidelight. It was the last piece of music we recorded that day at Goldwyn. Sam Spiegel was present, seated with some guest at the rear of the stage. We made the whole six minutes in one take. As the last bar was fading away Sam sneezed and we had to do it all over.

On one of my statements the picture earned $680,044 from theatrical exhibition in the U. S. Deductions included fees for Distribution, Advertising, Prints, Freight & Cartage, Duties, Foreign prints and one for $7,859 called, on this statement, Sundry. The film earned money in foreign countries and $45,648 from U. S. television stations. The producer's share of the proceeds after deductions appears on the statement as $489,633.

So how come I didn't get my $5,000? According to the statement there was a line ahead of me including:

De Luxe Laboratories	37,500
Walter E. Heller Co.	275,846
Motion Picture Center	7,719
Various individual investors	97,129
United Artists	33,710
I. H. Prinzmetal (Sam's attorney)	37,726

All that, oddly enough, adds up to 489,633. You may think I did the picture for nothing but Sam had a smart fellow named Irving Friedman figure out I owed him $1,200 for overtime. (Must have been that sneeze). Anyhow that's what it cost me to get my first picture credit. But I don't mind, and I think it is a good score. Alex North called and said he liked it.

Saturday the something or other—I've lost track.

More beach. Nina drove into town and brought back a letter from my mother who bears up under all the trouble they are having, with typical English cheerfulness.

For a recording at Coral I have to make arrangements of two songs from *The King and I*, the Rodgers & Hammerstein musical version of *Anna and the King of Siam*. I am also going to record "Hoofbeat Serenade," one of the songs from *Slaughter Trail*, with Terry Gilkyson for Decca. I hope I get my energy back in time.

Tuesday March 6

Having the most awful time with the music for Hallmark. I have scraped together a couple of tunes but the whole thing has no meaning. Uninteresting story so the music won't come. I tried to read *From Here to Eternity*, a first novel by James Jones. Too rough for me but he is a writer. Nina has disappeared with the book since Sunday. I am now reading Schoenberg's *Style and Idea*. Very interesting. "The great artist must be punished in his lifetime for the honor which he enjoys later. The music critic must be compensated in his lifetime for the contempt with which later times will treat him." Wow!

I have seldom felt so dull and logy and crass. I feel as though I will never write a decent note. I believe this comes from devoting so much time and energy to nothing music like Hallmark. I really must give it up next season. So very rarely does something come along on this program that lifts me up to an interested inspiration. "Cinderella" was one such. I enjoyed writing it and performing it. I am facing making eight records for Decca and Coral in the next two or three weeks and I don't have much of any go for that either. Maybe it'll come.

Benny Herrmann just called. He is back from a trip east. He is like a big goose to me. He certainly never gets bored with music.

Wednesday March 7

I have finished Hallmark and it is not so bad. At least today I am feeling fine. The weather is beautiful. I broke up two slices of bread and threw them piece by piece to the seagulls who hover and swoop for it against the sun. One of them has a distinctive habit of standing for a long time on one leg. I thought he only had one leg but before taking off he puts his other one down. The gulls skim silent downwind and execute a tight hairpin into the wind for a landing. There are several different kinds. The male-ish looking ones have large corporations and walk arrogantly. The female-ish ones are less affected and smaller. Some are dark brown, most white. Jean Hughey says the one with the one-legged habit has been here for eight years.

I was thinking last night of the day I introduced Terry Gilkyson to Irving Allen. He had never done a picture and Allen opened the interview saying, "What we're making here is a six-day piece of shit." Terry, being a gentleman from the Philadelphia Main Line, blanched. Sid said, "Pay no attention, Terry. We only allow him to talk that way because he owns a Renoir."

The Theatre Guild did *Hamlet* Sunday last with Gielgud, Pamela Brown and Dorothy McGuire. The music was appalling except for the finale which was some dark chords punctuated by the heavy and solemn firing of a gun. Dirgelike salute for the deaths.

Arnold Bennett has separated from his wife and in his *Journal* sounds even more pleased with himself than ever. He was a man who most of the time was very pleased with himself. He seemed to like sitting next to titles at dinner parties.

Saturday March 10

Hallmark last Thursday was another Opening of the West and I dummied up one of Fred's scores. (Fred Steiner who contributed a score now and then.) It was OK. Came home after carousing in the Derby with Bob Nye, Fred Harpman and Lonnie, the boy on the door at the Playhouse, and wrote with great rapidity a song called

"It Takes Millions of Civilians" for the Police show. Next day, Friday, we demonstrated it for a lieutenant from the LAPD and he lit up. It's for the Prologue of their show to be done with the Police band and some Police singers.

Met Mike Shore who may do some publicity for us on the picture company. Comes well recommended. He did all the publicity for Madman Muntz, a seller of used cars.

Benny Herrmann and Lucy and the Alexanders down here at the beach Friday night. We had dinner at Jay's. Very nice. Jay wears a small diamond in the lobe of his left ear, serves good food, and Cary Grant or Gary Cooper are usually there.

Fred Harpman here doing water colors.

During the week in town went to the Burbank High School and rehearsed the choir in "Lonesome Train." (The teacher in charge of music at the school has our Decca recording of this Earl Robinson work [produced and directed by Norman Corwin] and had called and asked if I would prepare and conduct a pair of performances at the school. I never say no to such requests from Academe.) The singers not bad but the orchestra is pricelessly high-school.

Monday March 12

Big day yesterday. The Gays here, Fred Harpman house guest, the Herrmanns dropped in. Benny told me how to write the opening and closing of this week's Hallmark. Very good. Lucky Bill Gay was here so he won't be surprised when the show opens with a chime solo. Harpman is talented and has all the faults of the very young. Said he heard an album of mine. Turned out to be the Christmas Carols. Said he thought they were horrible. Kids haven't learned you shouldn't say such things.

Benny said someone had referred to Richard Strauss as a "road hog." Priceless description of his orchestration. Benny said he once asked Elisabeth Schwarzkopf how it felt singing Strauss with those enormous orchestras he used. She said, "It's like being raped."

Tuesday March 13

Bored with Arnold Bennett. After success came he got awful stuffy.

Harpman in Alburquerque looking for subjects. Found an ancient adobe outhouse with thick walls, the door hanging open, throwing a nice black shadow. He sketched it. As he was putting in the colors a few Mexican kids gathered round—dogs and children are fascinated by artists—and saw the outhouse taking shape. A little Mexican boy said something to his sister in Spanish and ran off to the outhouse. Fred asked the girl what he had said and she said if he closes the door of the house will the door in the picture close and he was off to try it.

I have been reflecting about my income. It is down about one-third (last year's gross, $34,000). In addition to that, taxes have at least doubled. All in all I figure that with alimony (25%) agents commission (10%) taxes (20% at least) business management and lawyers another 7% and state unemployment, etc. 3%, all I see of my income is about 35%.

Monday March 19

Went into town last Thursday and did Hallmark. That was the day Larry Parks testified before the House Un-American Activities Committee that he had been a member of the Communist party from 1941 to 1945. I realized then that the committee is calling only known commies and that my theory that some of the ten might not have been is probably flooey. I have been thinking that I don't have a single friend who is a right winger. I never have agreed with Republicans; result—all my pals are liberals. How many of them are c———s?? I notice Hugo Butler is on the list of subpoenas this time, as is Georgia Backus.

Friday March 23

Bought a Chevrolet convertible for $2,600. Very nice. Nina sold the Buick, or rather dug up two guys who wanted to buy it. We got $800 which shows how big cars depreciate. I paid $2,500 for it in 1947.

Sid had a brilliant idea that we ought to publish a version of a folk tune we used in *Slaughter Trail* called "I Wish I Wuz," or "Woolie Boogie Bee." I pointed out that in dealing with public domain material you have to pin down a source for your steal. I had a hard time persuading him. He was all for taking it off the Burl Ives recording on the grounds that such a badly constructed song could never have been written by anyone. It just grew. Anyhow we wrote an original verse which under the law makes our version copyrightable.

Sunday March 25

Herrmanns and Jeff down. Benny and I called on John Brahm who directed *Hangover Square*, a 1944 film Benny did the music for. (Benny once said of Brahm: "What a difference an 's' makes.") Brahm has just returned from Venice where he did a picture called *The Thief of Venice*. He has an aerie above the coast highway, with horses and a collection of Strindberg. I didn't have time to see much of the library. He married an Italian woman when he was in Venice and has built an extension to his house—a sitting room for her when she gets here. She has never been in this country. When we left him Benny commented that on Sundays Brahm is surrounded by German refugees and that this is a kindness.

We called on Franz Waxman who, with his wife Alice, was entertaining Isaac Stern and a Miss Freedberg. Stern told wonderful jokes and anecdotes. Huberman, playing with the Perth, Australia, symphony, gets through a big cadenza and the orchestra doesn't come in. He asks the conductor if he may try the cadenza again. "Why certainly, old boy," says the conductor. He does it again, and again the orchestra doesn't come in. Huberman walks over to the podium and says, "In Vienna the orchestra comes in *here*," pointing to the score. The conductor says, "Well you're not in Vienna now, old boy."

And the story of Spaulding going to Denver to play the Mendelssohn Concerto and forgetting it. Later, a little shaken, he is telling a colleague about it (can't remember the colleague's name) and the colleague says, "Why that's impossible! You couldn't forget the Mendelssohn! Any schoolboy, etc., etc., etc." Next week the colleague is playing it with the Philadelphia and forgets it. Stern said the most fun he has had recently was playing in Copenhagen. A nice relaxed orchestra. Stern is small, a little overweight and hyperthyroidal.

Waxman has a little place here on the beach fixed up for him to work in. He has a whole wing at home, quite private, but discovered he can't work there, so he rented this place. I suspect he is tired of Alice and needs a place to lay a few friends more than anything else. I wonder if they have an agreement? I wonder if Europeans make these agreements. You let me have a little place to do some discreet banging and we'll keep up the larger front at home. Wouldn't be surprised.

At dinner Benny and Jeff harangued me for an hour about wanting to give up Hallmark. They are both very anxious for me to have an income to keep me independent of recording companies and picture studios. Maybe they don't want any competition. They have just about sold me and if Hallmark asks me to do it next year I will hire an orchestrator and at least keep part of the income. Of course the way radio has gone I am not at all sure they will invite me back or that there even will be an orchestra on the show or that they won't ask me to take a cut. Mr. Petrillo settled our hash by asking for 5 percent of the gross time sales on film made by the networks. The first big network production after the agreement was signed was "Amos 'n' Andy," a $40,000 show. It will be done with a choir singing "oohs and ahs" and "scooby doos" with no orchestral accompaniment.

I am reading Mizener's biography of Fitzgerald. Most depressing. He married the wrong woman in some ways. She put a price on herself and he met it year after year, driving himself and turning out *Saturday Evening Post* stories, etc. They were on the move all the time from Montgomery to New York to France to Hollywood. They did the stupidest things. In New York they jumped into the Plaza fountain. After a big night on the town they would motor to their house in Great Neck and go to sleep on the lawn where their "man" would find them in the morning and carry them to bed. In France he threw a ripe fig at the bare back of a lady guest at a dinner party. He kicked a tray of souvenirs out of the hands of an old lady standing at the entrance to a night club. Driving home from a shindig in France or Italy, I forget which, he and Zelda turned off the road onto some trolley tracks and stalled the car. They fell asleep. They were awakened by a farmer and pulled from the car a few minutes before a trolley came along and demolished it.

The most fun I am having is reading Manchester's biography of

Mencken. Mencken is my great man. In 1908 he decided that democracy was "fantastically corrupt and mismanaged; America was led by idiots and represented in both literature and drama the cultural nadir of the world." As far as I can gather he has no reason to change his opinion.

Tuesday March 27

Jack Husband, 20, Oklahoma City, has been accepted by the Army in spite of the fact that his head ticks and has ticked since he was nine. The sound is audible four feet away and has been recorded.

Finished scoring the Elizabethan music Benny laid out for Hallmark in approximately ten hours of comfortably paced work. The new car came yesterday and is a beauty. I think anyone who lusts after a Cadillac for town driving in Hollywood is out of his head. The Chevrolet is attractive and well engineered.

Mencken went into eclipse during the first World War because of his strong pro-German sympathies. By the early twenties the public had forgotten its rage and he was riding high again. During Prohibition he attended Oktoberfests in Baltimore. The revellers drank apple cider out of gourds and ate terrapin. He wrote a friend after one of these bouts that his "liver was seven inches thick and I have spiders in my urine."

Sunday April 1

We are back at the beach with my daughter Ann, who is recouping from chicken pox, not to mention the removal of her adenoids and tonsils. She is delightfully feminine but not musically talented, a bit timid and quite the opposite of Joyce.

Hallmark went well. Benny was not demonstrative about it. I would say he didn't think much of it; neither did Tony Collins, whose house we visited after our usual dinner at the Derby. Jimmy Hilton was talking about sex which he often does after five martinis. He said that, speaking anatomically, the difference between Adele and Betty Grable couldn't be more than ⅜ths of an inch and he personally wouldn't be able to tell the difference.

I have finished Manchester's Mencken and it is all right but not more. With the exception of the information about his last stroke, which occurred while he was visiting his secretary, and what happened after he came out of Johns Hopkins the last time, I knew all that was in the book. And Manchester is dull alongside the copious Mencken quotes, as indeed who wouldn't be? Mencken could neither read nor write after the last stroke. A cruel blow to a reader and a writer. Mencken's blind spots about Roosevelt and Hitler and anything German didn't seem to bother me. I guess I am enamored of his talent and personality aside from his Republican-isolation cum pro-Germanitis.

I recorded with Terry Gilkyson Friday night last, four sides, "Hoofbeat Serenade" again (which I have lost faith in) and some of Terry's things. Some of the orchestration and ideas very good; even Victor Bay (he was playing in the orchestra) came up after one of them and asked me who had scored it. Point is he didn't believe I had. Between the rehearsal and the actual recording I sat in the Melrose Grotto with some of the singers. A trombone player with a box of good cigars in his drunken hands came over. He had had a baby girl and he said in an accusing tone, "I bet you don't remember me, do you?" I said, "Not very well," and he said, "You always were a bastard." Turns out he played in the "Sound Off" orchestra when I was doing it, and thought I was a son of a bitch but conceded before he rolled off that I had a good down beat, which to musicians out here seems to be the mark of a good conductor.

Friday night after the recording, Norman and Betty Luboff, Ray Charles (the white one) and Nina and I went to hear Matt Dennis at a restaurant called the King of the Sea. I had an excellent English rarebit. Matt is fabulously inventive and sings a very boppy arrangement of "My Blue Heaven" which goes through such harmonic convolutions that it affected me like a tongue bath. Nina said Matt Dennis's work made her back ache.

One day last week when I was orchestrating the Elizabethan stuff I called to Nina, "What position is the cello in for the F above middle C?" and she replied, "Between his legs."

We finished recording the music for *Slaughter Trail* Wednesday last. Pretty awful when you add it all together. Darrel Calker did the underscoring and what I heard of it was badly played, badly conducted and of medium inspiration. And on top of that it was at RCA, the worst place I have ever heard for recording.

Monday April 9

With the help of some material Benny wrote for me I finished the Hallmark with an expenditure of about nine hours scoring. Tuesday I got on the phone to everybody and set up a showing of *The Prowler* so that those people at William Morris can see it and find out what I can do.

I wrote three songs without words yesterday and several letters. Benny's Sunday help gives me time for this sort of thing.

Tom Mack called. He spent yesterday recording Ethel Smith. Two p.m. to 11 p.m. on two sides. Involved a lot of overdubbing. She wants the record called "Ethel Smith and Her Organs." She'll be the only woman whose organs are available for 85 cents. (That's the current cost of a single record.)

Tuesday April 10

Last Thursday morning I had a date with Philip Waxman. He is getting ready to produce a picture called *The Big Night* based on the mystery novel *Dreadful Summit* by Stanley Ellin. The screenplay is good except for the ending which is pat and sudden. Joe Losey, who may direct, is fixing the screenplay to be more like the book. I read the book. It is about a 16-year-old boy who kills a man who beat up his father. He is a potential sexual pervert always thinking about shooting women in their business where it hurts. He is a tormented virgin. The story goes with him through a dreadful, evil night.

Anyhow, Waxman was not at the studio when I arrived. I found his office, one of several in a dank musty passageway in an obscure corner of Eagle-Lion. The people in the other offices seemed hopeless, trapped, look through the glass at you as you go by with either hatred or supplication. The offices are dusty—strictly low-budget. Waxman's was locked and there was no girl so I left. We spoke later on the phone and discussed a deal. He had just seen *The Prowler* and liked the music.

Lunch with Lud Gluskin, Charley Levene, my press agent, and a man named Zito from *Billboard*. I am trying to find out about the record business.

Hallmark was my amplification of the three cues Benny wrote for me last Sunday. His are economic, sparse and *correct*. From the first bar the orchestra looks appreciative. My style is overdone and tends to use the full orchestra too much. Benny started with two horns. Hugo Friedhofer called and said he liked it. After the show briefly at the Derby before going to John Burroughs High school. Jimmy Hilton presented me with a certificate from the Board of Education at Barrow-in-Furness, where I went to school, stating that Her Majesty's Inspector had passed "Lionel Breeze" in 1885. Lionel is the name I was given at birth and Breeze is my family surname. I invented the name I now bear for two compelling reasons. When I started performing on the radio in Philadelphia my father did not approve. He thought I should get a proper job and, furthermore, he did not want his name bandied about on the airwaves. When, as Lionel Breeze, I began to get fan letters addressed to "Line O'Breeze" and "Lima Beans" I thought I would get further with a simpler name and chose Lyn Murray. [When I became better known, signing insurance policies, contracts, driver's licenses and leases under one name and performing under another became just too complicated and I felt obliged to go to court and get a paper legalizing the change.]

Rehearsed successfully at the high school in Burbank. The kids are good. As I was leaving a group of three girls aged 14 or so ahead of me were exclaiming, "Am I *tired!* That maaaan!" I caught up with them and told them I was tired too. As a matter of fact, these kids have too much to do. I am afraid the kind of schedule they are on will break down their constitutions. Dances, track meets, endless rehearsals, sewing costumes for the play, etc. Maybe the plan nowadays is to keep them so busy they will be too tired to get pregnant, smoke marihuana and strip cars.

On the way home visited my neighbor Helen Schuchman who has had a tumor removed. At 11:30, at home, Sid Kuller, Jackie Gayle and Ada (last name unknown) arrived. Played our new version of "I Wish I Wuz." Gayle is going to publish it. Ada had a small vial of tea with her and made a cigarette which we all smoked. Nina for the first time, I for the second. The first time for me was in New Orleans in 1928 when I was a messman on the *Pueblo,* an oil tanker belonging to the Houston Petroleum Company. I dimly remember getting lit up and cleaning my dirty finger nails and straightening up my room on the ship. Tonight, perhaps because there was so little grass, nothing happened except my voice got husky. Nina got a headache.

Friday Sid Kuller, Norman Luboff and I went to Music City where we made a demonstration record of "I Wish I Wuz," then took it up to RCA where Henry Rene was recording Dale Evans, the girl in the Roy Rogers pictures. We got there ten minutes before the end of the session. Frank Worth, a very solid musician, was conducting. Rene was called out of the control room to take a long-distance call. I read a memo on his desk saying he was to contact Jackie Gayle (our publisher) and get a copy and a demo of "I Wish I Wuz." The tone of the memo was urgent and I was naturally pleased. Rene came back and finished his date. We asked if he would listen to our record and he said he hadn't time. He would pass it on to Dale Evans who in turn would give it to Roy Rogers but he himself was not enough interested to devote three minutes to listening to it. I heard later that he iced us because I was present and I represented competition. He is a conductor as well as an A & R (Artists & Repertoire) man. These guys are in a revolving door. Two flops and they are out. It happened to Rene's predecessor. He read in the trade papers he was through. And he was. Even in big corporations like RCA and Columbia the A & R guys are on the take. Payola. Drive Cadillacs. A good record can make a song and that means $30,000 or so to the publisher and the song writers. So the publishers grease the ways.

We left RCA and Sid and I had our picture taken in front of the drop that will grace our police show song. There was the usual dumb girl with legs to make sure the papers will run the picture.

Monday I scored "Joy Street" (Hallmark). I had collected a few ideas Sunday and finished it all Monday. These last few weeks at the beach I have been able to score the show in one day, usually with Benny's help. I can't explain why in town I debate and debate and then write something down. Here I don't debate as long, put it down and it gets done quick and sounds OK. Benny says the best way to start is to write a note for the bassoon.

Sunday April 22

Last weekend my daughter Joyce was here. She was difficult, reminding me of myself at her age. (At six I threw my younger brother into the fire. My father rescued him). But she is talented. She wrote and illustrated a story. One panel had her and her sister Ann basking in the sun. The sun was winking at Joyce with one eye, the other eye was glaring frostily at Ann so that she was not getting as much warmth as Joyce. This was explained in the caption which said the sun was being nice to Joyce but not to Ann. Three unexplained creatures appeared in another panel. Their function was to transport the human beings in the story back to home sweet home. They were identified toward the end as petrified seaweed.

Joyce has developed an embarrassing device which she first tried out in the Tick Tock restaurant where I frequently take her. She leaned over to me and in the politest possible way whispered that she thought the lady in the next booth was quite ugly. Driving down to the beach last weekend we stopped at a Thrifty Drug store to buy a pail. As I was paying the cashier, a hefty lady wearing a large button saying she was Miss Goldberg, my daughter beckoned me down to ear level and said, "She has fat cheeks." The jolly cashier wanted to know what the little girl was whispering. I thought fast and said, "She thinks you are pleasingly plump."

Hallmark had a gay 1905 piece about the automobile, written by Leonard St. Clair, a harassed young writer who has more dandruff than I, possibly because he seems to wear blue serge exclusively.

That day I had a call from Tom Mack at Decca. General MacArthur's mention of the song "Old Soldiers Never Die." has created a demand for it and would I record it immediately with Herb Jeffries? He would record another song on the date, something called "Unless." Pleading the pressure of the two concerts coming up at the High school, I arranged for Jeff Alexander to write and conduct the "Old Soldiers" and I agreed to do the other song. This was satisfactory to Tom. Jeff conducted his side first and I followed with the other tune.

Herb Jeffries is a large, good-looking man with more sex appeal than I have ever noticed in a man before. He has a Heidelberg scar down the side of his face and when he sings, his high breast bone makes him look as though he were in a prize fight. I mean in a nice way. He is very pleasant to work with and loved both arrangements.

Friday and Saturday nights. Concert including "The Lonesome Train" at John Burroughs High School, Burbank. A beautiful school with a magnificent mural framing the entrance doors to the auditorium. The children did very well at both performances. I had an outburst of trouble at the dress rehearsal Wednesday night. One of the boys got obstreperous and I threw him out. He apologized the next night and sang. So many of the kids came to me and thanked me for being with them that the teacher's hand in it was obvious. Too many. He is that kind of man. A simple, fighting kind of guy but exhibiting a sort of fear of the children I can't explain. At one of our meetings at the beach he brought one of the little girls with him and I couldn't help thinking he was laying her. They are all such well equipped young animals. The orchestra is a panic of course. At the luftpause in "Alice Blue Gown"—"I'll *Primp* Passing By"—the whole orchestra suddenly plays twice as loud as they have been playing. The first trumpet on two repeated notes would always fluff the second note a tone down.

Wednesday June 27

Jeff Alexander is at Metro and excited by the people he works with. Leonard Spiegelgass, a talented writer, discussing creativity at the luncheon table, says he is not creative—he is skill surrounded by flesh. He is gay, or as Jeff says, slightly gay. So is Roger Edens, a musical director-arranger-producer. Spiegelgass says Edens is the type who sits at a bar and when he catches sight of himself in the mirror throws his glass at the image because he can't have him.

Thursday August 16

I have been at Paramount since August 6 working on *Son of Paleface*, a Bob Hope film with Jane Russell and Roy Rogers. (There's a parlay.) Frank Tashlin is the director, Bob Welch the producer and Joe Quillan the principal writer. I have had a wonderfully good time. Everyone is cooperative and you have the feeling you are among friends who are vitally interested in getting a good result for you. Roy Rogers is nice to work with and so are his horses Trigger (he has three of them). They are trained to respond to visual cues. These cues can be given by anyone.

Yesterday, Wednesday August 15, in court. Florence is asking a review of her alimony situation. She gets 25 percent of my gross less agent's commissions. I was represented by Milton Tyre, brother of Norman Tyre of Gang, Kopp & Tyre; Florence by Jerry Ralston. When we arrived, Commissioner Brock was hearing a case. Gerald T. Brandt, son of a rich father who owns Brandt Theatres, was being sued by his ex-wife for falling behind in his alimony payments. He is supposed to pay her $300 a month alimony and child support. It was the most embarrassing thing I have ever heard.

Two things interested me about this case in relation to my situation. The judge did not seem overly sympathetic to the woman, intimating once that she was living beyond her means. He apparently thought Brandt could manage $300 a month and suggested he go into some other line of work. Doesn't think much of producers, I guess. When our case came on and the judge heard the details he scheduled another hearing for some months away and that's the last I heard of it.

I liked the scene they were shooting today: Hope in an antiquated car driving through a mud puddle and splashing the bystanders. A pressure hose was run under the street and into the puddle. When Hope in the car hit the puddle the pressure hose went into action and sprayed the extras with much force.

In Hope's dressing room, a suite complete with kitchen, he was talking on the telephone to Violet Hylton, one of a famous pair of Siamese twins. He talked to Daisy, the other one, and when he hung up Barney Dean whispered to me, "If I could get in there it might revive my thing."

Barney, one of Hope's writers, was reminded of a famous story about the Hylton Sisters. They were touring in vaudeville, booked into the Earle Theatre, Philadelphia. At the music rehearsal Violet saw a handsome, brawny stage hand in the wings. She said to Daisy, "Come on," and they sidled over. Violet made a date with the guy for after the show. He came to their hotel room and while

Daisy read a book Violet and the stagehand made love. It happened every night for a week. A year later they were back at the Earle. The same guy was at the switchboard in the wings. They went over and Violet said, "You may not remember me..."

The publicity department fixed up a gimmick. They had Trigger give a lunch for Hope and Russell in the studio commissary. Barney Dean was at the music table when this thing started and all the people in the commissary craned their necks to see what was going on. He said, "I saw a horse having his lunch in Ashtabula once. Nobody paid any attention."

Monday August 27

Start of the fourth week. When we are watching the dailies Bob Welch will cry out from time to time, "What producing!" and once, when Hope was looking at a rather violent scene involving the car, he said, "Anyone who quits this picture is chicken." He said he would rather be in Korea.

We were getting ready to shoot the number "Wing Ding Tonight." The eight dancing girls and Jane Russell were up on the runway in the Dirty Shame saloon. Barney Dean said, "That's a lot of knockers." I said, "Yeah. Nineteen of them." He said, "Don't give me the answer, the feed line's funny enough."

Tuesday August 28

Last night to the Herrmanns' rented house in Los Feliz where his two children Taffy and Wendy, by Lucille Fletcher, are spending a month with them. Benny is in a restless mood. He has finished *The Day the Earth Stood Still* (20th Fox movie about a visitor from another planet) and hasn't the energy to buckle down and proofread his opera, *Wuthering Heights*. Just wanted to talk mostly. He has been reading the new Toscanini biography. The main message is Toscanini's uncompromising attitude to the business of music. If the opera house wouldn't give him what he considered enough rehearsal he wouldn't perform. When he was quite young he had periods of a year or more when he didn't conduct. He fired the whole Salzburg orchestra once saying they were not good enough to recreate Wagner's music the way he dreamed it. Threw out a politically placed tenor for the same reason.

Benny said he was present at a rehearsal of the New York Philharmonic when Mitropoulos fired a drummer. The player came around begging for his job back. Mitropoulos told him he had no right to the job, wasn't a good enough musician. Right on the line. (I've seen Benny give many a timpani player a hard time.) Mitropoulos, says Benny, is only interested in music that challenges his powers. A piece, to command Mitropoulos' attention, has to present technical problems and also has to be intellectual. He is not concerned much with orchestral colors. Benny was on a Couperin kick last night and showed me where Couperin had influenced Brahms and of course Ravel and Debussy. Remarkable considering Couperin was a contemporary of Bach.

We talked a lot about CBS. The most extraordinary thing to me was his defense of Zack Becker, a lawyer in the CBS Artists' Bureau, whom I had always thought to be against the artist. Benny said he had letters from Becker saying he had no objection to CBS driving hard bargains (I wrote an opera for Corwin's CBS series and was paid $75), but that they were getting dishonest and he didn't want to be a part of it.

I am having a big hassle about billing on *Son of Paleface*. Louis Lipstone, head of the music department, insists no one around here gets half a card. (Most of the composers get a full card but he is fighting half a card for me.) At the same time he is talking a deal for four pictures over two years. We are fighting the billing battle of course.

In the song "Buttons and Bows," Bob Hope attempts to lift Jane Russell on to the bar. He fails. Roy Rogers then lifts her up with ease. That's what the script says, but Roy couldn't get her up either. Jane said it would be just as good if she lifted herself up. Hope said, "Save that for RKO." (Jane is under contract to RKO and Howard Hughes.) Bob Welch said the RKO commissary had the best food in Hollywood. Hope said, "They should release the food instead of the pictures."

Monday September 10

Hope told me today about the two nuns who went to see *Mister Roberts* (Thomas Heggen's and Joshua Logan's play about sailors in which there is a lot of profanity). When the play was over one of the nuns started rooting around on the floor. The other one said, "What's the matter?" The first nun said, "I dropped my fucking gloves."

Looks like my agent Jimmy Townsend has made a deal for me at Paramount. Five pictures in four years. $10,000 for twelve weeks per picture. One dramatic picture for $6,500.

Hugo Friedhofer told me he knows a girl who is listed in Duncan Hines.

We went to Frank Tashlin's house yesterday and sat around the pool. His wife is lovely. To the Academy Theatre in the evening to see *The Bells of Saint Mary's*. After a Leo McCarey picture I always feel like going out and being mean to somebody. They are so full of sweetness and light. But that's a great picture. They didn't miss a trick. Bobby Dolan did the score.

We recorded "Wing Ding Tonight," "Harvard," "Am I In Love," Trigger's dancing music and the march for Bob's walking up and down in the corridor outside Jane's room while she is taking a bath. The prescoring is now finished and I am waiting for the rough cut.

Wednesday October 10

Last Saturday was the last day of shooting on *Son of Paleface*. There was a wrap party. Diplomas were handed out by Don Hartman, head of the studio. The degree mentioned in the diploma was YTT. Translated that means You're Through Tonight.

Big bombshell. Tashlin has left his wife and turned to religion. Here is what happened:

Jane Russell owns a big piece of property out in the Valley. On it are two houses. Her mother lives in one and her brother Jamie and his wife in the other. Jane's mother is an ordained Pentecostal minister and Jane built a charming little chapel on the property for her mother to preach in. All through the shooting of the picture, every Thursday night, Jane took Tashlin to the service in the chapel. He loved what went on there, got baptized and pretty soon was speaking in tongues. He told me that every day at lunch time he, Jane and Carmen, Jane's stand-in, would have prayer sessions in Jane's dressing room. He said they were very helpful to him. I believed this because the first time I reported to Jane's dressing room to set keys for some of the numbers, she and Carmen knelt and asked the Lord to make sure we picked the right keys. The keys were fine.

Tuesday October 16

Nina and I are in splitsville and I have moved into the Chateau Marmont. (Tashlin must be catching.) I am sitting here in the middle of piles of books, manuscript paper, scores, paper cartons and records but I have to write down the things I heard in The Players just now. Exhausted by the moving, I had dinner there.

Sturges is presenting *Room Service* in the theatre upstairs. The actor who plays the Senator arrived at the same time I did. There were two young duos sitting at one of the tables. When they finished their dinner there was a big to-do about splitting the check. One of the boys said, "Well, I had the green salad and four Old Fashioneds." The man who plays the Senator was joined by Julius Tannen, a famous old vaudeville comedian. There is a story about him being interviewed by a young producer for a part. The producer said, finally, "I am sorry, Mr. Tannen, but this part calls for a bald man." Tannen wears a toupee. He whipped it off revealing a totally bald head. The producer studied him for a while then said, "I am sorry, Mr. Tannen, but I don't see you as a bald man."

Tannen noticed that the Senator was finishing a slab of rare roast beef and said, "What's the matter. Afraid they'll hire a heavier actor?" The Senator ordered a Napoleon for dessert. He told a story about the time he was playing in *The Merry Widow*. His wife came down with a case of Rocky Mountain Spotted Fever. He said it set him back $5,200.

Thursday October 18

Spent the morning in court. Florence is asking for an accounting of the alimony again. The agreement calls for her to get 25% of my gross less agent's commissions. Her attorney explained to the judge that I take package deals. For example, if I get $650 to deliver a score and I pay an agent $65, an orchestrator $225 and a copyist $100, I should, under the agreement and according to the law, pay her 25% of $585 (the gross after agent's commission). It didn't take the judge long to figure out I would be working for $113.75 and the alimony would be $146.25. He said a line I don't think I'll ever forget: "This is going to take a long time. Postponed until next June." Incidentally, Nina said she would testify that Florence had agreed to the principle of deducting orchestrators and copyists from the gross when I was up for the Sinatra show in 1949.

I returned to the Chateau Marmont, had lunch, hung some more pictures and was preparing to do some desultory work when Bob Welch called. He asked me to come up to Lester Linsk's (his agent, but a *nice* one), where he and Tashlin were sunning themselves round the pool. I went and Frank was lying along the diving board like a blond walrus with a book on his belly. "What are you reading?" I asked. He said, "The Bible." He had been having what he called "bad thoughts" about his wife. If he called her and she wasn't home, he imagined she was up to all kinds of hanky panky, and reading the Bible helped. He had brought the subject of his "bad thoughts" up at the chapel and Mother Russell said that was the devil working in him. The way to handle it was to say, "Satan, I reject you." Frank says it works fine. He knows he is a battleground for good and evil. God and Satan are fighting it out in him. I said it was only jealousy. Perfectly normal thoughts for a man to have about a woman he has spent so many years of his life with. I must have spoken with some conviction, for he broke off the conversation and left for his chapel meeting. The conviction was there, of course, because this same feeling made me marry Nina. She was going around with Stickney and a man named Jerry Rudner and although I had no right to, I got jealous. She was on her own—a free agent—and so was I. But she played me like a salmon. To fend off the competition we got married.

Saturday October 20

Today Hal Levy, a lyric writer, came to lunch. We sat at the pool and Phil Weltman, a William Morris agent who lives at the Chateau, joined us. He asked me if I wanted to do a television show, and had I had any experience in the pit? This sort of inquiry from your agent is infuriating. I told him I had played piano for a flash act in vaudeville for a year and in the whole year I never got the tempo right once.

I spoke on the phone with Florence today and I am taking Joyce tomorrow for the day. I have decided it might be better to have the children one at a time. Apart they are so different.

Sid Kuller called and came over for a while. He is writing the Donald O'Connor TV show. Needs money. I have seen the new tax schedule and all I have to say is, "Jesus!"

Spoke to Nina today and she seems to be quite active. I really believe that if she accepts our break as a break, which I think she will, I won't have to carry her for long, that is after the inter-locutory year.

Sid told me he was writing with a man the other night and when they finished about eleven o'clock the man said, "How about getting some dames?" They picked one up in Beverly Hills then drove to what turned out to be Florence's house. Sid said she won't get marriage out of this group, but they are plenty wild and she'll get lots of laughs and loving.

Monday October 22

Beginning second week at Chateau Marmont. Had two de-pressed days which is about par for my weekly course. Had Joyce for three hours yesterday. We went to a drive-in and she didn't want anything to eat. I showed her the view from the top of Laurel Canyon and she didn't like it. I asked her how she was doing in school, and I of all people can't fault her answer. She said she hated mathematics, didn't even like the art course. I planted the idea that she was so talented at art she really ought to enjoy it and that I would arrange for her to have some special training in it later on. We went to a movie theatre but before we went in she decided she wanted to go home. We stopped at the kiddie park for an hour with all the divorced fathers and their Sunday children. Perhaps that accounted for my depression yesterday.

Nina came over with some things today and as expected we went to bed.

Tuesday October 23

Attended a running of the rough assembly of *Son of Paleface* and this is a very funny picture. I might run out of money before they put me back on salary. It will be three weeks before I start writing the underscore.

Went to a cocktail party Coral Records gave for the Ames Brothers, four tall and darkly interesting looking Syrians or Armenians, very warm guys. After that to the Palladium for dinner with Sonny Burke and Tom Mack. Sonny's band is playing there. Excellent dinner which Tom paid for so it is very unkind of me to say that the band didn't grab me. Of course, there were four substitutes playing. This is something I couldn't stand, four strangers coming in, reading the book and doing incidentally two broadcasts. Their lack of precision and general sloppiness made the band appear loose and under-rehearsed. Oh, the hell with it. What do I care about any dance band and its problems?

Wednesday October 24

Saw Max Showalter briefly today. He is here trying to get an acting contract out of Fox. (He did. He became Casey Adams for a few years then gave it up). Mike Zimring, another William Morris agent, took us to dinner at the Players. We sat with Bill Robson, the CBS director, who was attired in a rough tweed suit with a red shirt and matching tie, and horn framed half glasses. Irving Reis sat with us for a while. He has just finished shooting *The Fourposter* and got along fine with Rex Harrison and Lili Palmer, and with Stanley Kramer. Robson called the waiter and asked who the very attractive woman across the way was. He still believes in adventure. He's honest about it.

Thursday October 25

Nina here in the afternoon. Bed again. John Abbott here with a German song Jackie Gayle, our publisher, is interested in.

Dinner with the Herrmanns. Lucille very thin, full of service for Benny. He looks at wrestling on the television with the sound turned off and the radio tuned to KFAC, the good music station. I am not interested in wrestling but he got me to look at one of the matches. KFAC was playing the Faust symphony of Liszt which Benny conducted right there, calling off the entrances correctly. He conducted with great vigor, and that started him talking about the time he conducted this work with the Halle at Manchester. He got out the notices and they were simply wonderful. One said the orchestra had delivered itself of its best playing of the season. I don't suppose John Barbirolli was too mad about that.

During this trip to Manchester Benny had the orchestra manager take him to see High Wythins and High Sunderland. He took pictures of the approach to Wythins and shots of the ruined farm itself and the three lone trees nearby. High Sunderland which is outside Halifax, whereas High Wythins is outside Haworth, is in a dangerous state of decay, gargoyles and decorative stonework in imminent danger of falling on the visitor. Benny has compiled a scrap book of Brontë material, photos, prints, chapters on the subject as a guide for the set designer of his opera *Wuthering Heights*, recently finished. It has occupied his life for seven years and he knows all there is to know about the Brontës. In a piece on his visit to the Brontë locale, the *Manchester Guardian*, or perhaps it was the *Yorkshire Observer*, remarked on his complete knowledge of Emily's life. A wonderfully stimulating evening, and I came away with a copy of *Wuthering Heights*, which I am going to re-read, and Phyllis Bentley's pamphlet on the Brontë sisters.

Friday October 26

Benny reported he had lunch at Fox with Earle Hagen (arranger) and Oscar Levant (ex-composer turned actor). Hagen said, "I am glad I am not a composer." Levant said, "Did you have the choice?"

Went in the evening to the Villa Nova for dinner with Eddie Powell and Robin Combs. Powell is Alfred Newman's number-one orchestrator at Fox. He has three daughters, 19, 14 and 5. He is always around alone. With the exception of once at Waxman's I have never seen him with his wife. We went to the Palladium to pay our respects to Sonny Burke, the Decca A & R man, whose band is playing there. Burke happened to have been duck shooting during the day. "Who presses the duck at Decca?" asked Powell. We then, sinking deeper into the mire of the music business, went to a place called Bob Dalton's on La Cienega where a disk jockey named Don Otis was making his farewell appearance. Disk jockeys are in on the payola. They can make songs happen, too. The place was full of record people, band leaders, songwriters and songpluggers and a painfully thin man with a parrot on his shoulder, an unexplained habitué of the place. Most dull and depressing.

Herrmann's dictum about accepting the fact that people operate on
different social and business levels is okay but I do not enjoy this
particular branch of society. The business of the popular song is a
rapacious and cynical racket. (Herrmann's dictum that any composer who writes on any level lower than symphonic stinks—
including Richard Rodgers—is nonsense and based on the fact that
he can't write a pop song.)

Saturday October 27

Arose with a hangover from the music business night. Worked
on the Main Title a bit. Sid Kuller called and reminded me it is his
birthday and I am expected for dinner. However, I have a date with
Tashlin for dinner. He called in the late afternoon and told me we
were taking a female named Jan Merritt to dinner with us. She had
called and declared herself in. They arrived at my apartment and
she struck me as being not at all bright. After a drink or two she
became full of nervous movements and giggled a lot. She insisted
we take her to a cocktail party she had been invited to, so we
shoved off.

The party was in an apartment in one of those new paper-thin
Hollywood apartment houses, wall to wall pastel carpets, modern
furniture, indirect fluorescent lighting and jammed full of people.
All the women were dressed in *Vogue* black, some with the new
hoop skirts, some wearing small hats. The men were all of a type.
The party was for a Colonel Shade and his wife of a few days. The
Colonel was loaded and his wife was introducing herself as the new
Mrs. Shade with an unmistakable air of accomplishment. The colonel
is Air Force and all the young men seemed to have something to do
with flying; anyhow there was plenty of talk about revolutions-per-
minute, props, etc. The hostess was a 35-year-old big-eyed thyroidal
type wearing a dress that punched up her bosoms so that they
seemed to be pouring over the top of the ruching, and they didn't
need to be punched up much. She had a wild nervous eye and
announced to us as we came in that although the party was for the
colonel and his new bride, she herself had just become engaged and
pointed out a man with patent leather hair. I ordered scotch over ice
and when it came it was literally half a tumbler of straight scotch with
a little ice in it. Frank, dazzled by the group, leaned over to me—he
was sitting on the floor while I was in a low comfortable chair—and
said, "Top this."

It seems to me this line can stand a little examination. Since Frank has turned himself over to God he has become driftish. He doesn't arrange his days, he just lets the Lord send whatever He will and Frank goes along on the rather unassailable assumption that what the Lord sends will work out in whatever fashion the Lord wants. Take this girl inviting herself to dinner and scooping us up and taking us to this cocktail party. (It isn't over yet.) The girl called Frank, the Lord got us to go to this party and Frank is bedazzled.

Jan Merritt, the lady who started this phase of the Lord's evening, introduced us to one of the lovely young things in a *Vogue* hoop skirt, a relative of the guest of honor. Her husband operates a sportsmen's flying service, away at the moment flying a group of customers around Mexico looking for ducks or trout or something. Miss Merritt introduced us to a bright-eyed, sensible-appearing girl named Shirley. We invited her to join us for dinner and things seemed to be looking up, but when we got to Villa Nova it turned out Shirley was desperately anxious for a career in the movies. Frank, or the Lord through Frank, is going to arrange a test for her at Paramount. Miss Merritt started trying to tell a lot of jokes I would not allow, and Frank was beginning to berate this poor Shirley girl because he felt she exuded a remarkable lack of confidence in herself which as everyone knows is not helpful in the picture business. We went into this very thoroughly and got the child all confused. Then we went to my apartment for an hour of soft music, and nothing else, until Jan Merritt persuaded us to adjourn to her house to hear tape recordings of her colored maid telling stories to her five-year-old son. They were bloodcurdling fire and brimstone Methodist, proving to me at least that the Lord works in mysterious ways. I suppose we left at some point because Frank said on the way home that he had not experienced such an evening since the twenties. It reminded him of Gordon Jenkins's "Manhattan Tower," that chi chi, sexy, drunken, exposed fleshy hysterical mad waltz done by guys with stiff prix and dames with itchy coos. And I was supposed to top it.

Monday October 28

Played Daddy to daughter Ann today. We went to the kiddie park (where else?). I had to ride on the ferris wheel twice. To a drive-in for lunch, then to *The Day the Earth Stood Still* for the second time. Still very good, especially Herrmann's score. Took Ann home and in the evening to Villa Nova for dinner with Tashlin and Bob Welch, who was in great form except for a skinned knee he showed to everyone in the bar. Then to Josephine Earle's and her husband's house. She's the lady who did the dances in *Son of Paleface*. Some of the dancing girls were there. Crazy kids. Hal Bourne was there and played the piano very well. Met a man named David Ledner who is working on a show with Lou Holtz, one of my favorite comedians. Ledner is an old pal of Tashlin's. They were in San Diego on D Day when the Navy took over, raping girls in doorways and turning over street cars. All the stores were closed and hot dogs were selling for $1.

Monday October 29

Florence telephoned to say she was calling off the suit. Scared of the money it will cost, although, if she won, it is I who would pay. She is aware that any surplus I have usually goes to the children. Victor Bay here for lunch, full of an idea to buy 20,000 acres of land at $10 an acre and look for metals or oil on it. (With his violin bow?) Finished a story about the making of *Slaughter Trail* today. Heard from Maurice Gardner, now a music publisher, who likes my arrangement of "Little Black Train." If we can find a PD source for it he will publish. Am going to the ASMA (Amrican Society of Music Arrangers) dinner tonight. Benny Herrmann is to talk about *Wuthering Heights*.

He didn't talk much about the opera but instead told a very small meeting that the networks are determined to get along without music on their television dramatic shows. There is a feeling here that in another year or so television will be a tremendous user of original music but I am of the opinion that as long as Petrillo insists on the payment of 5 percent of network time sales into a fund for indigent musicians all over the U.S., the networks won't allocate much money to the hiring of composers and orchestras. After a long time on this subject I tried to get Herrmann to talk about his opera but it didn't take. He did say something that struck me most forcibly. He said that when you sit down to write a work of art you tend gradually to throw off your conditioning and influences and begin to get things down the way you want them. I do know that in commercial work you tend to conform to the opinions, dogmas, policies and restrictions laid on you by others. You don't write with true freedom. I personally have always been writing in someone's footsteps, except in the very beginning when I was myself mainly because I had not had much education in the art. The pace of the emancipation process is determined by the strength of your own personality and in my case I am late but I am starting to lose a lot of my timidity and conformity.

I asked Benny to talk about his visits to Vaughan Williams. He first visited VW in 1936, having lunch with him and the head of the Royal Academy of Music. After to one of VW's classes. A student played a choral work. Asked for criticism VW said he enjoyed the work and would offer no criticism. He said, "However you want to write is fine with me." Everyone has his own way and he would not presume to suggest that anyone else's way was better.

The next visit was in 1949 after the war at VW's home in Dorking, a plain rambling house with plain furniture. He writes on a kitchen table next to a beat-up upright piano. His wife is paralyzed and is only able to move her eyes. VW told a story about Adrian Boult giving the first performance of one of his symphonies with the BBC orchestra. There was an ovation and he was called out to take a bow. He said to the concertmaster, "What's all the fuss about? Is my fly open?" He also told about an incident at the rehearsal. Boult questioned a chord. VW sat at the piano, picked out the chord note by note and said, "It looks wrong, it sounds wrong, but it's right." Manuscript paper is costly in England. Benny promised to send him some. VW said, "Don't send me too much. The younger people need paper too." He also quietly supports a lot of composers. Benny said he is very like Charles Ives.

When he was 13 years old Benny came across a book of 114 Ives songs. Benny looked up Ives in the phone book, called him and asked if he could come to see him. The old man agreed and since then Herrmann has seen him regularly. Every time he sees him Ives tries to give him money because he feels that no composer can possibly be making a living. He is an energetic old man who every now and then talks himself into the necessity of lying down. He says music is like bicycling, you have got to work at it—this accompanied by violent gestures. Ives's father was a professor of acoustics who conducted experiments in his own home. He tuned the piano in various temperaments and made his children sing in one key while he played in another. He said it was good for the muscles in the ear to get accustomed to two or three keys. As a result of diabetes Ives is somewhat deaf and consequently has not heard much of his own stuff—aside from the fact that it is not played much. (One piece he wrote in 1911 got its first performance in 1946). Ives doesn't care. He says when he is finished writing a piece of music he is through with it. Benny points out the difference between certain kinds of minds: Toscanini, after 60 years of playing the "Eroica," is still working on it but Beethoven was through with it when he finished it.

Carl Ruggles was mentioned. He received $20 or $30 a week from a Mrs. Gardner, a Boston art patron. After 20 years she persuaded Koussevitzky to play one of Ruggles's pieces. He destroyed the parts saying, "If she ever heard the music she was subsidizing she would stop the stipend." Benny said Ruggles was also a successful painter—hung in the Museum of Modern Art and the Metropolitan—and that if Benny ever went to his place in New Hampshire Ruggles would give him a picture.

Tuesday October 30

Worked on the Main Title most of the day although I am not on salary. There is a disturbing thing blowing up about this picture. With all the process stuff and special effects they have to do, it may be a long time before I get it.

In the evening to Tashlin's new apartment. Bob Welch and a rather plain-looking psychiatric nurse there. Name of June Tillie. Frank had been to the manager's office to borrow a screwdriver and the manager, a matchmaker, said there was a nice girl in the house who did ceramics and weaving and Frank ought to have her in for a drink. The manager called and June Tillie showed up right away. But that's not all. Lester Linsk showed up a little later with Chili Williams, a girl who achieved fame during the last war with one pin-up picture. They made a line of Chili Williams clothes and she was on the cover of LIFE, etc. While under contract at one of the studios she went around with Jack Carson for a long time. He tried and failed to get a divorce and eventually they broke up. Since then she has been banging from man to man. She drinks heavily and is one of those unfortunate people who have boundless energy and no brains. I have seen this a lot in actors.

Lester and Joe Linsk live on a two-acre estate at the top of Coldwater Canyon. Joe lives in the main house and Lester occupies the very attractive, small, country barn-like guest house. One night Frank took Chili to Lester's house where she proceeded to get loaded and tell all her troubles. Frank took her home. As soon as they got inside she took all her clothes off. He said he ought to go. Standing there naked she wailed, "After every date I come home and the man leaves and I am left alone." She turned and ran out onto her balcony threatening to throw herself off. He pulled her back into the room and escaped through the kitchen leaving her standing there with all the pain of her situation written on her face. He came back to Lester's where Lester was playing the piano for me. He is studying one of those Learn to Play the Piano in Ten Easy Lessons. He was attempting "Where or When," pausing at every bar line to contemplate the problems of the next bar. I don't know if it took Frank's mind off his experience.

Wednesday October 31

Worked some. Nina here in the afternoon. To Alexanders' for Halloween party. Herrmanns there. They had me on. Why I always choose the wrong women. Why I get involved instead of having arms' length affairs. Jeff's solution: divorce Nina (my third wife) remarry Florence (my second) and have an affair with Carol (my first). Maybe Carol would chip in some money towards the alimony. [Note: Both of these oracles were divorced by their wives later].

Thursday November 1

Went to see Lester Linsk in his Beverly Hills office this morning. Bob Welch there. He is having some sort of trouble with Tempy, his wife, and looked depressed. Gave Lester my *Slaughter Trail* story to see if he can do something with it. Had the children over in the afternoon for swimming. Cyril Cusack, the Irish actor, is here for a picture. He has brought his children Paul, Jane and Sally with him. Ann and Joyce had a good time in the pool with the Cusack children and their Irish maid Bridget, a woman with big legs, big torso, big busts and I doubt if she shaves—anywhere.

Monday November 5

Daughter Ann was run over Saturday morning, riding her bicycle near her house, by a woman named Dorothy Shearer. She is in the Children's Hospital. I went to see her this afternoon. She has a tiny fracture of the skull, a broken collarbone and many scratches and bruises. The X-rays show no serious trouble and she is getting along well.

In the evening to dinner with Frank Tashlin and Carmen Nesbitt, Jane Russell's stand-in. After dinner I sat down and did some work on an arrangement of "Sixteen Ghosts" for Maurice Gardner, the publisher. Normally at this hour I don't feel like working but I seemed to have ample energy.

I went to bed and was awakened by a draft from the window. I got up and closed it. I went to the bathroom and noted that it was 3:45. I got back into bed and presently my body was filled with circular rushing motions, head to toe, but my body was stationary, warm and comfortable. Then a voice very close to my ear said in a confidential tone, "Listen to him and he will tell you what to do." Then another voice, far off, stentorian, declaiming like an actor, spoke. It was in English and I understood each word but when the message was over I could not retain the meaning of what had been said. Just the sense that I had understood the words but not the whole. The first voice's line I remembered distinctly. Then the rushing came up to a sort of climax and stopped. I felt very relaxed and I thought, "You made this whole thing up." Then just above the level of my eyeballs and only for a second I saw a cross made of bright light with the figure of Jesus on it. I felt very thirsty, got up and went into the kitchen and poured myself a glass of milk. I noticed it was 4:45. The manifestation, demonstration, or whatever you want to call it, had taken exactly one hour.

Tuesday November 6

I got up and the first thing I noticed was that the occurrence of a few hours ago had changed my habits completely insofar as starting my day with pills was concerned. I just could not take the thyroid, or the liver, or the B 1 or any Benzedrine. (I had taken small amounts of Benzedrine for years for a condition diagnosed as a pseudo-narcolepsy.)

Today I did the radio program for Jeff. Ordinarily conducting for three hours tires me, but today I held up strong and tireless, not only through the program but through the evening which lasted till about one o'clock. I had dinner with Tashlin, Linsk and Joe Quillan (one of the writers on *Son of Paleface*). Bob Welch joined us. I told them of my experience in the night. Except for Tashlin, who seemed pleased, they were skeptical and tried hard to make me think I had made it up. All day my contacts with people have been pleasant and successful. I mean the little filling station, parking-lot type of contact which sometimes, with me, can be abrasive.

Wednesday November 7

To Paramount to have lunch with Louis Lipstone my boss. He is the type of man who starts the converstion with the remark that I am going to bullshit him and he is going to bullshit me. I didn't get far with him about getting started on the picture but maybe between Bob and Frank and me we can bamboozle him into putting me on salary sooner than he wants to.

To dinner with Nina at the Heinemanns. They have moved into town and have fixed up a flat with great style and charm. A white painted bird cage hangs in a window, nice dark walls and neat wallpaper, a brass bed they bought for $8 somewhere and some lovely early American furniture. Jo and Benjy, last name not known, there. He is a young writer, she a high-powered designer of clothes and bikini bathing suits. Saks has bought her line and is opening with it next month. Most of the conversation was about clothes and rather dull for me.

On the way down I told Nina about my experience of Monday night and she seemed impressed. At one point in the conversation at dinner Jo said she had seen in the paper that Jane Russell (then married to Bob Waterfield the football player) had brought a baby back from Europe. Jane had said in an interview before she went that she felt there was a baby for her to adopt, maybe in Germany. Jo scoffed at the idea of a movie siren adopting a baby or knowing what to do with it if she did adopt it. I talked for a while about Jane and what kind of woman she is. This led to stories of the Chapel and the few things I know about what has happened to people there, and while they didn't believe in a higher spirit and said so, they were just a bit impressed with some of it. I did not feel right talking about myself, but said I was going to the Chapel Thursday night. They said they would be interested in hearing what happened.

Thursday November 8

Good high today, no pills, worked well. In the evening to the little Chapel next to Mother Russell's house where a man named Batima preached a sermon about how good life can be once you accept the Lord. Jan Merritt sat next to me and confided she was disappointed in it because it was the same stuff she has been hearing since she was seven years old. This was my reaction too. I drove there with Tashlin and Chili Williams (he must have got over his fright) and before going into the Chapel we dropped in on Jamie Russell, Jane's younger brother. He is married to a beautiful and delightful girl named Pamela whose strong suit is definitely not housekeeping. The place was a mess. They have two children, one nine weeks old.

After the service a group of us went again to this little house and sat around talking and drinking coffee. Gale Storm, a young actress who has three children, and her husband; Carmen, Jane's stand-in; and her roommate whose name I didn't get, Velma somebody who has asked us to dinner Friday night; a model named Angela Foster (her first time); and Edna Skinner. Skinner is a writer who came to the Chapel about six weeks ago mainly, if not to ridicule, to say she had been and it was not for her. She thought everybody was slightly nuts when they started speaking in tongues, and not a little hammy. In the middle of the tongues stuff she got a strange feeling she was going to do it too. She fought it. She didn't want to appear as silly as the rest of the people. But she opened her mouth and started babbling in tongues along with everybody else. Then she had the horrible thought that she was going to sing. She had always possessed a not unpleasant low voice. Now she throws her head back and out comes an unknown song in the highest register. She began to perspire and as she looked at the roof of the Chapel it opened up. She thought, "I'm a heavy girl. Somebody hold my feet, I'm going through the roof." At the end of this demonstration she calmed down and saw Mother Russell smiling at her. She got baptized that night. Next day she went out to see Mrs. Russell who explained the phenomenon. She said that amid all the feeling of physical disturbance and upheaval the spirit had entered her body. Edna Skinner said if she had not yet become a true believer, what happened next clinched it.

Late one night a girlfriend telephoned and said she was going to commit suicide. She worked for a real estate agent, hadn't made a sale in nine months and was down to her last dollar. Edna said, "Wait a minute..." put her hand over the phone and asked the Lord what on earth was she to do. She took the phone into her bedroom, grabbed the Bible and read to the girl for twenty minutes until the crisis seemed to be over. She said, "You go to bed now and call me at eleven o'clock tomorrow morning." Edna went to sleep. At eleven the next morning she was awakened by the girl's call. The girl said that even though the implements she was going to use were on the bed beside her she fell into a deep sleep. Edna told her it was prayer that had done it. Now the girl calls her every day at eleven. She has made her first sale and collected a commission of $2,500. Her sister paid off a long-standing loan and patched up an ancient quarrel. She is going with a nice fellow.

So Edna Skinner finds God and has been able to perform a few little miracles with whatever power she has discovered.

The coffee session in the messy little house and Edna's tale prompted Tashlin to tell something similar. A woman called him in the middle of the night and said she had caught her husband playing around and she was going to take her children and leave. Frank said he talked her out of it by reading parts of the Bible to her. I said, "This has got to give you a sense of power." He said, "You'll be doing it too before long." I said, "Not me. I'm not the type people appeal to for help," and he said he hadn't been the type either but since he got the message he has made more friends, particularly women friends, than ever before. I said something like bully for you, thinking of the opportunities for sex. As though reading my mind he said, "And I'm enjoying these relationships more because there is no possibility of sex interfering and messing things up." I found that a little hard to swallow, but we drove Chili Williams home and I *felt* the changed atmosphere from just a week ago. There was a palpable feeling in the car that nobody was going to make any passes and we all knew it. The evening had passed without drinking anything except coffee and we all felt just as high and good as though we had been boozing it up all night as we used to.

Saturday November 10

Picked up Chili and Angela Foster (the new recruit) and drove them to Linsk's. We were intending to swim but the day was overcast and chilly so we spent the afternoon in the house. Ernie Gann, a writer (nine books) and a flyer (pilot on the San Francisco-Tokyo run for Transocean), is staying with Lester. He's a rugged, hard drinking geisha-house frequenter and a Japanophile. Bob Welch was there. We had a hilarious first hour on the Chapel. Tashlin has named Lester "Beezle" (short for Beelzebub). Lester and his brother Joe are up in arms about Tashlin taking all the tail to Chapel and getting them converted, making it difficult for the boys to get laid. Ernie Gann was entertaining a very nice girl named Kay Womack who works in the Hoffman Travel Bureau in the Beverly Wilshire Hotel. He had gone in to buy a ticket and she had recognized him from a jacket picture on one of his books. They are enjoying a romance. She served in Japan with the Army and she and Ernie play Japanese records and get nostalgic.

We had a few drinks, then went to Dominick's, a very nice little restaurant on Beverly Boulevard near Chasen's. After dinner a comedy writer named Hank Garson persuaded Lester, who was getting loaded, to play the piano. We all cheered him on when he started on "Where or When." He is normally slow, but drunk he is practically at a standstill. He strikes a chord, thinks, then strikes another. It was very funny until Garson figured one chorus would take all night and slammed the cover on Lester's fingers. The talk was mostly about who was going to boff whom and got dull.

Sunday November 11

Went to pick up Joyce to take her for the afternoon. She had been sick in the night; Florence looked like she had had a bad night too. Joyce again determined not to enjoy the day. In the car I told her she could be happy very simply—ask God to make her feel good. She said she would try it. At least half of the afternoon when she wasn't holding on to feeling bad she felt good. I caught her smiling a few times and every now and then, in spite of herself, she would get carried away with something that caught her interest. We saw *The Day the Earth Stood Still.* I for the third time. (The record is held by *The Greatest Show on Earth.* They made me go to that six times.)

Met Tashlin, had dinner at the Villa Nova then drove to the Chapel.

We started with some songs. By now they had found out I could play the piano and we always started and ended with some stomping, rocking, holy-rolling hymns. There was a big turnout. Carmen, Jane's stand-in, Edna Skinner, the new convert, Rhonda Fleming, Velma, Yvonne de Carlo, Tashlin, the usual group of star-gazers and Ray and Conrad.

These two brothers are recent additions to the cast. Ray comes to lech after the girls. One of the first he made a pass at was Pamela. Her husband Jamie, instead of punching the son of a bitch in the nose, nails him every chance he gets and tries to interest him in the Lord.

When the squares had left Jane came in and organized a group pray-in for a girl who is in jail downtown on a drug rap. They all took off in tongues and my reaction was the same as it always is: A mixture of incredulity and embarrassment. They all sounded as if they had gone completely nuts and for fifteen minutes I thought I can't get this crazy even if it leads to peace and happiness. This went on for about an hour and Edna Skinner who was near me went off into a most beautiful song. Her voice soared. The piece, sung in some strange Asiatic-sounding tongue, had form and line and ended the way it began with a re-statement of the theme. Astonishing to my analytical musical mind. They took a break. Mrs. Russell came and talked to me. She asked, "Are you hungry?" I assumed she was talking about spiritual hunger but not being sure asked her what she meant. She said, "If you are ready to accept the Lord you *know* you want it. You open yourself and the spirit comes in and takes over." I said I did want it, but being English, shy, reserved and reticent, almost totally wrapped up in myself and the problems of writing music, I didn't think I *could* get it. I thought if I went off into this crazy thing everyone would notice me, my appearance, etc. But Mother Russell is tough. She looks like one of those pioneer women who came across the country in a Conestoga wagon. Nothing stops her.

The lights in the Chapel were turned low. She asked me to lie down. Frank put his hand on my shoulder, Carmen knelt to my left, Jane put her hands on my temples and Jamie started poking me in the belly. He said the idea was to praise the Lord. Start for instance by saying, "Hallelujah," over and over then let the tongue say whatever words or sounds that come to it. The spirit moves in and has the tongue say what the spirit wants. I started, feeling mighty silly. For about fifteen minutes I got nothing—no outside manifestation. We stopped and talked. Jane said that making vowel sounds then adding consonants before the vowels helped to get it started. We tried again. During these efforts of mine all the others were off in the strangest tongues, Carmen occasionally breaking out into an Oriental tune. This time I was able to forget about myself and concentrate on having what I was saying go straight up through space and beyond the stars to the Lord. Every now and then when my concentration was total I was taken away in strange and wonderful-sounding tongues. My sincerity at this time, the complete elimination of self consciousness—the thing we were doing becoming less important and the meaning of what we were doing all important—gave me a sense of contact with God. Then Jamie shouted, "Louder! More voice!" and I came back to reality. "Do it again!" This time it was easier for me to start the concentration process and in a moment there was a new flight of tongues and new sounds.

When we stopped I had been on my back for two hours and these good people had been working with me all that time. It was considered only a partial baptism. I knew perfectly well a good deal of the time my literal, natural being was fighting it but it was clear to them when this fight was momentarily in abeyance. I had periods when I forgot myself and the others, when there was a sense of oneness between me and the person to whom I was praying. I was weak in the knees.

A group of us went to the Round Up, a restaurant on Ventura that served breakfast from midnight to noon. Most of them ate like cowhands in from a grueling cattle drive. Frank and I had coffee. I said that Edna's song was so beautiful I would like to record her sometime, make an accompaniment and release it as a commercial record. (Shows you how much I know about the record business.) We had a lot of laughs. Wouldn't it be great if she went into a studio to record and the orchestra had to wait until the spirit moved her?

Monday November 12

Tashlin and I to the Herrmanns. I mentioned the experiences we were having at the Chapel. Herrmann put it down. "The thing you are going through produces a state of euphoria. It won't last." He said, "It's all right to lean on religion if you are not strong enough to stand the pressures of the world without it." He said the religion of musicians, painters and all creative people should be their art. Herrmann changed the subject and discoursed for a couple of hours, bolstering his arguments with copious quotes. It was a long evening and on the way home Tashlin said, "All night your friend gave us the views of Wagner, Vaughan Williams, Charles Ives, Shaw, Voltaire, Anatole France, Reiner and Toscanini and Dimitri Mitropoulos. Except on the subject of religious experience, you never hear what Herrmann thinks."

Benny does have a rare quality. He can read something—a book or a piece of music—and he's got it forever.

Tuesday November 13

Worked well again. The euphoria is lasting and I feel physically and spiritually wonderful. No pills since the beginning.

Saw a picture Sid Kuller has just produced: "Actors Blood" and "Woman of Sin," two stories by Ben Hecht to be released under the title *Actors and Sin*. Except for a draggy start, very good. The music by George Antheil is fairly good; the leitmotifs for the characters are original and he is a good orchestrator. The playing was ragged but Antheil said they didn't have enough time to do it well. The budget always comes first.

Nina came by in the evening with a stew which we ate as we watched television. She is all fired up about the Chapel. Sees the difference in me. She had an hour's talk with Tashlin and asked him if going to the Chapel would bring us together again. He said she should not go with that idea, that whether we got back together or not she would be able to accept it without pain.

I told her in great detail about the baptism experience. She doesn't know why the acceptance of Jesus should make such a difference in one's life. She has always believed in Jesus and whatever happened to her she accepted as God's will even if she didn't always like it. Knowing me as well as she does and adding what little she knows of Tashlin, the change she sees in us both is very puzzling to her.

This character Ray who goes to the Chapel to get with a female—any female—has been talking to Tashlin. (He gets them all.) He has twice attempted suicide. Walking down a street late one night he smashed his fists through plate glass windows. He called Chili for a date. She called Frank, who warned her off saying Ray might get violent. She called Carmen and Velma who both have been propositioned by Ray and they urged her not to see him. She saw him and he ran smack up against God. Couldn't get to first base and Chili talked him blind about accepting religion.

Next night at Chapel Mrs. Russell said, "God so loved the world—the world—" and looking at Ray, "and that means all the stinkers too."

Wednesday November 14

Nina and I to dinner with Robert Russell Bennett and his wife Louise at Chasen's. Topic A must have come up, for Russell told about his communications with the spirit world. He said he contacts a woman named Betty White. She says she knows a certain Shakespeare who is an actor and a playwright. Betty White will find out some day that Russell Bennett is the greatest theatre orchestrator of our time here. He has done shows for every theatre composer including Richard Rodgers, who, says Russell, is a chaser. (On shows I did with Russell I never saw *him* go to lunch with less than six chorus girls.) Max Dreyfuss, the founder and head of Chappel & Co., the great theatrical music publishers, according to Russell said he never got inside of Rodgers. I asked how Rodgers worked. Russell said, "I don't know. Hammerstein turns over a lyric he's been working on for three weeks and Rodgers brings in the tune the next day." (I once asked Rodgers how long it took him to write "Oh

What a Beautiful Morning" and he said, "How long does it take to sing it?") Rodgers' wife Dorothy, the most charming woman I have ever met, is ill. Russell thinks that Rodgers must be a difficult man to live with. (The impression I have of Rodgers socially is that he is most solicitous of his wife.) Russell thinks that because he is such a barracuda in business he must be cold at home.

(Intermission at the opening of a Rodgers & Hammerstein show. Woman to Russell, "What would Mr. Rodgers do without you?" Russell, "Hire another orchestrator.")

Thursday November 15

Had a talk with Milton Tyre, lawyer, who is handling the recovery of some money from the insurance company representing the woman who ran over my daughter Ann. He requires an authorization signed by me and Florence. When he called her to explain this she could not understand why I was interested in the suit. Milton explained that the purpose of the suit was to get enough money to cover the doctors and hospital bills. Florence said all she wanted to get out of it was enough for a week in Palm Springs.

Went to Chapel. Nina's first visit. Mrs. Russell in great form. She talked about their being in London for Jane's appearance at the Command Performance. They stayed at the Savoy. There was so much publicity they got baskets of mail. One letter was from a woman who sounded destitute and desperate. Mrs. Russell got a cab and went to the address. The cab driver wouldn't let her go into the building alone. Together they climbed three dark flights of stairs striking matches. They knocked on the woman's door. No answer. They knocked on the next door and a Dickensian character opened it crying that he knew nothing and to go away. When she got back to the hotel she wrote a note to the woman, who eventually appeared and said she needed a winter coat. Mrs. Russell arranged for her to get one.

Another woman telephoned. She had a baby she wanted Miss Russell to take to America for the chance of an education and a good home. The woman brought the baby to the Savoy. It was wearing a little suit and a pair of shoes, never walked on, that Mrs. Russell thought must have cost someone a week's wages. There is a

law, Mrs. Russell explained, that forbids an English child being
adopted by foreigners and taken out of the country. The woman
said the child was an Irish citizen. Jane and her mother were flying
back to the States the next day. They all arranged to meet at the
Irish consulate the next day at four. Tea was served in the suite.
The woman refused the pastries saying she was not used to such
rich food but took two of them home for her children.

At the consulate the next day papers were signed and the
question of vaccination and a visa came up. Both of these items
were available and were attended to then and there. Jane decided
to take the baby on the plane with them.

The woman met them at the airport and handed the baby,
wrapped in a Turkish towel, to Mrs. Russell saying, "I know you'll
always love him." Everything had happened so quickly there had
been no leak to the press. A newsman discovered there was a baby
traveling alone on an Irish passport: He played his hunch, got on
the plane, found Jane and asked her if she was taking a baby with
her. She burst into tears and the thing was out. They took off,
landed in New York, went to the hotel and Jane gave the baby a
bath while her mother went out to buy him some clothes.

The abduction was a big story on both sides of the Atlantic. The
papers say that a question will be asked in Parliament today
(Thursday), "Are we raising British babies for export?" Earlier
today Mrs. Russell had a call from London. "If Jane Russell was the
woman they thought she was, she would return the child to
England, and did Mrs. Russell have a statement?" Yes she did. She
said the parents had had offers of adoption in England but wanted
the child brought to America. "Since it is the wish of the parents
we will give the child a home here, educate him and love him. He
will not be returned."

Friday November 16

Went to CBS to watch Dick Mack taping the Martin & Lewis
show. Dennis Morgan the guest. Wacky and bad. The writers said
he wasn't as bad as Shelley Winters the week before. They said
Dennis Morgan has piles and what's Shelley's excuse?

Saturday November 17

Didn't work today. In the evening to Mary and Harry Ackerman's for dinner. Took Nina. Very nice party. The only real square
there was a young, hard-driving CBS lad named Lester Gottlieb.
Others present included Howard Meighan, a pleasant CBS vice
president, Larry Berns and Sandra Gould, a marvelous funny
couple, and Guy Della Cioppa, the only friend at CBS who tipped
me off I was on the blacklist there.

I don't think women know what they are getting into when they
break the pattern of a good married life. It stinks sometimes, but I
know, for example, that Florence would rather be married than
not. I saw more of Carol, my first wife, after she married Paul
Hollister than I saw of her during the last two years of our
marriage. We would meet more or less surreptitiously at Pierre's
on 53rd street, our old lover's restaurant. When it got around that I
was going to get married again, Carol put together a dossier on
Florence. An orphan, no parents, no education, ill equipped to run
a ménage for me, a mistake. A lot of this was communicated to me
over the backstage telephone at the "Hit Parade." Her facts were
unassailable but I went ahead anyhow.

But back to pontificating about marriage. No woman should
marry a composer, of course, but if they do marry a composer or
anyone else who fills empty sheets of paper with stuff they pull up
out of their guts, a little time invested in learning to help the work
and the marriage along instead of hindering it might result in fewer
failures. I think women should be independent; then if they marry
a son of a bitch they can walk. A woman who loathes housework,
has a couple of children to bring up and is not too mad about her
husband is in a spot. That's a fairly apt description of Florence.

Right now money is running short, we can last about two weeks.
Florence has put her maid on notice. I am suggesting we borrow
money on one of the insurance policies in trust for the children
until Paramount puts me back on salary.

Sunday November 18

After insufficient sleep drove Joyce to that fabulous phenomenon
Knott's Berry Farm where Doy O'Dell, a hillbilly TV star, was

doing something billed as a turkey chase. Knott's Berry Farm has a large and complete replica of a mining village, a gold mine, stage coaches for the kids to ride in, a few stores for the tourist trade with very high prices, a couple of restaurants and a lone Indian dancing in the streets to his own tom tom accompaniment. At the end of the dance he said to the gawkers, "That's the Ghost Town Boogie Woogie."

Joyce very bad tempered. Making remarks about fat people and ugly people. I reasoned with her on the same basis as last week. She said, "You talk too much about the Lord." I turned mean and took her home before the turkey chase. Four hours driving in Sunday traffic bumper to bumper.

I was exhausted when I got to Chapel. Seemed almost none of us felt like it but the spirit the people generated gradually gave us a lift. I think Nina is about ready to accept the gift of tongues. Her presence made me self-conscious and I had trouble praying. Pretty good demonstration of how self-conscious I am about everything.

Friday December 14

Flew to Philadelphia where my father is in the terminal stages of kidney cancer. He is in the Abingdon Memorial Hospital and looks like Gandhi. His eyes and Adam's apple are life size, the rest has wasted away. Mother is behaving with typical English cheerfulness, full of faith that he will get better.

Since 1923, the year my father emigrated to America two years ahead of the rest of us, he has been having an affair with a Miss Partington. A regular Mr. Pennypacker. He spent three or four nights with my mother and four or three with Miss Partington. My mother has raised no objections to Miss Partington visiting the old man in the hospital, absenting herself at such times. This compromise with a situation she could not control has had a price. Last summer she was given shock treatments.

Visited first wife Carol's mother Daisy, a spry 67-year-old. Saw brothers Alan and Kenneth briefly at the North Philadelphia station where I caught the four o'clock to New York.

Had a nice dinner with Gene and Helen Loewenthal. He managed and sang in my choruses in New York from 1934 to 1946. Checked into the Ambassador where the room clerk said he thought the score for *The Prowler* was superior, and what nicer welcome could a composer wish? Called Deems Taylor, who is separated from Lu. (Deems married her when she was 20 and he was 60. Three weeks after the wedding I asked him how he was doing and he said, "No complaints, yet.") Went to the James Melton rehearsal and saw a lot of my old singers. Then to NBC to see Englebach. I wanted to pin him down to get me a TV show but all he talked about was how good he would be on Broadway. While there Henny Youngman came in with a comic named Archie something who had just returned from England. We talked about how tough the English critics are on American productions and performers. They had just wiped *South Pacific* off the map. Archie said he got good notices. "We took two critics to dinner the night before I opened. I have a beautiful and charming wife and we bullshitted them."

Had lunch at Al & Dick's with Carol (first love-first wife). Dick brought out a bottle of champagne. Carol looks older and is not winning the battle of blubber. When she was younger and more vivacious, whenever she laughed her eyes went into straight lines. Now her eyes disappear and you see only the ends of her false eyelashes. She produces a TV show called "Mama" based on *I Remember Mama.* Norway offered her a St. Olaf medal for her work but for the sake of the publicity she is having it presented to Peggy Wood who plays the lead. She says New York is tough, a fight all the way. I pointed out she hadn't done so badly; she was brilliant, brainy and charming and twice as tough as New York. I told her I had seen her mother in Philadelphia. She said she had not seen her mother in many years. When I asked why, she said, "Since I've been analyzed I no longer feel guilty about not seeing her." A rather sad occasion. I had loved her.

I went to my old offices in 52nd Street near Madison and saw Mike Ellis, Jimmy Russo, Paton Price and Ralph Alswang who took over my lease and are now producing plays. I walked round the corner to CBS and saw a number of people: Lucille Singleton, who had hired me to take over Kostelanetz's job in 1934; Jim Fassett, happy running the cultural programming; and Julius Mattfeld, who has run the music library for well over twenty years. He is a thin, nervous man with a high penetrating voice and, as he was when I first met him, full of complaints. He stormed and paced and cried that the network that commissioned pieces by composers like Roy Harris, Deems Taylor, etc., introduced Earl Robinson's "Ballad for Americans" and "The Lonesome Train," Sandburg's "The People Yes," and others—on that network music is dead. Killed by people like Hubbell Robinson. He says he gets memos from people he has never seen, that there are secretaries and others who don't know who he is or what he does. When I joined the network in 1934 he somehow got the idea that my father was an Episcopalian priest, probably because Carol's father *was* an Episcopalian priest. He would call me down to the library and show me some piece of music I had sent down to be copied. Waving it under my nose he would cry. "Your father would be ashamed of you!. Using parallel fifths!" I left him remembering and crying.

Saturday December 15

Dad died at 3:45 p.m.

Tuesday December 18

A most touching thing happened today. I haven't been doing radio for six months, and members of the Hallmark orchestra sent me a pair of antique gold cufflinks for a Christmas present.

1952

Monday April 14

Tonight at about six Terry Haskin called. She sounded disturbed and in fact said if she didn't get some help she would throw herself off the Malibu pier.

She is married to Bunny Haskin, 53, a fairly successful writer-director in Hollywood for the last 30 years. He is an alcoholic. A bodyguard has been engaged for the sole purpose of keeping him away from the bottle when he is working.

She came over. I gave her a drink. She didn't touch it because suddenly she had to be taken to Lucey's, the restaurant near Paramount, to drop something off for her husband's agent. I took her there. While I talked to Herbert Wilcox in the bar she telephoned their Malibu beach house and spoke to her husband. Robert Newton, the English actor, sat near the door attired in rough sea-going clothes waving a bottle of gin. He had that day finished retakes on *Androcles and the Lion.* Between his legs was a bag containing $20,000 in cash. He was about to leave for Jamaica. To the movie executives pushing in and out he addressed such remarks as, "Got everything pinned down, gentlemen?" or "How many actors did we screw today, chums?" Terry came back from telephoning and said she did not want to go back to her husband. I persuaded her to reconsider.

Driving down to Malibu Terry told me her life with Bunny had turned into a nursemaid's job, trying to keep him sober while working, hiring people to watch him when she was away, and furthermore she was in love with someone else who would have nothing to do with her because she was all loused up and drank too much. She insisted on stopping at the Malibu Inn for a drink.

In the Inn we met Larry Daniels, June Eckstine and Bunny Haskin's bodyguard, who was drunk at the bar. Terry told me, trying to focus her eyes, that Bunny was used to money and high living. If she relaxed her vigilance for a moment he would be finished in Hollywood. Bunny claims, she says, that if she left him he would die.

We stayed an hour and I persuaded the bodyguard to take Terry home. After they had gone Larry Daniels, very drunk, said, "She's a nympho."

Tell me where but in good old Hooray for Hollywood, Movietown, U. S. of A., could you assemble in one evening such a sorry collection of wasted, hopeless, lost souls?

Sunday April 27

Spoke to the graduating class at John Burroughs High School. Subject: How to make a living in music. Painted a bleak picture of the prospects because of the unemployment among musicians here and the pervasive use of recorded music on radio and television. I spoke encouragingly about the demand for music cutters. (Music cutters splice music tracks into the pictures.) Kenneth Helvey, head of the music department at Burroughs, came to me after the talk. He said that teaching takes so much energy the idea of becoming a music cutter appealed to him.

Nina has been going through a mess. She was at the Chapel one night when they were having a message session. One of the girls got a message straight from God that she should not sign our divorce papers.

Nina has moved in with a woman she recently met named Ann Grevler, a South African here on a visitor's permit. Grevler claims to be an emissary of God. Her name in this role is Michael and she gets messages too. One of them was that Nina and I were going to be reconciled.

One morning at three o'clock my telephone rang. It was Grevler-Michael saying I should come to her apartment immediately. Nina was there in a trancelike state. Her clothes were dirty and she obviously hadn't bathed for days (most unusual in a woman who when we were together bathed three times a day and whose cleaning bills were larger than our mortgage payment.) She transmitted messages. She now has a brilliant mind, even more brilliant than mine, and we are to be together again. She had not been to work for several days and looked so ill I telephoned her sister Dody in Jacksonville. She suggested I ask the Schuchmans to go round to see if they could get her out of the place.

I have heard she has returned to Blair Drive, gone back to work, and seems calmer. If these reports are true there is a possibility she may sign the papers soon. She is considering going back to Jacksonville to think things over. Why always to some remote point to think? On the whole a nightmarish situation, one that points up the dangers of evangelical teaching to emotionally unstable women. The business of getting messages not to go to work, messages not to sign papers, messages that there will be an earthquake at six p.m. Saturday, that *this* place will be destroyed, *that* place blessed, the placing of responsibility for everything on God seems to me not only ridiculous but dangerous.

Paramount is giving me a bad time. The contract which should have gone into effect February 21 is not yet signed. A big story in the trade papers about Howard Hughes denial of billing to Paul Jarrico who refused to tell the Un-American Activities Committee whether or not he had been a Communist. Jimmy Townsend at William Morris was talking of submitting me to Hughes. I asked him if he knew I was listed in Red Channels. "Jesus," he said, "Thanks for telling me. Maybe I'd better not submit you."

The political situation here is frightening. I can't help but think Paramount is holding up the contract on this account, although I have no definite reason for thinking so. More probably they are changing their plans at the studio and don't need me. In the meantime I turn down conflicting radio engagements and don't look elsewhere, since William Morris and Norman Tyre, my lawyer, assure me the deal is set. Money pressure is terrific. Florence has had her house up for sale for months with no takers.

Tuesday May 20

Been working on a television audition for Joan Davis titled "I Married Joan." Jim Backus is in the cast playing her husband. A Backus-ism: Never get involved with an out-of-work actress. First thing you know she wants to borrow $500 till Flag Day.

I have been going down to Lewis Milestone's beach house weekends where Bob and Marsha Presnell are installed. Drove out late last Sunday night and they and an English actress named Dawn Addams, a real prig, were taping excerpts from *Cyrano*, *Glass Menagerie* and other acting exercises. I am tremendously impressed with Marsha's and Presnell's qualities.

Abe Frisch, a lawyer I met in New York, here briefly. Had dinner with him at Dominick's. He is exploring a field of science which might lead to something. He makes dies, a strip composed of tiny bars of varying measurements—.0027 of an inch is an example. He places these bars on magnetic tape, runs a magnet over them, and produces tones. By removing every fifth bar, or every third, et al., he gets different fundamentals and different overtones. His tone colors can be varied too. I gather his experiments are creating a stir—professors visit him to examine the gadget.

Wednesday May 28

There are lots of Joseph Pasternak stories. This is one Andre Previn told me. The MGM producer was examining sketches of costumes for a schoolteacher character. "Looks too expensive for a schoolteacher," he said. "What do they make—$200 a week?" The designer said, "More like $200 a month." Pasternak, "So—$200 a month, $200 a week, what's the difference?"

Signed the Paramount contract. They paid me retroactive to February 20, 1952. Term is for 30 months.

Jimmy Russo (stage manager of *Finian's Rainbow*, partner of Mike Ellis), Milton Rosenstock (conductor of "This is the Army") and Charles Sherman (writer primarily) in town to sign Bette Davis for a new revue, *Two's Company*. Spent a delightful evening with Presnell and Dawn Addams (no longer identified as a "prig"), then to her house. She went in. We stood outside and loudly sang "Juanita." Why "Juanita?" I don't know. We went in and stayed until five o'clock, trying to get her to set up a ménage à trois.

We read John Collier and poetry. We were expected at the beach where Marsha was awaiting us. We never made it. (All married men have a roving eye.)

Herrmann thinks Presnell and Marsha are not as close and together as they seem. How could she have any respect for a man who is so mixed up that he worries more about the condition of the world than his work? (He doesn't know Marsha. She worries more about the condition of the world, and people, than even Presnell.)

Frank Tashlin and Bob Welch have sent me the script of *Red Garters*. It is a film to star Jane Russell, Rhonda Fleming and Yvonne DeCarlo, not to mention Jimmy Durante, Donald O'Connor, Dan Dailey, William Demarest and Eddie Quillan. The cast will cost $850,000.

Tonight I got all steamed up and resumed reworking my ballet "Camptown" but my early-to-bed neighbor, Dr. Popper, complained and I had to stop. Fletcher Markle and Mercedes Mc-Cambridge were at the Herrmanns Sunday. They are planning to go to Europe this summer and asked me to take their house for nine weeks. I will if they go. Fletcher is not at MGM any more and if he got a picture somewhere I imagine they would call off the trip. I must find some place where I can work. More and more I get nothing done in the morning, a bit in the afternoon, but really get rolling at night.

Nina still has not signed the agreement. She is asking for the right to live at Blair Drive another two years rent free. Showed her it was not possible and she said she would sign the agreement as it stands. Lucille Herrmann told me Nina is interested in a man. Maybe I'll get out with less than two years' support if she behaves and doesn't beat the man down. We were married for a year and a half.

Wednesday June 11

Nina has signed.

Saw Bretaigne Windust tonight (director of *Finian's Rainbow* and a lot of Theatre Guild plays). He bought a house in such bad repair that he engaged a Swedish contractor to put it in shape. This man was so sly and bitchy he brought back Windy's ulcer. Needed five transfusions, and of course he's now on a diet. I had an ulcer in 1931 and after two years on a diet of scraped lamb got rid of it by going to Howard Johnson's and drinking scotch and soda and eating ice cream. I hope the pressure of the last few months doesn't bring it back.

Victor Bay and I got together recently and decided to write the books for a dozen or so short Biblical operas. We have finished five. We did Adam and Eve, Samuel, Solomon and the Baby, The Exodus, and Lot's Wife, which we call "Pillar of Salt." I read them to Windust tonight and he thought well of them. We propose to get all the best known composers from Stravinsky on down to write the scores. Victor met a rich woman who has promised to do some of the spadework when we get ready. Publicity and money from the Ford Foundation and such.

Thursday June 12

Saw the Joan Davis film. Not good. Worked unsuccessfully with Victor Bay on "Ruth." We didn't lick it today. Tough story to do.

Had dinner with Inge von Schoenfeldt, an interesting woman, correspondent for the Cologne *New Illustrated,* a sort of German LIFE. She is from Mannheim, has worked in Rome and is here to cover Hollywood for the magazine. She is fascinated by the 254 religions operating in Los Angeles, so I took her to the Chapel. Mother Russell in fair form. Something must be bothering her. She said in Hollywood it is dog eat dog, and the last one goes bust.

Inge has a sharp mind. I met her at the Hollywood Christian Group where I had been taken by Melody Lowell, one of the dancers in *Son of Paleface.* The three of us got in my car and since I am into minds these days it was no contest. We dropped Melody off and went to Inge's apartment. She dresses and wears her hair like a lesbian. Tonight in the Chapel I thought I saw her chest heaving when Rhonda Fleming came in.

Friday June 13

Wrote a tune today and composed a nice ungrammatical lyric for it.

Went to a party at Ann and Bill Lester's (he's an actor). Jeff and Connie Alexander, Bert Freed, the Presnells, Selena Royle (black-listed actress) and her new husband, a delightful Frenchman named Georges Renevent. He started a story about an incident at the Comédie Française by saying, "You don't know you've got a hat on when you are wearing a wig." Elderly actor standing in the wings wearing a wig and a top hat. Someone hands him another hat. He thanks him and makes his entrance wearing both hats. Left the party at twelve, picked up Dawn Addams and followed the Presnells to the beach where, in the guest trailer, I spent the coldest night I have ever experienced. If it hadn't been for Dawn Addams' dog Whistler getting into bed with me I would be dead of pneumonia. Spent a lovely day. Read the *Love of Four Colonels* by Peter Ustinov. Dinner at the Holiday House. The sleeping arrangements at Milestone's house are weird. To get to the bathroom I had to go through Dawn's room. When I went through she was sobbing hysterically. She had a letter from Aberdeen. "It's Nanny," she wept, "she's dead." Pause. Then I said, "Why does death upset you so much?" She said, "Because I don't like it."

Saturday June 14

My first (ungrammatical) song lyric goes as follows:

You and me and the sea around us,
Stars gleam like lanterns in the velvet night,
You and me and the world behind us,
Moon beams a path of shining silver light,

Long before we met, I would walk with the tide,
Dreaming empty dreams while the moon
looked down and cried,

Now there's you and the sea to bind us,
Soon the sun will arise and find us,
High as the tide on its moon-mad ride,
Lost in the wonder of love.

So it's ungrammatical and worse, but it's my first flight and everybody, but everybody, thinks he can write a song.

Today the children were here at the Chateau swimming. Joyce's marks in math on the whole very good. Dropped in at the Herrmanns and met his mother. His daughters Taffy and Wendy there, also the Alexanders. Jeff is taking pictures in stereo. Frighteningly lifelike. Like Madame Tussaud's.

Tuesday June 17

Grace LaRue, a famous old vaudeville performer, called on me today with a song. She talked mostly about the songs she had made into hits in her Palace days. She belongs to a religious cult called Ba'hai. Aside from talk of this group she spoke mainly of the past.

Jackie Gayle (the music publisher) was here complaining about business being off and wishing for a war with Russia so that things would pick up. I played him my "The Sea Around Us" song and he launched into a lament about how there weren't any good lyric writers around anymore.

Thursday June 19

Got up early this morning and started studying Jack Hayes's Trumpet Concerto which I have promised to conduct. To Schwab's for lunch where I read the fourth installment of Lillian Ross's piece in *The New Yorker* on the making of *The Red Badge of Courage*. In it Dore Schary (studio head at MGM) remarked that music in movies should be cliché. If it's a picture about the Marines, play "Halls Of Montezuma." I thought that if this kind of mentality was in charge of production at the studio in England where they made *Hamlet* and *Henry V* we would not have those magnificent William Walton scores. I am despondent about the state of music in this town. Mostly idiots running it—except for Al Newman at Fox, of course, who has created a fine orchestra and pioneers improvements in the sound. The recorded sound in movies mostly way behind the times. (However, it was the sound of the Waxman, Korngold scores at Warners that made me want to become a movie composer.)

Inge von Schoenfeldt telephoned today and we made a date to spend Saturday at the beach. Feeling what she described as "an adventurous spirit" she and another girl have been visiting old Hollywood mansions. They saw Valentino's house and one that used to belong to Carl Laemmle. This one has a swimming pool surrounded by a large sandy beach with a palmetto shack for a bar. She is doing a piece for her magazine on these relics of the glorious past.

At the Chapel tonight I got an idea for a rocking hymn and got the tune and the lyric in about five minutes. I taught it to them and we made the joint jump. [It was later published and recorded. Called "I'm Really Livin'."]

Thursday June 26

Dinner with Presnell. In a moment of weakness he accepted my invitation to come to the Chapel. We picked up Inge and Fritz Lang, the great motion picture director. Presnell hated it. Later I went to Presnell's house on Magnolia in Sherman Oaks. Marvelous rambling hacienda, swimming pool, tennis court, a barn and a guest house. I am hoping they will let me stay in the guest house. Perfect place to work.

Ed Murrow has a five minute radio program called "This I Believe." Last night he had a cartoonist on who said he thought the word "love" in the Bible meant "respect." What a difference it would make if everyone who loved you respected you.

To a party at Sheila Cole's. She lives in a strange, old little house in a jumbled street near the beach. She is writing a musical comedy version of *Don Giovanni* with Herschel Gilbert. The lyrics she read me were filthy.

Friday June 27

Hugo Friedhofer called and we went to dinner at Dominick's, then to Bob Welch's but he was out. We segued to Presnell's who was in the middle of clearing out books and was not pleased to see us so we went to Hugo's where we listened to a new recording of the Vaughan Williams "London Symphony," which for depth, breadth and nobility is untouched. Adrian Boult, who played the first performance in 1914, conducted.

Hugo told a story about L. B. Mayer and Arthur Freed. Freed was having an affair with an actress named Lucille Bremer. He was producing a picture called *Yolanda and the Thief* with Fred Astaire and Miss Bremer. Someone went to Mayer and said, "You gotta do something about this picture. Bremer can't dance, sing or act. You are going to have a one million eight stinker on your hands." Mayer is reported to have said, "Oh, let the boy get her out of his system."

Tuesday July 15

Bill Schneider here. Talked about his analysis, which he says has helped him greatly. How? I gather it breaks bad patterns somehow. He is one of the most satisfactory friends I have. This evening conducted Jack Hayes's Trumpet Concerto at Plummer Park with the augmented MGM orchestra. Fun. Good piece.

Son of Paleface reviewed in the trades this week. Very good notices.

Joyce was run over by a car yesterday at Malibu and is in the Children's Hospital. No bones broken but plenty of lacerations. It was only a couple of months ago Ann was run over.

Went to Venice Monday night with Inge von Schoenfeldt. A real estate man's dream of about 25 years ago which didn't come off. A strange, neon-garish, ghostly town with an amusement pier.

Went to a Whittier Drive-In Sunday with Mrs. Russell and a group from the Chapel. They allow people to have services at the Drive-In on Sunday mornings. We have a singing group at the Chapel, called "The Four Girls" because it is composed of Jane Russell, Rhonda Fleming, Connie Haines and Beryl Davis. I write the arrangements. We have made some records. One, "Do Lord," was a hit. Connie Haines is a well-known big band singer and Beryl was on the "Hit Parade." We were all there at the Drive-In. We performed and Mother Russell preached to about 12 people. Velma Nideffer and Fred La Porte rode down and back in my car. Velma told us the gossip in the Chapel; La Porte is a Red spy and I am a reformed communist. Had a long talk with Tashlin about this gossip phenomenon. He said you can't drive a girl home from Chapel without the gossip crew getting to work on it.

Welch and Tashlin have a new script almost ready so I ought to be going back to work at Paramount any month now.

Wednesday July 23

Paul Santoro called. We were discussing Sammy Fain's marital problems. Sammy is the composer of "Let a Smile Be Your Umbrella," "Wedding Bells Are Breaking Up That Old Gang of Mine," "Was That the Human Thing to Do?" "That Old Feeling," "I'll Be Seeing You," "Dear Hearts and Gentle People," and "Love Is a Many Splendored Thing" among others. He married a girl he found living in a tent in Tennessee, installed her in his house in Beverly Hills with the swimming pool and a Cadillac. At parties when Sammy sat down to play his latest creation, she would come into the room and say, "Oh, is he at it again?" She put him through a hamburger machine for ten years and at the divorce hearing testified that he subjected her to cruel and inhuman treatment and got $185 a week for herself and $55 a week for her son. Santoro says you get one from the Ozarks and as soon as they find out about shoes you are dead.

Monday July 28

Bill Schneider, advertising man and part-time sculptor, and Al Dorne, great magazine illustrator, are buddies. Bill showed Al one of his bronzes. "Heavy, isn't it?" said Dorne.

Jeff Alexander and I have been buddies since he walked into my office in 1941 and I hired him. Myer Alexander he was then. Jack Kapp, president of Decca Records, did not like Jewish names and changed Myer to Jeff. (He also changed Jake Schwartzwald to Jay Blackton.) But that has nothing to do with heavy bronzes. I took Jeff to see *Son of Paleface*. He said, "A lot of music." On the way out he started humming my Torch theme. "Sounds like Rozsa's theme from *The Killers*."

Saw *Call Me Madam* Saturday with Presnell. We took Elaine Stritch, who plays the Merman part, to supper at Frascati in Beverly Hills. She is young, vivacious and funny and turned Frascati upside down talking to the customers, singing, drinking champagne, calling New York and generally carrying on. Went to Presnell's house. Cy Gomberg, Betty Carr (a dancer in Yip Harburg's show *Jollyanna*) and Elaine went swimming at three a.m.

Today worked with Sid on a tune for Joe Losey's picture *The Big Night* called "Within Me." Finished it finally after struggling with it for days. Jeff and I had supper with Joe and Eddie Quillan at Villa Nova, then to a couple of colored pros in St. Andrews Place. Mine was elegant. Showed me drawers of cashmere sweaters all carefully wrapped in tissue paper. I guess the Chapel is losing its hold on me.

Copies of the sheet music and records of "I Wish I Wuz" arrived from Denmark, where it is a hit.

Sunday August 24

Eddie Cantor is to do the "Colgate Comedy Hour" on NBC. Sid Kuller, who will produce and direct, told Cantor he wanted to use me to write musical material and brought up the fact that I am in Red Channels. Cantor said that if the NBC brass vetoed me to use me anyway—without billing. Sid went to Tom McAvity, an old friend of mine now a VP in charge of production at NBC, and laid the problem before him. McAvity said, "Use him. And give him billing."

Friday we had a long session with Cantor. He is a young and energetic 61, has a brilliant comedy mind and is altogether a terrific human being. He told anecdotes. He played Detroit during the heyday of Henry Ford's viciously anti-semitic *Dearborn Independent*. He had a telephone call from Mr. Ford and in a curtain

speech—he says he has been making curtain speeches for 35 years—
he said the real reason Mr. Ford is mad at the Jewish people is that
they can get more for second-hand Fords than he can get for them
new.

Back in Detroit a couple of years later Mrs. Edsell Ford asked
him to do a benefit for her church. Cantor, taking a small band
with him, entertained the folks and before he left handed Mrs.
Ford an envelope containing a check for $250. "So when Mrs. Ford
tells the old man about it," he said, "who feels like a prick—the old
man or me?"

He said Cardinal Spellman was a good man. He spent two days
on the telephone contacting delegates to the UN—delegates from
Catholic countries—urging them to vote for the resolution which
made Israel a nation. I said, "What about Cardinal Spellman's
attack on Mrs. Roosevelt over the issue of federal aid to parochial
schools?" Cantor said that Spellman had subsequently apologized
to Mrs. Roosevelt, proving he was a human being capable of error.

Tenney (chairman of the California Un-American Activities
Committee) accused Cantor of being a Communist and urged a
boycott of his sponsor's products. Cantor called Tenney and stated
he had belonged to the Hollywood Anti Nazi League and had
resigned when they had refused to change their name to the
Hollywood Anti Nazi and Communist League. He reported this
incident to Cardinal Spellman. One month later at a dinner at the
Waldorf-Astoria the Catholic War Veterans presented Cantor with
its annual Americanism Award.

He also told us how he raised over 100,000 pints of blood for the
Red Cross. He gives a two-hour one-man show accompanied by
two pianos. He pays the pianists $600 and transportation. The
papers have criticized him, saying he does it for the publicity. He
said, "If they take a few pictures it doesn't reduce the number of
pints of blood."

He was going to vote for Eisenhower until he found out
Eisenhower supports Joseph McCarthy. Now he is planning to
make four speeches for Adlai Stevenson. There is no doubt he has a
powerful appeal. He said he can influence about 3,000,000 votes in
this country.

As we left Cantor got into his car, backed out of the garage,
pressed a button in the car closing the garage door by remote
control. He said, "And Abe Lastfogel thinks he's a genius" (Last-

fogel, head of William Morris Agency, his agent). He called to us, "Sometimes I take the car out for a ride just to work the door."

Last Monday, Tuesday and Wednesday in Las Vegas working on the Cantor material and some stuff for the Sands show. As usual depressed by the vulgarity of this town and the waste of money.

Last night to Bill and Ann Lester's for one of those gatherings of fairly intelligent people who argue endlessly about religion, politics and the motion picture business. Julie Mitchum and a friend named Trudy there. They are Ba'hais. They say that in Ba'hai they are not entitled to an opinion of their own but that this represents free will on their part. They do not vote in national elections for the office of President. They believe the Messiah appeared in 1884 and that the millenium is now. They are taught that you cannot hate anyone—only yourself.

A couple of Eisenhower people there. One was Lester's agent, Sid Levy. He says his goal in life is to provide security for his wife and children and to prove it he said he had read of an earthquake in Chili that killed 15,000 people then turned to the sports section, but when he came home one night and discovered one of his children had pneumonia he cried.

Presnell wild and drunk. Criticized everyone's grammar.

Lester very emotional and immature about the picture business. Says they are interested only in sure things and making money. If he had more work he would probably change his tune. He suffers from a silly but widespread conflict—he is an artist working in commercial media and is miserable because the commercial media are only interested in making money.

I am writing the music for a picture at Paramount called *The Girls of Pleasure Island.* When I played the themes for Louis Lipstone, head of the music department, and Paul Jones, the producer, Louie didn't say much but made a good suggestion which I will adopt, about the structure of one of the secondary themes. Jones liked everything except the love theme. He wants it to sound more like "L'Amour, Toujours L'Amour."

Monday September 1

Saturday night Presnell and I had an expensive but fairly good dinner at the Tail o' The Cock then drove to La Jolla.

Tried to get something on the radio worth listening to and settled for Dana Andrews doing "I Was a Communist for the FBI." The most puerile drivel I have ever heard anywhere. We were going to La Jolla because Marsha is appearing at the Playhouse in *The Lady's Not for Burning* with Vincent Price, Beulah Bondi, J. M. Kerrigan, Phillip Tonge and Sean McClory. We picked Marsha up at the Valencia Hotel at 12:10 and went to a cast party given by a lady named Longstreth who works hard raising money and running the social end of things. Mel Ferrer and Dorothy McGuire there but not Gregory Peck (the three of them started the Playhouse). After to the Beach Club to join Ollie Carey and our hostess. There was a party going on straight out of F. Scott Fitzgerald. Most of the men handsome, still thin, wearing white dinner jackets and short haircuts. The women were handsome, expensive looking and everybody was drunk. Our hostess, an attractive gray-haired lady, bought us a drink before the bar closed. We met Gus Muller, Jack Thomson and a woman named Mike Lavender who seemed to have difficulty speaking. Muller invited us for a drink at his house. Ollie and I dropped Mike Lavender off. On the way to Muller's house Ollie explained that when cancer of the thyroid was discovered this lady had part of her jawbone removed.

Muller's house, which he rents from a man named McConnell, is the trap of all time. Modern, cantilevered over the ocean, a steeply slanting roof making the living room two storeys most of the way, the bedroom a balcony hanging over the living room. Opulent lounges facing an all glass front; $40,000 worth of everything I like. Someone asked what we meant by the word "trap." Presnell said, "When you bring a girl here what can she say but 'I'll stay'?" Marsha was very tired after giving two performances and was running on actress energy, so Bob took her back to the hotel.

Ollie and I went to Jana Running's nice little La Jolla beach house but the hostess had retired. Ollie showed me the room she was going to sleep in and took me across the hall to show me the attractive den-type television room where I was to sleep, when a bare arm appeared around a corner and beckoned. The hostess showed herself, still quite tight, and said, "Who do you want to sleep with, Ollie or me?" Well, I don't mind sleeping with people on short acquaintance and the temptation was strong but Ollie poked me and said, "We'd better switch rooms or you'll get raped."

With disappointing emphasis she added, "You like to do your *own* raping, don't you?" We fixed Jana a ham sandwich and a glass of milk, gave her two aspirins and put her to bed. Ollie slept on guard in the TV den and I spent the night in the other room, out of harm's enticing way. We got up about noon, Jana feeling guilty but claiming not to remember much.

She has a seven-year-old adopted daughter, is divorced from a doctor, has a walking-out fellow who arrived shortly. We went to the Beach Club where I met a very funny, very attractive lady named Peggy Thompson. She had seen the play and admired whatever it was Vincent Price had in his tights. She thought it might be mangoes except for the stringent fruit fly restrictions they have in this state. This woman is bright and witty and has been married three times. That makes one thing we have in common.

Tuesday November 25

Ollie Carey and Fran Ferrer have found me a place to live. (Fran is divorced from Mel Ferrer. She is a dear and wonderful woman who fell in love with Howard Warshaw, the artist, and refused alimony. Just takes some child support.)

The place they have found is a guest house on Douglas Fairbanks's 15-acre estate at 1515 Amalfi Drive in Pacific Palisades. The main house is a mansion and was built for Helen Twelvetrees a long time ago. The Fairbanks are in England. George, a caretaker, delights in conducting people on tours of the main house. There are seven garages. My little Jaguar nests in one of them looking lonesome. The "cabin" is charming, set among cycas and eucalyptus, with a fishpond just below the balcony. A perfect place to work. Ollie tells me Alec Wilder had it once when he was doing a picture at Fox.

I am tired from working straight through on *Pleasure Island* and segueing to *Here Come the Girls*, a Bob Hope picture.

Thursday December 25

The children came home from the Ojai Valley School for the Thanksgiving holidays and they are turning out very well. I guess the discipline at the school has something to do with it. They have come for Christmas and look more ladylike than ever. I am very proud.

We have finished the pre-recordings for *Here Come the Girls* and on the whole the results are good. Rosemary Clooney, Arlene Dahl and Tony Martin are in it. I think I could make a place for myself as a musical director—I mean of musical pictures—if all it took was conducting. But I am lousy at the politics and selling. Al Newman said it: Music in pictures takes 10 percent talent and 90 percent selling. For example we had made a take on a number with Tony Martin—40 minutes of high tension, nerve-straining concentration. As I laid the baton down Louis Lipstone brought the head of the studio to the podium. He said, "I've just been telling Don here what a wonderful main title we got. Play it for him." I said, "I've just had the orchestra pressing hard for 40 minutes. We've got to have a rest." He looked aghast. "But this is the head of the studio!" I said, "My health comes first." Don Hartman was nice about it but Louis looked like he was going to fire me then and there. Results are not enough, really. You've got to have the BS.

We have fallen into a routine on Sundays. Breakfast at the Herrmanns, then to Olive and George Behrendt's house in time for "Omnibus." The Behrendts are wonderful people. Olive used to be a singer, George is a big man, a native Californian with a prosthetic leg and "Omnibus" is the Ford Foundation's television hour and a half, produced by Bill Spier with Alistair Cooke host. They do all kinds of things—one week a play by Saroyan, next Helen Hayes playing Barrie's *The Twelve Pound Look*, a continuing Life of Lincoln by James Agee interspersed with interviews with people like Julio Diego and Roland Emmett, the Englishman who draws the funny train. Then we see Ed Murrow's "See It Now," always tremendous, then we have music. Sometimes Olive sings and all in all it is a wonderful day.

George and Olive introduced me to Helen Barnard Gruenberg and I have fallen like a redwood. She is the mother of two boys, 17 and 13, was married to a doctor and makes her way as a psychiatric social worker. I have seen her in the bosom of her family and surrounded by friends but the Friday after the Sunday we met she departed for Chicago to attend a family reunion. We corresponded. I must have bared my soul, for in a letter I had from her she said, "I am wistfully hoping that the things you say about me are not just projections of the beauty and serenity within you." It isn't every day you read such a warm and touching sentiment. I told Benny this is the first time I have been accused of harboring beauty and serenity within me. The damnable part of the relationship so far is that it is being conducted in absentia and when she returns I will be leaving for New York for *Carnival In Flanders*. It is virtually settled. The only thing that could change it is the schedule of the picture. If I read the signs right they will be editing well into February which would give me time to go and do the play and get a New York recharge. I have been here too long.

I have met several women in the year since I have been separated and going through the divorce but not one of them struck the chord, and now in one little day one's whole life takes on color and excitement. I am filled with warmth. I had it once before with Carol but she, poor girl, destroyed it. I say poor girl because now she thinks we made a mistake and when drunk wants to go back 12 years and recapture what we had. But my heart is clean and can be offered again. Helen is well educated and is the only woman I have known in years to whom it is no problem talking. She talks and I talk and there is a sense of much ground to be covered. It is a miraculous wonderful thing to be able to love someone again and I am thinking it must be a fearful responsibility for a woman to have this precious offering and spurn it.

The Herrmanns have given me a wonderful Christmas. Without them it would have been dull and perhaps lonely. Benny put me on to a novel I found a great experience, Ford Madox Ford's *Good Soldier*, and for Christmas he gave me *Parade's End*, Cecil Gray's autobiography and a book called *The Perfect Conductor*. I gave him eight volumes of *The Spectator*. He has finished *Wuthering Heights* and last Sunday at John Brahm's I played and he sang the fourth act. He gets into a perfect lather of re-creative excitement and one gets the impression that if one interfered with his trajectory at a time like this he would explode and leave nothing but a smoking crater for miles around. The opera is tremendous and contains some of the most beautiful songs I ever heard. He has spent $4,500 on the physical reproduction of the score. Rebner, the pianist at Republic studios, has done the piano-vocal reduction. Herrmann and I are planning to drive to Dallas about the 5th of January then fly to Washington and visit his children in Arlington, Virginia, then on to New York where he will try to interest the Met. He then goes to England and I have a feeling there is a better chance of a production there than in America.

Today, Christmas Day, went to the Alexanders and I got a beautiful cashmere sweater. Jerry Fielding gave me one too. I dropped in at the Presnells and collected some loot there. They are very nice to me. Then home to see if there was a letter from Helen, which there wasn't but I hardly expected one today. I was supposed to make a few calls but didn't feel like it and drove to the beach and had dinner in a dreadful tea-roomy sort of restaurant and then back home. I have been reading the diary of Dr. Campbell, an Irish minister who visited London in 1776. His eye for detail very rewarding. So are his conversations with Dr. Johnson. Asked what the two best things in life were, Dr. Johnson tells the minister, "F———g and drinking and it is surprising there are not more drunkards, for everyone can drink and not everyone can f———k." Remarkable stuff for a minister's diary. Also the anecdote about Johnson being given a lift in a carriage by a Dr. James who was riding with his "whoor." Johnson complained on finding out what the woman was, and Dr. James apologized and said that if he went longer than a month without it he got a swelling of the stones. Johnson replied, "You rascal, you are over sixty and the swelling wouldn't go any further."

I have been invited (or ordered) to do some arranging for the testimonial 90th birthday dinner for Adolph Zukor, which Rouben Mamoulian is staging on January 7. I met Mamoulian and liked him and he liked me, but as I said in a letter to Helen everyone likes me right now and that is her influence.

Saturday December 27

The John Huston film *Moulin Rouge* on its opening day at the Fox Wilshire was picketed by the American Legion. Next day in the trades the Legion said the picketing was wildcat and not official but the Los Angeles *Times* said that the Legion would picket the film nationwide. The Herrmanns and I want to see it. We drove by the theatre and were glad to see no pickets and a line around the block.

Monday December 29

A bit depressed. Guess it has to do with Helen's reiterating that I have her on a pedestal which makes it difficult for her to keep her footing and that my feeling for her is a projection of a need of mine. Smart lady. Can we work it out when she returns? I am beginning to wonder if I can live and work in a noisy family atmosphere. Smart fellow. Right now I am looking at one of the worst "Studio One's" ever. Story of a nasty young ambitious singer. All the songs done with three players (oh those budgets) and added to the puerile story, it stinks all the way.

Wednesday December 31

Having the Herrmanns, Victor Bay and the Berenbaums here to see the year out. Picked up Benny to go shopping for food and booze and on the way he told me Helen had written to George Behrendt saying she was alarmed by my letters. She called from Chicago at 10:15 our time and sensed immediately things were perhaps not all well with us. I feel low. And that's the way this year ends.

1953

Thursday March 12

About three weeks ago Bob Presnell asked me to have dinner with him and he brought Betty Hayden. She is small, thin and beautiful. Breathtaking face and eyes, lovely skin, neck and shoulders and a tense and serious mien. She has been separated from Sterling Hayden for 12 weeks and has four young children, 4½, 3½, 2½ and 7 months. She has strong opinions about how to bring up children—let them do as they please. A week later she invited me to her house for dinner. The Piroshes, Mel and Ann Frank, Carol and Larry Dudley (non pros) and Presnell. I stayed after all had left. We talked into the small hours and made a date for Wednesday, March 4. I took her to Holiday House for dinner then to her house for another long session of talk ending in some heavy necking. I have spoken to her twice a day on the telephone. Monday March 9 we went to a running of *Shane* at Paramount. A fine picture although Betty had some valid reservations—fights too brutal and long, Jean Arthur's hairdo, the boy running after Shane and getting to town at the same time though Shane was mounted, the boy on foot. We held hands and kissed in the movie. Then to her house for more long talk about ourselves and more passionate kissing. We have talked a lot about Hayden's problems, his relationship with his psychiatrist, his depressions, his violence and her fear that he might do something. She believes his mother has ruined him and their marriage.

She is the most fascinating woman I have ever met. She has dignity and poise and is remarkably mature for her age. She has definite opinions and is thus predictable. I imagine every man she meets falls in love with her. She is quite aware of this and admitted that since she and Sterling broke up 12 weeks ago she has been filled with a desire to destroy a few men. She has an analytical mind. She analyzes everything and is completely open about her feelings. If I did not feel that I understood this she could be difficult to be with. As it is I am totally relaxed with her and continually interested and stimulated. She is an uncompromising and fiercely independent woman. She takes her colored maid, whom she insists is not a maid but her friend, to places like Romanoffs, expeditions duly noted in the columns. We have a date for tomorrow and Sunday and though she has been busy all week with other friends I don't resent them. I am filled with thoughts of her. Whenever I am with others I think of introducing her into the circle, whether she would enjoy them or be bored. She has said often she would like me to meet so-and-so, that I would like him or her. I suggested that we take her children to the beach now that the weather is nice, but she thinks it would be confusing for them to begin with another man so soon after their separation from their father. We have talked a good deal about sex. She says she is not ready and the odd thing is I am not ready either, and it doesn't seem to matter at all. She has lent me some books and our telephone conversations run about an hour or an hour and a half each. I have spruced up my appearance and start with the dentist tomorrow. I feel more complete and fulfilled than I have in a long time.

Friday March 13

Dinner date with Betty at seven. She called in the afternoon and said she thought she ought to have dinner with the children. We could meet later. She called again and changed the signals. She felt like dressing up and going out. Would I come at seven and bring the closed car? When I arrived the two little boys were running around in their little nightshirts. We roughhoused a bit before they were taken to bed. In the car Betty said she had been suffering from anxiety all afternoon. After dinner at the Drake, to the Presnells. Betty hadn't seen Marsha since the trip to Washington a group made to protest the Un-American Activities hearings, but had seen Bob a few times. Marsha is going to play *Private Lives* at Palm Springs and was busy memorizing her lines but joined us for an hour. Betty was rather reserved all evening. When we left, Marsha called after Betty, "Take care of my Robert." Rather a strained evening and a more or less silent ride home. I went in and the baby sitter left. Shortly Betty said she was uncomfortable and would I go? I called her when I got home and we had a very short conversation.

Saturday March 14

This morning I called and we had a long conversation. The gist was that the anxiety she felt yesterday was caused by our relationship. I was becoming too possessive. I countered that I had tried very hard not to feel that way about her. When she was with someone else I suffered no jealousy pangs and was perfectly satisfied with whatever time and attention she could give me. She is quite discerning however and probably experienced at looking inside her men and insisted my feelings were becoming too strong. I said I had been able not to demand anything from her in the way of sex and she thought that was a) insulting and b) if I had she could have handled it. (I have been feeling way above this phase of male-female relationships, which perhaps annoys her. I knew eventually something would happen in this department and would probably be fine.) She would not tell me what it is that is causing her to begin to break this off but did say that if I described it to a professional I might get an explanation. Maybe she is doing a little destroying because of her recent separation? She suggested I see Norman Levy, a psychiatrist I have met at Ollie Carey's but he was too busy and suggested I go back to Judd Marmor. [I have no recollection of this but it is possible I had seen Judd professionally, although I have always resisted analysis.] I guess the time has come for me to find out what is preventing me from fully realizing whatever talent I have and enjoying better relations with people.

I must say that since leaving Nina I have been mostly happy. The trouble is I only feel attractive and *somebody* when I am in love with a woman whom I respect and am proud of. It is easy for me to get into bed right away with women I don't care about. Then I get guilty and break it off. I suppose I have hurt a lot of women this way who just don't have it for me. Betty has it for me. These last few weeks have not been the greatest. Helen Gruenberg and I stopped before we started, largely because George Behrendt said to someone I was so stuck on her I would marry her in a minute and neighbors began referring to me as her boy friend. Gave me pause.

I met a girl named Helen C. and we went to bed a few times, not too successfully. Another woman I met at the Presnells' became too possessive after a few times in the hay and I ran. I had three dates with Joan Elan, one of the English girls brought over for the picture *Girls of Pleasure Island*, who barely spoke, and with whom I did not dream of doing anything. Dawn Addams attracted me greatly but had absolutely no interest in me. I felt inferior with Elan and Addams but the non-affair with Betty Hayden gave me what might be described as a sense of superiority—not to her, but more of a sense of confidence in myself. She liked me enough to spend time with me and produced in me a reaction I haven't felt in a long time. I spruced myself up, got my hair cut, paid some attention to my clothes and felt an urge to fix up this cottage so it would be attractive to her although I never asked her here.

In sum, the approbation of a woman like Betty Hayden makes me feel important and attractive. I haven't felt that way since Carol. When a woman who is intelligent, attractive and conversationally adept shows interest in the little things I have to say about what happens from day to day and makes these little things seem interesting, I am a pushover. When I am not the object of this kind of woman's affections I feel I am not interesting to other people. One knows immediately when the chemistry is there. For example, Jack Hayes introduced me to a very attractive woman who lives with her 14-year-old daughter on a farm above Malibu. We both felt an attraction but both of us sensed it was not enough and I did nothing about it.

All day today I have been wondering about accepting an invitation to dinner at the Herrmanns. Victor Bay, John Houseman and his wife are going to be there. I think I will go and be determinedly not down about this. Betty is spending the evening with Jack Sher, who has been separated from Matty for some months now. Betty told me Sher has tried to get her in bed but so far she has refused on the grounds that she could do this with every man she likes but why should she? Sher's only answer was that it would be different with him. He is well along in analysis. He is a talented writer riddled with neuroses and I believe even less mature than I. Nina has been after me to have dinner, but I have ducked it because even the appearance of "cohabitation" can negate a divorce action.

In one of our necking sessions Betty admitted she wanted me and I was thrilled. I told her she should not do anything like this in her own house until her divorce was arranged. She was annoyed with me for presuming to tell her what to do in this regard. She knew what she was doing and Sterling wouldn't make trouble for her. She is an anomaly. She admitted that during her first divorce her husband had detectives watching her, that she did not propose to do anything that would interfere with this divorce but did not like people telling her what she could or could not do. She disagrees with her attorney on many points. She feels he is "interested" in her and gives advice based on his personal feelings not professional ones.

Another anomalous item: on the telephone this morning she told me a man had called and invited her for a drink. She suggested Romanoffs, he refused; she suggested the Beverly Hills Hotel, he refused, explaining that he was in the wholesale liquor business and called on these places. Since he was married he considered it too dangerous to be seen with her there. She called it off. She said that her mood of last night was not entirely to do with me but partly to blame on this incident. She had lunch with a woman named Francesca Cabot, aged 21, an erudite European who thinks every woman should have a husband and a lover. Betty said she thought I would like her and wanted us to meet, but the turn of events would seem to have ended all these plans we had for exposing each other to our friends. Well, it was wonderful and exciting and I guess it is over before it began, and getting used to the idea will be intermittently tough. Maybe I should go to see Judd Marmor after all.

Wednesday March 25

The above has simmered out. Last Thursday, the night of the Academy Awards, I had dinner with Joe Quillan at Villa Nova and Betty came in with Warren Stevens. It was nice to see her again and talk with her briefly. There does not seem to be any pain connected with the demise. Joe and I had a wild night and I slept at his crazy Beverly Hills Spanish manse, a house with seemingly endless rooms. Two pros there. On the day of this entry I was at the studio and Van Cleave, the orchestrator and dear friend, and Steve Czillag, head of the music cutting department, depressed me as usual. They loathe Paramount. One cannot do good work there, they argue, because of Lipstone imposing his philosophy of music in pictures. There is no respect, no dignity and no sense of importance.

Tonight to Bob Presnell's for dinner. Bert Freed there. I had received a magazine from the Ojai Valley School containing stories and poems by the students. I read them one each by Ann and Joyce. Both fabulously imaginative. Now comes a transition. After dinner we went to Polly Adler's. We got to her little house in Burbank at about nine o'clock. We stayed until nine the next morning. Polly has written a book called *A House Is Not a Home* to be published in June, and we talked most of the night of her experiences purveying sex in New York. An elderly man used to come and have one of the girls link her thumbs together and walk about the room as he called out "Pretty Peacock." A married man told her he was unable to perform with his wife and could he bring her there? He did and a routine was worked out. The wife went to work on two of the girls à la dike, and when the girl being worked on became excited the man got aroused enough to have his wife. This routine was varied on occasion. Once a colored man was the subject of the wife's oral attentions. When he came near orgasm the husband moved in on his wife.

Polly told about flagellators and masochists she helped, although she claims it made her blush at times. The girls who got whipped were paid $100. Ben Marden, the night club operator, was a steady customer. Once came in drunk and wanted to give the four girls he had ordered $500 each. Polly wouldn't let him. She took his money away from him to hold—$10,000. The girls told her later he had given them each a $50 bill he had secreted in his shoes. One of Polly's inmates, a French girl named Mimi, when drunk became inordinately over-sexed. After a really busy night she would wind up in the kitchen at dawn, throw a couple of the girls on the table and, calling for salt and pepper, eat. They are mentioned in the book. She has cleared these references with the principals, whose names have been changed. Only one objected. This was Polly's personal maid, a colored woman named "Showboat," who wanted several thousand dollars and has been written out. Polly told about serving a 30-day sentence in jail with five days off for good behavior. The day she left, 10th Street was crowded with photographers and reporters. She eluded them, leaving in a wagon that had just dropped off a load of prisoners.

Batten, Barton, Durstine & Osborne, the advertising agency, had an account. One of the biggest, she said, but was quick to add that Mr. Barton was never there. (Mr. Barton wrote books of inspiration.) After serving the jail sentence she went to Chicago. As always, when in a strange city, she wanted to visit the whore houses. The most famous one was operated by a madam named

Shaw. Polly got into a cab and asked to be taken to Shaw's. They went in and a slatternly maid served them liquor. It was six a. m. She gave the maid $5 and asked to see the madam, who was taking a bath. Upstairs Polly was received by an elderly woman. Asked why she was still in the business, the madam said, "I was born in a whore house, spent my life in a whore house and intend to die in a whore house." They drank and talked till noon. Back at her hotel there was a large amount on the meter and Polly asked the cabbie up to her room to give him a check. She fixed him up with her colored maid and realized she had to stay in the madam business. She is retired now, of course, partly because of her brother Sam (who was there briefly tonight). She was putting Sam through college and when he found out where the money was coming from he left school. She convinced him that most of her money came from the sale of liquor. Incidentally, the spotless little house she lives in now is furnished like a whore house. Gewgaws all around, over the sofa a lurid picture of two women kissing. All her perfume is in fancy colored bottles.

Polly did most of the talking but Presnell, not changing the subject, told about Proust. He would go to a house, lie on the bed with a girl while two plump boys paraded up and down. When five white mice were released the boys were required to wring their necks. On this cue the girl would touch Proust and that was it. Polly's reaction: "Where would you get the mice?"

Polly Adler is filled with the need for people to accept her. She mentions often that her career began when she was seduced at the age of sixteen at Coney Island. She quickly saved $6,000 and opened a lingerie shop. She was robbed and went back to whoring. She is smart. In my opinion she could have been a success at anything.

At 7:30 a. m. we turned on the television set and watched McCarthy's committee, Roy Cohn chief counsel, grilling Dashiell Hammett. McCarthy said that the State Department library was full of books written by Communists. He asked Hammett what sort of books he would put in a library devoted to fighting Communism. Hammett said, "No books." McCarthy said, "That's a funny answer for an author to give." Then the import of Hammett's remark struck him.

We left at nine a. m.

Wednesday July 15

One needs to break through to a kind of plateau above the effects of criticism. I am talking about music, At my stage I tend to avoid violating form, try to please, and worry about criticism. Not much freedom in what comes out. This morning I have a glimpse of what one must do to achieve freedom. Do what you think is right and to hell with criticism. A fiercely individual individual like Herrmann does not allow his creativity to be poisoned by becoming a salesman and pleasing others. I'll come to my senses tomorrow.

The gap in this journal was caused by a visit to San Francisco in April to have a detached retina attended to. I have an eye man here in Los Angeles but Herrmann would not hear of his doing the operation. He found out there were two great men in this field, one in Vienna and one in San Francisco. So Dr. Dohrmann K. Pischel in that city pasted my retina back where it belonged. I had to be quiet for six weeks. Now for the first time since March 15 I am engaged in writing some commercial music. Bob Welch is producing a pilot for NBC with William Demarest, shooting at the old Hal Roach studio in Culver City, and I am doing the music. When I paused to make this entry Demarest was on the roof of a building and I have to go and write something that will get him down safely.

Saturday July 25

Yesterday to Laguna with Bert Freed to see Selena Royle in a much cut version of *Mourning Becomes Electra*. Had a wonderful dinner with the Presnells at the Keg served by a red-haired French waitress with a behind as hard as a tennis ball. Three good performances in the play—Betty Paul as Vinnie, Selena's daughter, a talented fellow named Frank Jurovich and Selena, who went up a few times but otherwise was very good. The preview of Welch's film went off fine Thursday night after a false start. No sound for the first half reel. Reminded me of the preview of a film called *High Conquest*. I had written the Main Title and a few other cues for Lud Gluskin. We went to the Picwood for the preview and they forgot to open the curtain. Couldn't hear it at all. Robert Russell Bennett took me to the Radio City Music Hall a long time ago to hear his Main Title for

Wuthering Heights. We got there while Dick Liebert was doing his number on the organ. He took his bow and they started the picture. Liebert played the whole main title. It was the policy of the Music Hall designed to give a sense of continuity. The Main Title is the one piece of music in a film the studios spend the most time on and Russell's was never heard. I told Alfred Newman about it and I believe he got that policy changed.

Thursday August 13

Last night to Laguna to see a new comedy written by Selena Royle and her husband Georges. Some good performances. Louise Lorimer, John Hoysradt (Hoyt), Ilse Joslyn Drenick (daughter of Warwick Evans, the cellist), Stephen Voit. (Marsha said Voit's Stanislavsky key for his performance was a man who badly needed to go to the bathroom. He crouched slightly and kept his knees together.)

John and Clyte Mundy came to dinner Saturday last. He used to play the cello in the CBS symphony and is now the orchestra manager at the Met. We asked John about the orchestra at the Met. He said, "The bassoon is not the best in the world, my dears, but we do have a nice clarinet player." John taught the cello once at a nunnery in Ireland. Since they were not allowed to open their legs to accommodate the instrument, they played it, he said, "Side-saddle." Later to a party at Joan Weldon's who had sung tonight at the Bowl in a Cole Porter evening. Dixie Bowers was feeling no pain and introduced three esthetes to Joan's 73-year-old grandmother as follows: "This is the handsome one, this is the intellectual one and this is the shitty one." The old lady was unfazed. She is very worldly, and occasionally has to be spoken to by her granddaughter about her language.

Tonight William Walton conducts "Belshazzar's Feast" in the Bowl. I am going to sit with Victor Bay and the Herrmanns in a box they have borrowed. Tomorrow night SCA (the Screen Composers Association) is giving a dinner for the Waltons at the Beverly Hills Club. I am going.

Friday August 14

The first half of the concert was devoted to performances of "Orb and Sceptre" (composed for the Coronation) the Piano Concerto and "Façade." Sir William was only fair on the podium and the orchestra played very badly. The brass were missing all over the place and the woodwinds played wrong notes. Met Ignatz Hillsberg in the intermission. Herrmann did not criticize the bad playing, only talked about how great the music is. Odd thing about Herrmann when it comes to (pardon the expression) symphonic jazz. He is all for pieces like "Façade" and Lambert's "Rio Grande" but knocks Bernstein and while he's at it puts Rodgers down, though as far as I am concerned Rodgers wouldn't know a jazz riff from a bagel. "Belshazzar's" was a performance that got off the ground right away. Roger Wagner's Chorale was perfectly trained and the orchestra sounded like the management had flown in a new one. The extra brass were on the left side of the stage and the fanfares coming from the right then left were immensely effective. I was transported and thought the performance was better than Rodzinski's in Carnegie Hall. To me the piece sounded better in the open air. Thrilling and moving.

After the concert we went to the Presnells where a lot of people were playing charades. Judy Holliday, Warren Stevens, Bert Freed and Peggy, Dixie Bowers, Jack Sher, Cy Gomberg with a Hawaiian girl named Moana and Louise Losey with a new fellow who is going to marry her, she says. Some of the women went swimming in their underwear. A dull party. I don't know why I find these parties at the Presnells so dull. Bob and Marsha are very dear and entertaining. It must be the people. All the same I didn't get home till 5:30. Up at nine. Bert Freed was moving to a new apartment. He and Bill Lester and I moved his stuff in a rented truck from Sam's U Haul. We had a ball considering we couldn't figure out how to get it out of reverse.

At the SCA dinner for the Waltons, I sat with Hugo and Ginda Friedhofer; Sandy Courage and a very wholesome clean-looking girl named Jan; Connie and Jeff Alexander; Betsy and Andre

Previn. (That marriage did not last, for Betsy, a nice girl and a good singer, was fond of making remarks about Andre's height, saying things like, "What are you—standing in a hole?") Much conversation about what a shit Johnny Green is—he and Bunny were at the next table with Martha and Al Newman. All the movie composers were there and I got a chance to tell Bronny Kaper how much I liked *Lili*, and I introduced myself to Helen Deutsch who wrote the screenplay. I talked to George Antheil and Castelnuovo-Tedesco who said he had heard the first performance of "Façade" with Edith Sitwell in the twenties. Sir William, whom I talked to briefly, looks like a well-to-do shopkeeper. He is about 51, quiet and charming. He told me he lived in London but worked in Italy and that his opera would be finished by the end of the year. I told him I was much moved by his performance of "Belshazzar's Feast," as I was by a performance of *Parsifal* at the Met a year ago Easter. I felt I was hearing it for the first time. I told him Herrmann had had all his great musical experiences when he was 12 or 13, but I was having mine late in life, that I had been a musical virgin until I was about 35. He said, "That's an awful long time to be any kind of virgin."

Saturday August 15

At a Beverly Hills party Lois Harrison (a lady who is currently being very nice to me) thought all the women were beautiful, thin and exquisitely dressed. She thinks she is fat. A man came over to her and said he had nothing to offer but money and would she sleep with him for $2,000? Howard Warshaw was here one night and Lois told of this incident. Howard asked if she had accepted and Lois said, "No. It's only worth 35 cents anyway." Howard said that a commodity that fluctuated so much in value could not be reliable. Lois is very jolly and accommodating. When there are three of us in the Jag she doesn't mind riding on the gear shift lever.

Barbara and Mindred Lord [a writer] came in to pick up a roasting pan they had left the night they brought the food here. Barbara claims that Mindred walked into one of their favorite neighborhood bars and said, "I can lick any woman in the place."

Sunday August 16

With Helen Deutsch and Elsa Lanchester to Chuck Walters' for curry. Leonard Speigelgass was there, so was Jack Smith, not the singer, the one who lives with Chuck. It was a fast and conversationally furious evening. At one point Spiegelgass was making up names of movie stars. Flame Ricochet for a girl and Lance Pierce for a man. Elsa, who is appearing at the Turnabout Theatre, was complaining of difficulty parking at the theatre since she arrives at about nine o'clock when everyone has gone in. "I park," she said, "in the white space in front of the theatre and the police think I am unloading." Spiegelgass said, "I have seen your performance and that is a very good way of describing it." They play a game called "Casting." For example Spiegelgass cast me as an embassy attaché entrusted with secret papers who sells them to the Spanish Government. Chuck cast me as someone's older roué brother. The food was spectacular.

Monday August 17

Helen Deutsch is an extremely bright lady. This evening she told me two stories. She was married three years ago to a school teacher from Whittier who said he had been married once before. She blocks out the intimate details of what led up to their appearance before a Justice of the Peace in Las Vegas. The teacher shielded the documents they signed so she didn't know till later that he had been married several times. They spent the first night in a hotel. She prepared for bed. He did not. He went out. She went to sleep and didn't know when he returned. They spent the next night in her apartment at the Shoreham in Hollywood. The same thing occurred. As she was getting ready for bed he came in with his coat over his arm. He looked gray. He said he was going to the drug store and would be back shortly. He came back in an hour looking pink and glowing but went to bed in another room. In a letter to her sister Deutsch mentioned this incident. The sister wrote back and said the man obviously was a drug addict. On the third night (this would make a good piece on the order of 12 Days of

Christmas) he telephoned to say he was spending the night at his apartment in Whittier. In one of their conversations he said he had six months to live and was impotent. Strange that a smart woman like Helen Deutsch would not recognize the physical ups and downs, the gray and haggard to pink and blooming as symptoms of drug addiction. Writers usually know a little about everything. She said the studio, Metro, was hardly aware of her marriage. I have often wondered what happened in ten-day marriages. Deutsch has a steel trap mind and whether as a result of this experience or because she is not superficially attractive she now is very spikey and associates exclusively with homosexuals. She claims no experience with her own sex.

The other story was about an affair she has been having for two years with a homosexual. He is away but when he gets back she says she is going to break it off. Their sexual relations have been satisfactory. She says often that she is a normal woman. We sat in her living room until six in the morning. Once she went out of the room and as she passed planted a wet smack on my mouth. When she came back she said, "Come and sit here," patting the couch. I went. She lay back with her knees doubled up. She said, "Lie on top of me," then immediately, "No. That was an impulse." She straightened up. "My estimate of you," she said, "is that you have a wide homosexual streak." I laughed and said, "You may be right." She seemed pleased and said she was sure I would be angry and loud in denials.

She started talking about a trip she made to Rome last year. She stayed with a friend, Donald Downes, who had just had a book published in England concerning his service with the OSS during the last war. He introduced her into his circle in Rome which was—one guess—completely homo. She wanted to go to Sicily and went to an American Express office. The young American who attended to her asked her to have tea with him. She accepted. While they were having tea he mentioned that the two references she had posted with the American Express were both homosexuals. He told her he had been married for a short time in the States but had left his wife for a man—a masochist. The young American Express lad discovered he adored flagellation. He served in the American Army in Italy and when the war ended elected to stay on. Deutsch said she got the distinct impression that for some reason he could not return to the U. S. She also got the impression that she was being ribbed. Not wanting the young man to think she had swallowed his story whole, she confided to him that she was a canary crusher. She said she liked to trample on canaries with her bare feet. She loved the sensation she got when the bones broke and the blood oozed up between her toes. When he didn't bat an eye, it struck her that probably his story was true.

Tuesday August 18

To a delightful black tie dinner party at Admiral and Mrs. Dianopoulos's. John and Clyte Mundy are staying with them because in a way they are related. The Mundys have a daughter, Meg, who's latest husband is a son of the Dianopoulos's. The Admiral and his wife most charming, made me feel very welcome. Mrs D. referred to me all evening as "little one" and I can tell you that is a sure way to any 43-year-old man's heart. I sat next to one of the most beautiful women I have ever seen, a Mrs. Reed, wife of a retired diplomat. I was amazed to learn she is 62 years old. She has the complexion and body the average 30-year-old has lost, and spectacularly tinted gray hair molded in the Grecian style. Her daughter Rosalind, a plain, horsey looking 20-year-old, must lead a life of total frustration. Every boy she brings home has got to fall under the spell of the mother.

After dinner the Admiral—he served in the Greek navy, naturally—told a story about a World War I engagement between 100,000 Italians and 10,000 Englishmen. The Italians were badly beaten. At this moment King Victor Emmanuel arrives to review his troops and demands of the commanding general and explanation of the ignominious defeat. The general lines up his 100,000 men and cries, "All musicians step forward!" 10,000 musicians take a step forward. "All tenors one pace forward!" 10,000 tenors leap forward. "All painters!" 20,000 painters take their places with the others. "But," said the king, "you have 60,000 men left. Why did they not defeat the 10,000 Englishmen?" The General said, "Because, your Majesty, the rest are ruffians." Which in our vernacular means bums.

I noticed that while the Dianopoulos's were gay, energetic and sparkling, toward the end of the evening they let down and I realized what an effort they had been making. The Admiral has had a few heart attacks and is supposed to be careful. His wife was fine and fluent but after awhile tended to deflate. But this was not until most of the guests were gone.

Wednesday August 19

Tonight with Bert Freed and Helen Deutsch to Robaire's for dinner. We had cous cous. Then to see Billy Wilder's film of the play *Stalag 17*. On the way home from the picture Bert suggested we stop somewhere for coffee. I said since Helen had such a lovely home we could make some there. She said, bridling, that she was not used to being ordered about and if we wanted coffee we could damn well get it in a restaurant. I said I didn't want coffee anyway and we went to her place.

Her last assignment at Metro was a screenplay Richard Brooks is shooting in Rome. She says Brooks is a favorite of Dore Schary's. Bert Freed had recently done a picture with Brooks and said he was extremely unpopular with the actors and crew. Bert said that Richard Widmark and Karl Malden had staged most of their good scenes. Deutsch said she knew Brooks was no good but if the picture was a success he would get all the credit. We talked about the Brecht play *Galileo* Charles Laughton had appeared in at the Coronet. It was directed by Joe Losey. Deutsch asked Freed if Losey was a friend of his. Bert said, "I don't know him personally," whereupon Helen launched into an attack on Losey. The kindest thing she said about him was that he had no talent. She said, "He's been a promising director for twenty years. Why, he left out the most important scene in the play! If he was a good director he would have fought to keep that scene in." I said, "Why didn't you ask me if Losey was a friend of mine, Helen?" She turned to me, alarmed, and said, "Is he?" I said, "Very close. Very close indeed." We left and I was disturbed and annoyed by the whole evening.

She called me the <u>next</u> morning and asked that I not say she had attacked Brooks and Losey. She said, "In this town things get around. I could lose my job at Metro for talking that way about Brooks." She said she felt guilty about it.

Sunday August 23

Bert Freed and I are off toomorrow for New York driving my Chevy. To see the shows, survey the situation, dig up work maybe because everybody is complaining, and they are right, about how lousy business is. Had a letter from Laura Rogers [my old secretary] yesterday. She said Earl [her husband the singer] had no steady show this season but his teaching kept them going.

To Ollie's last night. Deedee Windust, Dean Jagger, Wendell Corey, Bob Mitchum and a lot of others there. A yacketta evening, everyone talking at the top of his voice. When Ollie heard Bert and I were going to New York in my Chevrolet she wouldn't hear of it. Insisted we take her Cadillac which is rather aged. It cost us $40 to get it in shape to leave.

Monday August 24

Left at four p. m. Here are the notes I made on the trip.

Through Santa Ana—the expanse of parking space at the track—well-kept buildings. Arcadia hot. We will not pick up thumbers, especially 120-pound blondes. In Cajun Pass the car began heating up. Dinner at Barstow (where we shot *The Prowler*), mediocre. Across the Colorado River, a bridge to the left and one to the right. The one on the right a square-rigged railroad bridge, the other a beautiful arc, white in the bright moonlight. In the Arizona desert the car ran dry and we are debating whether to turn back or nurse it on to Yucca a mile at a time. Bert flagged a kind-hearted motorist who gave us the contents of his waterbag. We made Yucca an inch at a time but Yucca appeared to be a single light 500 feet off the road. We stopped at a shack with a gas pump before it, and three puppies set up a howling. We could find no water. A voice from the dark called, "What do you want?" We saw a man naked from the waist up leaning over a half-door in a shack some distance away. We bought some water from him. Next Kingman for a cup of coffee in a dreary standardized sort of place—the customers fairly original looking, western clothes, etc,; then Flagstaff. Most of the roads have no white dividing line and I find it difficult to drive on the right. To Winslow, then Holbrook, and on to Gallup for a poor breakfast in another dreary place. Gallup to Albuquerque, Indian huts along the side of the road; a long drop down into Albuquerque, a large town, all public buildings constructed in the Spanish adobe style. For the rest it seems we drive through nothing but gas stations, motels and automobile agencies. We are lunching in a place furnished in red leatherette and chrome. Much trouble with the car. Two flats so far. Had to buy another spare tire.

The Lincoln country—Vandalia. Sign in Effingham: Wessel & Fulle, Grocers. Countryside familiar from Agee's Lincoln film. From St. Louis east the older buildings contrast sharply with the shoddy new of most of the West. Bert and I are getting bored with one another. I wrote down "Estimate the esthetic quality of the individual and act in accordance with the Christian Science ethic." That translates to: When one meets a lack in a person one must give much more of oneself to make up the lack. Picked that up somewhere. Must have been from Ernie Chappell, a Christian Science announcer I used to work with.

Saturday August 29

Arrive Fire Island to spend a day with Bill and Neil Schneider. Caught a beastly cold. Can't find the notes of what shows and friends we saw.

Monday September 14

Leave New York five a.m. We have been joined by Jordan Snyder, a friend of Bert's from Philadelphia. He's in the contracting business and has an unerring nose for good places to eat. Every meal we had coming was ghastly. As we climbed the Skyway to New Jersey the radio was playing a sad, sensual arrangement of "Manhattan" featuring Georgie Auld on tenor sax. Breakfast at Lesher's Hotel, Shartlesville, Pa., deep in the farm country. On the table stewed peaches, apple butter, tapioca pudding, prunes, apple sauce and doughnuts. They served plates of ham, pancakes and fried eggs. Heaven.

Three blowouts in the last 24 hours. We have seen Bryce Canyon. We arrived home Saturday September 19 at four p. m.

Monday September 21

Reported to Paramount to start work on *Casanova's Big Night*. Fine cast. Bob Hope, Joan Fontaine, Basil Rathbone, John Carradine, Paul Cavanagh, John Hoyt. The 18th-century period appealed to me and I saw many opportunities in the chases and sword play to use the wonderful sounds 18th-century composers got in their overtures. When I mentioned this to Louis Lipstone he had a fit. He said, "Just play Hope music." I went ahead and did it my way and it turned into a big fight, still going on. Louie suggested we hire Roy Webb and Leigh Harline to help me. I am using Leo Shuken, Sid Cutner and Fred Steiner as orchestrators. We went to preview once with a dreadful dubbing job but it was successful. I am extremely unpopular with our music department head at the moment.

On October 1 I moved into 20140 Pacific Coast Highway. Nice little house with a slanting roof rising above a balcony and extra bedroom. In our business things are tight and getting tighter. The Union reports only 18 percent of the membership working. Lowest figure in its history. We are forming a Composers Guild, twenty years late. The situation in radio and television frightening. Virtually no music being written and recorded for these media. Mostly tracks from abroad, and the music cutters are very clever with it, too. Even the film studios are tracking more pictures. The only good thing about it is that the composers, traditionally individualists, are now of a mind to unite.

Monday November 30

To the airport to meet Bert Freed. He deplaned from a DC 7 with Bill Schneider, whom I was delighted to see. Bill says at 47 he has never given a thought to getting old, but if he had to get a job in advertising at his age it might be rough. He has just returned from North Africa. The Bousbir is a walled-off section of Casablanca where young girls who have committed misdemeanors are incarcerated. They work their way out by prostitution, usually in about a year. A night with one of them costs 23 cents. She cooks breakfast, washes your clothes in addition to other things. When American women go into the Bousbir sightseeing, the inmates cannot understand how they rate shoes.

The investigations have the country in a turmoil. The Harry Dexter White case the big thing last week. Velde (chairman of the House Un-American Committee) subpoenaed Harry Truman, who refused to appear. The House committee was here last week and put out a subpoena for Jerry Fielding. I don't know if he is off his shows yet.

Friday December 4

In a meeting of most of the composers in Hollywood, one hundred and twenty composers present voted unanimously to form a Guild. The first step.

Tuesday December 8

Last Thursday preview #2 of *Casanova*. OK. Three comments on the music. Norman McLeod, the director, thought the first four bars of cue 1C could be gayer. Mr. Balaban, a director of Paramount Pictures Corp., and owner of the Balaban & Katz theatres in Chicago, thought the music fine. (Lipstone introduced me to him as "the kid who did the music." I was 44 last Sunday.) Dear old Louie the Lip intimated on the way home in a roundabout and circumloquacious manner that the music came out all right in the end by the grace of God.

Saturday Corwin came down for the weekend. Ollie Carey brought Richard Brooks and his wife down. Brooks talked about a picture he had just finished shooting, *The Flame and the Flesh*. He likes [Dimitri] Tiomkin and I said, "Kindly leave my house." He said Georgie Stoll was doing the music for *Flame*. I said Stoll did not write. Brooks amended his statement—Stoll and his *men* were writing the music. As Andre Previn said the next night at the Alexanders', "If Stoll could prevent World War III by scoring a unison C for the orchestra he couldn't do it." Jeff refers to the quartet composed of Jane Russell, Della Russell (Andy Russell's wife— replaced Rhonda Fleming), Connie Haines and Beryl Davis, for obvious reasons, as the octet. Corwin has written a screenplay of *Hedda Gabler* which is fine and a stage play based on Eric Knight's *The Flying Yorkshireman* which I think less of. Perhaps because I know the territory, having been brought up in Lancashire.

Last night I had a vivid dream. I was working at a desk in an office. Suddenly my heart stopped beating. The beat that did not take place was ten thousand times as loud as the beats that preceded. I let out a yell—I knew I was dead—and woke up.

Sunday December 13

Last Tuesday to Fran Ferrer's house for dinner. Ollie Carey was minding the children—Mark, 8, Pepa, 11—while Fran is in Juarez getting a divorce from Mel. It is a warm, countryish house full of the comforts of money and it made me feel sad to think that Fran is giving it up for love and Howard Warshaw, a painter of great integrity and no money. The children are typical. They have everything they could possibly want and lots of things they don't. I helped Pepa with her French homework, Mark showed us some card tricks, then we played a card game or two before they went to bed. Always nowadays there is a record player playing, usually records of the New York shows. Drives me crazy. Muzak is everywhere. At the Lindomar, a motel at Sunset and the coast Highway where I usually have breakfast when I have to go into town, the damn intrusive Muzak fights the jukebox blasting away in the bar. While I'm bitching, a few unkind words about Hollywood. Most of the people I know came for fame and money in the movies. I'm convinced we stay because of the climate. It is nice living among trees and flowers or at the ocean's edge.

Wednesday at the studio to work out the articles of association for the composers guild with Sandy Courage. He is a free enterprise Jaguar owner who when he doesn't have a job writing music for the radio picks out cues for the networks to play. His philosophy is that if he doesn't do it somebody will. Thinks there's nothing wrong with the way composers are treated in this country. Serious composers can get a job teaching and can write in their off hours. You wonder why he signed the proposal to start a guild.

Dinner with Victor Bay at Lucey's to discuss the final script in our opera series—the Crucifixion. We had an argument about the mechanical problems of recording music for films—which should come first, the orchestra or the voices. Never having done any, he thinks the voice should come first, then add the orchestra. In practice this is damn near impossible. (When I did the main title of

Disney's *Cinderella*, I did it that way and there were so many nuances of tempo in the chorus I had an awful time putting the orchestra to it. Ollie Wallace, head of music at Disney and a dear sweet old man, let me hang myself.) Victor's argument was if you could accompany opera singers from the pit you could do it listening to them over headphones. I almost forgot the most recent argument against this technique. In *Casanova* we had to sweeten (that's the term for adding something) a section of the Main Title. The original had a mandolin solo accompanied by strings. The producer wanted more strings on the melody. Because I had taken many liberties in the phrasing even Irvin Talbot, the Paramount house conductor and the best cue catcher in the business, couldn't get the sweetener in sync with the mandolin. Victor's clincher in the argument was that I am not enough of a conductor to prove to him it can't be done. Annoyed me.

Thursday so depressed all day I called the lady with the dress shop in Santa Monica. She came down for cocktails and stayed for dinner. She is a Texas farm girl who dresses very *Vogue*. Complained about her business being slow, her help inadequate and her body too fat. She is rather Rubens but is properly proud of her breasts. When it came down to it, I couldn't.

Friday to Bob Welch's for dinner. Due at seven I got there at six-thirty. Parked in front of the house. It was dark. I switched off the lights and sat listening to the news on the radio. A Beverly Hills prowl car pulled alongside. The cop said, "Hi." I said, "Hi." He said, "Do you live here?" I said, "No." Pause. I said, "I am having dinner here." He said, "Where?" I said, "Number 610." He said, "Okay," and drove up the street where he waited until I went in. I claim he questioned me because I was driving a Chevrolet. If I had been in the Jag I don't think he would have bothered. Welch is letting himself get fat and has an ulcer probably brought on by NBC not letting him do anything he considers startling or original.

Saturday December 26

Wednesday last Jerry Fielding in executive session with the Un-American Committee conducted by Jackson and Doyle, two representatives from this area. He does the Groucho Marx show and "Life of Riley." When he got the subpoena, "Life of Riley" dropped him immediately. He gave to NBC, Groucho, John Guedel (producer of the show) and their lawyers a written statement saying he had never been a member of the Communist party and was not now one. (He sent me a copy.) He had belonged to the Arts, Sciences & Professions group (so, incidentally, had Groucho), the Civil Rights Congress and the Committe for the First Amendment, all named by the Attorney General under Truman as communist fronts. He told them he would answer any questions the committee asked about himself but would not give any names of people who had belonged to A. S. P., C. R. C., and the First Amendment Committee. In view of Jerry's statement Groucho and Guedel thought they could keep him on the show. After the hearing Jerry told reporters that since this was an executive session he was not privileged to make a statement to the press. Jackson came out and said Fielding had refused to answer certain questions. It hit the papers and I did the Groucho show that night and the following Monday. He is dropped and at the end of the 13-week cycle the whole orchestra will be dropped so that Groucho, Guedel and the Plymouth De Soto Motor Company will not be in danger from employees of Jerry's who might have become "tainted."

I have decided that if and when I am called I will say I am not now and never have been a communist but will refuse to give the names of friends in A. S. P., and "People's Songs" (the latter a subversive project supported by me and Leonard Bernstein among others) and take the contempt rap which carries one year in jail. In this way I hope people will begin to realize this investigation is now concerned with ordinary liberals and not just communists. [I was never called.]

Last entry for 1953

One day at Metro recently Jeff Alexander, Andre Previn and I looked in the *ASCAP Biographical Dictionary* to see how old everybody is. Roy Webb is 65. The oldest, Rupert Hughes, 82. Andre sat at the piano and underscored Jeff's reading of Rupert Hughes's biography. When he came to age 82, Andre played the "Battle Hymn of the Republic" with sevenths in the bass and atonal triads above.

It's been a rather dreary year. Paramount a bust for me. Hate the pictures and have decided to get out of Hollywood. This is a provincial and dull place. No young people on fire about anything except acclaim and money. I am barren in the woman department. No one to fall in love with, too many mixed-up divorcées with two children, and I get impotent the second time out with women I don't care about. I have not met a solitary woman secure enough to give friendship. They are conditioned to take. My estimation of the crew I have run with is they are full of self and scared.

1954

Tuesday January 26

In response to a telephone summons I went to William Morris to see a man named Bob Coryell. He had had a request from Paramount to give them an extension on my contract. We both agreed no. (I wonder why?) We talked about Red Channels (I am in it)—it was in my mind how nasty William Morris had been to Jerry Fielding when he got into trouble with the Committee. Coryell said he had argued with Carl Foreman when he was up before the Committee that the only way he could preserve his career was to cooperate. Foreman, who is not a communist, refused to cooperate and Stanley Kramer bought him out of his contract. Foreman went to England where I am sure he doesn't have too much difficulty looking himself in the eye each morning. To Dr. Albaugh [my eye doctor] today and he saw nothing in my eyes to worry about at this time, although he did say I could expect cataracts in the future.

Friday January 29

Saw Odet's *Country Girl* at the Players Ring.
Sandy Courage and I have finished the first draft of the Constitution and By-laws of the Composers Guild of America.

Wednesday February 17

Drove up the Strip to see Mike Shore and John Hubley in a hilltop house with swimming pool and a separate little house for

Hubley to work in. They are preparing a feature length cartoon of *Finian's Rainbow* from key oil paintings by Ben Shahn. Tony Leader [director] was there. It is exciting and I might possibly do it.

Friday February 26

Went to see *Captain's Paradise*, the latest Alec Guinness picture, which I didn't like, and *The Cruel Sea*, which was very well done except for one scene when Jack Hawkins' eyes were too full of glycerine tears. *Captain's Paradise* had a lousy American-style Mickey Mouse score but *Cruel Sea* had a wonderful one by Alan Rawsthorne. The sea vistas with lots of freighters and escort vessels were accompanied by a solo flute—the exact opposite of the Paramount style. When Hawkins takes over his new command after the loss of *Compass Rose*, a violin starts a kind of siren song of the ship, other instruments coming in gradually. We would have done it with full orchestra playing the English equivalent of "Anchors Aweigh." ("Rule Brittania?")

Sunday February 28

To Judd and Suzanne Kinberg's who have taken a house down the beach a bit. A lovely party. Judd's father, the warmest man I have met in a long time, played the perfect host. Eartha Kitt, a man named Loew (can't think of his first name), Millard Kaufman and the Herrmanns there. I was talking to Kinberg when a man came up and said, "There's a strange man in the bedroom by himself reading a magazine." I said, "That's Herrmann." At dinner at my house Herrmann sounded off about Corwin and accused me of using Red Channels as an excuse for not working in radio and television. Jim Beach had Hunt Stromberg, Jr. call me up and offer me a big TV show they are planning. I told Stromberg I would let him know if I could do it. I called Jim and asked him if he knew I was in Red Channels. He didn't. He is new with ABC so I wanted him to know what he was doing. He might get himself into trouble proposing a listee. He said he would find out ABCs policy. Two days later he called and said he was going ahead with me without asking the policy and we would see what happened.

Tuesday March 2

Went to a party at Ollie Carey's after dinner with Larry Thor and Alice Kohler. Oll was entertaining James Barton and his wife, the Mitchums, the Wendell Coreys, the Harry Morgans and Richard Breen. It was the most fabulous theatre evening I have ever had. Barton was hilarious. His father was a minstrel man, "A good knockabout comedian, a trouper and a good acrobat." He told of his father parading in Galveston when the band leader, an Italian, came alongside and handed him a telegram. Barton's father took the telegram as he marched, opened it and read that he had a son. He saluted this information with a special pivot at the next corner. With a stylish sideways kick he spattered the horse manure and shouted, "I've got a son!" Then, with his top hat tipped further over his eye and his cane pistoning backward and forward, he went into that wonderful minstrel strut, proclaiming his pride. Barton, who is 64, said his father died at the age of 33. He told us he was a "good drunk."

Barton was in O'Neill's *The Iceman Cometh*. Eddie Dowling (Wendell Corey calls him "Saint Eddie Dowling") sent Jim the script and asked him to pick his part. He chose Harry Hope. O'Neill asked him to play Hickey. Jim said Harry Hope was the gravy part and Hickey was a son of a bitch and anyway he knew Dowling wanted to play Hope. O'Neill prevailed and Barton opened as Hickey. Barton regards Lawrence Langner, Terry Helburn and the Theatre Guild as a bunch of amateurs. They tried to get him for $750 when his salary elsewhere was $3,000. He says they are the only theatrical producing company that uses prompters as in opera. In the play Hickey has a 26-minute speech delivered from a rocking chair. Barton told Dowling he didn't want the prompter cueing him. If he got lost he would find himself. Dowling protested that he wouldn't be saying the lines— O'Neill is hell on actors who change a word. Barton said O'Neill's style was to repeat everything three times so if he blew, he wouldn't be far from the play. [Aside: I could kill myself but I had tickets for the opening and gave them to Lee Sabinson because I had to work.] On the opening night Barton made his entrance and saw that "every son of a bitch in the front row had the book in their hands," following the printed words. When he got started on his 26-minute speech he heard the words being whispered at him from the wings. He said, in character, "Shut up you lousy bastards. Quiet, you lousy sons of bitches." The prompting stopped as the people with the books looked up, startled. Jim looked down at the front row and said, "I lost you bastards, eh?" then resumed the speech.

He talked about a protégé of Armina's (Armina is apparently a woman he doesn't particularly like—married to Lawrence Langner) who had been engaged to understudy him. To this young man, Jim said, a character aged 50 is an old man and you play him bent over, limping and with a high cracked voice. With fine scorn Barton said, "I'm 64 and if I hadn't had that stroke last year I'd go out in the hall and do a handspring for you right now." He is very athletic and finely balanced and during the evening he was on his feet most of the time, acting out things, boxing, moving like a dancer.

Wendell Corey is the loudest and most profane man I have heard lately. Norman Cousins came in while Corey was in the middle of a story about how an actor on some TV show was so soft he couldn't hear him. Corey said, "I ate his ass out so I was a shit. *He* thought I was a shit—when you complain about *anything* you're a shit." Every so often he would shout at Barton, "Do the fuckin' moose-head." We never did hear the moose-head but Barton did do one of his parrot stories. Mitchum told about driving through Virginia one morning and getting nailed for speeding. The police took him to a general store-filling station court. The judge was an old man with a dirty vest and steel-rimmed specs halfway down his nose. Charge: doing 65 in a 55-mile zone. $10 for speeding, $10 for court costs. Judge, to the cop, "What kind of a car they drivin'?" Cop, "A 1953 Cadillac coupe de ville." Judge, "That'll be an extry $45."

Norman Cousins is a young, dark, intense man and although he had never met Ollie before seemed immediately to understand her and was warm and affectionate. Giving him that lovely open early-American look of hers she said, several times, "I'm pissed." Ollie had an amazing run-in with Dobie her son. She ripped into him for being overshadowed by his father [actor Harry Carey]. "You only have balls to knock up your wife, you aren't a *man*." Dobie is a man from what I can see and is suffering from what every young actor in this lousy town is suffering from: no work.

Saturday March 20

Saw Herrmann Saturday afternoon. CBS has commissioned him to do an opera, *A Christmas Carol*, with a libretto by Maxwell Anderson. He is starting a picture for Zanuck called *Garden of Evil* and is doing two television shows. Louis Lipstone died this week and was buried Sunday. I didn't go but everybody else was there. The Paramount strings played Tchaikovsky. Friedhofer said they never sounded so good. Y. Frank Freeman (head of the studio) put on a yarmulke and did the eulogy. Herrmann told me Franz Waxman's wife Alice thought Lipstone was a wonderful man. I only knew him in his last two years and he was pretty tyrannical and made life miserable for a lot of composers and the little people around the department. He was paid $1,250 a week. Last year in one of the economy drives they put a $175-a-week assistant librarian on half time.

Sunday March 21

ASMA (American Society of Music Arrangers) concert. First half: Elmer Bernstein's Viola Sonata, Jack Hayes' Rhapsody for Two Pianos, two saxophone quartets, one by Warren Barker the other by Lou Maury, whose square first name, I discovered from the program, is Lowndes. After the intermission three of my choral pieces, "Peace Comes to Me," "Anna May Millie" and "Sixteen Ghosts." Three songs by Sid Cutner on Joyce's *Penny Each Poems* and three pieces from Joe Mullendore's setting of *Shropshire Lad*. Thirty people on the stage singing the stuff for nothing (very nice of them to give their time) and about thirty people in the audience.

I have been working steadily on *Peg O' My Heart* (trying to make a musical out of the old play) but slowed up a bit because we are having trouble getting the rights—French's want to know who the book writer will be, etc. (Never start something without getting the rights first). I have spent the greater part of the last three days trying to complete the verse for the waltz—sometimes it takes a long time to boil the ideas down into a lyric.

Monday April 12

Ed Murrow in a devastating hour on television has exposed McCarthy. McCarthy asked for equal time and put on a very limp hour in defense of his tactics. The televised hearings of McCarthy's fight with the Army over favors he asked for Schine and Cohn due April 22. Counsel are meeting to discuss who will testify and what they will testify. Looks like a whitewash.

I have started a nice relationship with Ed Beloin, a very good comedy writer who is a producer at NBC. Might do a series with him this summer. He is bright and seems to appreciate me. Bob Welch was given up two weeks ago. The nuns and the doctors and everybody at St. John's thought he was a goner but he fooled them. He is leaving the hospital this week. I have seen him twice and he looks remarkably well considering his liver is shot. I have been rehearsing with the girls. Della Russell is ill and Rhonda Fleming is back to fill in for her. The other day, before we started to rehearse, they had a pray. They asked for help for Rhonda who is separated from her doctor husband. (Why do movie stars marry doctors?) They talk of the most intimate things in front of me as though I were another girl or not there. Or maybe they trust me. Rhonda said one night she got home from a Hollywood Christian meeting to find her husband sitting on the steps. They had a crying scene. I remember when she brought him to the Chapel I thought they did not seem to get along very well. He was jealous of the Chapel. Didn't think she needed that sort of thing.

Wednesday April 14

Tonight to dinner at Greta Peck's. The cast included George Chasin and wife (he's an MCA bigwig—lawyer, raconteur), Dean Jagger and wife (Ollie had warned me she was very reactionary but he was the one who couldn't understand 90 percent of parity for farmers or why the Government spends half a million a day storing subsidized produce), and Dan Melnick, a bright young fellow who works at CBS on the Bob Crosby show and devotes spare time to the Hacker Clinic on criminal therapy.

Friday April 16

Last night, Thursday, I conducted Victor Young's TV show again. Lucille Norman is a very good singer. It is an easy show and a rather pleasant way of spending an afternoon and getting paid for it, though not much. Had dinner before the show with Lloyd

Ulyate, trombone, Bobby Bain, guitar, and Jack Hayes, who arranges some of the stuff. When we got back the makeup girl had gone so the pretty bass player made me up. Very foggy drive home. The city quiet and mysterious, empty pairs of headlights suddenly appearing and disappearing. The streets I have driven dozens of times seemed different, wider. Everything seems bigger in the fog.

Saturday April 17

Joyce's birthday yesterday. Easter Sunday coming up. Went to the Brentwood Mart, bought some eggs and things. Florence and the kids were at John Payne's house in the Uplifters. I drove there to deliver the eggs and a check for Joyce's birthday present.

A few Saturdays ago I went with Ollie to a party at Carol Saroyan's. She is separated from Saroyan but he was there. I met Lion Feuchtwanger. I asked him about his work schedule. First he lays in the fact that he is old. He gets up at seven, has orange juice and sits on the patio with his wife enjoying the sun until she goes for her swim, then to work. A secretary arrives at 10:30. He writes in German and complains about the translations of his work published here. I said, "How do you know they are bad?" He said, "I know enough English to know that." Stops at one o'clock for a breather. No food. Works until seven, has a big dinner then back to work till eleven. Adolph Green, Betty Comden, Gene Kelly and his wife Betsy Blair there. I knew Betsy when she was in the chorus of *Panama Hattie*. She seems sad and hysterically gay at the same time. Saul Chaplin played the piano. Richard Conte's wife, whom I complimented for doing such a good job in *What Every Woman Knows* at the Circle Theatre, said nothing had happened for her since. Joan and John Houseman there with his mother who runs a hospital in New York. Fletcher Markle and Mercedes came in later. They had had dinner at a Chinese joint downtown. Mercy said that driving through those mean streets in Chinatown and seeing the slums people lived in depressed her. She wished she could bring some beauty into their lives. I told her that on average she might find more contentment down there than on her own Bel-Air level where everybody is preoccupied with money and all the strange ridiculous values movie folk seem to hold so dear. A few of us hung on after the sensible people had left.

Saroyan talks the way he writes. He can say the most inconse-
quential things and make them sound pregnant. A songwriter was
playing some things he had written. Saroyan said in essence they
were good revue type tunes but the language he used made it
something the young fellow could remember and treasure forever.
Saroyan says he has been a failure for ten years. He writes for
himself. In the case of plays he says he doesn't expect anyone to
understand them or to produce them right now; if they are worth
anything they will come into their own. He says in the last year he
has written twenty short stories, three plays and a couple of novels,
none of them any good. He has a loud rough voice and it dominates
a room. He is 45 and lives alone down the beach on Old Malibu
Road.

I called him on the phone today and asked him if he was
interested in having dinner. He said he would call me later. After I
got back from delivering the money to Florence I sank into an
antisocial lethargy and did not answer the phone when it rang
twice. But I do want to see him. He is interesting. I shook myself
out of the lethargy and went to see a Disney film of animal and
plant life in the desert. A remarkable picture. The Paul Smith
score on the whole very good. I didn't approve of the playing of
"Home Sweet Home" as the camera shows us how rats live, but
every now and then there would be a fine piece of ballet music for
the insect battles.

Roy Fjastad, a very nice man who has succeeded Lipstone as
head of the music department at Paramount, told me he is trying to
sell me to Bill Perlberg of Perlberg & Seaton to do the music for
The Bridges at Toko-Ri. I wrote Perlberg a note saying I would like to
do the picture for two reasons: 1) I heard from musicians that he is
difficult and since I am difficult too maybe we could do something
good together, and 2) So far at Paramount I had only hors d'oeuvres
and would appreciate some meat. Yesterday at lunch in the commissary Fjastad told me Perlberg had called him and wanted to know what
the hell I meant saying he was difficult, so my long shot only stirred
him up the wrong way. Mistake to take a chance on producers having
a sense of humor. A few days ago to Ed Beloin's office for a reading of
the script of *Uncle Dudley* with Rudy Vallee in the Edward Everett
Horton part. I worked for Vallee on the Fleischman Hour on radio.
He was very nice to me. He gave me a pipe. I was paid my regular fee
by the agency (J. Walter Thompson), but one day a check for $250

from Vallee came in the mail. A bonus. Vallee is now 52 and still thin. He says he takes only 1,500 calories a day but does a lot of drinking. He had on a business suit, white shirt, conservative tie, weirdly tinted glasses and a pair of loud ankle-high suede shoes. He was smoking a thin cigar. He asked me if I wanted one. I said yes. He waited while I lit it and said, "If you like it I'll tell you how to get some. I have them made especially for me in Pennsylvania. The great secret of the taste is the man puts a drop of honey under the mouthpiece. The only trouble is they are expensive." It was awful but I said I liked it and how much were they? He said, "Four cents apiece."

I have finished reading Gene Fowler's continuation of his chronicle of John Barrymore, John Decker, W. C. Fields and Sadakichi Hartmann titled *Minutes of the Last Meeting*. Very sad. It is easy for me to identify with these misfits, since they were in later years in such conflict with everything that has the upper hand in pictures and the other media. Who really grows old with serenity? Not artists.

Easter Sunday April 18

The Herrmanns, the Kinbergs, Danny Melnick and a man named Olvin here. We listened to the NBC under Katims playing Benjamin Lees' "Profiles." At the conclusion of the piece the following dialog took place:

HERRMANN: Guy hasn't got an idea in his head. Might pass as the first movement of a symphony then go ahead. Everybody was writing that kind of stuff in the twenties, there's no personality there. The orchestration in the beginning sounds like Bartok, then the "Roumanian Rhapsody" of Enesco. I only know when the local crowd tells you somebody's gifted you can rest assured he's as dull as dishwater. (In this kind of dissertation Herrmann gets loud.) These guys are only interested in building up mediocrity. Lukas Foss likes to have mediocre composers around him. Ingolf Dahl, who's mediocre, likes to find one who's even more mediocre and God knows George Antheil's as mediocre as the underside of an omelette, so if *he* thinks someone's got talent you can be sure he has none.

Freud was a great man because he invented something which has an element of truth, like every religion has. Today if an artist has an escape world he is naturally regarded as an escapist with either a mother fixation or a father fixation or he's homosexual or likes women too much. Something's wrong with him. I mean he isn't *normal*—normal has become a level of mediocrity. Analysts. These bastards are the worst people for normality. When you meet one of them they're so smug. Next to meeting a Republican from a steel company you can't meet a more smug individual than an analyst. He's so normal, have you noticed he's trying to goose every woman in the room? But that's alright, he's normal. He's having a fine life but he doesn't speak to his wife when they're alone.

We have another bromide in our life and that's the word "success." There's only one rule of success in the whole world— each individual is the one who is the best judge of it. It doesn't matter if I think you are a success or you think I am, each individual knows if he's been a success. That's the yardstick, it doesn't matter what the world says. That's why highly publicized people of our time are such miserable failures later on. An example at random: Leonard Bernstein. Lennie reads all the things they say about him and he knows himself he isn't that good, that he's a phony and a failure. [Not my view - Herrmann's.] Same goes for Marlon Brando.

KINBERG: How do you explain this psychosis—I think it was Hemingway said it—that America is filled with young writers who start out well and are never heard from again?

HERRMANN: Including him.

KINBERG: The last twenty years are filled with people who started out well and never did better than when they started, which is the real test of genius. Some French writers are better at sixty than they were at twenty.

HERRMANN: Take Ernest Hemingway. He's the one example of a writer who started out with so much talent and look at what a complete piece of corn he's been for twenty-five years. Done nothing better than game hunting. He never has a pronouncement to make about the world of any interest, he never has a literary criticism to make. All he can do is talk aboout hunting or getting a new wife, which is his own affair—who cares if he has a harem? What kind of a literary figure is this? He was the same age when he wrote *Across the River* as Thomas Hardy when he wrote *Jude the Obscure*. That shows you the difference between the two men.

OLVIN: Better still, how about Faulkner?

HERRMANN: He follows his own personal vision. D. H. Lawrence was a man who followed his own personal vision and for my money was the last really first-rate writer the world has had. And before him was Thomas Hardy, one of the last great Titans of English literature. Now Hardy was a man who had his personal world, he had social feelings. As you know *Jude the Obscure* was banned in England, the Archbishop of Canterbury had it burned because it revealed that the church didn't want a person who believed emotionally in the church. It wanted a person who could advance the position of the church. I always remember the opening of that book. Little Jude goes out into a road full of puddles after a heavy rain. Worms are struggling to get back in the water and little Jude hops from rock to rock so he won't step on them. Hardy says a person of that sensitivity is going to have a very hard and wretched life. Right off the bat he tells you what's in store for this poor guy. But I read that last piece of crap Hemingway wrote. What kind of a writer is this? Here's a man of great gifts. Why is he so shallow? After all, why should I go into a bookstore and see all those crappy novels lying around at $3.50 or $4 and you read the blurb and you say, "Yes, that sounds very good and Zanuck might make it?" Why should I buy something they might do on CBS or Bob Montgomery's show? You can tell by the blurb it's a lot of garbage.

Wednesday May 12

The gatebell clanged yesterday. It was three small boys. The ringleader said, rather belligerently I thought, "You wanna contribute to the Cub Scouts?" I said, "What are you raising money for?" The ringleader turned to a smaller boy but he didn't have an answer either. I said, "For equipment? Catcher's mitts?" They said yes. I said, "I am sorry I don't have any money but I will write you a check. To whom shall I make it?" The boy thought a minute then said, "Steve Tomkins." So I made out a check for $5 to Steve Tomkins and they accepted it incredulously. They hung around the gate for a bit, then I went back to work and forgot about them. Next day I was getting my mail out of the box and there was the check. On the back, in pencil—twice—was written: "Counter-fit."

Roy Fjastad called yesterday and said he had succeeded in selling me to Perlberg and Seaton to do the music for *Bridges at Toko-Ri*. He said they would find it difficult to give me the upper half of a card for my billing since there was no one on the picture who could contractually accept the lower half. Would I accept the top line of a card (with multiple credits on it)? I have thought it over and today I must tell him, in spite of the fact that he is very friendly to me and that I hold him in the highest regard, that I cannot accept this kind of billing. Today Jane Russell and I lunch with the brass at Paramount about a proposed VistaVision short with the Four Girls.

Thursday August 5

Dream last night. Walking along a street I come upon a silent crowd of children standing round a stricken bird with a horribly shattered leg. A mother comes out and I tell her to have her husband bring an axe and chop the bird's head off. Quick and humane. Thought better of it, picked the bird up and it turned into a little girl with a shattered leg. Took her up the street to a clinic and went in. A railing separated the clinic from a cigar counter. The clinic was busy. Girl at the switchboard surrounded by patients lying on the worn wooden floor having their metabolism measured, etc. A doctor who reminded me of Paul Lynde, the excellent comic in *New Faces*, took the child. He came back shortly and said she would live. All around us people were singing a song on the order of "Tumblin' Tumbleweed." The doctor and I joined in, he in a fine stentorian Tennessee Ernie sort of voice. We went over to the cigar counter and bought two 26-cent cigars.

A few Saturdays ago I went to a place called the Cottage, a small bar full of Malibu beach bums. The drill is you have a drink at the Cottage, then go across the street to the Seacomber have one there, and go back to the Cottage. There was a middle-aged lady in a sun suit sitting at the bar exposing her tits. I engaged her in conversation and she turned out to be quite interesting though dreadfully drunk. We watched a young couple dancing. The boy had on white socks, no shoes. End of dance they sat down and the boy's socks were not dirty. He had been dancing on his partner's feet. The plumber from Koontz & Babineau is the bartender. For the extra loot, he says. The lady followed me home in an ancient Lincoln.

I have finished *The Bridges at Toko Ri* and it was previewed in Santa Barbara last Friday night. Very successful. It is a fine picture and I enjoyed working with Perlberg and Seaton tremendously, and they liked me. Both thoroughly tasteful and intelligent.. The score is good and well dubbed although we are going to dub it over again. Rode up to Santa Barbara in a company limo.

Friday August 6

I have just been to the Country Store up at Malibu. The signs on the wall interesting as usual. An announcement of a raffle, the prize a small sailboat, the proceeds for "Sande's Get Well Fund." No identification of Sande or what happened to him or her. A man employed at the Albatross Hotel across the street is advertising for a room and the use of "a small area of the refrigerator."

During the evening I read a song of Bernice Holden's called "Orphan Angel." It gives a nice slant on her lyric ideas. It is about a young couple whose child dies and they call upon God not to take her. They don't want her to become an Orphan Angel. I have just finished reading *A Child of the Century*, Ben Hecht's autobiography. I was moved by his account of the Jews for the first time in their history fighting back against their persecutors. Loved his story of an uncle showing up during a big weekend party at Nyack. A bunch of actors, writers and duchesses sitting round the pool. The uncle announced he would take a swim. Ben said, "I'll get you a suit." The uncle said, "Never mind, I got mine underwear on," and slipped out of his clothes and plunged in in his union suit. He retells the story of Barrymore at a hot dog stand presided over by an ugly woman with a wart on her nose. He climbs the counter crying, "My last Duchess! Lift your skirts and let me see Epping Forest again!" I heard it about a nurse in the hospital where Barrymore was dying. And the account of a dinner party for a group including Charlie Chaplin. Hecht's house was staffed by Croatians. The three who served the dinner dropped their dishes when they saw Chaplin, crying, "We luff you, Sharlie!"

I always get impatient at the end of books, mainly because when one gets near the finish one encroaches on one's schedule to finish, instead of leaving the last few pages for the next session.

Monday August 16

Up the beach near the restaurant with a tank of seals to attract the tourists is a row of dilapidated houses, broken up into apartments, available any way you want them—by day, week or month. The electric wiring is exposed, creating a fire hazard, but if the installation antedates current law the landlord need do nothing about it. The real beachcombers inhabit these places. Larry Thor (radio announcer-philosopher) has moved into one with a woman named Alice Kohler. She is a smug intellectual girl whose ambition is to get to Cambridge to earn a Ph.D. Earlier this summer she was casting about for a quick way to earn $2,000. She thought of television but didn't make it. I don't know if she is going to get to Cambridge. Each week there is a rumor she is about to take off but she's still here.

Next to them lives a young woman named Lavonne who has just had a baby. The father is married but he had told Lavonne he would divorce his wife and marry her. It didn't happen. She could not abort. She came back to the beach without the baby. I suppose it was put up for adoption. She lives in a little place full of paperbacks—Thurber, avant garde short stories, philosophy. She has snaggle teeth and drooping breasts and paints weird distorted clowns. She lent me Artie Shaw's book *The Trouble With Cinderella*. One passage was marked. Shaw says that John Donne was wrong. Man *is* an island and communication between islands is difficult. Lavonne had marked "Amen!" in the margin.

This lad [Shaw] is bad off. At least he was during the period he writes about. His conflict is the old one between art and commerce. He hated radio and dance music, liked jazz. Angry because people don't buy guys who play what they like; embittered by the troubles a Jewish kid runs into growing up in a town like New Haven; and he was not exactly fond of his father and his mother.

There is a naiveté about the way he puts down the most alarming stuff. It is embarrassing to read. He has been analyzed and that explains a lot. His father walked out one day, and, saddled with his mother, young Artie took up music as the quickest way to get out of New Haven.

I am at the studio redubbing *Toko-Ri*. Bill Perlberg has promised to speak to Hitchcock about getting me *To Catch a Thief*. My contract here is up in five days. I have been to see Martin Gang about getting off the blacklist. We made an affidavit describing everything I did during the war years; that is, every cause to which I contributed—good and bad. Russian War Relief, Red Cross (they should change that name), playing at Army hospitals, recording for the Navy, contributing a cantata for the U. S. Treasury broadcasts, that sort of thing. This affidavit (containing the statement that I am not now and never have been a communist) has been mailed to all the advertising agencies and the networks, the idea being to get off their blacklists. The first reaction was from NBC who said I am not on their blacklist but admitted that sponsors are the ones who raise the objections usually. (Guy Della Cioppa had told me some time ago I was on the blacklist at CBS.)

Friday August 20

Saw *Dial M for Murder*, the Hitchcock film version. Too much music (by Dimitri Tiomkin).

I have to go into the Presbyterian Hospital Tuesday at 8:30. Wells Cook will do a hydrocele. Today I offically started with Lester Linsk as my agent. Tuesday night gave a little party for Lavonne, the unwed mother, and some of her friends who are leaving for Mexico.

Wednesday September 15

Louis Armstrong and Robert Merrill opened at the Sands to good notices. [Sid Kuller and I wrote the material for the Sands shows at that time] "Mambo Fire" (how's that for a Vegas title?) the opener, turned out very well. The first finale we wrote Jack Entratter vetoed. He wanted something more commercial like jazz vs opera. We wrote one. Merrill comes out of the Met stage door, top hat, tails, Louie comes out of the Basin street door wearing a beret. Louie sings Pagliacci (he pronounced it Pagliacho) and Merrill does "Honeysuckle Rose." And a lot of other stuff running about 30 minutes. Killed the people. Ed Sullivan there and signed them up to do it on his show.

I haven't seen Louie for 19 years. In 1935 we made some records for Decca. "Shadrack" was one. A big hit. We made friends on that date and we corresponded for awhile—his letters, most amusing, came from all over the country and were done in elite type. Later we did "Shadrack" at a jazz concert in Carnegie Hall. Big thrill for me. Louie is a wonderful, original man. His autobiography *Satchmo* is out now. He is working on a sequel and let us read a chapter (in elite type). The chapter we read deals with marijuana. He smokes it every day and feels that J. Edgar Hoover is wrong to put it on the same level as hard stuff like heroin and cocaine. He says his book wouldn't be honest if he didn't talk about "shuzzit" (his name for marijuana), since he has blasted with hundreds of friends all his life. To preserve his health and happiness his mother told him to do three things: gargle, move your bowles (that's Louie's spelling) and smoke a stick of gage (marijuana) every day.

Thursday September 16

I have met a woman here in Vegas whose name is LaVeeda Scherer. Small, plump and rather vivacious, she has a 15-month-old child and a dusty Cadillac convertible. She writes phone numbers in the dust. If she had it washed she would lose track of her last month's contacts. We horsed around, lay on the bed and she burst into tears and ran away.

Friday September 17

Sid and I had a breakfast date with Louie in his bungalow at three p. m. Colored acts are not allowed to stay at the Sands so we went up the Strip a hundred yards to the Bon Aire Motel. He was in #7 naturally. We knocked on the door. Miss Preston his secretary opened it a crack, saw who we were and invited us in. Louie was in the bathroom following his mother's advice, gargling, moving his bowles and smoking. The air in the bungalow was nice and thick. He came out of the bathroom with a white towel round his head (he wears it in his dressing room between and after shows), a pair of nylon shorts, which didn't quite cover everything, around his loins. He gave us a big happy greeting, led us into the kitchen and presented us with two B-52s which we lit up. The tape machine was going. He listens constantly to all the current music. He had his supply of "shuzzit" in a Sucrets can. At one point he went into the bathroom and came out with a herbal laxative called Swiss Kriss. He said it was basically "gage" and it was good to stretch out the real stuff if you were running short. Velma Middleton came in with a perfectly beautiful little girl, daughter of Trummie Young the trombone player. Louie gave the child one of those dime slot machine banks. The back door of the bungalow was open so the little girl didn't get high. I took about six drags and held the smoke in my lungs as best I could but was not aware of any effect.

I have been invited by a music teacher at the Las Vegas High School to talk to his kids tonight and run them through a couple of my published choral pieces. Sid and LaVeeda went with me. When we entered the classroom there was a gasp. LaVeeda's picture had been in the paper that day illustrating a follow-up story of how she shot her husband. Driving to the airport she told me that the man she is divorced from is Tutor Scherer, a large stockholder in El Rancho Vegas. When she caught him cheating on her she shot him. In the leg. (Probably aiming higher.)

Saturday September 18

George Corey came down and told the story of Hollister Noble. (I met Noble some years ago at George Kast's house and we did his novel *Woman With a Sword* on Hallmark.) He and George worked at CBS in the early thirties in the news department. Noble had three wives. No. 3 wrote pulp stories at two cents a word. They lived in a house in Laurel Canyon where he kept a set of electric trains in the basement. They fought, and the marriage disintegrated. They saw lawyers. Both wanted the house. Finally in a knock-down-drag-out fight he said she'd get the house over his dead body and left. He had disappeared many times before. Whenever he got writer's block, or just plain nerves, he would hop a train for anywhere. Sometimes

Seattle, sometimes New York, in a day coach. This time he was gone four or five days. She got worried and called the lawyers. They had not heard from him. She noticed an unpleasant ordor, and thinking the drains were stopped up called a plumber. He traced the lines and found Noble under the house with his brains blown out.

Corey brought Kathy Iles with him. She is 5' 9½", well proportioned, blond, steel blue eyes, chic bright and unconfident though she runs the advertising for the May Company, a large department store outfit here (four stores). The only difference between Kathy and Carol is her insecurity and lack of confidence. And of course their ages. It is not very often one meets a woman who, in the current phrase, one has eyes for. I knew in the first thirty seconds I had eyes for her. She appears shy. She is more loquacious after the third martini but during Corey's long Hollister Noble story she fell asleep. When she came to she was apologetic. I was sorry she was sorry. I would have liked her to feel comfortable enough here to fall asleep and not feel sorry about it. Anyhow I asked if she could come down Sunday and she said she could.

Sunday September 19

She came with George. He had called and said she was shy and he was coming "for protection." While they were here George called New York and spoke to his wife Fran. The problem is she has a big new job with Macy's and George is trying to decide if he wants to go and live in New York. He told her he was at my place with Kathy. A one second beat and (he reported) Fran said, "I wonder what will come of that?" Kathy worked for Fran at the May Company. She got on the phone, talked, and hung up upset. Didn't say why.

I made a date with her for tomorrow. I will take her to Dominick's then we will go to her place and talk for a few hours. I like her looks. What about what's inside?

September 20 Monday

Took Kathy to dinner at Dominick's. Back to her apartment on Olympic in Beverly Hills where we talked until two.

Saturday/Sunday September 25/26

Kath down here. She was tense the first time. Alarmed. Sunday I talked her tenseness into the open and then it was better. Odd note: I have no pubic hair from the recent operation. She didn't notice. However, I like her. She is friends with Harry and Polly Tribolet who live up the beach. They came in on Saturday and stayed for dinner, which was a big stew. They lived in Mexico for a year on $60 a month. I guess they ran out of loot—he's now working at Douglas.

Monday September 27

Jerry Fielding has returned from a tour of one nighters. The troupe consisted of Danny Dingle, a "has-been singer" (Jerry's quote), the Vocalites, a quartet currently big on records, and Jerry's band. They toured in a bus. Jerry hired a singer named Tingley Bell. When he mentioned this to friends around New York they yelled in unison, "Tingley Bell ! ! ! !" Turned out she had the reputation of being the greatest cocksucker in America, so Jerry allowed that the band would be happy. His group was almost 100 percent Catholic—Dingle, the Vocalites and most of the band. The head Vocalite, whose name I don't know, was the only one who was true to his wife in the sense that he didn't go out and get himself laid. He necked and did everything but put it in—he was true. According to Jerry, Dingle is a swordsman. Several times a day. When he saw Tingley, that was it. They flew into each other's arms and stayed there. They did it in the bus, in the wings between sets, in hotel rooms with thin walls—constantly. There was one hiatus in Dallas or Houston—somewhere in Texas. Dingle had a previously arranged assignation with a female disk jockey. He disappeared into a hotel room with this woman and they stayed there all day. At dinner with Jerry they did nothing but talk about how great it was. Miss Tingley was almost suicidal until this interlude was over. There was a big dinner at the end of the tour. Tingley gave Dingle a set of rosary beads inscribed, "To Danny in memory of many precious moments." Being a pious Catholic he couldn't throw the gift away, and being happily married he didn't know how he would explain it to his wife.

Jerry is bitter about this kind of life. The sort of dance halls they played drew a lot of wild kids. "Not one of them" he complains, "can tell you the name of the Vice-President of the United States." They come with liquor in wet and dry states and Jerry says, "You'd be surprised how many dry states there are." They get piss-assed drunk and in the rest periods the band can't get into the bus, it is full of kids fucking. All the unattached girls count it a triumph to lay a third trumpet player who is here tonight and gone tomorrow. The band got laid in every town they played. In the bus one night driving from one town to another Tingley Bell happened to mention she was against war, "Like this one we got in Korea now." Jerry said, "The war in Korea is over." Tingley said she hadn't heard.

Fielding surprised me when he said the kids in Salt Lake City were as bad as anywhere else. He found Iowa the most nationalistic state, worse than Texas. He had some colored men in the band and the audiences in Iowa were more obstreperous about them than those in Texas. And about music, he said the kids always ask for the tripe they have made big on records like the current #1, "Sh-Boom." And the others climbing the charts are just as frightful.

Thursday October 7

Met with Bob Welch and Sid Smith [director] at NBC about "Revenge With Music." Colgate is sponsoring and in view of the blacklist situation I am doing it for the credit.

Friday October 8

I am going to do Hubley's *Finian's Rainbow*. Went to the Beverly Hills Hotel to meet with Fred Schwartz, a theatre owner from New York who is putting up the money. Maurice Binder, who is working on the film, and Burton Lane there.

October 11 to 23

Rehearsing "Revenge" at NBC. Anna Maria Alberghetti and Ray Middleton. This is the old Dietz & Schwartz musical. Hardest work I have ever done.

Sunday October 24

The performance of "Revenge." Never again.

Tuesday October 26

Roy Fjastad called me into Paramount to discuss a weird problem. Paramount has some hazy connection with Forest Lawn. Mr. Eaton, the owner, has a meeting once a month with his 1,000 employees. The meeting opens with the Forest Lawn song. Mr. Eaton doesn't like it—"Doesn't have enough balls." It is a bit like the song Ford employees sing at their meetings, the one that ends with "And to hell with Chevrolet!" Fjastad asked me if I would write one for them. I said I would try.

Wednesday October 27

Fjastad sent a lady named Bebe (didn't catch her last name) down to the beach to write a lyric for the song. I don't know how good she is at lyrics but she had the largest bust of any lyric writer I have ever seen. We wrestled with the problem for an hour or two and I realized I could not write a song whose burthen was to get out and sell, sell, sell more grave sites. I passed. In the afternoon another meeting on *Finian's* with Hubley and Binder. In the evening a date with Kathy.

Thursday November 18

Had lunch with Hitchcock. I am going to do the picture. He is a very funny, bawdy man. His views on American women are similar to Hilton's. (Jimmy says that American women look like they will and won't while English women look like they won't and will.) Hitch says American women are teasers. Grace Kelly and Cary Grant are in the picture. Hitchcock said Grace Kelly has an affair with every leading man she works with but blushes when you tell a dirty story. He said, "You can't say 'shit' around her."

Bob Welch went back in the hospital and they took his stomach out. Such a lot of bad luck he has had this year. He did two Colgates and I have never seen anyone work so hard. He is thin and does not look well but seems to want to prove he *is* well by working his tail off.

Wednesday November 24

Ran *To Catch a Thief* all by myself. Took my tape recorder and taped all the dialog. It is a wonderful picture, one of Hitchcock's best, and is full of marvelous chances for music. I am elated.

Thursday December 2

I have seen a great deal of Kathy and she is a case. She has a great drive to destroy relationships. Tonight she told me that when I don't check in after a recording she has tears. I told her I could not guarantee to see her at all for the next few days, that I had a heavy schedule and that recording sessions never end on time. Mostly her problem is booze. She is out of control when she is drinking. She knows well enough not to lay this kind of responsibility on me, but ordinary common sense goes out when booze comes in.

Friday December 3

Ran *To Catch a Thief* with Hitchcock. In the big party scene near the end of the picture Grace Kelly is wearing a gold lamé dress, very elegant. Hitchcock leaned over to me and whispered, "There's hills in them thar gold." Afterwards in his office he gave me three pages of single space notes about sound and music. He knows exactly what he wants each of these elements to accomplish. For example, in a scene on the beach at Cannes with Grant the wind is whipping the umbrellas and the canvas on the cabanas. He said there would be absolutely no sound in this scene—just music.

Adele called tonight and said Jimmy (Hilton) is very ill. It looks bad.

Monday December 6

Forty-five today and Al Sendrey and his wife gave me a party. Kathy was, or pretended to be, annoyed with me because I had said I was going to work, which indeed I was and should have, but when Helen Sendrey baked a cake and invited a group, I wanted to go.

Tuesday December 7

Ran into Corwin on Hollywood Boulevard tonight. He was walking along alone and I was going to the Derby to get some dinner and he joined me and we had a long talk. Just catching up on stuff—what he is doing and what I am. He has just written a cantata commissioned by the Jewish community of Cleveland.

Wednesday December 8

First orchestra recording of *Finian's* at Goldwyn. Wonderful band. Andre Previn is playing the piano for me. We recorded Ella Logan singing "Gloccamorra" and "Look to the Rainbow." Outside of the fact that it took too long—5½ hours—it went well and the Goldwyn sound is superb. Al Sendrey did the orchestrations. Yip Harburg and Burton Lane were at the recording today—worrying. They are nice to me, though. The whole gang on this picture is nice to work with. We have Sinatra, Ella Fitzgerald, David Wayne, Louis Armstrong, Barry Fitzgerald, Jim Backus, and we have hired Oscar Peterson's trio plus Red Norvo to do some sequences.

Ella Logan has a tendency to sing flat. A few days ago I went to her house, a very pleasant one on Bristol Circle, to rehearse. Among other things she told me she didn't think people should walk around naked just because they are married. Guess that's one of the reasons she divorced Freddie Finkelhoff.

Friday December 10

Frank Sinatra and Ella Fitzgerald today recording with a temp rhythm section. We'll add the band later.

Saturday December 11

Finished the orchestra prerecording today. Mostly Frank. Very good. He was in a gay mood. It is his birthday today and he sang very well, making us do take after take until the brass cried for mercy. Nelson Riddle's arrangements spectacular. Had the usual drink with the crew after we finished, and the usual warm feeling on breaking up.

Monday December 20

Louis Armstrong arrived. We had lunch in the little commissary at Goldwyn and then went and added him to the stuff we had previously recorded. Marvelous in "Begin the Begat," and astonishing in a scat blues Frank had ad-libbed, leaving holes for Louie to do something. He is on his way to Palm Springs and Australia, and how's that for a parlay? Frank is going to Australia too. Our performers are big there.

Tuesday December 21

Jimmy Hilton died today.

Thursday December 23

Went down to Long Beach for Jimmy's funeral. Very short service in the mortuary chapel—coffin closed. Went with Adele to their house. She took me up to his work room and I cried when I saw he had a picture of me on his desk.

Saturday December 25

The children here for Christmas. A rather joyless day for me.

Wednesday December 29

To New York to record David Wayne to the orchestra tracks we have made.

Friday December 31

Came home and saw the New Year in with Kathy. [Sadly *Finian's Rainbow* was never finished. Fred Schwartz and the group of New

York theatre owners he represented ran out of money. They were counting on the cash flow from a film they had made called *Long John Silver* with Robert Newton to keep us going but it bombed. We spent $40,000 of their money making the tracks. One day we did a rough mix and that is all that survives of what could have been something wonderful. The tape is a collector's item now.]

1955

January

I am writing *To Catch a Thief.*

Hitchcock is shooting another picture, *The Trouble With Harry.* He told me he doesn't have a composer set for it yet. I now make what is probably the biggest mistake of my life. I recommend Herrmann for it. Hitch does not know Herrmann. I introduce them. [It was love at first sight. Hitchcock had Herrmann do all his pictures until he fell out of love with him on *Torn Curtain.* By the time of *Torn Curtain,* Hitchcock was in a very lucrative arrangement with Lou Wasserman at MCA. It is said that Wasserman had suggested Hitchcock have a lighter, more pop-sounding score for this picture than Herrmann is capable of writing. Hitchcock is said to have transmitted this request to Herrmann, who brought in his usual marvelous-sounding eight-horns-blowing-their-brains-out score. After the recording of the main title the musicians say Hitch came out and stopped the session and the rest of the score was not recorded. John Addison did another one.]

Wednesday February 2

Recording *Catch.* In the main title there is a section played by three pianos (with the orchestra) in which I used the Effenbach sisters and the studio pianist, Harry Sukman. It sounded puny and ineffectual to me. You just can't record a lot of things going on at once on the Paramount stage. [I must admit that hearing the film on television years later it does not sound as bad as I thought it did then.]

Monday February 14

Georgie Auld, the tenor saxophonist, recorded some sequences with Jack Costanza the virtuoso bongo player today.

Thursday March 10

We rescored a couple of scenes today. In the fireworks scene with Grant and Kelly I had Auld playing the tune in a very sensuous manner. The front office brass wanted the whole scene toned down and Hitch thought if I rescored it in a more conventional way, like with strings, he might get to keep it. Hitchcock amazes me. He has an innocuous scene where two French plainclothes policemen are staking out a villa hoping to catch the thief. It is a long shot and they are looking at what one imagines are dirty French postcards—a wry Hitchcock touch. Don Hartman, one of the studio brass, objected and Hitch took it out. I said, "Why would you take that out? It's charming." He said, "The picture doesn't stand or fall on one little shot. Besides, if I take that out they won't complain so much about the fireworks scene."

Friday March 11

Herrmann recorded his score for *The Trouble With Harry* this week. Strings and woodwinds. I introduced him to the orchestra. He had a hassle immediately with Charlie Strickfaden, the first oboe. He is a saxophone double and is not really the best first oboe in the world but we all love him, he is such a nice man. But Herrmann is a martinet. Charlie did not please him. After the session Steve Czillag, head of music cutting, said to me. "He may be your friend but he is a prick." Herrmann has always been very superior about our complaints concerning the acoustics of the stage at Paramount. He said, "You guys who can't conduct always blame it on the acoustics." Then he did this picture and they recorded it very close. After the dubbing session he admitted he was physically ill.

Thursday March 17

Previewed *Catch* in Pasadena. Smash.

Monday/Tuesday March 28/29

Working with Sid Kuller on material for the *Zeigfeld Follies* which opens shortly at the Sands with Sinatra. This is our last show there. Sid has accepted the position of entertainment director of a new hotel called the Royal Nevada and I am assisting. Helen Traubel is going to headline the opening show.

Saturday April 9

Rehearsing with Helen Traubel. (We wrote some special material for her.)

Monday April 11

They are doing a little redubbing on *Catch*. Hitchcock told Fjastad he likes the score.

Wednesday April 20

The Royal Nevada opens. Miss Traubel is a simply superb singer but she has a husband, Bill Bast (I think that's right) who is a real HOSA (Husband of Stars Association) and a blocker. She isn't so bad. Gets a little iffish about some things, some of them fair, some of them not. For instance there was a picture of Marilyn Maxwell outside the entrance to the showroom. Standard display of the next attraction. Traubel insisted it be taken away. She didn't like to look at "her puss" every time she came into the room. The microphones were bad at the opening show, and Bast went into the bar and got drunk. His complaints could be heard in Los Alamos. There is an installation of the so-called "Dancing Waters" on the stage run by a tall German general type named Hans Hasslich. A lovely interlude which closes the show. After a few days Miss Traubel wanted them moved up ahead of her for some reason. It was done. Georgie

Tapps did some very fine choreography and Jerry Fielding is conducting the orchestra. He loathes Las Vegas but can't get a job right now in Hollywood.

Friday April 29

Drove up to Ojai to see the Ojai Valley School's production of *Ruddigore*. Very funny. The kid playing Mad Margaret had talent and worked out a sort of twitching gimmick which she did all the time even when others were supposed to have the ball. Joyce was in the chorus of professional bridesmaids and Ann led a hornpipe in a sailor's suit. Very nice. Spent an hour afterwards admiring the kids' hamsters.

Friday May 6

To Greta Peck's who was giving a going away party for herself and the Mitchums. Bob is going to Spain and other countries for *Foreign Intrigue*, Greta to New York for fun. Lots of people. The ubiquitous Dean Jagger, Harry Morgan, Dick Widmark and a fascinating lady named Barbara Cruikshank, related to the illustrator. She spent a lot of time telling me about a drink called Pisco Punch. Ollie claims it originated in Chicago. It is a fresh peach floating in Southern Comfort and you can have it. Mitchum is a throwback to the days when actors used to raise hell and have fun in the John Barrymore tradition. For that matter so are Wendell Corey and James Barton. According to a story in the paper yesterday, Mitchum is suing *Confidential*, the scandal sheet, for stating that he went to a party given by Charles Laughton, took his clothes off, smeared himself with ketchup and announced he was a hamburger. Seeing Mitchum reminded me that last year at the Cannes Festival a wanton imitation actress named Simone Silva took the top of her bikini off for the photographers. Mitchum was reported to have placed his hand on one of her mammaries and a French photographer uncharacteristically fell off a rock into the sea. *Confidential* is the paper that did a story on the Four Girls giving the impression that the girls and others who take part in the festivities at Mother Russell's Chapel sort of got their agates off for a finish.

Saturday May 7

To the Presnells. Marsha is doing "Anniversary Waltz" at the Carthay Circle with Howard Duff, and came in later. Jack Goodman, an editor with Simon & Schuster, was telling Corwin he should write a novel. He said, "It is getting late, you know." Corwin said, "Do you want to commit me? That's the only way I'll do it—if I owe it to you." Kate (Norman's wife) wasn't there and I don't know why. I listened later as an intense young woman talked to Norman. She never came to a period or a question mark. She was a script girl on a picture Corwin had written that was shot in the Philippines. She told Norman she had majored in Television at some university or other. Corwin said, "What was your minor?" She said, "Psychiatry." Later she told Kathy she had majored in Art and minored in Physical Therapy as related to Art. She also claimed to be a Phi Delta Kappa.

Anne Shirley and her husband Charlie Lederer were there. She talked about Lederer's *Kismet* when it played in London. (Actually it opened in Oxford.) She said the actors who had played the piece in New York had to slow up their delivery about half for the English audience. Same with some of the music. They had a 24-year-old conductor named Cyril something who was very good but his gold collar button showed. Reminded me of Franz Waxman who is always so afraid *his* collar button is going to show he is forever shrugging his collar higher even in the middle of Mahler.

I am reading Lionel Barrymore's autobiography and it has a rolling reverberant style. I have been dipping into Schillinger again [the teacher of a mathematic basis of music] and am agonizing a piece using some of his devices. It certainly is slow work. (You have to make graphs.) Well, back to the drawing board.

Wednesday May 11

The Schneiders (Bill and Neil) are here. We had dinner with them. After, Kathy told me they had said they didn't like me. (I didn't believe it.)

Thursday June 2

Saw *The Cobweb*, a far-out film with a 12-tone score by Lennie Rosenman. First class. I like to hear people taking chances with film music.

Friday June 10

Zipped up to Ojai for the graduation ceremonies at the Ojai Valley School and zipped back in time to receive Bob and Eileen Bassing for dinner. She is working at Columbia Pictures in the Screen Gems division, more popularly known as Screen Germs. They make television series—ten this season and next year they will be doing 21. None of them uses music. They are tracked with foreign recordings.

Eileen tells the story of the new Herman Wouk novel and Mr. Harry Cohn, the tyrant who runs Columbia. The studio had a great success with Stanley Kramer's film of Wouk's *Caine Mutiny*, and optioned his next novel for a hefty price, sight unseen. The galley proofs arrived and at four p. m. a reader named Jack Fleischman was told by his supervisor to read the novel and be in Mr. Cohn's office at ten the next morning prepared to tell the story. The novel was long but Fleischman got through it and reported to Mr. Cohn's office, accompanied by his boss, the story editor, ready to do his number. Mr. Cohn always has a few piddling phone calls to get out of the way—making a deal for a television set at wholesale or something. This over, Mr. Cohn said to reader Fleischman, "Did you read the book?"

"Yes."

"Did you like it?"

"Well—I don't think there's a picture in it."

Mr. Cohn looked at the reader as if he were an alien from another planet who had somehow insinuated himself into an important meeting at Columbia Pictures.

"You don't think there's a picture in it. I *know* there's a picture in it. For two reasons. Number one it is by Wouk who wrote *Caine Mutiny* and number two I *bought* it."

"Well, sir, there's the question of the story."

Mr. Cohn: "Start telling the story. You got fifteen minutes."

The panic-stricken reader says it is a 1,000 page novel and he doesn't think he can tell it in fifteen minutes.

Mr. Cohn says, "Try."

The reader talks for seven minutes and is interrupted by Mr. Cohn: "How far into the book are you?" The reader says, "About 200 pages." Mr. Cohn says, "You got eight minutes. I don't think you're gonna make it." The reader ploughs ahead and sketches in the story line and finally Cohn says, "It stinks." He turns to the reader's boss and says, "How can you hire people like this? I give him a Wouk novel to report on and he comes in with this shit." The boss of the story department protests that it isn't the man's fault. Cohn comes up with the solution. "Wouk didn't write this. He's probably big enough now to hire people to write his books for him."

Eileen's boss at Screen Gems is a man named Briskin. He supervises all the television production at the studio and for the last four years has suffered from an annoying ringing in his ears. Doctors suggested that Briskin describe the sound he hears so that they can duplicate it, and base a therapy on the idea that the patient can combat something he becomes familiar with from an outside source. Briskin could not describe it satisfactorily. One night, unable to sleep, Briskin became aware of a toilet dripping. It sounded something like the tone of the ringing in his ears, but not quite. The next day he had the studio sound department come to his house and they recorded the toilet, added some crickets, and approximated the original sound more or less. Footnote to this story: Mr. Cohn occasionally leers at Briskin and says, "Falling apart? Hearing noises again?"

Monday June 13

At the Royal Nevada. Rehearsing Anna-Maria Alberghetti, an elaborate presentation full of problems. Sid Kuller under stress tramples on everyone but lacks the innate authority to pull things together. There are gripes from the crew, even the waitresses and bartenders who apparently cannot get the room set up because we are encroaching on their time.

Tuesday June 14

The opening. It all comes together and is immensely successful. At the end Alberghetti emotionally introduces her father—"It is his day, not mine"—tears streaming. Jerry Fielding told me she did it the same way every night. Well, why not? She's an actress. Bretaigne Windust was there for the opening and introduced me to Hank Greenspun, the fighting editor of a local paper.

Thursday June 16

Date with Kay Marx, Groucho's ex. A nice girl with her share of insecurities. Wants to go back to singing. I am helping.

Monday June 20

Talked to Edward Heymann, the great lyricist. His songs include "Body and Soul," "Through the Years," "I Cover the Waterfront," "You Ought to Be in Pictures" to name four. He is going to put lyrics to some of the tunes in "Catch a Thief." I am honored.

Thursday July 18

Kuller has made a deal with Frank Loesser and we are going to do *Guys and Dolls* as the next attraction at the Royal Nevada. This is taking chances in a big way. Some years ago Jack Entratter produced *The Student Prince* at the Sands with Jan Kiepura and Marta Eggerth. Nobody came. As a result of this fiasco none of the wiseacres up and down the Strip believes the audience in a Vegas showroom, drinking and eating, will listen to a book show. If this jinx can be broken it would seem we have the perfect show to do it. We have virtually the original cast: Sam Levene, Vivian Blaine, Robert Alda, Stubby Kaye and B. S. Pully playing Big Julie. We started to rehearse in Hollywood. There were problems, mostly having to do with Pully. He didn't pay his rent at the Hollywood Kinickerbocker hotel. The lady who owns it called Sid. Pully said he didn't have any money. He was sending whatever he could to the Edison Hotel in New York where, he said, they had his wife chained to a bed until he paid his bill. Sid made arrangements to deduct a certain amount weekly from Pully's paycheck and give it to the lady.

Friday August 5

Rehearsing at the Royal Nevada. Pully is to get $1,500 a week when we open. He lost that much at the tables the first day of rehearsals. Sid had to cut off his credit. Pully, who is a tall, heavy, foul-mouthed bruiser and a compulsive gambler, did a nightclub act with a partner before he was cast by Loesser and Abe Burrows in *Guys and Dolls*. One day he locked his partner in a pay toilet at Penn Station, had him hand his suit over the door, hocked it for $2 and put the money on a horse. The horse paid off.

Thursday August 9

Guys and Dolls opened and made history. [It probably started the dinner theatre business. At any rate book shows have been playing Vegas since.]

Wednesday August 31

Lunch with Stephen Bosustow at UPA, the high class cartoon factory in Burbank across from Warner Bros. UPA makes enchanting short films. notably Thurber's "The Unicorn In The Garden," "Gerald MacBoing Boing," the "Nearsighted Mr. Magoo" series and many others. CBS has ordered 26 half hours and Bosustow wants me to be his musical director. I am thinking it over.

Saturday September 3

Lud Gluskin at CBS wants me to do a "My Favorite Husband." The scoop is he gets $400 and gives the composer $200. We compromised on $250.

Thursday September 15

Started at UPA. I have to hire composers, supervise recordings, write some myself, stay within a budget. I don't know how good I'm going to be at that.

Monday November 14

I am in New York seeing some shows and looking up old friends. Saw Deems Taylor, Jim Fassett and Lucille Singleton today. Deems is always a pleasure to see, although he hews to his rule of never picking up a check, but who cares? He's always been so supportive of me and I am truly glad I know him. He lives in a beautiful apartment on Fifth Avenue overlooking the park at about 60th street, and is still bitching about the rent—$250. Fassett is still sitting behind his desk at CBS, puffing his pipe, and running what's left of CBS's cultural affairs. Lucille, who gave me my first job at CBS, is nearing the end of her working life and is looking forward to going back to Alabama.

Tuesday November 15

Went to see Larry Lohman at CBS, the only high-up exec strictly on the business side I really liked. In 1934 he sent me a note out of the blue saying he liked something I had done and to keep it up. Lunch with Bill Schneider at the Illustrators Club and in the evening to *Cat on a Hot Tin Roof*. Burl Ives, my old comrade in arms against CBS, was very good. He's become an actor.

Wednesday November 16

Saw Englebach and Deems again and touched base with Millard Lampell who wrote the libretto for "Liberation," the cantata based on Pres. Roosevelt's D-Day prayer which we broadcast on a Treasury Department radio program, incidentally with Burl singing the leading part. Saw *Silk Stockings* in the evening. Love Cole Porter. [This journal starting as it does in 1947 makes no mention of the fact that I did the vocals on two shows for Porter, *Panama Hattie* and *Let's Face It*.]

Tuesday December 6

Got to be 46 today. No mention on my calendar of any celebration, and indeed what's to celebrate?

Thursday December 8

Went to Fox and had lunch with Ted Cain who is now running the business end of the music department. He offered me a film called *On the Threshold of Space*, which of course I accepted sight unseen. Love working at Fox.

Friday December 9

Bright girl named Betsy Beaton down here. Ex of Keenan Wynn's and as mixed up as they come. She slept in the upstairs bedroom which may or may not have surprised me. I am as different from Keenan as you can get. I drive a Jag, he drives a fire engine.

Thursday December 15

Start on Fox's payroll today. They assigned me one of the nice old bungalows built circa 1930 to work in. Met producer Bill Bloom, a nice man.

Tuesday December 20

Ran the picture with Mr. Zanuck from eight p. m. till midnight. (He's a late starter and that's to my liking.) He's a very, very smart picture-maker and as tough as they come. He chewed Bloom out on a dozen points.

Wednesday December 21

Ran film with Bloom, discussing where music and what kind.

Friday December 23

Ran it with Lionel Newman, Alfred's brother, who does a lot of conducting around here and has an immense vocabulary of four letter words.

1956

January

Finished *Threshold* and returned to UPA. Mel Leven, songwriter, one of the delights here. He and Dory Langdon (she later married Andre Previn) have written most of the songs for this series UPA is making for CBS. One night I invited Leven to dinner and to spend the night since he was leaving on a fishing trip at three a. m. from the Malibu pier. He got down to the house at 6:30, we had a martini and went to the Golden Bull for dinner. After the usual two martini wait in the crowded bar we got a table. He is a warm and lovable man with a most unusual songwriting mind. Titles of some of the songs he wrote for us: "Miserable Pack of Wolves," "The Average Giraffe" and "People Taste Terrible but Make Nice Friends," sung by the lions in a film about Nero.

They are making 78 films at UPA for this CBS series—three per half hour. A sweet soft man named Bobe Cannon (almost everybody in the cartoon business has a funny name—remember Tee Hee?), who takes forever to make up his mind, is supervising the films. The talented underpaid people at UPA bring him wonderful funny ideas and he can never make up his mind. The result is I have plenty of time off and have no difficulty getting permission to leave the little lot to go and do a feature picture.

Alfred Newman has invited me to do the score for a Charles Brackett film entitled *D Day, The Sixth of June* with Robert Taylor and Dana Wynter. (Miss Wynter is one of the three English girls Paramount brought over for *The Girls of Pleasure Island.*) When I went to see Mr. Brackett in his office he was lying on a sofa. He apologized for not getting up, explaining he had "policeman's toe." He is a delightful humorous man who did a lot of films with Billy Wilder, also a funny man but a son of a bitch. Ivan Moffatt wrote the screenplay, a trite wartime romance. He gave me three pages of close-typed notes about what he thought the music should be. I love Ivan. He is an erudite, charming Englishman, superb at conversation, has an admirably keen mind and loathes the typical Hollywood score. In his notes he said he abhorred strings and thought that in this picture they would be "very dangerous." He said he longed always to have a score played by a very small orchestra and that wind instruments seemed to him ideal to underscore emotions such as love, etc. We are at Fox, remember, the studio with the best orchestra in town, run by Alfred Newman, whose use of strings in his film scores is so exquisitely moving he is the envy of us all. Ivan's ideas did not survive.

I went to see Alfred, who lectured me in the nicest way about doing a commercial score and not trying to express myself too much in this kind of picture. He wanted me to use as the love theme, "You'll Never Know," a song by Harry Warren which the studio owned. I fought it, wanting to write my own, but he was adamant, and "You'll Never Know" it was. The score was finished in a few weeks and Alfred conducted it sensitively and the orchestra played beautifully. In the dubbing Henry Koster, the director, objected to a piece of music in one of the early reels. I said it was important to plant it here otherwise it wouldn't pay off later; if the audience heard it here it would be more effective there. Mr. Brackett backed me up and it stayed. Odd how few directors (and writers) know anything of the mechanics and art of constructing a film score.

Wednesday May 30

D Day, The Sixth of June opened yesterday at the Chinese Theatre, Hollywood, and in another 119 theatres including the Roxy in New York. I went into UPA early today, having read the reviews in the trade papers. I tried unsuccessfully to find out who wrote the very fine and literate review for the *Hollywood Reporter*, and called Mr. Brackett. He said that among the hundreds of pictures he has produced many had been released "quietly" but this is the first picture that has been classified "Top Secret." It is true there has been almost no advance publicity or advertising. Mr. Brackett said he knew of five people who attended the premiere—he and his wife and three friends.

Thursday July 5

Working at UPA is largely a pain in the ass. An atmosphere has somehow been created there that makes everyone feel completely unimportant. It is not a happy ship. All the brilliant artists complain that they are paid almost nothing. It is nice working with Jules Engel, Fred Crippen and other fine talents but it is Mel Leven who cheers me up no end. I have just done a score for a delightful picture called *The Unenchanted Princess* in which Edward Everett Horton does the narration in his usual enchanting style. Andre Previn played the harpsichord, and in one of the breaks told me he was going to conduct a performance of Boris Blacher's "Romeo and Juliet" for the Monday Evening Concerts and asked me to prepare the singers. Delighted. Andre told me he once played in an orchestra that recorded a movie score written and conducted by Buddy Bregman. Bregman had written a cue in 5/4 and had difficulty conducting it. In the men's room on a break, Previn offered to show Bregman how to conduct 5/4. Bregman said, "Fuck it. I'll never write a 5/4 cue again."

At UPA the composers are supplied with "bar sheets" with all the action and the footage at which it occurs indicated. In the case of *Unenchanted Princess* I used clicks so that I could catch every important piece of action accurately. (Clicks provide the sound of a metronome in the proper tempo fed to each member of the orchestra through earphones.) When I put the music into the film, nothing fit. The bar sheets were out of sync anywhere from six frames of film to two feet. Joe Syracusa, the music cutter, and I opened up the score in nine places to get everything in sync with the action, thereby ruining the flow of the music. I had an unlucky session for *Brother John*, a little film about a French town. We used "Sur Le Pont D'Avignon" and "Frère Jacques." The film was directed by a nice bright fellow named Bill Scott who does a lot of bitching about how the properties we do have to conform to Bobe Cannon's leanings toward Christian Science and his subservience to the PTA. Scott systematically took out all the poetry and charm.

Wednesday July 18

Jerry Lawrence and Bobby Lee are making a musical out of Jimmy Hilton's *Lost Horizon* to be called *Shangri-La*. They were kind enough to ask me to do the score. After much consideration I declined. [It eventually opened in New York, with a score by Harry Warren, and closed after two and a half weeks at a loss of $2,500,000.]

I am rehearsing the singers for the "Romeo and Juliet" at night in my office at UPA. Herrmann has advised me to stay away from it. He doesn't like the work. He and Lucy have just returned from England where he conducted some concerts for the BBC with the London Symphony Orchestra. On one of the concerts, appropriately enough, he did Vaughan Williams's "London Symphony." After the performance the old man came down the aisle and grasped his hand. Herrmann says it was a supreme moment for him. Then the papers came out and said he didn't understand the work.

I have two cats, Charlotte and Jane. Jane is a male but got named before I found out. They are both in the hospital, Charlotte with worms, Jane with an infected toe which had to be amputated. I have been having cesspool trouble. The erosion in the last few months has been severe and a bulkhead is being constructed. The only trouble is that the trench which two men spent two days digging, got filled in last night in about 15 minutes of a high tide.

Two young men have taken the house next door. I knocked on their door. When one of them answered I said, "I am your next-door neighbor." He said, "I know. We can smell you."

I see that Larry Thor is about to be divorced by his wife Jean. She claims he took a pet monkey on a tour of the bars on the Sunset Strip and thereafter showed more affection for the monkey than for her.

I feel I am laying a bomb at UPA. I just sent a long powerful memo to Steve Bosustow pleading with him to allow me more freedom in running the music department, which is in as much confusion as all the other departments here. I don't know if it will work. Probably not. No one has any authority and Steve is as cautious a postponer as Bobe. I am not liked here so I'll probably get postponed and fobbed off and frustrated until I quit. Too bad because I actually like having a job, and while I don't readily fit into organizations, I like having something of this nature to do every day. The big problem in being a writing musician in Hollywood these days is lack of work. Very doldrumsy right now. There are compensations, however. I invited dear Mario Castelnuovo-Tedesco to do a score for us. He accepted and did a delightful one. (We were running it against the picture one day and Herb Klynn—he's the business mogul here and by far the nicest thing about him is his secretary—objected to a pizzicato passage. Tedesco said, gently, as though addressing a backward child, "But, my dear, it is *right.*")

Fred Steiner, one of our better composers, is doing a score for a film about Rousseau. He and I had lunch with Tedesco one day. Tedesco was full of stories. As a young man in Florence he wrote an overture and sent it to Toscanini. Months passed before he got a summons to come to Milan and discuss it. At Toscanini's house he was shown into a room. The maestro was standing in the bend of the piano deep in thought. Tedesco did not know whether to advance or retreat. Toscanini saw him and said, "There is a wrong note in the score." Tedesco knew which note he meant. It was part of a bass line. Toscanini sat at the piano and tried several ways of getting round the problem. None worked. Tedesco said he had tried everything and couldn't solve it. Toscanini admitted he had called Tedesco's teacher and he couldn't find an improvement so Tedesco suggested the masestro play it the way it was written. Tedesco went home to Florence and in due time Toscanini notified him the overture would receive its première in Vienna and would he come?

Tedesco and his wife arrived in Vienna at 8:30 in the morning, went to their hotel, bathed and proceeded to the concert scheduled for 11:30 a. m. (Don't ask me why they give concerts in Vienna at 11:30 a. m.) Now this overture ends with a long diminuendo punctuated by a soft chime. The chime was too loud. Later at lunch with Toscanini, his wife, his daughter and Vladimir Horowitz, the program was discussed in detail. Tedesco, when they got around to his piece, said he enjoyed it very much. Toscanini said, "How was the chime?" Tedesco pondered whether to lie or tell the truth and finally said, "Too loud." Toscanini broke out into a terrible tirade about women and music. He had been worried about the chime and had his wife stand in various parts of the hall. She couldn't hear it so he had the percussionist play it louder. "I should have trusted my own judgment," he shouted. Turning to Tedesco he said, "We play it in Budapest Wednesday. Tedesco, you come." They went to Budapest arriving at 5:30 p. m. for the eight o'clock concert. When the orchestra got off the train they were surprised to learn that a rehearsal had been called for six. It was to check the chime. Tedesco sat out in the hall while Toscanini tried different hammers, finally settling on a felt one. It was fine.

Tuesday August 7

The kids and Florence have gone to New York and are staying with Bill and Georgia Johnstone until they find a place. I am advertising this house (20140 Pacific Coast Highway) in *Variety*. I want to move back to the Chateau Marmont for six months until I finish at UPA.

In the evening to see Lawrence and Lee's *Inherit the Wind*. A two-level set, the lower the courtroom, the upper the town where they staged crowd scenes. Herrmann was there. Didn't like the two levels. Would have preferred it all done in the courtroom. I wasn't mad about the way they wrote Mencken, but the actor played it very well. I did not like the man who played Bryan, but Herrmann thought him a good likeness. I simply could not stand the actress who played the sweetheart of the defendant. She practices the style of acting which calls for a lot of swallowing before delivering a line. Later to Billy Gray's to see Sid Kuller's parody of *My Fair Lady*, this version called "My Fairfax Lady." Herman Levin who produced the original show (incidentally it cost $400,000, all put up by CBS), has ordered them to stop. Billy is infuriated. Thinks because he pays ASCAP he can do all the tunes from the show. He's never heard of Grand Rights. (In a club, or anywhere else, you may do four songs from a musical but not the whole score without making a deal for what are called Grand Rights.) Milton Berle was there and we sat with Senator Richards and his wife, who are friends of Kathy's. He seems all right. I voted for him. His wife is lively and fun—plump, dark and kind of hip.

Wednesday August 8

To see Bobby Clark in *Damn Yankees*, book by Douglass Wallop (he's married to Lucille, Herrmann's first wife) and George Abbott, dances by Bob Fosse, orchestrations by Don Walker, who is almost as good as he thinks he is.

Thursday August 9

Recorded a couple more for UPA. That's my theory—to do two at a time—they don't understand this saves money. Betty Hayden called me. She is living at the beach with her four children. Kathy was sore. Kathy generally is sore about something.

When I started this UPA gig I hired George Cates, a friend and a very experienced record producer, to be in the booth for all our sessions. I wanted record quality. Now I am having a vendetta with Herb Klynn, the money man. It started with a memo from Steve Bosustow to me stating that henceforth we were to record only "film quality" not "record quality," that we were not planning to have phonograph records made of our soundtracks. I called Steve on it and he said Klynn wanted him to send the memo. I asked for a meeting. Steve postponed for a few days then called and said there wouldn't be any need for a meeting since Herb Klynn was being removed from the production department and transferred to commercial spots. (I hope that's a demotion, anyhow it can't help but make life easier for me.) Interesting sidelight on this memo. Kathy thinks Klynn regards "film quality" as not as good as "record quality" and therefore must be cheaper to attain. I think he is just plain annoyed with me because I have been treating him with such love and affection.

Tuesday August 14

To Vegas to see Harry Belafonte, Judy Garland and Louis Armstrong. Went backstage and talked to Belafonte. He is afraid his contempt of Vegas shows in his work. I asked him what he wanted to do. He would rather play colleges and concerts. Says playing the Greek Theatre this summer was his greatest experience as an artist. Saw Judy's show. As usual she tore the place apart. Went back to see her and she was mortified I had seen that particular show, she thought it so bad. I told her she was truly great but of course she didn't believe it. Then to the Sands where Louie and Bob Merrill were doing some of our old material. In his dressing room Louie said he ain't mad at nobody. He has had four wives and they are all friends. The second and the fourth "run together" and when anyone says "Miz Armstrong" they both turn round. We made a date to meet after the Billie Holiday show to "talk over old times" but I folded. Billie Holiday walked on and off the stage as though she was made of glass. I read her book when I got home and she has a chip on her shoulder—the exact opposite of Louie. She has been on H off and on the last ten years. They never beat that one. Looked tonight like she might be on it again. Sad.

Sunday September 2

To Alice and William Woodrow's with Kathy. Jules Engel the artist, Rosenthal the sculptor and wife, Lee Wainer the songwriter and wife, May Collins (Alice's sister), a pediatrician named Tobias who raises tomatoes. He injects cognac into the tomatoes before picking them. It doesn't work. Squirts right out again.

Wednesday September 5

I have moved back to the Chateau Marmont. I am in 3C, a small apartment fronting on Sunset boulevard with an irritating view of a 40-foot-high woman dressed in a bathing suit, wearing a cowboy hat. She turns slowly and endlessly, advertising the Sahara Hotel in Las Vegas, and the sight of her is driving me insane.

Had a rehearsal today with the eight singers, drawn from the excellent Roger Wagner Chorale, who are going to do the Blacher "Romeo and Juliet." Previn is to conduct it for the Monday Evening Concerts and came to hear what we were up to. Tonight at Glen Glenn, Freddie Steiner recorded his score for "The Merry-Go-Round in the Jungle," the film about Rousseau when he was with the French army in Mexico. I insisted on a one-mike pick-up and Glen was aghast. He said, "We haven't recorded that way in twenty years." Sounded super.

Last Friday (August 31) did a Workshop at CBS with Stan Freberg, a weird and wonderful talent. Bill Robson directed. I got up in the morning with quite a thrill of anticipation to be doing a radio show again. The actors—Alan Reed, Dawes Butler, June Foray and Sam Pierce—all had fits of nostalgia, especially when we recreated a bit of the Fred Allen show. Played the theme "Smile, Darn Ya', Smile" and everything. Alan Reed and I had both worked on the Allen show. At that time Alan's name was Bergman. He decided to change it to Reed. Fred asked why? Alan said, "Who could make it with a name like Bergman?" Fred said, "Ingrid?"

Freberg's show was called "Colloquy 3—An Analysis of Satire." Not much music but some of it got laughs from the cast. Incidentally, Robson lives in a dirty, miserable little guest house out in the Valley. I was there one night trying to pry some script out of him. (In that respect he hasn't changed. He hasn't changed in any respect.) We drank and he talked about his long dry spell on the blacklist when he lived on money borrowed from his insurance, now all gone. He put the knock on his analyst, a Dr. Hacker, and while I was there the doctor called. He asked for some of the $3,000 Robson owes him and told him to stop knocking him.

The day before the show I went into Robson's office at CBS to see if there wasn't a bit of script I could work on and he was dictating revisions of Freberg's gems to his secretary. He paused, sighed, and asked her for a pill. It was dexedrine he wanted. He told me about his current lady friend. She is given to saying things like, "Have you ever had such a delightful companion, so sexy and all?" When they get in bed she has to be on top. He told me his take-home pay for directing a Workshop such as this one is $47.50. If he doesn't write the script—just directs—he spends two weeks hanging around CBS and collects $47.50. In the Italian restaurant across from CBS where we had lunch he drank five vodka martinis.

Monday September 10

Lunch with Mel Leven and Dick Walton's wife Vanna McCain who makes animated television commercials in Reno. Dick Walton is a fine artist who comes down once a year with a car trunk full of paintings he sells to all of us. I came home at four in 100-degree heat. Previn called and can't make it tomorrow for the Tedesco score. Having a hell of a time finding a classically trained pianist who can work to clicks pounding in his ear. I called Lukas Foss who turned me down coldly. He doesn't do "commercial work."

Saturday September 15

Wednesday night (12) to a CLGA board meeting. (We are now called the Composers & Lyricists Guild of America.) Dull, as usual. David Raksin was chairman and fussy as an old maid. Thursday I went to CBS to pick up an assignment. It will be the first time I have written music to be recorded out of the country. (Artistically it is most satisfying. Gluskin uses large orchestras in London and the stuff sounds magnificent. The English players are a sensitive and well trained lot.) This recording abroad is done all the time now. Herrmann's done some. It puts our players out of work because Petrillo won't relent on the 5 percent. (If a network wants to use American players they must pay 5 percent of their time costs into the Trust Fund.) Outside the Italian restaurant I ran into Robson who was drunk because he had just signed papers declaring voluntary bankruptcy. Sam Pierce, the actor, and Robson were on their way to barbecue some chicken and invited me. I went to UPA to rehearse "Romeo and Juliet," then to Robson's place.

While the food was cooking Robson and I went round the corner to register to vote. This took place in a rather littered modern house. The registering paraphernalia was on a long table in the living area. On the end of the table was a pile of film cans. The husband of the lady of the house was cutting a film featuring Dr. Baxter, a local TV celebrity dedicated with irrepressible enthusiasm to bringing Shakespeare to the masses, which I may say he does with enormous success. I told the lady I was a Democrat and asked what she was. She said, "We are not supposed to say, but I am a Democrat too." She said, "Most of the people around here are Republicans." Even the two old ladies she had just registered, who were living on pensions.

"Raise your right hand and swear these statements are true."
"I do."
Robson said, "What, no so help me God?"
The lady said, "I never looked." She looked. There it was. You are supposed to say, "So help me God."

Wednesday September 26

Friday last went to the première of *Lust for Life*, a good picture with a script by Corwin. Bleachers, lights, TV, stars and social folk. Miklos Rozsa score rather modern with some good effects. I am plugging away on the chorus of "Romeo and Juliet," which goes

Monday 15 October. Did a date with the Andrews Sisters at Capitol Monday. Christmas songs. Voyle Gilmore produced. He's a love. Patti Andrews, who used to be married to Marty Melcher before he traded her in for Doris Day, is now married to their piano player, Wally Wechsler. I got the sense that he is an intensely ambitious man. For what, I don't know.

I had a real nightmare last night. I am rehearsing a group of singers. My old friend and benefactor at CBS Lucille Singleton tells them I don't like them. I am furious and leave the room. I go to where my car is' parked and someone has attacked it with a hammer. It is a mess. Scene II. Lots of racing down flights of stairs to get to where I live. It seems I live with a large group of people. About three o'clock in the morning a gaggle of dentists led by Adlai Stevenson come in and tell me I have to have all my teeth pulled. We go to a dental office but the dentist has taken his chair and equipment home. I suggest we go upstairs to another dentist's office but Adlai and his crew veto that. Why? Because the dentist would know we had used his equipment. Adlai gave me two codeine tablets and advanced with a pair of pliers to pull out my teeth. I woke up very short of breath.

There may be simple explanations for this dream. I bought a new Jag recently and almost immediately got side-swiped in Beverly Hills. I have had eight of my teeth capped. Herrmann put me on to his dentist, a man named Reagan. I told this man I wasn't worried about his bill, I was expecting a $1,200 refund from the IRS. The bill was $1,200.

Monday October 15

The Blacher "Romeo and Juliet" at the concert tonight went very well, the chorus performing with such flight and emotion I was thrilled. Andre was meticulous and considering the lack of rehearsal time the orchestra played correctly, if without much sing. It wasn't their fault really. The orchestra parts are rather dry. Johnny Green and Hugo Friedhofer came back after the performance. Green ignored me and Hugo just said he hated the work. My thought about Andre is that he has courage. I wouldn't have gone on with such skimpy rehearsals. The problem is that the players are all busy studio musicians and getting them all together on their free time is jigsaw impossible.

Wednessday October 17

Recorded two more little films for UPA. *Tingley's Tangle* and *The Last Knight*. UPA is in a mess. The show opens December 16 without a sponsor and CBS is mad at UPA for being so late with the material. The studio is grinding to a standstill. It is still the most disorganized place I have ever struck. The jealousy is unbelievable. Memos about music problems go to other people without even copies to me. I find out about things by accident. Intentionally or not the bosses are rude, treat the talent with icy disdain and minimize their contributions. I suppose it is all designed to keep their salaries down. It is a hotbed of dissatisfaction.

Thursday November 1

Lud Gluskin has hired me as musical director of "Shower of Stars," a television show for Chrysler starring Jack Benny. We did the first show tonight. It is produced and directed by a very talented man named Ralph Levy. A nice group. Jack Meyers is the assistant producer, Miriam Nelson the choreographer, both very nice and pleasant but this is still the hardest kind of work yet invented. (The prerecording session last week ran from 7 until midnight.) They decided to do the commercials live. They were staged by a man from the agency named Bud Cole whose favorite expression is "Down in Flames," and most of the time during these three long, elaborately scored commercials, we were indeed down in flames. They were cutting the commercials until the last moment and I didn't have time to give the orchestra all the cuts, so on the show we were flying blind most of the time. Television, however, smooths out a lot of minor disasters. At least on the playback of the kinescope they weren't quite so disastrous as they seemed when they were happening. I came out of the show with immense respect for Benny and Nanette Fabray the guest star. She is a comic genius and he is simply remarkable, full of taste and the discipline of years of performing.

Tuesday November 13

Victor Young died last Saturday. The funeral was today at the Hollywood Cemetery. This cemetery is midway between RKO and Paramount. Crowds of people could not get into the chapel. We stood on the grass and heard the service over loudspeakers. You could hear the warning buzzers from the Paramount lot signalling for quiet during takes. Victor would have approved. A red-haired woman sat on the outskirts of the crowd on a chair provided by one of the cemetery attendants and sobbed throughout.

Wednesday December 5

CLGA gave a lunch to George Jessel in the Patio Room at the Beverly Hills Hotel today. We had informed him we were giving him honorary membership in the Guild and then asked him to perform at our dinner. He was unable to appear at the dinner and we got Peggy Lee instead, but we are stuck with giving him this scroll anyway.

He was funny. He screwed his monocle into his right eye and talked a lot. In his stentorian Capitol Theatre delivery he told a joke that brought conversation at the other tables in this intimate little room to a halt.

Man and a woman in a bar getting loaded.

Woman: Tell the truth. What do you want?

Man: I'll tell you the truth. I'd like a little pussy.

Woman: So would I. Mine is as big as a hatbox.

Our group consisted of Leith Stevens, president of the Guild, Abe Marcus, lawyer, Buzz Adlam and Russ Garcia.

Friday December 7

Yesterday I was 47. The Red Cross was at UPA collecting blood. I gave some. Not sure I can spare it. Kath put on a party but we are at loggerheads. Same old problem; If I don't see her for a day she is hurt. If I don't see her for two days it takes a week to get back somewhere near where we were. There is not much fun anymore.

I heard from Dan Golenpaul (my "Information Please" friend in

New York). He says my kids are unhappy there. They are in a public school with 45 in a class and he thinks they ought to come back to California and go back to the Ojai Valley School where there are 12 maximum in a class. I called the school, reserved the space, called Dan and he is arranging it. And that is a friend.

We recorded a new opening for "Shower of Stars" today with members of the MGM studio orchestra. We could not get into Goldwyn or Republic or Glen Glenn so we did it in Studio 31 at Television City. Very poor sound. When it came to cutting the tracks together with the visuals, it turned out CBS does not have a three-gang synchronizer nor a three-headed movieola. We built the tracks blind and at the dubbing they were out anywhere from 2 to 3 frames. Incidentally the film we underscored was animated and processed in France. My first reaction was that the unions involved should squawk, but my second was that maybe all work in our fields should be on an internationally competitive basis.

Mark Smith (writer friend from CBS days) here. I haven't seen him in about eleven years. He is now married and has two young children. The oldest is a boy of 3½ who was born with a club foot and to date does not speak. Mark is supervising four shows for MCA. One of them is the GE Theatre. Each episode costs them about $35,000. The music budget is $85. This week he is spending $400 on a composer, a cello and an oboe which he says he will have to defend to *his* supervisor. While I thought $400 is better than $85 I told Mark any show costing $35,000 that can't spend $2,000 on music ought to be ashamed of itself.

Saturday December 8

I have just returned from Corwin's piece called *Tonight! Lincoln vs. Douglas* [later to be titled *The Rivalry*] which is playing at the Circle Theatre. Most of the playing time is devoted to the debates on the slavery issue. In the first act there is some repetition, which may be necessary but not for me. The two best scenes involve Lincoln and Mrs. Douglas. One on a train and one in a hotel lobby. In these scenes the two of them are interesting as people and one gets the sense of a strong attraction between them. The scenes between Mrs. Douglas and her husband do not have the same effect. The style is classic and the actors who played Lincoln and Mrs. Douglas (Jeff Morrow and Mala Powers) are very good. I did not very much like

Phillip Pine as Douglas. He is swarthy, young and not at all like the man he was playing. There was no sword clashing in the debates and I don't know why the true excitement of conflict is missing. I was very moved by the series of narrations and vignettes covering Lincoln's defeat by Douglas, his subsequent election as President and Douglas's support of Lincoln as the country moves towards war. Ray Bradbury was in the audience but I didn't talk to him. The usher came over to me before the play began and said she was reading Corwin's books and noted that I had done a lot of his music. Just wanted to talk to a character she had been reading about, I guess. Mala Powers went to Korea to entertain the troops and caught an obscure blood disease which laid her low for three years. At first they gave her up but she licked it and is now active again in TV, movies and this play. Paul Gregory, the producer, is going to tour it. It should do well on the road.

Monday December 10

Lunch with Byron Kane at Frascati Sunset then to Alhambra. Alhambra is a sleeper jump but Byron wanted me to try one of those massage parlors with trimmings. You are put into a cubicle, told to undress and relax. After a bit a very plump blonde comes in. She is dressed in a nylon uniform which she takes off. Then the panties and the bra. Then on the massage table à deux and from then on it's just like Cincinnati. To Television City where I checked the new opening film for "Shower of Stars." Works fine. Then to Chateau. Called Norman (Corwin) told him how I felt about his Lincoln play. He was very warm.

Thursday December 13

Yesterday to UPA to prepare for cutting. Marilyn there. She is a sweet, simple, unsophisticated, darling secretary. We all love her. I, so much, that I gave her my old Chevrolet convertible. Her husband understandably thinks the worst, so to make it legit I let her give me $1. Dick Shaw, who does the Nearsighted Mr. Magoo films, brought Marilyn back from lunch loaded. She sat on my couch and Bill Scott and Jules Engel came in and we analyzed her for an hour. When Marilyn had gone back to her office Engel diagnosed her trouble. She is married to a man who works for

IBM. Their whole circle is composed of IBM types. She works at UPA and meets a lot of dizzy, bright, non-conforming screwballs and is now dissatisfied with Mr. IBM.

Monday December 17

The UPA show opened yesterday to good reaction and notices. Kathy and I went to Bosustow's to see it in color. All the directors and department heads were there, quite a crowd. Today I went to the studio. Four guys are installed in my office and all my stuff has been cleared out. No one knows where my own personal couches are or where the supplies etc. have been put. The piano is in the projection room. No notice to me about any of this. Typical UPA.

Wednesday December 19

A week or so ago I went to a party at Jane Russell's house. A lady came over to me and introduced herself as Adrian Brian. She was friendly, outgoing and not unattractive. She said she loved the songs I had written for the Chapel and since she had sung them so often she wanted to meet me. She pointed out her husband. David Brian is an actor fairly well-known from his appearances in a popular television series, "District Attorney." I liked him and made a date to have dinner with him.

During the war he was married to a woman named Winsome Courtney with whom he did a cabaret act. He volunteered for the Coast Guard. They offered to send him to officers' training but he rejected the offer, feeling he was not fitted to command. Winsome thought he was. They invited an old friend, now an officer in the Coast Guard, to dinner one night. He arrived wearing his officer's uniform; Brian was sitting around in his ordinary seaman's outfit. Winsome, to her husband: "Don't you get up when an officer comes into the room?"

Wednesday December 26

Kathy and I spent Christmas eve with her parents. Her old man is okay. When he asked me how I was, I said, "I have a brain tumor." He said, "I am working on my second." So we have a rapport. He was loaded as usual. His second wife, Elaine (not Kathy's mother), does alright in this department too. I was having a slight recurrence of the old iritis and someone was taking flash pictures. One of the symptoms of iritis is photophobia. I spent the evening with my hands over my eyes.

Christmas Day to a swinging party at Ralph Levy's (director of "Shower of Stars"). Janice Rule with her new husband, playwright Robert Thom, Paul Godkin, choreographer of *Around the World in Eighty Days*, an actor named Dean Cromwell who was in *Hollywood Pinafore* (a disaster of a show I did with George Kaufman), Jerry Lawrence, fresh from his *Auntie Mame* triumph, and an elegant young man named Robin Joachim with his friend Curtis Harrington. Harrington has just finished an avant garde movie. Ernest Gold did the score. Harrington didn't like it because Ernest used "too much celeste." Joan O'Brien and Rod McKuen, who are going to be on our next "Shower of Stars," were there. McKuen told me he had written a song yesterday called "The Big White Boat." He sang it for me. It is a song about a fellow who sees the Big White Boat leaving and he wishes he were on it. He has captured in it a feeling of hopelessness and yearning. The guest stars on "Shower" the following week are an interesting parlay: Jayne Mansfield and Liberace.

To Capitol Records today to see Voyle Gilmore about another album we are preparing for the "Four Girls." We talked mostly about Peggy Lee and Judy Garland and the problems he runs into producing their records. They are bundles of neuroses. Judy is currently married to Sid Luft, who manages her affairs. According to Voyle, she okays any recording date that is far enough away, then cancels the day before. And Peggy seems mainly to be riddled with the fear of failure. Then to UPA where everyone is ecstatic about a great notice the show got in TIME last week. Lunch at Paramount with Roy Fjastad. He is trying to get me *Chalk Garden*, a film Don Hartman is preparing. [The film was not made at Paramount. It was finally done, rather unsuccessfully, by Ross Hunter in London in 1964 with a very fine score by Malcolm Arnold. But a fine score does not a fine film make. As Adolph Deutsch said about film music, "We can't save a picture. We can only make the corpse look pretty."]

At an emergency meeting of the Board of the Composers and Lyricists Guild, the possibility of a strike against all the major studios was discussed. The last meeting between our people and the studios ended in deadlock over the question of rights. We want the publication and other rights, the studios to have only the right to synchronize the music with the picture. They laugh at us because we really have no power. They know we don't have the money to support a long strike. Abe Marcus, our lawyer, said he would hate to have to defend the suits the studios would bring against composers who walked out on their contracts. We are going to call a meeting of all the contract composers to see if they will support a strike. I don't think they will. We are on the horns, alright, since if we give up on the question of rights, we will have wholesale resignations from our songwriting members.

Thursday December 27

On fathers-in-law: I did not know my last wife's father. He was dead—probably from over-exertion. He sired 16 children. No one knows anything about Florence's father. She was brought up by "relatives." Carol's father, whom I knew and liked, was the Rev. John W. Irwin, a curate at Grace Church in Mount Airy, a suburb of Philadelphia. He maintained a home near the church supervised by his wife Daisy, a simple, country-type lady who bore her crosses with good humor and an attitude which implied: "Doesn't everybody?" From Mondays to Fridays the Reverend was in New York attending to publicity for the Church. That is, he spent the days in the office and the nights in a cozy little apartment in Greenwich Village with a plump, pretty young woman called, I think, Jeannette.

Tonight dinner at Kathy's for the Alexanders, Mark Smith, Robin Joachim and Curtis Harrington. The Bassings came very late. They had been evacuated from their beach house when a fire broke out in Carbon Canyon. For the last two days an enormous fire has been blazing behind Trancas, Zuma Beach and Point Dume. Hundreds of homes have been lost, including Irving Reis's. The police believe someone set the fire in Carbon Canyon and have evacuated the Malibu beaches called La Costa, Las Flores and Big Rock. Big Rock is where my house is.

The talk at the party was mostly about films and film music. Curtis Harrington has seen everything, and he and his friend Robin belong to the school that deplores the fact that composers like Roy Harris and Aaron Copland do not work in Hollywood. They asked me if there was any film current or about to be released that had interesting music, and I couldn't think of one with the possible exception of Hitchcock's *The Wrong Man*, which will have a score by Benny Herrmann. Jeff Alexander was funny and rather vulgar talking about Kazan's controversial film of Tennessee Williams's *Baby Doll*. Jeff said, "If you want the plain facts, Kazan always has to have someone pissing on someone in his pictures."

Monday December 31

Last night to the Vogue Theatre in Hollywood to see *Baby Doll*. A line around the block composed mainly of leather jackets with a sprinkling of persons wearing bottle-bottom glasses. The show broke and out came a lot of pock-faced toughs, a gaggle of teenagers and a few girls in twos. In *Variety* today Kazan says he is sorry there has been such a fuss about the film (the Catholics condemned it); that it was not his intention to make what it seems to have become—a dirty, sexy picture.

Nothing New Year's Eve—Kath ill—we sat and watched television until my eyes crossed.

1957

Wednesday January 2

Up early, drove Julie Cass and my children back to school at Ojai. When I got back to the Chateau Marmont Carmilla, our switchboard operator, told me Joyce had had to be restrained from climbing an outside fire escape and the two of them had been stopped from racing up and down the halls and disturbing the actors. (The Chateau, built by an actor named Percy Marmont, is where the New York performers stay when they are out here making pictures.) The kids do turn my life upside down. Their rat, Hanky, adopted me and spent his time crawling over me dribbling little droplets every ten seconds.

Tonight to Ralph Levy's for a meeting about "Shower of Stars." Liberace, his brother George, Rod McKuen, Joan O'Brien, and Lud Gluskin, the impressario of the CBS music department. After we settled on the musical content of the program, George and Lud left.

Liberace is an extremely nice, gentle man, naturally humble, very smart. He knows his outrageous clothes and candelabra have got him more publicity than his playing, and he has a knowledgeable and humorous view of his show business image. He told us about a recent trip to Rome with his mother. They attended a mass audience with the Pope but his request for a private audience was discouraged. The day they were leaving for London a messenger arrived with an invitation to a private audience at 11 o'clock. Liberace said he was honored but didn't think they could make it. He and his mother were on a 12 noon plane. The emissary was aghast. The entourage had left but Lee (that is what intimates get to call Liberace) telephoned London to change orchestra rehearsals, then rearranged the plane reservations. He said, pleased, "That's the first time I have ever done it myself and I found out I could do it!" The emissary conducted them to the Villa de Castel Gondolfo. Lee presented his invitation and the guard sprang to attention and gave him a royal salute. They were presented and Lee had a chat with his Holiness, who knew all about him. He blessed a pocketful of medals for Lee's friends and introduced him to some influential people from Spain and St. Louis.

Friday January 4

Kath to New York at 7:30 from Pasadena. The train is impressive, all gleaming stainless steel, and loses money on every trip.

Saturday January 5

The Four Girls are now three. Jane Russell, Beryl Davis and Connie Haines. To the latter's apartment on top of Bel-Air to rehearse. There were four children under two years of age in the room and it was a nightmare. Connie was bitchier than usual. Rather unsatisfactory rehearsal. We have twelve tunes to record for a Capitol album by the end of the month. Most of the arrangements are all done and copied and this gave Connie the feeling that she couldn't change anything. When it was made clear to her that she could change anything she didn't like, the reconstruction of every bar began.

Later to look at a dance routine for the "Shower of Stars." The dancers are small and cute. I went down in the elevator with one of them, a charming, dark little girl who chatted warmly then got into her Cadillac and drove off.

Thursday January 10

The show was funny and went well, and an arrangement I had made of a song called "Sinner Man" surprised me it was so good. After the dress rehearsal Al Scalpone, a CBS exec, said he couldn't understand the words in "Sinner Man" and we almost re-pre-recorded it at 4:30 but Lud Gluskin put his foot down. Nobody messes with Lud. Hubbell Robinson, now high up in CBS, New York, was there and didn't like the show. These guys are the limit. They have nothing to do with the planning of the shows and I can't think what we can learn from their not liking a show. Everybody has a different opinion anyhow. Mike Ellis and I caught the last act of *Janus* at the Huntington Hartford. We went backstage to see Edith Meiser, Joan Bennett and Donald Cook. Vivian Vance and Glenn Anders were visiting too. All very gay. When Mike and I left two taxicab drivers were having a fist fight in front of the theatre. We stopped it. At the Chateau I ran into Sylvia Sidney in the lobby. At 46 she is beginning to look old.

Sunday January 13

I have seen Lee Sabinson, the producer of *Finian's Rainbow*. *Finian's* was the first commercial success he produced and when the money started pouring in he misappropriated some funds due the investors. Now, a good many years later, a friend at William Morris has got him a job as a producer at Columbia Pictures. His salary is

$300 a week. He winds up with $85 after deductions applied to paying off his debts. He and his wife live in a cheap apartment, and, knowing the attitude of people in this town to someone making $300 a week, he must be having a rough time. He seems to have learned a lesson, but God knows how long it will take to pay off the debts. He is tough and I admire what he is doing.

Thursday January 24

I knocked out a score for a Columbia Workshop last week in 36 hours, taking the script over the phone, putting it on to my tape machine in short takes. It was the story of the Malibu fire. I thought it a very good score but Bill Froug, the producer, didn't care for it. Over the weekend I did a score for a Marie Wilson pilot. The music was put on a plane for Mexico City where it will be recorded tomorrow.

Wednesday January 30

To see *Anniversary Waltz* at the Ritz Theatre on Wilshire Boulevard, recently reopened as a legitimate house. Compared to the average movie theatre, where you sit up to your ankles in popcorn butter, the Ritz is clean and well cared for.

Had a drink at a bar where poor old Dick Aurandt and his ten clumsy thumbs were entertaining at the organ. Even during the short time I was in this bar three amateurs performed. In these places there is a bar built round the performer's instrument and there is always a soprano or two ready to sound off and annoy the customers. The other helper in this case was a plumber who pushed Aurandt off his bench and tried the organ.

I had a letter from Joyce who says that clothes, jewels and stuffed animals mean nothing to her anymore. She wants a horse.

Sunday February 10

To Herrmann's for dinner. He has done his house over in 18th-century English style (he's an 18th-century man) with Hessians guarding the fireplace, lovely little three-taper chandeliers around the room, all his scores and books neat in beautifully designed shelves. Wound up the evening, as usual, analyzing me. Conclusion: I am not as screwed up as David Raksin but generally I am a mess.

Monday February 11

Recorded four numbers with the girls at Capitol. Connie called Capitol in the morning saying she didn't think she could make the date—her legs were acting up—but she arrived in a wheel chair. Very harrowing. At one point Connie said in a loud voice that the drummer sounded like he was chopping wood and destroyed him for the rest of the date. Jane thought I ought to be in the control room so I turned the baton over to Van Alexander. Every note of these sessions is a geschrei. After the date I had cocktails with Jane and was late getting to dinner with Kath. We had a fight. Kath said Jane did her adopting of children and taking drug-addicted women under her wing for the publicity. Made me mad and I left.

Saturday February 16

Had lunch with Bill Schneider and Lee Sabinson at the Beverly Hills Hotel. We joined S. N. Behrman, who is here making *Jacobowsky and the Colonel,* and his producer Gottfried Reinhardt. Sabinson told a story about Burton Lane and his wife Marion. They have a retarded child and are on the verge of divorce.

One night Sabinson and his wife Billie took Marion Lane to Beau Soir in the Village and afterwards to Lindy's to get something to eat. Sabinson went to the men's room. When he came out the ladies told him a man had tried to pick them up. They pointed him out. Sabinson went to him and thanked him for the compliment. The man apologized, saying he didn't like to eat alone and Sabinson asked him to join them. He introduced himself as Judge O'Brien. They ate and talked. Sabinson brought up the subject of divorce. The judge said the terms of settlement usually depended on who got to the referee first. Marion blanched and the judge said, "So it's you, isn't it?" Marion said it was. "And your name is Lane? And you are Lee Sabinson, the producer of *Finian's Rainbow?* They admitted their identities and the judge said, "Then you are the wife of that wonderful composer and great genius Burton

Lane. How dare you let this great man down? You should be helping him to create those marvelous songs, etc., etc."

Sabinson suggested that the judge accompany them to the Lane's apartment. They would get Burton out of bed and maybe get the thing settled then and there. They went, Lee got Burton up, introduced him to the judge, who made his speech about how Marion should be a real helpmate to such a great man. Burton has a sweet smile and he smiled as he listened to the speech. The judge turned to him and said, "Don't smile yet. I'm coming to you." It got to be seven a. m. and Billie Sabinson said they really must go, their children would be waking up and wondering where they were. The judge asked Lee to call him in chambers later and have lunch with him. He gave him his number. They left.

When Sabinson called the number it turned out to be a Chinese laundry. He called the Superior Court and they had never heard of Judge O'Brien, neither had the lower court. Sabinson called a friend in the D.A.'s office and *he* couldn't find the judge listed. Sabinson called the Lane's apartment. No answer. He went there and Marion was radiant. The judge had got them to kiss and make up. They had even discussed the problem child and the judge had promised to get the girl into a special school, but he had to bribe someone. They gave him a check for $300. They called the bank. The judge had tried to cash the check, unsuccessfully because he did not have an account there. They ordered the check stopped. Two days later the Lanes were apart again and resuming divorce plans because the glib and distinguished judge who had effected the reconciliation was a phony.

Dinner at the Herrmanns'. He was suffering from a virus but we had an evening of laughs anyway, except when we were discussing a deal Lud Gluskin has offered us. CBS is making films for "Playhouse 90," to be released theatrically after their TV run. They will pay the full feature picture price—in Herrmann's case $15,000, in mine $10,000—in three instalments: one-third when the film is released over television, another third when the picture is released in European theatres, and the final third when it plays domestic theatres. The scores to be recorded in Mexico with Fred Steiner conducting. We decided to turn it down for three reasons: 1) No control over the recording of the music, 2) no guarantee to get the full price if they decide not to release theatrically, and 3) the scores would have to be redone to a certain extent because the TV version is broken up by so many commercial interruptions.

Sunday February 17

In the evening to dinner at Scandia with two friend's of Bill's, Ted and Marion Gallenter. He is a press agent at Columbia Pictures, late of MGM. She was apparently in the same business, for she told of once escorting the Goldwyn Girls on a tour of South America and Australia. In Bogota they were entertained at tea by El Presidente. Some time after they returned a story ran in LIFE about how their host had had some people shot for booing his daughter at a bullfight. He was not too popular. I said, "Suppose that had happened the day before your tea date. Would you have gone?" She said, "Of course. The picture was going to play there."

Friday March 15

Florence and the children at the beach for the weekend. I am taking the kids on a trip while Florence goes to New York to do the Robert Montgomery show. (She was an actress in a previous incarnation.)

Monday March 18

The children and I decided to go to Ensenada. Halfway there we stopped for lunch at the Rosarita Hotel, a large, rambling establishment built, they say, by a group of investors who thought they could get a license to operate a casino. Mexican law stymied them. It was deserted. Ensenada was up to its hubcaps in mud. Ann was reading from a brochure of the delights of vacationing in Ensenada when we got stuck. Two natives volunteered to push us out, and did. They started to walk away. I called them back and gave them $1. The didn't want to take it but I insisted. We found a place called Quintas Papagayos where we were given a fine bungalow with two bedrooms, kitchen, fireplace complete with a supply of wood, all for $19 a day. Joyce went immediately to the pool and dove into 50-degree water.

The people seem clean and happy. The young couple running the officina made up some match books with my name on the cover. We went to a market in town and brought some food and the children played at running a restaurant, a game we all enjoyed. Much more fun than eating out.

Monday March 25

Reported to UPA. Steve Bosustow seems to think because they are paying me I should show up. He put me into a room with a piano and handed me a book about Jelly Roll Morton, by Alan Lomax, based on tapes Jelly made at the Library of Congress. They are contemplating a film about Morton and I am supposed to do some research on his life, times and music. It is interesting but I don't think there is a picture in it.

Monday April 15

To Kath's house where I disturbed a robbery in progress. The man ran out the front door as I came in from the garage. Didn't get much. Called the police who came and dusted the place for fingerprints. It wasn't altogether a great day. I had a flat tire, I lost the crystal out of my watch and it occurred to me the CBS has not paid me for the Workshop I did February 27.

Saturday April 20

I am writing a "Magoo" to work out my time at UPA. [These Magoo films are still playing somewhere in the world. I know because they are on my ASCAP reports.]

Lawrence Morton is organizing the Ojai festival this year. Aaron Copland will conduct. Among other things he is going to do the second act of his opera *The Tender Land*. Lawrence has asked me to prepare the singers and I have accepted the honor.

Tuesday April 30

Lenny Adelson (lyric writer) and I have been productive. Songs to date: "Nice to Have Loved," "Ten O'Clock," "Maybe Love Me,"

"Mirror on the Wall" and "On Your Merry Way." We played the last named for Joe Linhart, West Coast rep of Frank Music, and he says we couldn't give it away with S & H Green Stamps. He showed us a resumé of professional activity at Frank Music. They have about 20 songs in release on records, a dozen or so coming up and not one of them is selling. Rock and roll sells, period, says he. Also some albums. *My Fair Lady* sold over 1,000,000.

First rehearsal of *Tender Land* tonight at 1st Baptist church, 8th and Westmoreland.

Monday May 6

I don't know about my depressions. One hit today and tomorrow we prerecord music for the next "Shower."

Tuesday May 7

Still down in the depths but I got through the prerecording. An arrangement of "On the Sunny Side of the Street" that Frank DeVol made for Georgia Gibbs gave me a lift. Reminded me of the time Sinatra came into a "Hit Parade" rehearsal I was conducting. He was down, down, down in the depths. I stopped what we were doing and had the band play an arrangement of George Siravo's. In half a chorus Frank lit up and became his usual swinging, professional self.

Wednesday May 8

The depression broke at eight p. m. Maybe the psychiatrists in the audience can explain it. This phenomenon bothered me enough to keep a meticulous record on my calendar of good days, medium days, bad ones, and it furnishes no clues whatever. The depressions are not related to things that happen, nor can I make a graph showing when to expect them. There is no periodicity.

Thursday May 23

Dress Rehearsal of the Ojai Festival concert. The orchestra is full of political refugees like Joe Di Fiore, viola, (who took a diminished fifth before the Committee), Milton Kestenbaum, bass, and Edgar Lustgarten, cello. Actually I think the Ojai Festival is benefiting from the blacklist. There are wonderful players in the orchestra. The rehearsal was exciting. Mr. Copland's presence casts a spell, although he is no Toscanini.

Sunday May 26

In Ojai. Orchestra at 11, singers at 12, performance in the little bowl at 4:30. A local lady gave us all a spaghetti dinner at her ranchito, a dozen long tables spread with red-checked tablecloths under espaliers of bougainvillea. Very gay and noisy. I guess we were a success.

Wednesday May 29

To the Civic Light Opera tonight to see *My Fair Lady*. Brian Aherne in the Rex Harrison part, Anne Rogers as Eliza. Alan Lerner has come a long way since he wrote scripts for the "Hit Parade."

Wednesday June 6

Seven p. m. recorded the music for a "Magoo" at Glen Glenn. When I got home George Corey was in the middle of a big argument with Kathy on the subject of Grand Passion. The result of the debate was inconclusive because everybody has a different idea of what Grand Passion is, but it served to launch Corey on one of his stories.

In the thirties he was in Buenos Aires representing a newspaper syndicate. One enchanted evening across a public room he saw a tall ash blonde. Their eyes met and held. When he got back to his room a note had been pushed under his door. It read, "London *Times*, 25. Gwendolyn." He bought the London *Times* on the 25th. There was an advertisement in the Agony Column. "Baden Baden, 8th. Gwendolyn." George (he says) went to Pernambuco and hunted up St. Exupery, who was flying the French mail between Pernambuco and Dakar. He explained the situation. St. Exupery threw off a few sacks of mail and flew George to Dakar where he caught a plane to Baden Baden or some point close by. He got to a hotel where he saw his fatal femme for two hours while her aged German husband was taking a steambath.

About a year later there was another assignation. Every 25th George watched the *Times*. The last meeting took place (George says) with the help of Jimmy Doolittle who happened to be in Santiago where George caught Gwendolyn's invitation. The only obstacle to Doolittle's flying George to his rendezvous was that Doolittle had just won a bet by jumping out of a second story window and had broken both his ankles, but I gather it was arranged somehow and George saw his amour again for two hours of grand passion. (If you knew George you might have a little difficulty swallowing this story whole; he is a short Irishman who looks more leprechaun than lover.) Nevertheless, I have a theory about Gwendolyn. Why could not such a woman, married to an impotent old man, have an arrangement with about thirty men, each having his day in the London *Times*?

Friday June 28

Made a deal with a company called Transfilm to supply the music for a cartoon designed by Ronald Searle, sponsored by Standard Oil of New Jersey, with the exciting and imaginative title, "Energetically Yours."

Saturday June 29

Had the Herrmanns for dinner. He is depressed about the current phase of movie scoring: theme songs are important. He can't write that sort of thing.

Tuesday July 2

Went to the Alexanders for dinner. (Glad it wasn't Wednesday. Wednesday is chicken.) Wrote a piece for the Hollywood Flute Club, a little suite called "Devoirs," the sections labeled Serge, Erik, Nicolas, Vladimir and Igor, each section being, of course, in the style of its namesake. It is scored for three flutes, clarinet and bass clarinet.

July 12 Friday

Bobe Cannon, late of UPA, now working for a new little cartoon outfit called Playhouse Pictures, has made three one-minute cartoons for the Navy recruiting department. I wrote the music and recorded it at Capitol with a jazz group. Bud Shank, flute, Art Pepper, baritone sax, Stu Williamson, trumpet, Shelley Manne, drums, and Red Callender on bass. Red arranged them. Turned out fine. How could you miss with a group like that?

Friday July 19

Kathy had wanted to go to Mexico City for her vacation and I wanted to, too, but it didn't work out because I couldn't get a paper in time proving I hold derivative citizenship, through my father. We went to San Francisco instead.

Tuesday July 30

Spent the day in the company of Jane Russell making the rounds of the local disk jockeys. We started at nine with Dick Haines, a very funny fellow on KLAC, then to CBS, where we taped an interview with a DJ whose name I have forgotten, then to KMPC and Ira Cook, who was dull and square. Next to KBIG (I've forgotten his name too), and back to KMPC to go on with Johnny Grant. I love being with Jane, who is nothing but fun.

Wednesday July 31

Reported to Warner Bros. to do the vocals on *Marjorie Morningstar*, a film starring Gene Kelly, Natalie Wood and Ed Wynn. This means I have finally broken the ice with Ray Heindorf (head of the music department).

Thursday August 22

I recorded four numbers with a 25-voice chorus for a Lawrence Welk album. George Cates produced and Welk was in the booth, too. The results were really good and Welk spoke to me after the date saying, "These are the first arrangements you have made for me and you have captured the feelings I have in my heart and when I put this out I know I won't hear from my fans they can't understand it." George Cates told me the next day that during the session Welk said, "This man is doing such a good job we should pay him more than scale." I am being paid $500 for the four numbers. Everybody was pleased, and I might as well do it until I get my back taxes paid off. They really hit me last year. I still owe over $2,300 plus interest.

Monday August 26

It is Heindorf's birthday today. I sent him 15 pounds of chateaubriand steaks from a fancy Beverly Hills meat store. They left it outside his garage and when he found it a few days later it smelled like a dead body.

Wednesday August 28

Franz Waxman is doing a film called *Sayonara* with a lovely theme song by Irving Berlin. Heindorf asked me to do a big choral arrangement of it.

Thursday August 29

Chorus call at Warners today to record the arrangement of *Sayonara*. Heindorf had some fancy ideas about how to record it. He put the girls on the left channel, the men on the right, then we did it in reverse, girls right, men left. Sounded big. [This is called overdubbing and is done every day now.]

Friday November 1

To the Shrine Auditorium, the worst theatre in the United States for anything except Police shows, to see the San Francisco Opera Company's production of *Ariadne*. Sat in a little valley and couldn't see a bloody thing.

Saturday November 9

May Collins (a mutual friend) called from Cleveland a few days ago and suggested I go to that city to marry Kathy. Sid and I went.

Monday November 11

This day is aptly called Veteran's Day. I got married for the fourth time. By a rabbi yet. George and May Collins put us up and did the whole thing in style. During the ceremony the rabbi read two poems, one by Edgar Guest and the other good. I asked him why the Edgar Guest and he said, "I didn't know what kind of people you were."

Monday November 25

We moved to the beach. Back to 20140 Pacific Coast Highway where the rent is still $150 plus $5 for water.

1958

February

Kathy and I have deserted the beach and moved into two (2) apartments at 748 N. La Cienega Boulevard. The building consists of two stores fronting on La Cienega and, behind a little courtyard, a two-story structure formerly occupied by *Fortnight*, a magazine recently overtaken by bankruptcy. The upstairs, which we rented, has a large entry hall leading to a small kitchen. On the right and left of the entry hall are two sets of large double doors. The right-hand set open on a spacious living room with fireplace. Two french doors lead to a roof patio complete with a little grass shack where the children lived when they visited. A bedroom and bath open off the living room. On the other side of the entry hall is a room identical in size to the living room, sans fireplace but having a mirrored wall furnished with a barre. Another bedroom and bath open off this room. I installed my piano and recording equipment on this side. It was a perfect arrangement because in times of stress I had my own bedroom.

Wednesday March 26

Adelson and I met with Ben Hecht and got his blessing to make a musical out of his "Spectre of the Rose."

Saturday March 29

11:30 p.m. Kathy and I to Europe.

Wednesday April 2

I got on a train at Euston bound for Ulverston to see my relatives. Uncle Willie met me at the station. In 1925 Uncle Willie had taken my mother, my two brothers and me to Liverpool to board the White Star liner *Cedric* when we left England for the United States. Before we got on the ship he took me aside, told me to take care of my mother and added, in his gentle and reasonable way, "Always remember, Lionel, that one Englishman is as good as five Americans."

Thursday April 3

To Barrow-in-Furness to see relatives and my old school where four masters who had struggled with me 34 years ago were still in residence. The headmaster gave us a concoction he referred to as tea but it had been stewing so long I thought it was coffee and when the Head excused himself for a moment, Uncle Willie said he believed it was cocoa. All the relatives we visited insisted we take a cup of tea. We stopped by Uncle Willie's stonemason yard where I saw Uncle Jack, a short, powerful 65-year-old heaving blocks of granite from a flatbed truck to the ground.

Friday April 4

Back to London. At five, in the Royal Festival Hall, we heard a performance of Bach's "Saint Matthew Passion." After that to dinner at Les Ambassadeurs.

Saturday April 6

To Westminster Abbey for Easter. The boys sang like angels but their surplices were dirty. A cat strolled up and down the main aisle on the icy stone floor. In the afternoon to Ronald Searle's house. He was charming and gave me a line drawing of a violinist which I used on the label of the album I made of the music from the Standard Oil Company film we had worked on together last year.

Monday April 7

In the evening to the Saville Theatre to see Wolf Mankowitz's *Expresso Bongo*. Not much. Their competition is *My Fair Lady, Irma La Douce* and *Where's Charlie?* I had a miserable dinner in a Greek restaurant on Shaftesbury Avenue. The waiter, learning I was from Los Angeles, asked me if I knew his brother there. I said, "Not very well."

Thursday April 10

To Paris. We have a suite at the Parc Elysées, a lovely little hotel on the Rond Point.

Saturday April 12

Eddie Constantine picked me up in his Buick convertible. We couldn't move for the crowd hemming us in and asking for his autograph. He is as big here as Clark Gable. I went with him to the Montana Bar, talked to a bunch of musicians and segued to an actors' club on the Rond Point where Preston Sturges was dining alone, reading a script. I didn't bother him.

Sunday April 13

Spent the afternoon with Constantine and Helene at Longchamps. They had a horse running. It didn't win but it was a lovely
though rather nippy afternoon. Monday we went to their farm,
about a 40 minute drive from Paris. It appears to have been built in
the 16th century and is staffed by a dozen warm and friendly
Spaniards. Constantine had hired one, Victor, as his chauffeur.
Within a week he had smuggled the rest of his family in, and there
they were. Victor refuses to wear a chauffeur's cap, feeling it
demeans him.

Tuesday April 15

Went to see *Irma La Douce*. Loved it and didn't understand word
one, but it doesn't matter—you get the message.

Wednesday April 16

To L'Opéra to see Constantine's daughter Tanya dancing in
"Giselle" and "Firebird."

Thursday April 17

To 108 Rue de Bac for dinner with Alaine and Margie Bernheim
and Richard Avedon. Kathy had Avedon take our picture with her
Kodak instamatic.

Friday April 18

To Milan on the Orient Express
After a very businesslike start from Paris to Dijon the Orient
Express turned out to be nothing but a milk train stopping every
five minutes. The dinner very good and most efficiently served,
the background music was the sound of corks popping. After all
the romantic notions one has formed about this train the aluminum
and formica sleeping compartment was a disappointment, but the

first views of Italy in the misty morning, the ice capped mountains, then Stresa on beautiful Lake Maggiore, the little towns along the lake all drawn by Bemelmans, were breathtaking.

Sunday April 20

Went to La Scala and heard *La Boheme*. The acoustics splendid, the singers not so.

Friday April 25

To Florence.

The only thing I care to record is that I walked over Ponte Vecchio and found Castelnuovo-Tedesco's apartment. Though he's been exiled in Hollywood for years his name is still on the bell. Walking to Harry's Bar through the narrow streets in single file, some young Florentians got between me and Kathy and did some pinching. I thought it complimentary. She did not.

Monday April 28

To Rome. I love this city much more than London, even more than Paris mon coeur. Ran into Corwin on the Via Veneto.

Thursday May 1

Flew direct from Rome to Los Angeles.

Friday May 2

I learn Frank Loesser has taken an option on "Spectre of the Rose." May 4, 5, 6 and 7: Adelson and I with Ben Hecht working on the book.

Friday May 9

Meet with Donn Arden. He wants Adelson and me to write material for a Moulin Rouge show to be called "Wonderful World." (The Moulin Rouge is the old Earl Carroll Theatre on Hollywood

Boulevard now run by Frank Sennes, featuring extravaganzas by Arden, who also does the Lido shows in Paris.)

Wednesday May 14

Today and Friday more sessions with Hecht on "Spectre."

Friday May 23

Received the contract from Loesser. Looks like he means business.

Friday June 6

Frank Loesser is staying at the Beverly Hills Hotel and wants to hear the book as far as we have gone. Ben Hecht, Lenny Adelson and I met him poolside. Frank was keeping a sharp eye on his daughter in the pool. He told Hecht to go ahead. Ben started reading and kept on reading through a hundred yells from Frank to his daughter to be careful. When we left I asked him how he could do it. He said, "I got my experience reading stories to Sam Goldwyn. He would take telephone calls, make deals, and look out the window at a natural gas storage tank located near the studio. If the tank was full you had trouble. He was convinced it was going to blow up. If it was low you had his attention, more or less."

Monday June 9

Another session with Loesser. Very productive. He makes good, solid suggestions even to an old pro like Hecht who makes all changes requested quickly and without cavil.

Wednesday June 25

To see Loesser's *The Most Happy Fella* at the Civic Light Opera. It is a great achievement, considering Frank's lack of formal training. It gave me a chance to say hello to Robert Weede whom I hadn't seen since the Squibb radio program in New York. The show was produced by Kermit Bloomgarden and Lynn Loesser, Frank's wife. [In the cast was Jo Sullivan, who became the next Mrs. Loesser.]

Tuesday July 1

The children arrived to spend most of the summer. Joyce bought an Indian head in one of the stores downstairs for $60 and named it Heathcliff, at the moment her favorite character. (When she tired of it she sold it back to them for $25. She has inherited my flair for business.)

Thursday August 14

A meeting with Donn Arden at the Moulin. An experience. He is an incandescent 1950's reincarnation of R. H. Burnside, the genius who staged similar eye-poppers at the Hippodrome in the early years of the century. If you want to re-stage the burning of Rome or the sinking of the *Titanic*, Arden's your man.

Thursday August 28

Decca. Recorded some tunes with Bing, among them "Harbor Lights" and the "Hawaiian Wedding Song." As is usual with Bing the date was relaxed and pleasant.

Thursday September 11

Two p.m. to six p.m. Lawrence Welk, in spite of his reputation for corn, has an eclectic taste in music. He admires Johnny Hodges, Ellington's phenomenal lead alto sax player, and made an album with him accompanied by a much enlarged orchestra. I arranged and conducted two of the numbers.

Thursday October 9

Moulin Rouge opening. Arden's girls are a mixture of French and American, all beautiful. Wandering about backstage I was struck by the difference in their attitudes. They all apply their makeup with their breasts exposed. When you go by the open dressing room doors the French girls pay no attention, the American girls squeal and cover up their breasts.

MGM wants me to run over to London to supervise the re-recording of a few cues for a George Pal picture, "Tom Thumb."

Saturday October 11

To London. Muir Mathieson, a charming man, took me to lunch at the Savage Club where we discussed the few cues we were going to redo. The following week the orchestra assembled at Elstree, the London MGM studio, and we did it. Mathieson and two flute players named Gordon and Eddie Walker, father and son, with whom I became friends on later pictures, had a very boozy lunch at a pub next door to the studio. In the afternoon session the father flute player handled the piccolo part from the "Stars and Stripes" with such bravura and accuracy that I wouldn't have believed he had drunk half a dozen scotches at lunch if I hadn't seen it with my own eyes.

Friday November 28

A call from Bob Finkel at Ramrod Productions, an aptly named company, to come and talk to him about doing the chorus on a new television show starring that great lover Eddie Fisher. Fisher was married to Debbie Reynolds but has become deeply involved with Elizabeth Taylor. Fisher marries so often Sid Kuller says he gets a rate from the rabbi.

Tuesday December 2

Tonight I paraded my chorus for the production people. One of them took me into a corner and indicated several members of the group who were not acceptable to him because they looked *old*. I said I had an obligation to them and if they went I would have to withdraw. I guess they didn't have the time to replace me so we stayed. Hours of meetings with all concerned, including the conductor, Buddy Bregman, and lots of hard, intensive work.

Tuesday December 9

On the show Fisher did the old Bill Gaxton trick of leaving out bars and beats. I was glad I was not conducting. The choral director on shows of this type stands out of camera range and relays the conductor's beat to the chorus and generally tries to avoid disasters. Now I know why everybody makes so much money on live television variety shows. It's to defray the cost of the ulcers.

Friday December 12 et seq

From the 12th to the 18th I spent 36½ hours in meetings and writing. The rehearsals were long and subject to various kinds of interruptions. One night at midnight all the lights went out. NBC was saving money. It took an hour to get someone with enough authority to turn them back on. Another night Miss Taylor showed up in high spirits and carried Fisher off to his dressing room. The ensuing delay was of such duration—everybody waiting around on double time—I wouldn't be surprised if it gave the man in charge of the budget a heart attack.

Tuesday December 23

After the show I told Finkel I wanted to quit. He asked me to do one more.

1959

Tuesday January 6

MCA is doing television under the name of Revue Productions at the old Republic Studios. Stanley Wilson is head of music. Met him, loved him and went to work for him, at first on a very small scale. He gave me a "Wagon Train" to do with a seven-piece orchestra.

Tuesday May 19

I have been having some fun over the last weeks. I met Mr. John Harris the owner of "Ice Capades," a remarkable, dynamic man who invented the ice show. They carry an orchestra from town to town but all the vocals are played in the arenas on tape. Today I and 25 of the finest singers one can assemble gathered at Radio Recorders and recorded all the vocal music for the next edition. Twenty-seven numbers. We went in at 10 a. m. and got out at midnight. We took a break for dinner. The whole 25 and I, and a couple of the recordists, went to Nickodell's an Melrose Avenue. The waiters came out with a birthday cake for a young couple and the group stood up—it was impressive—and sang "Happy Birthday." The young fellow was stunned. He said, "I hope this isn't on my check."

Monday May 25

Stanley Wilson has a show at Revue called *Markham*, with Ray Milland, and he asked me to do one. His notes on what the music should be: "Thin, mysterious, dark, foreboding, puzzling." Well, I know how to do that.

Tuesday June 2

To a cocktail party at Ralph Levy's for his mother, a delightful lady in her mid-seventies, who lives in Elkins Park, a suburb of Philadelphia. The usual all star cast: Jack Benny (I talked to him briefly but I always get the impression that in spite of working with him for two years he doesn't quite know who I am), Robert Tyler Lee, the set designer, who lives around the corner in a row of exceedingly quaint apartments Kathy calls Munchkin Villas, Ben Feiner with his nice wife and my one-time favorite supper club singer Greta Keller, alas looking old now and pinchy eyed and droopy breasted and hard lipped. I told her how much I had enjoyed her radio series for Tangee lipstick and she reacted predictably, for how many people remember radio shows of the 30's?

Friday June 5

I put Kathy on the Superchief. She is going to New York for the
May Company, which allows her $30 a day for room, food and cabs.
She stays at the Hampshire House and that blows the $30 and more
right there. I am not going to let thinking about that prevent me
from writing some nice foreboding music for Mr. Milland. It may
even help.

Friday June 12

Before Kathy left she had an idea it would be good for us to rent a
house at the beach in conjunction with two friends, Katie and
Barney Safford, for a period of six weeks. The first two weeks for
the Saffords, the second two weeks both families to overlap, and
the third two weeks for us.

Jimmy Dunn and Edna Rush live next door. I used to play the
piano for Edna in Philadelphia and worked with Jimmy in *Panama
Hattie*. One evening they came to visit and we told our Philadelphia
stories. Stories of Doc and Ike Levy who own WCAU and Manie
Sacks who worked for them and Delores Reade who was mad about
Manie. Jimmy was brought up in New Rochelle where he and his
family lived next door to the Foys. Mr. Foy [a vaudeville star of the
time] drove an Oldsmobile with a high contoured front seat and a
higher back one. One night he drove a friend, a Mr. Sullivan, from
New Rochelle to the Lambs Club, a distance of 17 miles. Mr. Foy,
who was driving, sat in the front seat and Sullivan sat in the back. Mr.
Foy kept up a running conversation for the entire 17 miles, the kind of
conversation that does not require answers. When they got to the
Lambs Club Mr. Foy turned around and Sullivan was not in the back
seat. He had been bumped out on the outskirts of New Rochelle, and
taken to the New Rochelle Hospital.

At that time there were six Foy children, two girls and four boys.
Mr. Foy was suspicious of all the neighborhood boys and would not
allow them in the house. When he drove off for the theatre, as soon
as he was out of sight, the boys piled into the house. Towards
midnight they would station a sentry to give the warning, and
when Mr. Foy was sighted, out they would pile again. One night,
all the doors and windows being full of escaping boys, one lad

didn't make it and hid in the coat closet, curling up on the floor. As Mr. Foy was putting his duster away he noticed this boy and said, "What are you doing down there, Carroll?"—then shut the closet door.

September

MGM is making *Bells Are Ringing* with Judy Holliday and Dean Martin. Previn is the musical director, I am doing the vocals, mainly to go through a big musical with Andre. Minnelli is directing, Jule Styne and Comden and Green are here to protect their interests and Arthur Freed is the producer.

Styne has the greatest ego I have ever encountered with the exception of Johnny Green's. Russell Bennett did the orchestrations for the Broadway show. Styne ordered Andre not to change a note of the orchestrations because he personally had spent three hours on each arrangement with Russell; further, they had cost $30,000; and last, any changes would "throw" Judy. I was most impressed with the way Andre handled Styne. One day Andre read through a number with the orchestra. Styne said, "I don't understand that trumpet figure." Andre said to the trumpets, "Take it out." At one point he remarked to Styne that *Bells Are Ringing* seemed to have more tradition than the Salzburg Festival.

We spent seven days with Judy and Dean Martin, four or five hours a day, recording eight songs, each averaging a chorus and a half in length. Dean is a consummate professional. He came in knowing his songs and recorded them fast. No trouble. Judy was a different story. She was living with Gerry Mulligan and he was around—helping. She was unable to record with the orchestra directly because of throat problems and panic. She recorded to earphones, and made numerous takes of each number, rejecting and rejecting until even Styne and Freed joined us in trying to tell her that what she had done was not only acceptable but quite often marvelous. She is a great performer but if perfectionism is a neurosis, then she has as bad a case of it as I have. Mulligan is articulate, intelligent and learned very quickly to express his opinions and to exercise the rights conferred upon him as "friend to the star." The fact that her sore throat delayed the start of the picture two days at roughly a cost of $50,000 a day didn't bother him, or her, or Julie, nor, apparently, Arthur Freed. When we finished this phase of the pre-recording the studio gave Judy a set of disks to take home and listen to. At MGM these are made at 80 r.p.m. Her machine revolved at 78. She came in and announced that the tracks were no good and she wanted to do them all over. Freed put his foot down and Judy did not show up for the next day's shooting. Freed backed down and agreed to let her do some of them over even though this means shutting down the picture until they are done.

Andre told me an anecdote about a Freed picture, *Invitation to the Dance*, starring Gene Kelly. Andre had a disagreement with Kelly about a piece of scoring. Impasse. He went to Freed to explain his viewpoint. Freed said, "Excuse me a minute," and left the room. Fifteen minutes later Andre went into the secretary's room and asked where Mr. Freed was. She said, "He's gone home."

Fred Clark is in the picture. One day he blew a few takes and Mulligan took him to one side and offered some suggestions on how to clear up the problem. Clark went to Minnelli and said, "This won't do. Call him off." Minnelli explained he couldn't do anything about Mulligan since he was so important to Judy and he didn't want to disturb anything.

I had a 28-voice group in the picture. We worked on the song "Drop That Name." When I had it ready I called Minnelli to come and hear it. We sang it and I turned to him for comment. He bowed his head and said, "I couldn't understand a single word." He stayed with us for a day and a half getting it exactly the way he wanted it. We went over every word a thousand times in a hundred different ways. When we recorded it Styne came on to the stage and said it was all wrong. So we went over it word by word for *him*, changing it to the way *he* wanted it. Minnelli didn't put up a fight for what *he* wanted. He just rolled his big doe eyes and pushed his lips in and out. I asked Bill Ryan why everybody rolled over for Styne, and he said Freed wanted to buy *Gypsy*, and the way to buy *Gypsy* was to keep Styne happy. (Warners got *Gypsy*.)

After a hiatus I went back to Metro to record "It's a Simple Little System," a wonderful funny song in which a character—played by Eddie Foy, Jr., with a Hungarian accent—explains to a crowd of bookies a system for using the names of composers for race tracks— Beethoven is Belmont, Debussy is Delmar. The big joke comes at the end of the song when Foy says, "What is Handel?" and the chorus answers, "Hialeah! Hialeah!" à la Hallelujah Chorus. I had 40 voices (Halperin the budgeteer is still on the floor) and we rehearsed for a bit and got it down. Minnelli came in and heard it. Comment, "Isn't the last note of Hialeah too short?" My answer, "No. It's the Hallelujah Chorus." Minnelli, "I know, but they didn't do the note that short in the show." He returned to his shooting and we continued preparing the number and then made it. Arthur Freed came down and heard it. Freed is an elderly man whose hearing is probably on a par with Sam Goldwyn's, whose ears cut off at about 6,000 cycles. When you play back for the producer he sits in a chair about 40 feet from three Voice of the Theatre speakers, and he hears the stereo track played loud enough to please even musicians. The clarity and the balances are superb. Freed: "I can't understand a single word." Previn was there. I said to him, "What can I do? It's perfect." Andre, cool as always, marvelous in these idiotic situations, said, "Let's sing the names of the tracks louder than the names of the composers." I went out on to the stage and we took it bar by bar and Mr. Freed okayed it bar by bar. Then we made it and Mr. Freed left—mad at me—and I left mad at him.

The solution at Metro is simply not to become involved in what you are doing. Rehearse it poorly, play it for them, let them suggest how it can be improved, do it, gradually making it better, or at least different; if they want it upside down, do it upside down. I have come to the conclusion that those who can do this succeed at Metro. I have failed. When Andre conducts the height of his beat is maybe a foot, the orchestra plays clean and meticulous but no head of steam is generated, no one gets up a sweat. Cool. When I work in front of a group I get into a lather. Discussions following a take are heated because I am flying. Opposite of cool. The hell with Metro.

Saturday October 17

J'étudie Francais avec Mme. Vessiot, professeur de l'école que s'appelle Marlboro, tous les samedis. Aujourd'hui ses enfants sont ici mais, a ce moment, elles sont prêtes de partir pour Ojai avec Kathy. Elles passeront la nuit et elles retourneront demain. Ann demeure maintenant à Palm Springs chez sa mère, Joyce va à l'école de la Coeur Immaculate. Elle y demeure.

Last night to dinner at Sandy and Marile Courage's. They live in a nice gray modern house in the hills above Beverly Hills. Previn, Dory Langdon, Connie Salinger and his friend David White, a doctor and his girl friend, who later sang "Widmung" and some other lieder badly. Previn told Benny Goodman stories. He was in New York staying at the Gotham. Goodman called to take him to lunch. Asked if he wanted a light lunch or a heavy one, Andre opted for light and Goodman took him to Walgreens. (That's a drug store, folks.)

Helen Ward sang on the date. When Andre mentioned Helen Ward he said her name with an exclamation point as though, because she had sung with Benny in the early thirties, she should be dead already. It was cold in the studio and after some hours Helen said to Benny, "It's cold in here." He took the clarinet out of his mouth, agreed, and put his sweater on.

Thursday October 22

I have been suffering from a sickness of the spirit lately due to a feeling that what I am devoting my time to is unimportant. That is, making money to pay tuition, teeth straightening, alimony, insurance, rent, etc. I haven't written a decent note of music for a couple of years and, with the way our business is, earning money is very hard. For example I made $750 for the last "General Electric Theatre" I wrote—85 pages of music, about 16 minutes, taking about six days over a period of eight days. I must say the producer, a very nice fellow named Joe Narr who used to be an agent, was complimentary about the music. This particular GE is a budget-maker upper. They shot it in two days with Ronald Reagan starring (costs the producer nothing since he is the greeter on the show) and two $750 actors. The music cost about $2,000. The five weeks at Metro were depressing. I earned $3,000, of which about $2,000 went to alimony, taxes, agents, etc. Tonight I have an appointment with Desi and Lucy to discuss the TV version of the revue Lucy produced at the little theatre on the Gower Street lot for which Jeff and I organized the music.

Yesterday Joe Nadell at Chappell Music sent me the score of *Sound of Music*, the new Rodgers and Hammerstein musical based on the story of the Trapp family, and each song is more delightful than the last. Masterpieces.

Thursday December 3

Met Stanley Rubin, producer, and Sherman Marks, director. They are going to do a GE Theatre based on Crockett Johnson's cartoon "Barnaby" to be shot on videotape at CBS. They have Bert Lahr to star and young Ronnie Howard, age five, to play Barnaby. On Sunday (6) Rubin and Marks came to the beach and we went over the script and agreed on solutions for all the music problems. They are both very pleasant and hardworking. Because of the mechanical problems of flying Bert Lahr, à la Peter Pan, and not being able to work young Howard more than three hours at a time, they took an extra half day for the taping. When they finished editing I went to a room in the basement of Television City, where they have the videotape editing machines, ran the tape and made my timings. Stanley Rubin, Sherman Marks and the tape editor (who collapsed) had been there for 24 hours.

We had engaged an orchestra for the evening of Wednesday 16. It was arranged that I would go to the studio at seven, an hour before the orchestra call, to rehearse with the tape by myself somewhat in the manner one rehearses with film before a scoring session. I arrived but the tape was not ready. The orchestra came in and we read the music starting at eight. At 8:45 we were ready to record but Gluskin said we would not have facilities until 9:30. 9:30 came and the technical people had forgotten, or not had time, to make a dupe of the color. We waited half an hour while that was done. They played the dupe over a monitor and we started to fit the music. It was not easy because, unlike film, you can't mark up a video tape with streamers and other visual aids for the conductor. We took it scene by scene, rolling the tape back and forth until everyone was satisfied. Then Sherman, the director, got into the game. Having a lovely orchestra right there and the wonderful possibilities of what you can do with a lovely orchestra right there struck him. It went like this. "Can you put something in here where the doctor shrugs his shoulders? Maybe just a little wood-wind effect with xylophone and bongos?" We manufactured a little something. "And here's a scene which now seems flat. It would be nice to play so and so's theme until he goes out the window." And we did that. It took us until three o'clock in the morning to finish.

One of the complications of recording to videotape is that you have to do a whole reel, 12 minutes, at a time. If you make a mistake it's back to the beginning. That is the way it was when sound was first introduced on film. They tell me you had to do it a reel at a time. [This reminds me of the night we recorded "The Lonesome Train" for Decca. This was before tape. One had to record a whole side of an LP record in one take. In the last 30 seconds of the first side Corwin cued Hester Sondegaard to read a line and she blew it. We had to go back to the top.] Still, recording on videotape is more fun than recording on film in the sense that you get a more theatrical performance out of the whole and in a way the sound is superior to film. Everything is so much more alive and every little music effect works because, other than the dialog, there is not much sound on the original track. Whatever sound effects are needed are added as you record the music.

I remember Mr. Paley and some CBS brass visiting a set at Paramount some years ago. Seeing the grips, cameramen, electricians, etc., milling about he said, "Let's not let this happen in television." During a break in our session I went into the booth and it seemed there were twenty technicians in there and the tape was coming from somewhere else. The cacophony on my intercom of various groups talking to each other, people giving directions, acknowledging them, the director talking to me over the hubbub and interested parties shouting suggestions as we recorded was unbelievably wonderful. And the coffee out of the machine you drop a dime in was good.

Wednesday December 16

This week Kathy became a Woman of the Year. Each year the Los Angeles *Times* chooses ten women from different fields, runs their pictures and bios and presents them with a little silver cup at a ceremony held in the Chandler's town house in Hancock Park. Among those honored were a singer, a designer, a painter, a woman who runs a clinic for backward children, some others, and Kathy who got hers for outstanding achievement in business. The *Times* has made these awards for ten years and about eighty of the past winners, including Irene Dunne and Hedda Hopper, were present and took a bow, Jeff and Connie Alexander and Kathy's father and stepmother attended. Mrs. Chandler in her capacity of Director of Public Relations conceived the idea of Woman of the Year. The Editorial board of the *Times* picks the nominees. In 1951 they quite properly gave one to Mrs. Chandler for her work in promoting the Hollywood Bowl. (Later she raised the money for the construction of the Music Center, a remarkable achievement.) As part of the presentation someone reads a little bio of the recipient. One sentence in the speech about Kathy told the audience that she administered a $5,000,000 advertising budget for the May Company. (They didn't mention that the *Times* gets about $2,000,000 of it.) Jeff, Connie, Pop and Elaine came to our place afterward. We served cocktails and celebrated the occasion. Pop was very proud of his daughter.

Since I am committed to telling the truth here I am ashamed to report that after a few drinks I ventured the opinion that outside the awards for medicine, art, music and literature I thought the whole thing was bullshit. As they say in France: Horreur!

A little innovation to round out the year:

Work done: Two "M Squads," 5 "Wagon Trains," 4 "General Electric Theatres," 2 "Markhams," a "Have Gun Will Travel," the "Millionaire," the "Clockwatchers," two unsung pilots, "Night Patrol" and "Guestward Ho!"

1960

Saturday January 9

To Las Vegas with Sid Kuller to do our bit for the Variety Clubs of the U. S., a charitable organization. Our contribution is a number for a show they are doing on Monday. All the comics, singers and dancers appear. Phil Silvers, one of the performers, seemed rather morose at the rehearsals. He is getting $40,000 a week for four weeks and he blew $50,000 at the tables the first day. There are a number of nude shows on the Strip and some of the local religiosos are mounting their pulpits and hooting about what devil's work is the female breast and, for all I know, doubling business. Our number—the poetry from Sid's fertile brain—is called "The Prudes Against the Nudes." God forgive me.

Tuesday January 19

CBS has this TV series called "Have Gun Will Travel" and good old Lud Gluskin asks me to do one now and then. Saw a very interesting one today with a Chinese theme. I went home and got the idea to do it with a lot of percussion and a flute. When I told Lud he said, "If I let you do that they'll fire me." We hired ten percussionists and Arthur Gleghorn, who is the best flute player on the Coast.

Monday February 1

Had a lovely afternoon at Goldwyn doing the percussion. Lud was scared to death. Still thinks he'll be fired but I must say it was a hell of a sound.

Tuesday February 2

Ran a wonderful GE called "Judith," a version of the biblical story, produced by Harry Tugend. I used the opening from my opera *Esther* in "Judith." Tugend's comment when he heard it, "It sounds Chinese." Alfred Newman said of producers, "They all know their own business *and* music." Take Eddie Montaigne. I did a Western for him and in the Main Title the four horns played a big, fine American-sounding tune. When he heard it he said, "Change that. I can't stand French horns."

Sunday April 17

Driving round with Kathy looking for a building to buy, or a house, went up Kings Road to visit Henry King and his wife, whose name before he married her was Ida King, so she is now Ida

King King. Henry King is an old, distinguished director. One of his early pictures was *Tol'able David*, with Richard Barthelmess. When we got there Mr. King was in a languor but the talk of pictures brought him to life. Stories of Orson Welles in Rome, Zanuck in Florence, talk of the recent actors strike (immoral). Ida King is an old friend of Kathy's. Though I was meeting her for the first time she was affectionate and called me "Cousin Lyn."

King went to Rome to prepare the shooting of the film *Prince of Foxes*. He thought he might like Orson Welles to play Borgia and talked to him for a few minutes in a hotel lobby. Welles was interested and made a date for lunch the day after next. He didn't show up. His secretary didn't know where he was. An abject letter came the next day asking forgiveness and another date was made. Zanuck called King from Florence to ask how he was getting along with Welles. King said, "So far he has eluded me." Welles showed up in Florence with his agent, Charles Feldman, and Zanuck sent them back to Rome to discuss the engagement with King. In the interim King talked to Gregory Ratoff, who had directed Orson in a film at Cinecitta in Rome. Ratoff told King that Welles did not like to start shooting before two p. m. but would work all night. Ratoff usually quit for the day at eight p. m. leaving Orson to shoot close-ups, etc. King told Feldman that if Orson wanted to do the part he must be ready to shoot at nine a. m. and if he wasn't there a substitute would be used. Feldman told King Orson was broke. He had borrowed 5,000 lire from his butler and owed Ratoff $5,000. King was willing to pay Welles $100,000 to play the role, although, he said, "Putting his name on the marquee of a theatre is the same as putting the word smallpox up." The deal was finally made and the company departed to start shooting in Sienna. The entire picture was shot in palaces. King arrived on the set at eight a. m., where Leon Shamroy was setting up lights. In the shadows he saw a figure wearing a black costume and cape. Welles. He is not needed for two days but is there, if Mr. King doesn't mind, to "get in the mood." On Wednesday, the day he was to start, Welles was there at eight dressed and made up. King said the only trouble he had with Welles was in a scene involving 400 extras.

King was up on a parallel looking down on a banquet scene. Orson called up to Mr. King that the people should show him, as Borgia, more respect. King called down that if Welles would just play the part the people would show the proper respect. A little later Tyrone Power climbed up to talk to King. He said Welles thought the people were not showing enough respect. King told Power he had carefully rehearsed the people in the proper amount of inclination of the head and Orson was just testing him to see if he could take over the picture and to go back and tend to his knitting. King is a very strong man. He said some interesting things about Orson's direction of films: He doesn't have the fibre to push an idea (picture) all the way through to the finish. He flies off at a tangent three quarters of the way through. On the subject of music King seemed very impressed with Herrmann. We talked about the score for *The Snows of Kilimanjaro*. Herrmann ran the picture with King and everyone else who attends the music run. Benny asked King if he would mind running the film again with him. They did. And the next day once more. After two lunches and the two runnings they had discussed every aspect of the music. This was very smart on Benny's part—any offbeat ideas in the music would be pre-sold. No surprises.

Tuesday May 17

Mrs. Burr, wife of the headmaster at the Ojai Valley School, wants me to write some material for their Spring play. It will be the story of Robert Louis Stevenson in Samoa and will be called *Home Is the Sailor*. Sid Kuller and I wrote several songs for the production.

Wednesday June 15

Kuller and I discussed the Stevenson play and thought it might make a full-scale musical. We talked to Norman Corwin about writing the book and made a date for tonight to lay the idea before Edwin Lester the impressario of the Civic Light Opera. We met at Scandia. Ed was not only interested but suggested that Corwin and I go to Samoa to see what we could soak up about Stevenson's last years there. At his expense.

Wednesday June 22

We saw a house we liked at 1227 Sunset Plaza Drive. The asking price was $62,500, I offered $55,000 and today the offer was accepted.

Saturday July 9

Kathy and I to San Diego. The 10th to Ensenada, staying at Quintos Papagayos. Kathy wanted to swim. The pool was full of children. She changed her mind when a navy wife, sitting poolside, said to her, "Think of the urine content," Returned home on the 14th.

Sunday August 7

Corwin and I leave Los Angeles by Pan Am at 11 a. m. arriving Honolulu 1:30. Staying at the Royal Hawaiian—louvered doors à la tropics. It is humid. Rented a car. My smallpox certificate not having arrived, we found a Dr. Devereux, originally from Illinois but now very Maughamish with an Oriental nurse, who gave me one. He had seen Norman's picture *The Story of Ruth* and had preferred it to *Ben Hur*. He was very interested in our trip and was shocked that we had not planned to see Stevenson's grass hut. He insisted we take time to see it.

Monday August 8

We drove up the center of the island through high passes shrouded in mist, then along the very beautiful coast road. Lunch at the Crouching Lion served by a voluble waitress named Evelynn. She volunteered she was "pushing 60." She has lived for 18 years in a house on leased land—$100 a year, and the lease runs 35 years. Back via Diamond Head, which went by unnoticed behind all the old residences. Stevenson's hut is maintained by the Salvation Army, and a lady named Mrs. Ann Leak showed it to us. It contains some good photographs of him. After this we went to the YMCA, sat in the steam room, showered, lay in a dark room for an hour then had dinner at the Tropics, a restaurant with grass and bamboo decor but an American steakhouse menu. To the airport, where the chap who checked us in gave us quite a welcome, laid on by Art Lavove, a friend of mine who works for Pan Am. At 11 p. m. we took off for Samoa in the last of the old-style double-decked non-jet Clippers. We are the only passengers in first class. The tourist section is half filled with returning Samoans in mu-mus. The steward told us they are an emotional people, partings bring on tears.

Tuesday August 9

The plane carries two crews. It arrives American Samoa Tuesday, goes to Fiji and New Zealand, returning the following Monday. We slept on banquettes in the lower deck bar. I photographed the dawn out of the plane windows and we touched down at Tafuna, American Samoa, at seven a. m. A large crowd of colorfully dressed natives greet the plane. Arrivals are apparently as emotional as partings. The airport building is small, made of wood, well-worn and bustling. Corwin and I, having a few hours before the DC 3 leaves for Western Samoa (pronounced *Sam*oa), hired a cab and bounced the short distance into town to have a look at the hotel used by Maugham in "Rain." We saw Centipede Row, with its signs in Japanese, and Van Camp's tuna canning factory. Their trawlers are manned by Japanese.

We took a car to Apia where we have reservations at Aggie Grey's hotel. Aggie is short, plump, half German, half Samoan and, as everyone knows, is supposed to be the model for Bloody Mary in Michener's *Tales of the South Pacific*. She is also an entrepreneur. She owns the hotel, a grocery store, the harbor launch service, and part of the Polynesian Airlines. We chose our space—separate new cottages on an inlet leading to the harbor—and were despatched immediately to the Police station to get our liquor ration. The natives are not allowed to buy liquor and visitors' consumption is strictly controlled. Aggie asked how much we drank. Corwin drinks nothing and since we are only to be here one week I thought a bottle of scotch would do me. Aggie said, "You make the chit out for four bottles. Give it to me. I give you all you want to drink." A fair number of New Zealanders and a man from *Time* staying at the hotel. Our first dinner at Aggie's consisted of chicken, taro, two cabbages, a special taro item, breadfruit, rice and chop suey, spaghetti. Ketchup on the table. There was a disturbance in the middle of the night. We learned later it was the *Time* man chasing Vaaki, one of Aggie's handmaidens. She apparently was not interested.

Wednesday August 10

Awakened at 7:15 by Shiela bearing coffee. She is one-quarter German (does that make her a quarter caste?) At eight the breakfast bell rang and we joined the other guests on the dining verandah. A piece of papaya, tomato juice, french fried potatoes, fried egg, baked beans and bread. Aggie knew the purpose of our visit, that we wanted to find out first hand something of Stevenson's life on the island. We knew he had been entertained at various native villages and we wondered if we could experience that, too. Aggie arranged it with a chief named Mamea.

We drove into the village where we were conducted to the meeting house. There the chiefs had gathered to welcome us. The house had the usual palm leaf roof, open sides, and matting on the floor. There were sixteen chiefs. We sat cross-legged in a circle on the floor. The first order of business was the choice of an orator to make the welcoming speech. All sixteen chiefs declaimed their unworthiness of the honor of welcoming the two strangers from America. Finally one was chosen by acclamation and made the speech, in Samoan, translated by Mamea. Corwin answered with a speech in English, translated into Samoan, comparing the Samoans to the ancient Greeks. He is good at this and spoke in long, beautifully constructed strophes. I tugged at his sleeve and said, "Give it to him in shorter bursts." I didn't think Mamea could possibly be translating Corwin, but was off on a routine of his own. After this ceremony we were taken outside to dinner, palm leaves on the ground for a table cloth. Chicken and taro were the pièces de résistance and I had a hard time. The main function of the women during the feast was to wave the flies off.

After dinner a Siva (entertainment) in the meeting house. The chiefs gathered in the hut. The women entered wearing long yellow blouses, green skirts, white flowers over their ears (the chiefs had red flowers over theirs). Each lady came over to us and shook hands. With the entrance of the women the conversation picked up. At length a wild cry from one of the women signalled the start of the entertainment. Sticks were handed to two men. They were the rhythm section. They beat the sticks on rolled up matting.

Mamea says the songs are composed by the chiefs. The history of the people is not written, it is handed down from generation to generation in song. A prayer bell sounded and a song about Stevenson was sung.

Throughout the entertainment a lady in an elaborate headdress was making the Kava. This is a root kneaded in water. The traditional way of making the Kava in Stevenson's time involved using spit instead of water. It is served in a small wooden cup, first a sip for the head chief, then the honored guests, until everyone has had a taste. It is not alcholic but numbs the lips.

There are no bare breasts. Since the advent of the missionaries, the Mormons, Catholics and the London Missionary Society, breasts have been covered. There was one exception. One of the women in the fields as we arrived had nothing on from the waist up. I imagine when they think the missionaries are not looking they revert to their natural way of life.

Finally all sang a hymn, and Norman played back a little of the tape to see if we had got it. They were worried about the sound. Norman explained that it would be played back on a big machine, that this was just for recording here, and they seemed relieved.

Tuesday August 16

Back to Los Angeles. Kathy has ordered the ceiling torn out of the living room at 1227 Sunset Plaza Drive, leaving the roof exposed, and has started people digging a pool. On Saturday August 27 we moved in.

In September I did a "Gunsmoke" and a General Electric based on the William Faulkner story "The Graduation Dress." The music for some reason caused a stir and the producer had Reagan mention it in his closing remarks, something so unusual it gave me quite a boot. Norman is busy making an outline for Mr. Lester of the proposed Stevenson show, to be called "Tusitala." Lester has always had a burning desire to do *The Count of Luxembourg* with the Civic Light Opera, and has hired me, Sid Kuller and Allan Scott to make a version of it.

Monday November 7

Twentieth Century Fox has engaged me to be the musical director of, and to provide a background score for, a film called *Snow White and the Three Stooges*. It is being produced by an affable man, Charles Wickes. [He later achieved some notoriety as a member of President Reagan's administration.] I started on salary today.

Tuesday November 8

Election day. John F. Kennedy vs. Richard M. Nixon. We are having a party to watch the returns. During the afternoon I had a telephone call from Bernard Herrmann. This is the conversation.

BH. I hear you're having a party tonight.

LM. That's right.

BH. And I am not invited.

LM. That's right. In case Kennedy gets defeated, Kathy wants only Democrats here. She doesn't want to hear any Republicans crowing.

BH. How do you know I'm not a Democrat?/

LM. Oh, come on. You're completely apolitical.

After a bit more he hung up. With the exception of a brief exchange on the street one day at Fox, we have not spoken since.

Wednesday November 9

I must describe this Snow White picture. It stars—besides the Three Stooges—Carol Heiss, a championship ice skater whom Fox hopes will become another Sonja Henie. It is to be directed by Walter Lang, of almost the same vintage, if not quite the stature, of Henry King. At any rate a tough, old, no-nonsense director. The cameraman is Leon Shamroy, one of the three or four giants in his department. The songs have been written by Harry Harris, not exactly a household name to me. I looked him up in the ASCAP Biographical Dictionary. His oeuvre includes "When I'm Walkin' Down the Lane With Jimmy," "Strollin' Down the Lane With Bill" and "I had Someone Else Before I Had You, and I'll Have Someone After You're Gone." Today I met Carol Heiss, a sweet, simple, darling little girl, and her dialog coach, Pamela Danova. We are not wasting any time. I have asked for, and the studio has okayed, Jeff Alexander to be the choral man on the picture.

Friday Kathy and I went to the symphony with George and Ruth Cates. He is still Lawrence Welk's major-domo and she is a total delight. They have a son who started at UC Berkeley this term. When he went away he was a polite boy with short hair and conservative clothes. When he came home for Thanksgiving they met him at the airport. He descended from the plane wearing long hair, a Nehru jacket and under the jacket a T-shirt bearing the printed message, "Help Stamp Out Lawrence Welk."

After television, which always has to be ready tomorrow, working on a musical at a big studio is heaven. At Fox especially because it is such a pretty studio and they give you an isolated, nicely furnished bungalow to work in, complete with bathroom, refrigerator, couch, a dartboard with a picture of Inger Stevens as the target, and, in case the Muse acts up, a piano.

Kathy is doing a bang-up job on the house, having ceilings torn out, a pool built, furnishing it and holding down her job at the May Company all at the same time. There are four bedrooms. One fixed up as a workroom for me, another for guests, one for Kathy and one for me. Conclusions drawn from the description of this arrangement of separate bedrooms would be right. So when I met this lady on the picture who, to protect the living and her husband, shall be nameless, and I took to getting home late, anyone inclined to think harshly of me should know it became a consuming passion and probably greatly improved the score of a mediocre picture.

For the balance of the year lots of socializing. The pre-recordings for the Wickes picture proceed at a measured pace, so measured that at one point tough old Walter Lang cried, "You guys are goofing off down there!" with some justification considering the long lunches in the commissary with jolly colleagues, and cocktails and l'amour in the bungalow at the end of the day.

Work done this year: 2 "Have Gun Will Travels," 2 "Gunsmokes," 1 "Twilight Zone," "Roy Coots," a pilot, 3 General Electric Theatres, the work on "The Count of Luxembourg," the pre-recordings of *Snow White and the Three Stooges*, a Capitol album with Salli Terri.

1961

Wednesday February 15

Dear Cyril Mockridge, a staff composer at Fox, got into trouble finishing his score for *All Hands on Deck,* a potboiler of a Navy film, and I did a few cues for him which were recorded today. He's a compatriot of mine, born in London and, next to Alfred Newman, writes the best string parts of anybody.

Thursday June 1

I have been engaged by Fox to do the score for *Tender Is the Night,* to be directed by Henry King. The film requires a few 1928 jazz pieces to be played by the orchestras in various Paris nightclubs.

Friday June 2

A writer named William Copeland came to see me. He has made a children's play out of Kenneth Graham's *Wind in the Willows* and wants some songs for it.

Thursday June 8

I ran into Herrmann on the street at Fox. He planted himself in front of me and said, quite out of the blue, "Kathy only works because she kisses Mrs. Chandler's ass." We never spoke again.

Today we recorded the 1928 jazz for *Tender Is the Night.* I spent the rest of the week on Copeland's project, which is coming easily. Songs written so far: "I'm a Lowly Mole," "Hi Diggety," "I'm a Rather Erratic Water Rat," "The Toad Song," "Watch for the Weasels in the Wildwood," "When You Mess Around in Boats," "It's Good to Be Going Home" and "Has Anyone Here Seen Toad?"

Tuesday June 13

Daughter Joyce graduated from Immaculate Heart High School today at a ceremony in the Hollywood Bowl. (Someone should write a piece to replace "Pomp and Circumstance.") Kathy got Joyce into Immaculate Heart and Joyce has become a Catholic convert. She is going on to the College for Women at El Cajon, near San Diego.

Saturday June 24

Just talked on the phone to Victor Bay. He came to this country in 1922, playing in a Russian ballet company orchestra, and still fractures the English language. Discussing President Kennedy's lack of decision at this moment, "It is surprising since he made mince pies out of Nixon in the debates." I told him I had seen the huge Moiseyev ballet company last night. He said socialist countries put people to work. For example, he went to Thomas Cook & Sons in London to change a reservation. Three people took him in hand, but the change was effected finally by a fourth person on a higher echelon. I said in Europe one sees people polishing wood and brass, holystoning steps, 14-year-old boys assisting waiters, and one-armed ex-soldiers, wearing ribbons of medals from ancient battles, operating lifts. Victor said, "Here is different. If we can eliminate seven people we do. There they put them all to work and so everyone is walloping in pastry."

Finished "Wind in the Willows" this week. Wrote to Frank Loesser about publishing; later we discussed a production here. Here are the economics of such a production: Assuming we get a 400-seat theatre and charge $1.50 a seat, at capacity we could gross $600. The five actors will each get $25; a four-piece orchestra will be paid $112.50 (three at $25 and a leader-player at $37.50); the theatre will get $100. All that comes to $337.50, leaving $262.50 for the director's royalty, writers royalties, advertising and promotion and 10 percent to the lady who organizes theatre parties. While I am in this mathematical mood—*Tender Is the Night* will pay me $10,000. I figured out what goes out of that. Commission $1,000, Composers Guild $190, Musicians Union $20, taxes about $3,300, alimony $2,250, Motion Picture Relief (a 2 percent voluntary contrib I happily make) $200, business manager $450, net to me $2,590.

Sunday June 25

Kathy has departed for Dayton, Ohio, for a course in new methods for retailing, at the National Cash Register Company.

Tuesday June 27

Jeff Alexander and Larry Orenstein came over and made a tape of the *Wind in the Willows* score for me. Audio Arts made a 12-inch LP which I sent to Frank Loesser. He wrote back in a week and said he was about to go into rehearsal with Abe Burrows on *How to Succeed in Business Without Really Trying*, but that he would have his staff think over our property and its possible uses. He said he had a song in his show that sounded like one of mine and that he had used the words "peanut butter" in one of his lyrics (so had we) and he was telling me this so I wouldn't think he was being "derivative."

Wednesday June 28

The course Kathy attended in Dayton was conducted by a charming Bogotan named Trujillo. It was so impressive, Senor Trujillo was invited to Los Angeles to give it to other May Company executives. Mr. Brunmark, Kathy's boss, gave a dinner party for him, the executives and wives, at the Key Club. This is a private dining club where business men over fifty are served hors d'oeuvres by sexy young women in very brief costumes, net stockings, and boobies at the ready. After dinner Mr. Brunmark introduced Senor Trujillo. He opened with a story about a farmer whose prize cow stopped giving milk. When asked by the disturbed farmer why, the cow said, "You have been pulling on my tits for ten years and you never said I love you." After the shock waves subsided Mr. Brunmark stopped by our table and asked us how we like the Bogota wiz. I said I had one observation, "If anyone told a story in my house with the word tits in the punchline, Kath would give him the Pasadena freeze and show him the door."

Thursday June 29

To Arthur Blake's opening at Billy Gray's Bandbox, now called Arthur Blake's Bandbox. He's an extremely talented female impersonator. The show, written by Sid, is called "Camp-a-lot." A middle aged lady put up the money required to open, under the impression Blake was going to marry her. It is not all that unusual for gays to marry rich old ladies but in this case, when Arthur kept her at arm's length, after two weeks she withdrew her support and the club closed. The notices were so good, however, it is now running at the Cabaret Theatre.

Friday July 14

Pamela Danova, the dialog coach on "Snow White," has been given the job of running Fox's talent school. There is to be a convention of the world sales staff at the studio to acquaint them with the product, and Pamela is going to do a show with her 23 talented students. For a fee of $2,000, Sid and I have written two pieces of material. The opening introduces the 23 members of the school and the closing is a piece mentioning by name all of the distinguished visitors from overseas. John Gregory has been engaged to stage the numbers. Fox is in quite a mess. The studio lost $15,000,000 last year and banker members of the Board of Directors are here to see if they can effect some economies. The first thing they did was cancel the sales convention, presumably to save money, or perhaps they have seen some of the product. I mean, think of *Snow White and the Three Stooges*. In any case Pamela is going ahead with the opening number and intends to film it to show the brass what their 23 contract kids can do. And we have our $2,000.

Sunday July 16

Helene Constantine came in from Paris with their two younger children. Tanya, the eldest, now 18, has run away from home and is shacking up with a young Algerian. Ed is furious and, consonant with his new personality as a great star, has threatened to disinherit her. The Algerian let him know that under French law he cannot do this. Helene and the children were here swimming today and we took them to dinner at the Cock 'n' Bull. Ran into Henry Alper [my agent] dining with Bobby Burns who used to manage Sinatra in the "Hit Parade" days. One of Burns's jobs was organizing the claque of screaming teenagers who, after doing their thing, would come to the stage door to collect 50 cents each.

I have been taken off *Tender Is the Night*. Henry King originally wanted Herrmann to do it. David Selznick, the executive producer, wanted to hire Sammy Fain and Paul Francis Webster to provide a commercial, pop tune for the theme. Herrmann won't work with other people's material so he made an attempt to write a commercial song, which was turned down. He quit and went to Europe. Fain and Webster wrote a nice song and I was engaged to do the score. As a courtesy to Herrmann, Ted Cain wrote him in London acquainting him of this development. Herrmann returned from London, went to see Henry King and Selznick in an attempt to get the picture back. (Henry King told me later Herrmann cried.) Ted Cain, as a courtesy to me, reported that Herrmann's maneuver had been unsuccessful. It was my practice to call Ted once a week to check on the progress of the shooting of the playbacks I had made, and to inquire if my presence was required to solve any problems. One morning at eleven I called and everything was proceeding satisfactorily. At two he called back, embarrassed, and said Herrmann was back on the picture and that he had been instructed to take me off the picture and put me on something else. The something else was a picture called *Watcher in the Shadows*, to be made in England, starring Gregory Peck. I was disappointed but told him this would be acceptable to me provided *Watcher in the Shadows* was ready for scoring not later than 30 days after my starting date on the underscore for *Tender Is the Night*. I called MCA and Alvin Bart told me Ted had already called and told them of the mess, and that I had agreed to the solution outlined above. Henry Alper, another agent at MCA, told me Herrmann had cut his price to $15,000 (he normally gets $17,500 because he does his own orchestration) and had agreed to use Fain's song. Alper also told me he thought I was making a mistake in letting Fox off the hook, that I should insist on doing the picture. I demurred. I did not want to be forced on King and Selznick now that they had re-engaged Herrmann and obviously preferred him. Then Alper told me they had not shown the script of *Watcher in the Shadows* to Peck, whom they represent, because MCA was not satisfied with it and that even if the script was fixed to their satisfaction, the picture wouldn't be ready for scoring for at least a year. He also pointed out that the Fox Board of Directors' investigations into the management of the studio could conceivably result in no production at all in the near future; that I should have a full payoff on *Tender Is the Night,* unless a comparable picture was forthcoming within the time limit, and no such picture was in sight.

Wednesday July 19

Recorded the music for a GE called "Wishbook" starring young Ricky Nelson, directed by Ozzie. Not very good but I got a charming, complimentary letter from Ozzie on the contribution the music made to the film.

Tuesday July 25

The Fox talent school has been torpedoed by Peter Levathes, new head of production. We are going to Europe August 12 with the Alexanders.

Wednesday July 26

The Alexanders came over to cancel their participation in the trip. Their daughter, Jill, has run away from home. The Alexanders have no idea where she is and they are going through the "Where did we fail" phase. So until this *crise* is settled they don't want to leave town.

Friday July 28

Stanley Wilson, my boss at Universal, and his wife Gert are going with us. We had dinner at Romanoff's to discuss it, and elaborate preparations are under way. We want to hire a cabin cruiser for a trip up the Thames, rent a car for a tour of the wine country in France, and maybe we'll drive to Venice and Rome.

Friday August 4

Dinner with Stanley and Gert to discuss the trip. Too much to drink, Kathy somewhat contentious, having definite ideas and not brooking too much palaver about them. Stanley wonderfully diplomatic and amusing, so maybe all will be well.

Saturday August 12

Leave Los Angeles 12:15 p.m. Pan Am for London.

Sunday August 13

Arrive London 8. At the Savoy we were shown our suite. Stanley loathed the space, and the fellow in the tailcoat showed us a suite overlooking the river. We loved it but didn't take it. We would have had to mortgage our combined salaries for a year to pay for it. We settled on one with awful Swedish modern furniture, but affordable. Good dinner at Trattatoria Tarrazo, recommended by Sinatra, a gourmet.

Monday August 14

Lunch at Cunningham's in Curzon Street, then Stanley and I to see the boat Basil Soper of MCA had found us for cruising up the Thames. It was sitting forlornly in the middle of the river. We were rowed out to it and found it cold, uninviting, austere, Spartan and, though it was supposed to sleep six, two and a half would be more like it. We passed. Dinner at Simpson's, then to the Palladium for one of those Val Parnell–Bernard Delfont extravaganzas with Harry Secombe and Terry-Thomas.

Tuesday August 15

Dropped in to see Teddy Holmes at Chappell. Great lunch at the Savoy Grill starting with a watercress soup, served by a waiter with a very dirty thumbnail immersed in it. To matinée of Lionel Bart's *Oliver.* Not so good. The best thing about it is Sean Kenny's set.

Dinner at the Talk of the Town. Two orchestras alternating on stage, the music non-stop, the working band is rolled off as the other, playing the same tune, is rolled on. Jack Costanza, the great bongo player I had in *Catch a Thief*, on the bill headlined by Frances Faye. I worked with her at the Russian Palace in Newark, N.J., in 1928 when she was doing an act with her sister. She is wild. Went back to see them.

Thursday August 17

The Golden Arrow to Paris. We crossed the channel aboard the *Invicta* in very mild weather, not much of a sea running. Lunch on the train; arrive the Elysées Parc, the delightful little hotel on the Rond Point, 7 p.m. Eddie Constantine met us for dinner at La Rive Gauche, one of the few restaurants open in August. He caused a sensation—customers getting autographs, etc.—and when we tried to pay the bill they wouldn't hear of it. His presence obviously worth money to the management. Afterwards to a samba joint, the dancers très supple and sexy.

Tuesday August 22

Saw Kathy and her friend Eleanor Morgan off in a rented Citroen for a tour of the wine country. They proceeded down Rue Jean Mermoz in such a jerky and erratic fashion I thought that would be the last we would ever see of them. Saw the film *L'Avventura* with Italian dialog and French subtitles which popped on and off too fast for us to read. Taxi to Orly, 17 francs. Had a croque monsieur in the snack bar. (Somebody should introduce this delicacy at home.) When we two middle-aged composers and one middle-aged wife arrived on the departure floor, the attendant asked, pleasantly, "Going far?" We said, "Nice." He said, "Ah, Nice est pour l'amour." When we alighted from the Caravelle at Nice, Gert looked around and said, "It looks like Santa Monica."

Taxi to Juan Les Pins, 28 francs. We are staying at Le Provençal, an old hotel with balconies and a casino. At dinner in the patio we were entertained by four girls and a gay man doing cancans, and a Spanish act called "Les Platters" who sang rock and roll and Spanish songs. The band incessantly played "Never On Sunday" and Tiomkin's song from *The Alamo*. Stanley and I went for a walk.

Juan Les Pins is crowded with très unchic people, and blasts of rock and roll assault you wherever you go. We passed two of the cancan girls in the street and said, "Hello," but they ignored us. Before turning in we inspected the beach which measures about 2 × 4, part of it covered by a wooden deck. The band in the patio kept me awake until it stopped playing at four o'clock.

Wednesday August 23

The most interesting thing I did today was buy a tube of toothpaste. Taxi to Cannes for a good dinner at Voile au Vent. Couldn't get in to the bicycling races, so before catching the bus back strolled the back streets. Wild ride back to Juan Les P in a bus driven by a noir who thought he was in a Hitchcock chase.

Friday August 25

To Monte Carlo by train (3 francs) where Stanley's rich uncle Harry lives at L'Hermitage with his very smart French wife, Irene. We took L'Hermitage's bus to the hotel's beach. Uncle Harry borrowed a franc off Gert to tip the driver. He handed it to Irene who, as we walked off, rummaged in her bag and came up with a 50 centime piece which she gave to the driver. Uncle Harry's suite overlooks the harbor full of graceful, expensive yachts, nothing under 100 feet allowed. Probably one of them belonged to Fritz Loewe, for *My Fair Lady* was a hit and when you have a hit musical all things are possible. We took a limousine to Nice where Stanley had arranged to meet Jack Andrews' wife Wendy in the bar at Hotel Ruhl. She is a small, well-shaped, over-made-up woman with a very hostile attitude. We were supposed to go to her house so Stanley could renew his acquaintance with Jack, but first she wanted to go to a cocktail party. I got the impression that my presence in the group annoyed her so I bowed out and went back to Juan Les Pins, had a sandwich in my room, and went to sleep accompanied by the sounds of an Irish Gala in the patio.

Saturday August 26

Took the ferry to Les Isles de la Reine, visited the fort, had a nice lunch at La Guérite, came back to find Kath and Eleanor safely arrived from their wine country tour and being very gay with Wendy Andrews, who had left her hostile attitude at home with Jack in Cagnes sur Mer. She was quite nice to me. We went again to Cannes for dinner at the Voile au Vent and the invitation in her eyes was unmistakable. [Later, when she visited California, the invitation was accepted. There was an odd sidelight to this encounter for, in what might be described as an intimate moment, she confessed to me that she had once left her husband for a woman.]

Sunday August 27

In the afternoon to a concert by a British fife and drum corps and the Grenadiers' band. Rather an odd program. "Sweet Sue," "Sweet Georgia Brown," "Greensleeves," "On the Sunny Side of the Street," "Get Me to the Church on Time" and "Yankee Doodle." It was hot. I noticed that one of the clarinet players, a kid who looked all of 16, had a drop of sweat hanging from his nose which, as the afternoon wore on, must have interfered with his fingering.

Wednesday August 30

To Rome, where *Cleopatra* is shooting at Cinecitta. Joseph Mankiewicz is writing by night and directing by day, Leon Shamroy is in charge of photography. We are staying at the Excelsior. In the evening to *Aida* at the Baths of Caracalla. Large orchestra, horses and other animals populating a stage with a decided rake. I was less worried that one of the animals might misbehave than I was that they would lose their footing and take a fall.

Friday September 1

To Cinecitta at 10:15 to watch the shooting of a scene staged by Hermes Pan, the choreographer, involving dancers, smoke throwers, horsemen, chariots, pole vaulters. Lunch with Pan, Shamroy and Walter Wanger, who is producing. Pamela Danova is on the picture. We went to her sister Rosemary's apartment for drinks with the Shamroys and Hermes Pan, then to dinner across the piazza, where we bought balloons from the vendors and sent them sailing up into the soft Roman night.

Saturday September 2

To Ostia Antica and the Kursaal beach. Drinks at the Grand with the Shamroys and Ken Crawford, Leon's assistant. Shamroy talked about this great folly of *Cleopatra*. When he arrived in Rome he discovered that the set was too big to photograph and impossible to light with the available power. They sent all over Europe for extra generators. He said the set designer has gone nuts. He has recreated the buildings larger than they were originally. He said, "Roman steps go up about eight or ten and then there is a plateau. This guy has about 100 steps without a break and Cesare Danova has to carry Elizabeth Taylor up the steps rolled in a rug." Shamroy says this picture is the biggest waste of money he has ever seen. Crawford says they have to wait eight days to get the dailies back from the States because they have to be reduced from 65 mm to 35. Shamroy said, "Who wants to see it? Let's just get the damn thing finished."

Fox has rented all 15 stages at Cinecitta. There are 250 locals working plus 65 English and Americans, exclusive of the top-lined cast. Spyros Skouras and a man named Engel are here to keep an eye on how the studio's money is being spent. The reason the film is being shot in Rome is that the Italian government has put up a lot of money at a very favorable long-term rate of interest. Getting off the subject of *Cleopatra*, Shamroy reminisced about shooting a dog picture a long time ago. He said, "Shooting dogs is better than shooting dumb actors." He had to film a scene of a dog eating with a knife and fork. How do you do it? You strap his front legs and fasten on phonies worked with a string, and when the SPCA comes around you dismantle all the gimmicks until they leave. For a big dog chase you smear the lead dog with stuff from a bitch in heat. He's a funny, tough, old-time picture man. Shamroy said Henry King gave him some advice once. "Don't fight them. Take the shots you can get, and enjoy yourself." I wish that worked with music, but if writers, directors and cinematographers run into delays, it all comes out of the time left to compose the music. We have to meet the date.

Saturday September 30

Back home.

At 9:30 a.m. met with Bill Stinson, the new head of music at Paramount, and Ronald Neame, the English director, who is finishing a picture called *Escape to Zahrain*. I am to do the music. Before reporting to Paramount on October 12 I did another GE and am writing a "Frontier Circus" (Universal TV show).

Thursday October 12

Escape to Zahrain stars Yul Brynner. Looking at this picture I couldn't imagine a) why Brynner would do it, b) why Paramount would make it and, c) why such a distinguished director as Neame would bother. Maybe Brynner and Neame need the money, and maybe a bunch of Arabs gave Par the money to film this drek. Neame has a problem. He is here on a limited visa and he has used up most of his time. After the conference with me he left for Mexico. When I finish, and we are ready to score, he will come back for the few days remaining on his visa. When one settles down to write a picture, no matter what its quality, it becomes *Tristan and Isolde*. You write the best you know how.

I took a half day off to record the music for *Frontier Circus*, then returned to *Zahrain*. I was bereft of ideas for the main title and Eddie Powell, bless him, came up with the solution and we are going to have a male chorus sing some kind of an Arab song, punctuated with exciting brass figures to keep the audience awake. The usual problem with such an approach: We had to find someone who speaks the language to check the lyric to make sure it didn't contain Communist propaganda, incitement to overthrow a government, or anything dirty.

Tuesday November 21

Finished writing the music. Thursday Neame came back and the first thing he asked me about the music was, "Do you like it?" I said, "I think it's okay."

Friday December 1

The last scene of *Escape to Zahrain* has Brynner and his group of Arabs arriving at the top of a range of mountains and seeing their goal, a coastal city, spread out below. This was to be a matte shot of the city, painted by studio artists. Nobody saw this rendering until we went to preview. In reel eleven, Brynner and his band having struggled to the top of the last ridge, we finally saw the shot of their promised land. It looked as phony as a five-cent postcard, and the audience woke up and laughed. We had a glum little meeting on the sidewalk in front of the theatre. The cards, distributed to the audience for comment, were not complimentary. Well, I really only did it to work with the man who made *Tunes of Glory.*

Work done this year. TV: 7 GE's, Hess's pilot, "Baron Gus," 1 "Have Gun Will Travel," 1 "Frontier Circus." Films: *Snow White and the Three Stooges, Escape to Zahrain.* Score for "Wind in the Willows."

1962

Thursday January 4

John Griggs, the New York actor who founded the Sutton Cinema Society to preserve and show prints of silent films and who once almost got me picketed by *PM*, a left wing newspaper, was here tonight and ran *The Kid* and *Phantom of the Opera.*

I knew Griggs in New York. When he saw the size of my living room at 322 East 57th Street he immediately organized a showing of *Birth of a Nation*, admission: bring your own beer. A motley quartet led by Edgar Varese, whom I was naturally more than delighted to meet, came in the afternoon, hung a screen, moved the furniture around and dragged in an organ. Someone from *PM* reportedly threatened to picket the apartment house if the showing took place. (*PM* objected to negro villains, Ku Klux Klan heroes and white actors working in blackface.)

Tonight after the films a roaring party with Max Showalter—who plays even louder than Johnny Green—banging out show tunes on the piano.

Sunday January 21

Saw *Fantasticks*. Don't understand it. I'm wrong, it's a big, big hit.

Friday January 26

Ran a CBS pilot, "Hercule Poirot," starring Martin Gabel, who is married to Arlene Francis, my favorite woman in her age bracket.

Friday February 2

Dear Norman Lloyd and Joan Harrison are going to produce "Alfred Hitchcock Presents" for television. Had lunch with Norman today to talk about doing some of them.

Friday February 9

Lovely day at MGM recording the Poirot music. The sound is super.

Sunday February 11

Spent the day writing a cue for Jeff Alexander's Presley picture. Elvis records the songs in Nashville with his group, Jeff adds strings etc. to the tracks, and an underscore, here. The only trouble with this arrangement is that the Nashville tracks are "in the cracks," that is, they don't tune to a recognizable "A." The orchestra here has literally to play by ear, tuning down a bit. Doesn't work for xylophones and glockenspiels, though. You can't tune *them* down.

Monday February 12

Dubbed the Poirot pilot. Sounded nice but I don't think it will make it. Martin is just not quite Hercule.

Thursday February 15

Spent five hours at the movieola looking at "Very Special Girl" and making copious notes. It takes time to write a score for one of these half-hour films. Example: Friday, 7 hours; Saturday, 6 ½ hours; Monday, 7 hours; Tuesday, 8 hours; Wednesday, 7 ½ hours; Thursday, 3 hours, Friday, 2 hours on the first cue (drawn from material already written) and 6 hours on the End Credits. A total of 53 hours writing, plus five on the movieola and one for the music run with Stanley Wilson. Altogether, 59 hours in 11 days.

Tuesday February 27

ASCAP meeting Beverly Hilton, five p.m. This is the semi-annual gathering of West coast members who hear the business report, make their beefs about whatever they feel is wrong, then swill gallons of free booze and descend like locusts on an enormous layout of hors d'oeuvres.

Saturday March 31

Jeff Alexander and I got away from it all and drove to Santa Barbara. We stayed at the Santa Barbara Inn. Walking through the lobby (Jeff was upstairs in the room) I ran into Norman Cauldwell, an executive of the May Company. He asked if I was with Kathy. I answered, perversely, "No. I'm with somebody else." On Monday morning Cauldwell reported this to Kathy. You can't get away with a thing around here.

Thursday April 5

To Warners to see about doing a picture Jack Rose is producing called *The Incredible Mr. Limpet*. Rose came to our house for cocktails. When he launched into an anecdote Kathy picked up a magazine and started to read. He said, "Kathy, you might be interested in this." She said, "Oh," and put the magazine down. This is called "How to entertain a Producer who is trying to give your composer-husband $10,000 to do a score for his picture."

Friday April 13

Some concert and moviegoing for the rest of the month. Went to a Tedesco concert and a performance of Verdi's *Macbeth* at U.S.C.'s Bovard Auditorium. When Verdi was rehearsing for the French première at the Paris Opera, after three weeks a delegation from the orchestra came to him and said the French equivalent of "enough already." He was outraged and said he would never allow the Paris Opera to do any more of his works.

Wednesday May 2

Spent the day with Jim Peterson, the conductor of the Ice Capades, going over the material needed for the new edition, and on the 10th we assembled at Radio Recorders and put on tape the arrangements I had made. I enjoy these long sessions. The chorus is marvelous. What would I do without Marni Nixon, Salli Terri, Bill Lee, Thurl Ravenscroft and Bill Reeves, to name just five of the 25?

Tuesday May 15

At Warners where I blew Mr. Limpet. The head of the music department had definite ideas about what size of an orchestra they wanted to use and what it should sound like. To be specific, 18 players doing an imitation of Harry Owens's Hawaiian orchestra. I disagreed and walked. Frank Perkins finally did the score and the picture sank without a trace. I don't want to imply that it was Frank's fault. No score can save a picture.

Spent most of the rest of the month on an interesting project for a producer named Zugsmith. He has an idea that an original TV musical comedy each week might sell. Half a dozen team of writers and composers would turn them out. Sid Kuller, Jeff Alexander and I are doing the pilot to be called "How to Break into the Movies."

Friday June 8

To Palm Springs for daughter Ann's graduation from the Palm Springs High School. I drove down in her graduation gift from me, a small, used Hillman Minx I bought for $250 and (surprise) we got there.

Monday June 11

Recorded an audio tape of "How to Break into the Movies." It was never filmed because Danny Melnick at ABC could not bring himself to believe that even six sets of composers and authors could turn out acceptable one-hour musicals. Also the form has never been successful either on radio or television. Rodgers and Hart did one I was involved in years ago for radio and as I recall, even with those illustrious masters, it was not a great success.

Thursday June 14

Ran the first Hitchcock with Norman Lloyd. It is called "Final Vow." I kept a record of how long it took to write. 57 hours.

Tuesday July 3

To MGM to meet Lawrence Weingarten, who has produced Tennessee Williams's *Period of Adjustment* directed by George Roy Hill. Mr. Weingarten is charming and sensible and very experienced. He hired me to do the score.

Thursday July 5

At Metro for the music run of *Period*. The pace, compared to television, is going to be leisurely. I don't start on salary until the 23rd but I have begun getting some ideas together. While I was working on Mr. Weingarten's picture I did two Hitchcocks, "A Piece of the Action" and "Don't Look Behind You."

Monday September 17

Having recorded the music for, and successfully previewed, *Period of Adjustment* I was taken to dinner at Hillcrest by Mr.

Weingarten. On a scale of 1 to 10 of the producers I have worked for he is an 11.

Wednesday September 26

Kathy has lost her job at the May Company. This is a big trauma, so she is going to run off to Paris for a month. I have arranged with Alex Trauner, the French art director who is here working on the film of *Irma la Douce*, to rent his apartment at 108 Rue du Bac in Paris for her. Today, after recording a Hitchcock called "Captive Audience," I drove Kath to the airport, returned, and in the great peace that has descended upon the house, started to write a "Wagon Train."

Thursday October 11

Joan Harrison has produced an ambitious Hitchcock called "Annabelle." There is such a rush on this one I was allowed to see it at what is called the network run. Hubbell Robinson, now high up in CBS, was here from New York. Hadn't seen him in years. Like all network executives he knows how to fix the flaws one can find in any hour television show—there just is not enough time to turn out perfect gems every week—and told dear, sweet, unflappable Joan what to do. The only problem is that to meet the air date the show has to record in five days. I spent those five days in the studio, day and night, working with the help of two orchestrators, Sandy Courage and Sid Fine, stealing a reel when we could pry one out of the cutters. One evening, however, Joan and her husband Eric Ambler gave a cocktail party in her bungalow and I must say two hours in such stimulating, entertaining company does something for the creative juices.

Wednesday October 17

We recorded starting at seven p.m. The unusual starting time was necessary, for we were still writing and the copyists were still copying until the downbeat. Stanley conducted and I sat in the booth and okayed takes so we would not have to take the time to play them back. We managed to finish by midnight. If we hadn't, the orchestra would have gone on golden time and the studio doesn't like that. Golden time pays double the ordinary rate. To everyone except composers, that is.

Sunday October 28

Left for London by Pan Am at 12:15 p.m. to do a picture for Metro called *Come Fly With Me.*

Monday October 29

Arrived London seven a.m. A studio limousine met me and took me to a flat they had arranged for me to rent for six weeks. Didn't like it. A Katherine Mills, who has a little list, took me to one on Eaton Square which comes with a butler for 50 guineas a week. The butler's name is Telfer. Mark it. He said he had shown the flat to a lady actress who had until five o'clock to make up her mind but, since he didn't like working for ladies, I could count on it. At Elstree, the British MGM, ran the picture with Anatole de Grunwald, producer, Henry Levin, director, and Frank Clark, the picture editor. De Grunwald and Levin charming, Clark my kind of a nice, tough movie man, and the picture is fun. I had someone call Telfer to see how I was doing. Telfer had got rid of the actress. My driver, Peter, drove me to Eaton Square in the studio limousine they have given me for the duration. Did I want Peter and the car after dinner? Not bloody likely. I want my dinner and then I am going to take my jet lag to bed. Telfer prepared and served the best dinner I have ever eaten.

Tuesday October 30

Started breaking the picture down. Discussed the orchestra with a business fellow. We are to have 70 men. What can I say? A limousine and driver, six weeks to write the music, Telfer, Eaton Square, Kathy in Paris *and* a 70-piece orchestra. It's pure Heaven, that's what it is.

Wednesday October 31

Finished breaking down, rented a piano, discovered my large stop-watch-clock won't work on the British 50 cycle current, a problem solved by Telfer who went out and bought me a converter. He set up a good solid card table for me to write on.

The flat is on the second floor of a Georgian mansion and Clive Brook lives in the one next door, but he is in Hollywood, poor fellow, making a picture. It is elegant. There is a large living room, a fair-sized bedroom and a tiny one, a grand luxe bathroom and a small kitchen where Telfer performs his miracles. He lives elsewhere, coming in each morning at 7:30, seven days a week. Peter, the driver, pops in at about eight to see if I need him and to have a cup of coffee with Telfer.

While Telfer was setting up my writing table the phone rang. He won't let me answer the phone. He picked it up and said, "Mr. Murray's Residence." It was Kathy. She is miserable in Paris, slowly starving to death because she can't communicate with the people in the markets or anybody else. She is going to join me here.

When Telfer arrives in the morning I ask him how he is today. His answer is always the same. "I never vary," he says. While he is clearing away the dinner things we converse. The previous tenant was Nicholas Monsarrat. Telfer said Mr. Monsarrat, besides having pals in for a poker game every Monday night, wrote a book while he was in residence. When the book was published he gave Telfer a signed copy. After a few days Monsarrat asked Telfer what he thought of it. Telfer said, "It's not you, sir. You just wrote that one for money."

In a day or so Kathy arrived and announced that she would take over the marketing. Telfer said, "No, madam." (Telfer is a short, thin man who got his training in the stewards department of the P & O line. Every morning he puts on his bowler hat, walks to Ebury Street, visits his friends the butcher, the baker, the greengrocer, the fruiterer, the dairyman, and comes back with the day's supplies.) Kathy tried to get Peter to drive her to a market. He was aghast. "It is not done, madam." He managed to convey in that one short sentence that if he drove his lady to a market and was seen following her out carrying the bags the whole fabric of British society would be somehow undermined.

Before giving up, Kathy made one more attempt to assert herself. On the occasion of my birthday on December 6 we gave a dinner party and invited Norman and Betty Luboff and another couple. Kathy gave the menu to Telfer. It was an ordinary, uninspired list and Telfer responded as usual. "No, madam," he said. "I will attend to it." He engaged a lady to do the flowers and a friend of his from the P & O to serve. The friend was, of course, wearing a tailcoat and white tie. All the best silver and linen came out and Telfer prepared a truly memorable meal, emerging from the kitchen afterwards to take his bow. Kathy left the next day.

The studio is giving me 100 pounds a week for expenses. When the first cheque came I wondered how I could get it turned into money. Telfer saw no problem. He put on his bowler hat and took me to his branch of the National Provincial Bank in Ebury Street. Three tellers with handle-bar moustaches stood comfortably in their cages flanked by the polished brass scales used for weighing specie. We passed them and went into the manager's room. Mr. Greenup, a man in his thirties, came from behind his solid oak desk, was delighted to meet me and when Telfer replaced his bowler and we left I was the owner of what Mr. Greenup referred to as an "external account." Each week I visited the bank. Over a cup of tea in Mr. Greenup's office I reported on the progress of the score and answered questions about life in Hollywood.

Monday November 5

I have engaged a small, thin, pale, frail English musician of great talent to orchestrate the music. His name is Wally Stott. [Years later he had a sex change operation and is now Angela Morley, an award winning composer living in Hollywood.]

The telephone rang today. Telfer answered it, asked 'oo was calling, turned to me and said, "It's Mr. Grumble, sir." Turned out to be Mr. de Grunwald, my producer.

Sunday November 18

I have developed a toothache. Telfer is sympathetic and is going to take me to his dentist tomorrow.

Monday November 19

Every few days Wally Stott comes and I turn over whatever sketches I have ready. The picture has to do with four American airline hostesses and the people they fall in love with. One scene takes place in Vienna with the palaces and parks of that beautiful city as a background. It is a long scene and I wrote, naturally, a series of waltzes. Maybe 40 or 50 pages of orchestra score. One day when Wally was visiting I asked him how the waltzes were. He said, "Tedious."

Wednesday November 28

People who hire orchestras in the States are known as contractors. In England they are called "fixers." My fixer is a lovely lady, recommended by Muir Mathieson, named Dusty Rhoades. She has engaged members of the London Symphony orchestra and the brass from Teddy Heath's band. The orchestra assembled today. The only players I know from my previous visit are Gordon and Eddie Walker, flutes, and a viola player whom I know only by his nickname "Flatiron." The orchestra is simply superb. When you write "p" on a part, meaning softly, that's the way they play it. I could go out on a limb and offend some of my colleagues in Los Angeles and say that in general the British players are better trained than ours but I believe it is a fact. It was a lovely experience and the sound on the Elstree stage, once they got it warmed up, was just fine. Everything stops at eleven for tea and at one we all go out for a heavy lunch. There is a feeling of goodwill and the lack of pressure is markedly different from the conditions we work under at home, where the prime concern is to get it done on time. Here there is a feeling of respect for the music and if it takes time to get it right, so be it.

Monday December 3

Recorded the chorus singers. They are good. When I sing a phrase in the American idiom, they sing it back to me with the accent and the loose feel I need, perfectly. Very professional.

Wednesday December 5

There is a heavy fog. Peter picked me up at 7:30 and we proceeded to Elstree at a crawl and arrived in time for the 9:30 recording. Only one member of the orchestra, the harpist, did not make it. We recorded all day, finishing at 5:45.

Friday December 7

After today's session, from two to five, the whole score is now recorded. I had a cup of tea with the gateman. He told me he earns 30 pounds a week. That is exactly what a musician gets for a three-hour session. Last night was the great birthday dinner party and today Kathy has flown home.

Sandy Courage arrived today to work on a picture and is going to stay with me. Telfer is delighted and is going to make Courage a haggis. Sandy had a little trouble getting here because of the weather. Pan Am sets down at Shannon. They decided not to chance flying into England but Air Lingus, the Irish Airline, was flying and Courage got himself on to one of their planes to Heathrow and delightedly reported that his seat-mate was Percy Grainger.

Tuesday December 11

Kathy called and told me she had read in the paper that Carol (my first wife) died. Since I am 52 she would have been 54.

Tonight Gordon and Eddie Walker and Flatiron entertained at the Savage Club. Courage and I went. Big dinner, lots of people, started with all standing up and holding hands and singing some kind of a song. Who said the British are reserved?—holding hands and singing is about as Rotarian as you can get. As a matter of fact Rotary is big in England. Eddie, accompanied by a pianist, played some lovely flute pieces. We are invited by the musicians to come tomorrow night for a farewell drink.

Wednesday December 12

Dubbing during the day. After one reel which was to my ear perfect, Mr. Smith, the gentleman handling the music tracks said, apologetically, he thought he could get a little harp phrase better. A little harp phrase! They did the reel over.

9:45 met our hosts in the Savage bar. A nice fire was going. There is a raised narrow seat curving around the fireplace and on it was seated a roly poly little man with a red face who looked like Mr. Pickwick. From time to time he would fall into the fire and be tenderly lifted out and set back on his perch. A large wing chair in the corner was empty. It was GBS's private chair and no one has sat in it since he died. At 11 o'clock the bartender called time and placed six drinks before us. Sandy was telling of his Irish airline experience. He has bought a Gaelic phrase book. One of the examples in it is, "Your ear trumpet has been struck by lightning," a phrase that could conceivably come in handy some time. At about three we made our tearful farewells to the Walkers and Flatiron and went to the Churchill Club where we made friends with two ladies. Telfer was unfazed in the morning, having undoubtedly served many a breakfast to such unexpected guests and possibly pleased that his boys were being boys.

Thursday December 13

Finished dubbing and ran the whole picture. Everybody, including me, happy.

I have changed my plane reservations and am going home in SS *France*, the 66,000 ton pride of the French Line, introduced into the North Atlantic service only last year. I called Mr. Greenup at the bank and he was quite upset that I would not have time to come in and pay him a final visit before leaving. (Bank of America, are you listening?)

Tonight during dinner we heard treble voices outside the apartment door singing Christmas Carols. Telfer said, ominously, he would take care of them. He opened the door, the singing stopped, he barked, "Little early, aren't you? Where are you from?" A boy said, "St. Stephens in Henley Street." I made him give them half a crown.

Friday December 14

Genuinely sorry to come to the end of this period when I lived like a Lord. After all, I was born in London and if I could have Telfer and Peter and Eaton Square I could live here happily for the rest of my life. I realize that Telfer is the last of his breed and to live this way costs money, but I do love being waited on and having the porter at the street door touch his cap when I come out and Peter holding the limousine door open for me.

Telfer presented me with a walking stick with a little silver band below the handle he had bought in Portobello Street, and when I left to catch the 7:20 at Waterloo I felt we had become friends although, even when I begged him to, he never bridged the gap enough to sit down in my presence.

The *France* departed Southampton 9:30. The Lunts and the Mona Lisa are on board.

Wednesday December 19

Arrived New York 5:30 a.m. Saw *Little Me* in the afternoon and *A Funny Thing Happened on the Way to the Forum* in the evening.

Thursday December 20

Took Deems Taylor to lunch at Pierre's. He is barely able to walk now. Sad. Went to Mitch Miller's rehearsal to see some of my old singers. They have been given a new lease on life by his show "Sing Along With Mitch." Saw Dave and Elaine Terry and Bill and Nell Schneider.

Got a plane home.

Work done this year: 6 GE's, 5 Wagon Trains, 1 Checkmate, 8 Hitchcocks, two pilots, "Little Amy" and "Hercule Poirot."
Movies: *Period of Adjustment,* and *Come Fly With Me.*

1963

Wednesday January 2

Back to the happy grind. Ran Hitchcock "To Catch a Butterfly." Have a luxurious seven days to write it.

Saturday January 12

To the studio to dub "Butterfly." They must be up against an airdate to pay the dubbers double time for Saturday.

Thursday January 17

Ran a nice pilot at Metro about a teacher called "Mr. Novak." E. Jack Neuman, producer, operates out of Irving Thalberg's luxurious quarters. I asked him if sitting at Mr. Thalberg's desk and thinking of all the great pictures that were planned, discussed and fought over in those illustrious surroundings did not produce a sense of historic awe in him. He said, "No. I just think of what those pictures *didn't* cost." The film is not ready but is going to be very good.

Thursday January 24

They are still fiddling with the film but I must start writing if we are to make the recording date next Thursday. Got a pretty good theme and wrote a commercial piece called "Assembly Stomp." Pete Rugolo is orchestrating because of the press of time.

Thursday January 31

Recorded the pilot. Very good. And it sold. That's news.

Sunday February 10

Went to Felix Slatkin's funeral. He was my concertmaster for the last umpteen years, a fabulous player, leader and founder of the Hollywood String Quartet. He will be sorely missed by me and a lot of other people.

Sunday February 17

Dinner for the Wilsons, Mancinis, Alexanders, Rugolos and guest of honor, Frank Cordell, the British composer.

Wednesday February 27

Ran the worst show I have ever seen (at CBS), a pilot with an all star cast that is bound to sink without a trace. "Hotel Paradise." How can they go so wrong? They scrapped it before scoring.

Thursday March 14

Hall Wallis's Paramount film *Wives and Lovers,* says my agent, will have my services as composer. Met with John Rich, director (his first feature). Wallis is in London doing a film.

Wednesday March 20

Start on salary at Paramount. Ran the film with Rich. He said, "I don't want a mickey mouse score." Five minutes later he said, "Every time the maid walks to the door I hear drums." That's mickey mouse, folks.

Thursday March 21

Saw John Hamill, a dear fellow who now runs the music cutting department. Never forget the music cutter is the composer's best friend. Chatting with Maggie Mascell on the phone. Having worked together on a couple of pictures produced by Irving Allen, his name came up. She said, "From Irving, don't tell me," and that pretty well sums up my attitude.

Thursday April 4

Bill Froug has been assigned by E. Jack Neuman to be the line producer on "Mr. Novak." Froug is not my favorite character. He produced a "Suspense" show about the Malibu fire on CBS and hated my music.

Monday April 15

Bill Stinson, now head of music at Paramount, and I go over copious notes received from Mr. Wallis in London about his thoughts on the music for *Wives and Lovers.* It is to have a title song written by Burt Bacharach and Hal David.

Thursday April 18

Bought a lovely little Lancia for Kathy. She didn't like it on account of the stick shift, prefers big American cars, bought herself a Lincoln Continental. So I will drive the Lancia.

Friday May 10

Had a good preview of *Wives and Lovers*.

Wednesday June 12

I have decided to become a promoter of my own music. Assembled a group at United Recorders and made demo records of the Novak theme, "Assembly Stomp" and three numbers from *Wives and Lovers*.

Thursday June 13

Played the Novak material for Hy Kanter of Robbins, Feist and Miller music. Bill Stinson will pass along the *Wives and Lovers* stuff to Paramount's publisher, Famous Music. [In due course all of it was handsomely published in sheet music.]

Sunday June 16

Boarded M/S *Berganger*, a Norwegian freighter, bound for Panama. Returned on M/S *Fernbank*, arriving Los Angeles Friday July 5.

Thursday August 8

Ran a Novak starring Lillian Gish with Froug. When we got around to dubbing it Froug threw out the whole score, replaced it with music from the pilot. I quit and he hired Leith Stevens to do the series. Well, that's show biz.

Thursday August 22

When I told Stanley Wilson of the above debacle he gave me a Hitchcock to do. Ran it today. Called "A Nice Touch."

Friday September 6

Ran a Chrysler Theatre called "The Fifth Passenger." These are nice little movies. It's TV but they manage miracles of production within the time limits.

Tuesday September 24

Recorded the Chrysler. Just had an odd thought. I have been working on and off for Chrysler since 1937 when we did a radio program called "Chrysler Airshow." Only 26 years.

Tuesday October 8

Lou Teicher of CBS is interviewing prospects to succeed Lud Gluskin as head of music at CBS. He was kind enough to ask me if I would be interested. I leveled with him and told him I was a lousy administrator and anyhow much preferred to write and thanked him for the compliment.

Tuesday October 15

I have written a clarinet concerto for Mitchell Lurie and orchestra. Tonight to rehearse with the Whittier Symphony, a community orchestra with some professional ringers judiciously spread about the sections.

Sunday October 20

To Whittier for the concert. Ruth Haroldson, the permanent conductor of the orchestra, turned the baton over to me for my piece. It was a hit. And I must say conducting an orchestra of mostly amateurs who are playing for the love of it differs radically from standing in front of a first-class band of bored professionals. A palpable difference. Kathy made a few wrong turns off the Freeway and missed the piece. At the end of the concert I asked the audience if they'd mind if we played the first movement again for her.

Wednesday October 23

Bill Schmidt, who runs a small publishing firm out of his garage, wants to publish the concerto, now called "Collage for Clarinet." Every time the title has been printed in a newspaper it has been College for Clarinet. He wants me to make the accompaniment for band instead of orchestra.

Monday November 18

Hitchcock, I thank God, goes on. All the titles of the Hitchcock films this month seem to have a special bearing on my life. Recorded one today called "The Dividing Wall," and one on November 20, "Goodbye George."

Friday November 22

My mother's 80th birthday and I will never forget it again, for President Kennedy was assassinated today in Dallas. Spent four incredible days watching television.

Monday December 2

Life goes on. Today we recorded Mr. Hitch's "How to Get Rid of Your Wife." (Hm.)

Friday December 13

Assembled 4 flutes, 4 clarinets, 2 horns, piano and harp and recorded the music for "Three Wives Too Many." Add one to that title and it describes my situation more or less accurately. Still paying alimony to number 2. I am not complaining, one gets used to it. Only wife number 4, who makes out the checks, bitches about it.

Saturday December 14

Tony Collins, the English composer-conductor, died and I attended his funeral today. He was a dear, funny man. I remember his talking about recording a large orchestra at RKO. The mixer stopped a take because a chair on the stage squeaked. Tony said, "How come we can never hear the 3rd bassoon but a chair squeak comes through loud and clear?" In the evening to a party at Bobby Bain's. He's the guitar player and a lovely fellow. It was mostly musicians and wives. Stanley Wilson was, of course, invited. At five a.m. he hadn't arrived and Bobby said, "Stan's late."

Kathy got drunk enough to fall down the steps in front of the house but, like all folks to whom gin is mother's milk, didn't break anything. We had come in two cars and I followed her home. She drove on the left side of the white line all the way except when she was straddling it.

Monday December 23

At nine a.m. we ran a pilot called "90 Bristol Court" with a terrible man named Joe Connolly. Sid Kuller has been engaged to write a lyric for the theme. Because Connolly is such a son of a bitch I am happy to report that the series was not successful.

Friday December 27

Today I drove to El Cajon to attend a Mass for the Veil at which daughter Joyce became a novitiate. She is going to become a nun. A beautiful ceremony.

Work done this year, TV: 3 "Mr. Novaks," 10 Hitchcocks, 1 Kraft Theatre, 1 Chrysler Theatre, 1 Lieutenant and two pilots, "Careful My Love" and "90 Bristol Court."
Movie: *Wives and Lovers*.
"Collage for Clarinet."

1964

January

Lawrence Weingarten has produced a little black-and-white picture at Metro called *Signpost to Murder*, with Joanne Woodward and Stuart Whitman, directed by George Englund. The action takes place in England and has to do with an escaped murderer, Whitman, who holes up in an isolated mill house where Woodward lives. Had a meeting with Lawrence and Englund to discuss the music approach.

Englund wants the film scored by a flute and a lute. After Englund left Weingarten agreed with me that scoring a picture full of dramatic suspense and moments of terror with a flute and a lute would be, to put it politely, inappropriate. I went home and pondered a while and decided to use 4 flutes (doubling on alto and bass flutes), 4 oboes (some doubling on English horns, baritone oboes and an oboe d'amore), 4 horns, 2 trumpets, piano (doubling harpsichord), Jack Cookerly on his magic electronic machinery, 4 percussion, playing—besides the usual—bass marimbas, cannisters and a strange double stringed instrument Maggie Mascell had found in her attic and graciously lent me; Laurindo Almeida playing the lute, tipple and guitars, and a string section of 6 violas, 6 cellos and 3 basses.

Monday January 6

I am on the Board of Governors of the Television Academy and this evening we met at the Los Angeles Country Club where, until recently, actors and Jews were not welcome. I left the meeting early. Walking down a long corridor I saw a woman. I thought to myself, "That's the most beautiful body I have ever seen." As we drew abreast this vision said, "Hello, Lyn." It was Nina, my third wife, married now to an official on the staff of the Club.

Monday February 3

One to six. First recording of *Signpost*. Elegant. As we finished reels they were whisked to the dubbing channel where the mixers were doing something quite unusual; probably because of the pressure of an imminent release date they were dubbing each reel while we recorded the next one. Margaret Booth, a very powerful lady at Metro, was supervising. From time to time Charley Paley, my music cutter, came to the stage to report that Miss Booth was eliminating whole chunks of music.

Tuesday February 4

Nine to five. Resumed the recording. As is my custom I rehearsed the sections separately. When I was rehearsing the woodwinds in the Main Title music, Englund made a suggestion;

he thought it would be interesting if we just used the woodwinds and left the rest of the orchestra out. Since this would have eliminated the main theme I was using throughout the picture I vetoed the suggestion as tactfully as possible. All went well. I am very happy with the sound of this score.

There is a long suspenseful scene in the picture that I had very carefully scored. In the dubbing session I attended the scene played only with the accompaniment of the creaking of the giant water wheel outside the mill house. The camera pans to the wheel revealing a dead body draped on one of the flanges, underscored only by a creak. Everyone, including Mr. Weingarten, agreed it didn't work. Charley Paley, beating me to it, said, "Maybe we ought to try it with the music." Miss Booth said, "I didn't know you had music there." Lawrence said, "Let's try it." They ran it with the music and it made all the difference. It stayed. We went to preview and for once there were no changes.

This score, along with all the others, is in my archive at the University of Wyoming.

Friday February 21

Les Remsen, who runs an outfit called The Los Angeles Brass Society, has asked me to write a piece for them and I told him I would think it over. In the meantime I am finishing a piece for six of the clarinet family (including Eb, bass and contra bass) called "Clarinet Capriole" for Bill Schmitt's Avant Music.

Monday March 23

Collected my unemployment today. Jeff says everybody does it when not working. (It is said that Adolphe Menjou, a notably wealthy actor, was occasionally seen in the unemployment line.) In the evening six clarinet-playing friends came to the house to tape "Clarinet Capriole."

Tuesday March 24

Called Bill Perlberg who, with his partner George Seaton, is making a film I would love to do, but alas they are committed to using Dimitri Tiomkin. Started writing the piece for Les Remsen. It is going to be a big Christmas Oratorio for all his brass, plus harp, organ, percussion and a large chorus; it will be called "The Miracle." Having been paid for writing so-called commercial music for so long, I like to think I am giving something back to music, and getting in a lick for the glory of God at the same time.

Friday April 3

Lunch with Mockridge, Rugolo, Kenton, Johnny Williams and Eddie Powell. To my house after to play tapes of new concrete music.

Sunday April 12

Dan Golenpaul here. He is devoting all his energies these days to producing his "Information Please Almanac."

Wednesday April 15

Norman Lloyd has given me another Hitchcock to do. True to the tradition that has sprung up, of the titles of Hitchcock's shows describing my marital condition, this one is called "Who Needs An Enemy?" We ran it today. Eager to get at it.

Thursday April 16

Wrote for seven hours and produced one minute 53 secs of music. On Friday and Saturday wrote for 13 ¼ hours, resulting in three minutes 33 secs of music.

Thursday April 23

To the Thieves Market, a sort of society rummage sale attended by lawyers, accountants, show biz execs and other assorted crooks. People donate things they don't want, to be sold to people who don't need them. I bought a lovely silver lamp with only a slight dent in it where someone probably threw it at someone.

Friday April 24

Usual colleague lunch, this one at the Kirkeby Center in Westwood, and in the evening to the Redlands University to see a musical production created by Sid Kuller's son Richie. After the performance I was nailed by a music major who wanted to know how to get into the business of writing music scores for films. He knew a lot about the financial side of it; e.g., he knew that Hank Mancini and Andre Previn get $25,000 per picture. He said he didn't want to spend all of his time writing for movies; two a year would be enough. On the $50,000 he could devote the rest of his time to doing what he wanted. I told him he would have to work up to the $25,000, that I only got $10,000 per picture. He was disappointed.

May 13 through May 18

With Sid, writing Donald O'Connor's act for the Sahara, Las Vegas. All the material based on the fact that in 1964 we are celebrating the 400th birthday of William Shakespeare.

Friday May 22

Spent the day sailing in the Catalina Channel aboard the USS *Yorktown*, courtesy of Cy Mockridge, who is a member of the Navy League, watching take-offs and landings, demonstrations of anti-submarine warfare and eating the good navy chow.

Monday May 25 to Sunday May 31

Sid and I exposed Donald O'Connor to what we had wrought for him and as usual he didn't think he could learn it in time.

Sunday June 7

Caught the 12 noon Western shuttle to Vegas for a four p.m. orchestra reading of the arrangements Pete Rugolo had made of the O'Connor material.

Tuesday June 9

Donald's opening at the Sahara. As Sid would say, "Smash."

Wednesday June 10

Daughter Ann wants to spend the summer at Grenoble University. This was discussed and the financial arrangements worked out.

Tuesday June 30

Took part in a recorded tribute to Lud Gluskin who is finally retiring from CBS. Herschel Gilbert organized it with his usual efficiency except for the singing group. It was bad either because a) they were doing it for nothing, or b) they are not as fond of Lud as we are; or both. One exception: Gloria Wood was on the date and she can sing anything you write and then do it an octave higher. The material was rather funny, spotlighting Lud's attitudes to money, musicians, and his wife.

Saturday July 4

Celebrated Independence Day by starting to write a "Virginian" entitled "The Brazos Kid." Reminds me of Jack Elliott complaining to a producer about these schedules and the fact that composers work Saturdays, Sundays and holidays. The producer said, "But, Jack, we're all in the same boat." Jack replied, "Yeah, but on Saturday you are *out* in your boat."

Saturday July 18

This is the day Ann leaves France for home. My Ann is a sweet, lovable girl but she had an adventure in France that I was not mature enough to accept in a civilized manner. She left Grenoble at the end of her session to stay in Paris with the family of a friend she had made at the University. She had an idea she wanted to go to the Sorbonne. Kathy was against it and we fought about it. I prevailed. Some sixth sense only fathers possess must have prompted me to call Helene Constantine to ask her to go to the address on Ann's letters and see what sort of a family she was living with. Helene called me the next day. Ann was living in a small apartment with a boy she had met at Grenoble, and I blew. After a recording session one day I had a drink with Bobby Bain, the guitar player, and unburdened myself to him. He asked me what I was doing at the age of 20 and I said, "That's different. I'm a man." He tried his best to make me see that I was behaving like a father whose daughter has suddenly become a woman, but I was unable to accept it and wrote Ann that if she didn't move to a hotel I would stop sending her money. Kathy was predictably "I told you so" about it. Anyhow that's what I did and Ann is on her way home.

Tuesday July 21

Recorded the music for "Brazos Kid." There was so much music I said to Stanley, "I wish I was getting paid by the pound for this score."

Friday July 24

To see Corwin's "Overkill and Megalove." He is a master of language and sets his ideas to such ringing cadences one would hardly blame other less gifted writers, on hearing the clang of his words spoken in a theatre, or reading them, if they contemplated cutting their throats.

On another subject, I got to a spot in "The Miracle" where I wanted to depart from the Bible as text and asked Norman to supply a poem I could set after Mary has given birth to the baby Jesus. He sent me a couple of stanzas called "Sleep Now On Thy Natal Day" and a note saying they were probably on a par with something a Hallmark writer would turn out on an off day. They were quite beautiful and, considering Norman is not exactly a WASP, certainly qualify as a tribute to his versatility.

Wednesday July 29

To dinner at Albert Rosenberg's. He's an executive at the May Company. Paula Kelly and Hal of the Modernaires there and we made some nice music. I also renewed my acquaintance with Walter Woolf King with whom I worked on "The Flying Red Horse

Tavern," a radio show we did in the mid-thirties. Bea Lillie was his co-star, Lennie Hayton the conductor, and I had a 16-voice male chorus on the show. One week Miss Lillie was appearing in Washington and the engineering geniuses at CBS hooked up a line between New York and Washington and "piped her in." We had programmed a duet between Walter and Lady Lillie. Walter listened to her on earphones and, being strictly a theatre performer used to having the leading lady within arms length, or at least in sight, couldn't get the hang of this modern miracle of radio communication. Hearing her disembodied voice over an apparatus completely threw him. I sang his part so I can claim, with truth, that I once sang a duet with the great Lady Peel.

Tuesday August 18

Mitch Miller is here with his TV show "Sing Along With Mitch" for a concert in the Hollywood Bowl. Tonight a big party for approximately 15 inmates of Miller's touring cornbin who served time in the Lyn Murray Singers and the Hit Paraders in the dear dead days. They were greeted by a dozen local survivors of the same servitude—the ones still ambulatory. Andy Love pushed Hubie Hendrie into the pool. (Hubie was the baritone in my quartet "The Four Clubmen" at CBS New York in the thirties. We did a show every Thursday morning and Hubie always sang flat; not at other times, only on Thursday mornings. Attempting to get to the bottom of the problem I discovered that Wednesday night was his night with his wife, Dorothy. I got him to change the night and from then on he sang in tune.)

Tuesday September 15

In the evening at the Alexanders, who are celebrating an anniversary, Jeff made me a martini. As he handed it to me he said, "This is the best martini you will ever taste." It tasted awful and I said so. Turns out he thinks putting onion juice in martinis gives them a certain *je ne sais quoi*. He's right.

Sunday October 4

Ran out to Pasadena for a get-together with Warren Marsh who is going to conduct "The Miracle." Had a session with Norberto

Guinaldo going over the organ part.

Monday October 5

Wrote a cue for Hugo Friedhofer who is in trouble doing a score for Glug Glug, otherwise known as "Voyage to the Bottom of the Sea." Visited with Lionel Newman at Fox trying to pry a little work out of him.

Thursday October 8

First rehearsal of "The Miracle" with the combined choirs at the Oneonta church; they seem rather excited at being in on the birth of a new piece.

Friday October 9

Herschel Gilbert is the new head of music at CBS and has invited me to do a score for something called "Gilligan's Island." We ran it today and in my opinion it is a ridiculous idiotic little sitcom. [It became one of the greatest international hit television series in history and undoubtedly made its producers and the actors rich beyond dreams.]

Monday October 12

Went to rehearse Lester Remsen's enlarged brass society in "The Miracle" at Sepulveda Junior High. After the rehearsal one of Lester's young trumpet players, tired of playing 12-tone music, Ives, and other non-consonant composers, came up to me and said, "It's nice to play some commercial music for a change."

George Cates called and wants an arrangement of "Cry Me a River" for a Lawrence Welk album.

Friday October 16

Went to Goldwyn to record the music for the episode of "Gilligan's Island." Herschel Gilbert was in the booth and, as is usual at Goldwyn, the sound was just lovely.

Monday October 19

Recorded the arrangement of "Cry Me a River." On these double sessions (six hours) Lawrence records twelve numbers, each number is allowed 25 minutes and no nonsense about it. This is because a recording hour is 50 minutes. The musicians rest for ten each hour. Lawrence doesn't conduct these albums. As George Cates said, "He's in the control room counting his money." Rather unfair, but Lawrence *is* a rich musician. [Today he owns half of Santa Monica.]

Friday October 23

All this week I have been seeing Dr. Hare. I have a return bout with the iritis.

We ran a "Kraft Suspense Theatre" two-parter called "In Darkness Waiting" at Revue this morning. I had seen Dr. Hare at 7:45 a.m. and through my dilated eyes I couldn't tell whether the show was any good or not.

Saturday October 31

Dr. Hare, after 10 visits, seems to have the iritis under control. Incidentally, Kathy goes to Dr. Hare. She thinks he has a crush on her. She mentioned this to the doctor's receptionist who said, "Don't be silly. Every time he gazes into your eyes he sees $15."

Saturday November 28

In the evening to Liz and Paul Hanson's house in Pasadena for cocktails. Friends of Kathy's. He is a doctor, she was a *Vogue* model thirty some years ago and still is a most handsome woman though thickened a bit since she was one of *Vogue's* willowy beauties. Roaring party, lots of doctors and wives. I played the piano and had no trouble with the repertoire; the newest number they requested was "Is It True What They Say About Dixie?" One of the doctors expressed his philosophy of medicine to me by equating the practice of medicine with the automobile business. He said, "If you can afford a Cadillac you buy one. If you can't you get a Chevrolet. Same way with medicine." I said, "Suppose you can't afford even a Chevrolet?" He said, "Then you don't get one." I said, "Then, if you have no money ... " He said, "You go to the General Hospital."

Liz Hanson walked us to our car. Kathy went on ahead. She always insists on driving, drunk or sober. Unmistakably I was attracted to Liz and I knew she was to me. I had my arm round her waist as we walked but she said, sotto voce, "No further as long as you're married to Kathy."

Sunday December 6

Combination marital and birthday note: There are two words scrawled on my calendar. HA! HA! What's wrong with arriving at your 55th year if you're working and you feel good?

Sunday December 13

Tonight was the performance of "The Miracle" at the Oneonta Church in Pasadena. I hired a bus and invited 20 friends to come. Kathy was against it but when I insisted that it would be fun I must say she rallied round and bought a few cases of booze for us to drink on the bus to ward off chills and to see that we arrived at the church in a proper frame of mind to enjoy the work. The driver of the bus wore a large cowboy hat and got into the spirit of the thing but didn't know the way to Pasadena. We got lost and were half an hour late. They had roped off a couple of rows down front for us and we got a lot of dirty looks from the faithful as we poured down the aisle and took our places. The piece went extraordinarily well. I took a bow, thanked Warren Marsh, blew kisses to the choir and tripped over the microphone cables going back to my seat. We got back in the bus—it's a little like playing one nighters—they toasted me and I toasted them for coming and we all concluded that this was the right and proper way to launch a piece to the glory of God.

Monday December 14

NBC has been talked into broadcasting the work as part of their celebration of the Yuletide season and we assembled at Burbank today and videotaped it. The performance was better than the one in the church except that during my introductory remarks my nose started to itch and I scratched it.

Thursday December 17

The Screen Composers Association gave a cocktail party at the Music Center for John Addison, the English composer, who has decided to become a Hollywood composer in order to escape those narsty British taxes.

Sunday December 20

"The Miracle" was broadcast on NBC from 1 to 1:30. Andre Previn called after and said he liked it.

In the evening to Leo and Ingrid Pollakoff's annual Christmas party, attended, except for me, exclusively by May Company employees. I had a good time because I sat with the wives having laughs while the men talked about what a mistake the purple blouses were, and why the sales of reinforced bras are not holding up.

Work done this year: 5 Hitchcocks, 1 Chrysler Theatre, 2 Kraft Suspense Theatres, 1 Virginian, 1 Gilligan's Island, and an Alan King pilot.

"The Miracle," "When I Survey The Wond'rous Cross."

1965

Tuesday January 12

Ice Capades has commissioned Sid Kuller and me to do an original score for an "Alice in Wonderland" section of the show. Ought to be fun.

Saturday to Monday January 16-18

Working with Sid. Got the titles of all the songs and made a start. The songs: "Whimsy Wonderland," "Tea Cup Train," "Mad Hatter's Party," "Snickersnack," "Jabberwock," "Pepper Pot Soup," "That Sounds Logical To Me," "Wonderland" and "Deal Off!" Lawrence Welk is going to let us use practically his whole cast of soloists for the taping. They'll be ideal.

Monday February 1

In the evening with Eddie Powell to Stan Kenton's First Neophonic concert at the Chandler Pavilion.

Thursday February 4

Kenton called and invited me to write a piece for his next Neophonic concert March 29. Accepted with pleasure and thought, "My God, I'm writing for Lawrence Welk and Stan Kenton and I wouldn't dare tell either one of them."

Sunday March 28

The Kenton rehearsal. He lets the composers run their pieces through with the band then takes over. The rehearsal starts at ten a.m. and goes to five p.m. I had them from four to five. Everybody, including me, writes the brass too high for this band and by the time I got them they couldn't blow a note. It was, as Milton Bernhardt the trombone player always says, "a bloodbath."

Monday March 29

The concert. My piece seemed to be well received although my stomach filled with blood when the brass got a bar and a half out for a couple of phrases; but nobody noticed. Shelley Manne was a tower of power and held everything together with his usual unflappable virtuosity.

Monday April 5

Morty Stevens is now head of music at CBS and today I recorded a "Rawhide" for him on the marvelous old Republic stage. It is interesting to remember that this is the stage Werner Janssen used when he recorded his album of excerpts from *Wozzeck* thirty years ago.

Tuesday April 6

Dick Walton, the Reno artist, here to dinner with a new wife and a car full of new paintings. He is a very articulate man and talks about his technique and the phases he is going through in a most interesting way. As usual I bought two. One was a Western subject and I gave it to Ollie Carey because she is a Western woman if ever there was one.

The big news this month is that Lucy Herrmann has left Benny. Surprised she stuck it so long.

Big news for me this month is that Leeds Music, a subsidiary of MCA, has accepted "The Miracle" for publication.

Saturday May 1

Poured Kath on the plane for New York. She is afraid of flying. Eight hours before embarkation she starts a course of phenobarbital and gin. It has got to the point where I balk at taking her to an airport alone. Sid came with us and lightened it up, his wit and upbeat chatter seem to take Kath's mind off her coming ordeal. Aside: Whenever Kath and I go to a movie there are three arguments—who's going to drive, which way to get to the theatre, and where we're going to sit.

Wrote an overture for the annual Share Boom Town party the movie ladies put on. It was called "Show Stoppers." The arrangers contribute their services and get two free tickets. I took Kath's friend Jeanne Rains. All the stars turn out and everybody wears Western costumes. I loathe this requirement. In a Western costume I look like a CPA.

Tom Poston borrowed a nickel off me to make a phone call.

Tuesday May 18

To United Recorders where we made an album of the "Alice in Wonderland" score with the singers Mr. Welk lent us, including Kathy Lennon, and which George Cates masterfully produced. They are going to sell the album in the Arenas.

Wednesday May 26

Jack and Patsy Melchior arrived to spend a few days. Love them. They perform the same function Sid does going to the airport. They lighten things up around the house and the bickering is muted while they are in residence. One night Jack, Patsy and I took a stroll along the Strip and stopped to look at the pictures in the lobby of a porno movie theatre. Patsy, staring at a big blowup of a frontal female aperture, said, "My God! Do they *all* look like that? I thought it was just me."

Sunday July 4

Big swinging July 4th party at Sunset Plaza. Hot dogs and ice cream cones. A rattlesnake attended. We called the fire department who sent two men to sever its head with a spade and cart it off.

Tuesday July 13

I am doing the John Forsythe show. Recorded the first one today. Bad. Mikes going out, equipment falling apart. They've got to do something about this stage.

Friday July 16

To Catalina for the weekend with Alonzo and Lee Cass. I was tired and while they went for a walk I took a nap. When they returned Kathy announced she had bought a house. They took me to see it. A nice little typical Avalon abode at 219 Clarissa Street. It is to cost $21,500. I raised no objections, having gradually come round to the opinion that one can't go wrong buying real estate in California.

Saturday July 31

The annual musicians' Christmas party. In July, you say? It is such a success at Christmas we have decided to do it twice a year. This one was held at the house of Dick Nash, the trombone player. The cast at these parties is composed of playing musicians so, being what is known as a "leader," I consider myself lucky to be invited. Stanley Wilson is always there and though he started as a trumpet player and is their boss he is there because they love him. These parties always start with Johnny Williams playing the piano and the celebrants singing Alfred S. Burt's lovely Christmas carols and once they are out of the way Jack Marshall and Bobby Bain, guitars, Jack Sheldon, trumpet, Shelley Manne, drums, sometimes Dick on his trombone and whoever else feels like playing, turn it into a jam session. As the evening wears on Sheldon and Marshall do their hilarious routines. Nash turns his tape recorder on and I have copies of the tapes to prove that the use of the word hilarious is an understatement. Everyone knows musicians are a funny breed and we non-blowers laugh ourselves silly at these parties and feel guilty if we have to sneak out at five a.m. because maybe Sunday we have to write something they are going to play on Monday.

Wednesday September 8

Stanley Rubin has made a picture in London called *Promise Her Anything* scored by John Barry. Barry is very good but everyone loses one now and then and the powers didn't like this score and have asked me to replace it. On Thursday and Friday we broke down the picture (I never heard Barry's score) with Bill Stinson, head of Paramount's music department and a gentleman, John Hamell, head of the music cutting department, also a gentleman; George Brand, the cutter assigned to the picture, is a dear man who brings his dog to work with him. Rubin treats his composers (except Barry in this case) with respect. We are going to record in London in a perilously short time.

Wednesday September 22

Started writing *Promise Her Anything*. Incidentally Leslie Caron and Warren Beatty, who are currently raising the temperature of London several degrees, are in it.

Monday October 4

I have hired Johnny Keating, a Scotsman who used to play trombone with Ted Heath, to orchestrate the score. Fortunately he is living in Hollywood at the moment and is free. He is a certified character. The first time I went to meet him—with a bunch of sketches under my arm—no one answered my pounding on the door of his apartment on Franklin. I hunted up the manager, explained my problem and she reluctantly let me into the apartment. I was just going to drop the sketches and leave but I was transfixed by the sight of a broken raw egg in its shattered shell on the coffee table. A hungover figure in pajamas appeared in the bedroom door. I said, pointing to the egg, "What's that?" Keating said, "Oh, that. Someone said it's no possible to break an egg in your hand if you squeeze it from its ends. It's not true."

Thursday October 21

Shipped a lot of scores to Doug Matten, the copyist, in London.

Monday October 25

Keating and I to the airport. When we got there he had forgotten his passport and had to go back and get it. They held the plane a bit—he's a charmer.

Tuesday October 26

At seven p.m. to the London studios of Decca where Tom Jones was recording Burt Bacharach's and Hal David's title tune. Bacharach was producing. At 11 o'clock he fired the guitar player. At 12 another one came in, a long-haired practitioner, and Bacharach

said, "I like it better already." I left at 1:30 a.m. in need of sleep. I
heard that Bacharach was satisfied by 4:30.

Friday October 29

Yesterday and today recording at CTS. An embarrassing episode
with the bass player. I had asked the fixer to get me a jazz bassist,
able to ad lib if needed. One of the cues had a bass solo on a blues
pattern. When we got to it the bass player stopped. I asked, "Why
did you stop?" He said, "Well, nobody else was playing." The poor
man was a pit musician and had never had a solo. He had to be
replaced.

In the evening Rubin and I to the Georgian Pussy club where we
ate a foul dinner, watched a worse show M.C.'d by a patent leather
haired shrimp with a hairline moustache, and fought off the $100
hookers.

Saturday October 30

To the greyhound races (a cruel sport much favored in England)
with Johnny and his lady friend, harpist Trephina Partridge, and
Stanley Rubin. My date was a beautiful girl named Maggie Wright
who belongs to Sam Spiegel. We went to Keating's apartment after
the races. Miss Wright wore a red jockey cap, white boots, a tweed
mini skirt with a white blouse attached—stained at the cuffs and
lipstick on the collar—and had a run in her stocking. In the
beginning she was quiet, almost introverted but after a few drinks
she became bright, loquacious and funny. At the hotel later Stan
was tired and wanted to retire. Maggie begged me to stay up and
drink with her awhile. She told me a lot about herself. She is
illegitimate, her mother died when she was fifteen, she was
brought up by two younger brothers. She is profane. Every other
word is bollocks, bullshit or fuck-all. Her term for sex is the
English one, "Having it off." She has been in a mental hospital.
One time, when her mother was visiting her, she put a knitting
needle in her mouth and threatened to ram it down her throat if
her mother didn't get her out of there. A month later her mother
died of a heart attack. When she asked the doctor if her behavior

might have been responsible for the attack, or perhaps hastened it, the doctor said it was possible. Much sobbing at this point and requests for another drink. She sleeps mostly with producers for the obvious reason—a part in their pictures. She is used by an Arabian prince as hostess at his parties but when Spiegel is in town she breaks all dates when he calls.

At one point Rubin appeared in the bedroom door and said to her, "I heard you also had an affair with so and so." (No one I knew.) She denied it heatedly then said, "Well, I won't put any bullshit on it, Stan. We did go to bed, but we were both too pissed to do anything about it."

Sunday October 31

Got up and went in the rain to St. Clement Danes for the morning service. Managed to squeeze in an evening with old friend Eddie Walker, the flute player, who was on all the dates. His father Gordon, the senior flute in the family, has retired from playing to manage the London Sinfonia, but Eddie's son occupied the second flute chair.

Wednesday November 3

A final session at 9:30 a.m. and we finished it. The pressure to finish this picture is so great we have to dub it at Shepperton from 6 p.m. to 3:15 a.m., the only time the dubbing channel is available.

Saturday November 6

Moved from the Carlton Tower, where it is too noisy to sleep in the daytime, to the Mayfair.

I did not enjoy this experience as much as I did doing "Come Fly With Me." I missed Telfer and the gracious atmosphere he created. This one was done too fast and under too much pressure. In a way, England depresses me, too. I don't know why. It has beauty and grandeur as well as ugliness. I was born in London and yet feel alien. Maybe my undereducated, medium mind will dredge up an answer some day.

Wednesday November 10

Leave London airport 12:37. 1:37 Passing the Outer Hebrides. (Here comes the navigator in me.) 3:10 Passing Iceland. 3:50 Passing Greenland. 9:17 Calgary, Ontario. Arrive San Francisco, short of fuel, 3:15 p.m.

Thursday November 18

Lulu given by the San Francisco Opera. Loved it. Remarkable writing.

Thursday December 16

Previewed *Promise Her Anything* at the Encino Theatre. Smashing.

Saturday December 25

NBC ran the tape of "The Miracle" again.

Tuesday December 28

In the last month I was fortunate enough to be chosen to provide the music for two pilots. At 55 I'm glad I've still got them fooled. Ran another pilot today with a strange title: "Noway Thataway" featuring two odd English clowns, Chad and Jeremy.

Work done this year, TV: 9 Forsythes, 1 "Rawhide," 1 "Gunsmoke," and five pilots.
Movie: *Promise Her Anything.*
"Alice in Wonderland," "Incident at State Beach."

1966

January

Dave Kapp, head of Decca Records, wants to make an album of the music from *Promise Her Anything*, in England. I can't go. Johnny Keating is going to do it for me.

Jeff is over at Metro where they make the "Dr. Kildare" series. They have made a story that takes four hours to tell and he needs help. We looked at the first two hours, wrote some themes and figured out a practical way to split the chore. A lot of telephoning to make sure the key I was writing in would segue to whatever he was going to follow it with and vice versa. It is like the early days of pictures when they would hand half a dozen composers a reel or two each and they would hemstitch a score together.

Thursday January 27

Recorded the first two hours and I will never forget it. The call was for seven p.m. I was driving down Motor Avenue at about 6:15 and ran over a little dachshund. I picked it up, took it into a candy store and asked the proprietor if he knew to whom it belonged. I explained my problem and said I would come back after the recording to see what I could do.

The Kildares are easy—they don't like anything later than Tschaikovsky.

After the recording I went to the candy store and was directed to a small apartment in a side street. A woman answered the door and said the dog, a pet of her 12-year-old daughter's, had died. I said I would get the child another dachshund. The woman's husband thanked me but vetoed the suggestion. "We've had three dogs killed on Motor Avenue," he said, "and I don't want to go through it again." I gave them my number and said if they changed their minds to call me. Later that night the woman called and told me her daughter was taking the loss very badly and if I really wanted to get another dog she would get round her husband's objection. Next day I drove to a kennel in Eagle Rock, bought a dachshund puppy and delivered it.

February

Johnny Keating, the arranger who is going to pop over to England to do the *Promise Her Anything* album, is in Hollywood trying to break into the movies. He is here with his mother and his harpist lady friend, Trephina Partridge. Trephina called and invited us to a surprise birthday party for Johnny. We arrived, as bidden, at seven p.m. It was a surprise all right. Johnny was asleep on the couch in the living room in his underwear. When Kathy asked for a gin martini Johnny got dressed and went out and bought a tenth. (He is a Scotsman, remember.) Guests—smart guests who had obviously had their dinners—began to arrive at about 8:30. Kathy had knocked back the tenth and went into the kitchen to see what food was being prepared. Johnny's mama had a plum duff cooking on the stove, "Johnny's favorite," she said, and that was it. We went to Bob's for a hamburger.

March

This is my Fox month. Love working here. Got my old bungalow back with the dartboard and the refrigerator. Happily churned out a "Jesse James" and was assigned to write a score for the last of a failed series called "Long, Hot Summer." This is an interesting show, produced by Frank Glicksman, who said he has hated all his music, directed by a young new hot-shot named Mark Rydell. Story of a modern composer holed up on a yacht at Cannes writing an avant garde piano concerto. Lionel Newman and I decided it would be silly for me to write such a piece since Leonard Rosenman is working on the lot. Rosenman can sit at a piano and ad lib stuff like this by the yard and that's what we had him do. I wrote the rest of the material, conventional scoring for a Cannes soap opera. The producer loved it and wrote me a letter.

April

I am scoring a two-part "Daniel Boone."
All studios have big, efficient police departments responsible for

the security of all the expensive equipment lying around. (Once at Metro two men in a truck drove on the lot, waved at the cop on the gate, backed up to the scoring stage, loaded a 9-foot concert grand and got a wave from the cop as they drove out the gate. Well, I guess the insurance covered it.) The point of this is the tape recorder in my bungalow picks up the police department short wave. "Car eight-oh to stage 12 to quell a disturbance," etc. Didn't hamper the composition of the "Boone" score. May have helped.

Ice Capades has been sold to Metromedia and things is going to be different this year. Had lunch with Phil Wyllie and a man named Jim Harbert who is going to do what he calls "A & R" our recording. (A & R stands for Artists & Repertoire and has come to mean "producer.") He gave me strict instructions to write everything in unison or thirds. I said, "That apply to the operas, too?" The new conductor Chuck Schneider there. Didn't say much. Harbert and his ego are in charge.

Wednesday April 20

Big day. Met Jack Webb and ran a World Premiere movie (that's what Universal calls its Movies of the Week) with him and Stan Wilson. It's called "Dragnet 66." More running on the 22nd. Like Webb enormously. Tonight to a Screen Composers Association dinner at the Friars Club. Johnny Mercer did his act. Astonishing the good songs he has written and more astonishing how modest he is.

May

Writing the "Dragnet." Wrote and recorded a commercial for Saul Bass for Rainier beer. Bass is a picky prickly perfectionist. Jeff Alexander is his favorite composer and does most of his work. I guess he was busy. I wish he hadn't been.

Thursday, Friday May 26 & 27

Recorded the "Dragnet" film. Webb was there through the whole thing. He's very perceptive about music and appreciative. I mark this as a good experience with a producing chap. A big booze session in his bungalow after with some of the musicians and Ray

Heindorf, a bosom pal of Webb's, visiting. To dinner, then to Webb's house. He has a great room with a bar across one end and a bank of 36 speakers across the other end. The bar registers 8.6 on the Richter scale when music is playing. There is a sign over the toilet saying "Fuck Communism." Heindorf says it's all right visiting Webb's house but he closes the bar at seven a.m. sharp. We wound up watching an old Fred Allen movie on Channel 11 at six a.m. Webb, once married to Julie London, goes with a delightful girl named Luana Patton who passes out promptly at three a.m.

Thursday, Friday June 16 & 17

Recorded Ice Capades. No fun. Normally I work the chorus up into a high tension sweat and you can believe me when I say it takes energy. When I've got them at the peak I signal the mixer to turn the machines and we get it while it's hot. I just call, "Turn it," and we're off. This time, after the first take, there was a long silence from the booth. They were having a discussion. All the energy ebbed out of us. Then came a few pronunciamentos. It was just Harbert establishing who had the upper hand. I complained. He said through the talkback that *he* was "A & R'ing" the session. I took him to one side and told him he wasn't A & R'ing a record session, he was recording a theatrical performance and that when I was ready that's when he would record. They would have plenty of time to set their balances while I was rehearsing, which we did on mike. I explained my theory of energy and excitement and that you can't get it through discussion. Harbert wrote a great deal of the material and it was bad Latin Quarter. I finished the sessions and when I left I knew it was goodbye.

Tuesday June 28

Went to see *My Fair Lady* and *The Loved One* at a miserable little movie house on Sunset Boulevard. The projectionist missed every changeover by three feet and did not have the right channel on until halfway through the picture. For the first six reels I thought Andre (Previn) had lost his touch but when the projectionist woke up it didn't sound so bad, even in that rotten little theatre. Enjoyed the picture and make obeisances to Rex Harrison.

Promise Her Anything has laid the biggest bomb in history. Nobody went to see it. It sneaked in and out of town as though Paramount/ Seven Arts were intent on hiding it. I guess what I like is not what the audience likes. One of the reviews of the album said, "Lyn Murray wrote the music, Johnny Keating performed it and it sounded like neither of them had anything to do with it."

Wednesday June 29

Had lunch today at Fox where I am going to work this season. Lionel Newman, Sandy Courage, Lenny Hayton and Arthur Morton. Lionel and Sandy had just returned from London where they had recorded some tunes for *Dr. Dolittle*, a film with Rex Harrison, Hugh Griffith and Anthony Newley. After the recording Griffith was banished to Wales to dry out before the shooting.

Newley lives at the Grosvenor, a staid hotel patronized by American tourists. He invited Lionel and Sandy to a party. They went. Steve, Newley's procurer-gofer, wearing only jockey shorts, let them in, conducted Lionel to a door and threw it open. To an unsurprised red-haired woman sitting on the john he said, "Daphne, the next time you go, let Mr. Newman hear you pee." (This is going to be a Hollywood on the Thames story but in truth I have never heard of a party in Hollywood quite like this one.) The living room was lit by three candles. Three 19-year-old girls wearing short skirts and funny stockings were talking to four men. Steve, the gofer, picked up the phone and while he was placing a call to Prime Minister Wilson one of the girls lowered his jockey shorts, roused him and gave him some attentions I don't suppose I have to describe further. A waiter in tails passed hors d'oeuvres. A naked man and a naked woman entered the room as another waiter arrived bearing steaks. The naked pair stood close and disguised themselves by putting a lampshade on their heads. Lionel, who is as bawdy and earthy as the next fellow, said he suddenly felt sick and he and Sandy left.

Kurt Frings is a Hollywood agent. Leonard Rosenman is a composer based in Hollywood. When Rosenman signed up with Frings, he asked to see him. Frings was too busy for a week or two so, as this tale begins, Rosenman has an agent but has not yet met him. An actress Rosenman knew invited him to a cocktail party at her house at the top of Laurel Canyon. He arrived at six, got squiffed and at eight everyone had gone save him. The lady had a dinner date and asked him to leave. He said, "I am too drunk to drive." She said, "Take a swim and sober up." He said, "I have no swimming suit." She said, "I won't watch." He went in and soon the girl appeared, starkers, and joined him. He thought that a good omen. She got out of the pool saying she had to go to her dinner engagement, gave him a key and told him to come back at twelve. Rosenman went home, did a little work, went back to the lady's house to find it dark. He let himself in, made himself a drink, played the piano for awhile and at three went to sleep in the lady's bed. At seven a man forced his way through the french windows. Lenny pulled the covers up. The man said, "Where is she?" poking in the closets and looking in the bathroom. Lennie said, "Aren't you Kurt Frings?" The man said, "Yes." Lennie introduced himself. Frings said, "You wanted to see me?"

Saturday July 9

To Stanley Wilson's for late dinner after visiting Sid Kuller in Valley Doctors Hospital where he is recuperating from a mild coronary. The occasion at Stanley's was a reception for Stella Adler who was recently married to Mitchell Wilson, Stanley's writer brother. A man was sitting by himself amid the swirl of actors and musicians. I did not catch his name and in a short while he left, probably angry at being ignored. I found out later it was the playwright William Inge. The usual Revue stable of composers and musicians present; Barbara and Johnny Williams, Judy and Bobby Bain, Eve and Jack Marshall, Howard Roberts (that's three guitar players in a row) and Stan Levy (he's a drummer.) Others were Sam Jaffe and wife, Norman Lloyd and his Peg, and writer Arthur Ross and frau. Stella is very grand and very well preserved.

Sunday July 10

To a brunch at Marlon Brando's house on Mulholland where Mitch and Stella are staying. Approximately the same cast as last night. Brando's garage houses four motorcycles and his bedroom is lined with conga and bongo drums. The house was built by Bob Balzer, the high-class grocer, and is sort of Japanese. It sits on the ridge between the Valley and the coast side with spectacular views of both.

Friday July 15

I am to do the music for an excellent "Chrysler Theatre" produced by Stanley Chase, directed by Joe Sergeant. Has to do with a private eye who gets involved with some visitors from the year 2372. I am planning to use some of Paul Beaver's stuff. (Beaver is a local pioneer in electronics.) He has an oscillator and a modified novachord. There is a knob on the novachord enabling him to slide up or down a minor third from every note. Could be valuable.

Lionel Newman told me a story you might label "Vicissitudes of Working in the Movies." The other morning during the regular production meeting at Fox there was a telephone call from the ranch where the animals for *Dr. Doolittle* are kept. The giraffe was passing blood in his urine. A vet was dispatched and reported nothing serious. The giraffe had awakened with an erection and stepped on it.

Dream. (Probably triggered by seeing the sci-fi Chrysler film and hearing about the amorous giraffe.) I am working at Paramount. Walking down the street at the end of the day Bing Crosby's secretary gives me the eye. She says, "We can go to my boss's office." The office is beautifully furnished, has a dropped ceiling and a bar. As we open the door we hear Bing's voice coming through a speaker. "Hi, Lyn. How's Sid? Heard he's laid up. Give him my best. Now here is a thing you arranged for me years ago. Thought you might like to hear it." Music plays. The girl tells me everytime Bing is photographed with someone an attachment on the camera feeds a profile of the subject's bone structure, facial characteristics and voice quality into a computer. When a person passes a photoelectric cell a tape addresses him appropriately from a memory bank of Bing's words put together instantly by the computer.

Tuesday July 19

Saw the UCLA Theatre Group's production of the Hellman-Bernstein *Candide*, directed by Gordon Davidson. Admirable work. Carroll O'Connor playing a couple of parts and Alan Gilbert, my chorus captain in *Finian's Rainbow,* is playing three.

When *Finian's* opened in Philadelphia I went down for a day or two. Gilbert met me at the train. When I asked him to report he said half my chorus has contracted a disease brought on by sexual contact. The chorus was half black and half white and the infection had spirocheted back and forth across the color line. According to Gilbert it was nothing to concern myself with because Mike Ellis, one of the stage managers, has a doctor uncle in Philadelphia who has the situation in hand.

August

At Fox I have been assigned to write some music for the television series "Time Tunnel," produced by Irwin Allen. That's not *Irving* Allen. In a meeting with Irwin Allen he instructed me to avoid the use of discords. I wrote and recorded the first episode and was at work on the second when the phone rang. It was Irwin Allen. He said, "We have just finished dubbing reel one. I *like it.*" Before I could breathe easily he added, "But that's not to say I am going to like reel two."

I wrote and recorded the second episode and started the third. Mr. Allen called me to his office and warned me I was getting too "discordant." Furthermore I was using too much percussion for his taste. For the guidance of future composers I will give an example of what not to say to producers in this kind of discussion. I said, quite seriously, "'Time Tunnel' appeals to a young audience and I think they will accept more adventurous music than you are limiting me to." He got mad. After finishing the third episode I was fired.

Wednesday September 7

Anita Nye, Louie's wife, has been deaf all her life. A so-called window operation has restored her hearing and tonight it was proved in spades. After dinner we went to Bonesville to hear Don Ellis's big band. Lots of brass and percussion. At the first blast Anita ran out into the street in pain. We stayed for a set and then, feeling guilty, joined her and left.

Tuesday November 8

Met with Jack Webb, Stanley Wilson, Harry Garfield and Bob Cinader on next season's "Dragnet." I am to do the music for the whole series.

Work done. TV: "Dragnet 66," 1 Forsythe, 1 "Laredo," "Mister Terrific" pilot, 1 Chrysler, 4 "Dr. Kildares," 1 "Jesse James," 1 "Long Hot Summer," 2 "Daniel Boones," 4 "Time Tunnels," 1 "Rounders." "In the Cross of Christ I Glory" sacred piece, "Canon à Go Go" piece for 4 clarinets. SATB version of "Sleep Now on thy Natal Day" published separately from "The Miracle."

1967

Work done this year: 24 "Dragnets." 1 Danny Thomas.
Movies: *The Smugglers, Now You See It, Now You Don't, Rosie!*

Donald O'Connor played the Greek Theatre using the Shakespeare material we wrote for him.

The 24 "Dragnets" kept me mighty busy, so busy I did not do the writing at home. Harry Garfield gave me Jack Benny's dressing room to work in. There was a small quid pro quo involved. Because from a distance I bear a resemblance to Mr. Benny, when the tour buses went by, I was expected to stand in the door and wave to the gawkers. Attended the booze sessions in Webb's bungalow every night. Webb is the compleat picture maker. He has a cutting room at his house furnished with a movieola so he can take reels home with him and recut them. Lots of times I would drive out there and pry a reel out of him when the time was growing short.

The Smugglers was a nice little movie produced and directed by Norman Lloyd starring Shirley Booth whom I hadn't seen since George Kaufman's fiasco *Hollywood Pinafore*. Had a bit of fun using

Rossini for police chases through the Dolomites, and a lot of fun writing a sort-of pop love theme, and assorted skulduggery music. We had a cymbalom and a zither in the orchestra. The cymbalom player was a tower of strength, the zither player couldn't tell a whole note from a meatball.

Now You See It was a different story. Harry Garfield, the executive in charge of seeing that music gets written on time and for as little money as possible, said that because of an imminent airdate the score had to be finished and recorded in three weeks. Sidney Fine, Van Cleave and a couple of other orchestrators and I burnt a lot of midnight oil and got it done somehow. Awful. Then they didn't release it for 18 months. Jonathan Winters was in it and his antics made it a pleasure to run back and forth through the movieola.

(Just to show that you never can tell, I had a letter from Henry Howard, a retired CBS exec, saying, "I have just heard for the second time your beautiful score for *Now You See It, Now You Don't*. The theme was especially lovely—even the 'button-ups' before the commercials were works of art. I really enjoyed it, etc.")

Rosie the film has an interesting history. It was based on a play by Samuel Taylor who based his play on a French oeuvre called *Les Joies de la Famille*. Rosalind Russell and Brian Aherne were in it. Ross Hunter produced it along with his close friend Jacque Mapes. No film score is totally easy to do. One Saturday at six p.m. I called Hunter's house to discuss a problem I was having. Jacque answered and I put the question to him. He said, "I can't talk about the picture NOW, we're having 12 people to dinner!"

Joseph Gershenson, head of the feature film music division at Universal, conducted, and very well too. In all the arguments with Hunter on the scoring stage Gershenson was very supportive of me. So was Harry Garfield. They talked Hunter out of most of his objections. I didn't go to the dubbing but Gershenson did and came out regularly with bulletins—we'd lost this or that—then later he'd tell me most of it was restored. Hunter would get a hate on some sequence and they'd run it without the music and always wind up putting it back. I got the impression Hunter didn't like me or the score and that is why I print the memo below.

Ross Hunter Productions, Inc
Inter Office Memorandum

To: Harry Garfield.

Subject: *Rosie!*

Dear Harry:

It's easy to spout off in loud terms how dissatisfied you are with this or that—and I guess I took that route when I told you about my dissatisfaction with the musical score for *Rosie!* The desire towards perfection evidently was steering my thoughts.

I've just looked at and heard the entire picture put together and want to tell you (very humbly) how wrong I was. The score is beautiful—almost remarkable at times—and does an awful lot to enhance this movie. My congratulations to Lyn and to Joe and to you, who never lost faith.

sincerely,

Ross

1968

Saturday September 7

All the television scores listed below were fun to do, particularly "The Virginian," a fine funny film directed by Charlie Dubin (who was once a singer in one of my theatrical choruses) and written by a first-class fellow named Robert van Scoyk. This is the first year I worked for David Wolper, who produces the National Geographic specials and other shows. I got to meet John Glenn when he came out to put the finishing touches on "John Glenn in Africa" and found him extremely charismatic. Naturally, in this film, I used all the exotic percussion instruments I could lay my hands on, including practically all of Emil Richards' enormous collection. Must have worked. Had a letter from Mel Stuart saying he thought the score "excellent. My sentiments are shared by everyone working on the project."

Both of the movies done this year were unhappy experiences. Universal bought *Destination Mindanao* from an independent producer who was sound effects happy. I had to fight him to get any music through his effects tracks and, even worse, after he left the lot, the brass in the black tower had the film extensively re-cut without regard to what happened to the music. One example of what this sort of messing about with a film can do: A young girl is looking at a silver framed picture of her dead parents. I underscored this moment with an alto flute solo accompanied by strings. In the re-cutting this piece of music turned up under a character breaking a door down and bursting into the room brandishing a gun. There were other similar mismatches. A session with the orchestra would have enabled us to correct these gaffes but the studio was reluctant to spend the money.

Angel in My Pocket starred Andy Griffith, whose favorite composer is Earl Hagen. The studio rammed me down his throat and when we met I got a freeze. Not the most ideal of working conditions. "The Lonely Doryman" is a good score and in "The Amazon" Alan Landsburg gave me plenty of opportunity and support. Mel Stuart, one of Wolper's producer-directors, dropped in at the recording of "Amazon." When I finished one cue he came over to me and said, "For that I forgive you *Rosie!*"

On December 6 I reached the chronological age of 59.

Work done; TV: 2 "It Takes a Thief," 1 "Virginian," 2 "Daniel-Boones," "John Glenn in Africa," National Geographic "The Lonely Doryman," "The Amazon," "Mannix," "Missy" pilot.

Movies: *Destination Mindanao, Angel in My Pocket.*

"Songs of Samoa" (SATB), "When I Survey the Wond'rous Cross," anthem, "Let His Name Be Sung," anthem.

1969

January

My brother Kenneth and his wife Leila have moved to San Pedro from Sugarloaf, Pennsylvania. With his arrival I am renewing my onslaught on Kathy (who is deadset against it) to get her to agree to let me acquire a boat. Ken is handy around engines. For the first time in my life I went to a boat show. I've got the bug in spite of the description of a pleasure boat as a hole in the water surrounded by wood into which you pour money.

February

Dear friend Alonzo Cass died February 1 after open heart surgery. He was a doctor and went in knowing he had only a fifty-fifty chance of survival.

Sunday February 2

Ken and I went to Long Beach to look at 40-foot houseboats. I like the space (one could work on a houseboat) but they are too expensive. A friend of Kathy's, an experienced sailor, put the kibosh on it saying they were unseaworthy. Funny, all this talk of buying a boat, since I am not working. I am collecting unemployment compensation.

Monday February 24

Eddie Constantine and daughter Tanya came to dinner. He is here on his annual pilgrimage to get the U.S. to pay attention to him. He is still riding high in Europe.

Wednesday March 6

A big day. Kenneth and I bought an old 32' Chris Craft from a retired Navy chaplain and his wife for $8,000. The boat's name is

Valido. On Saturday at eight o'clock in the morning we had our shakedown cruise. Very scary. It ain't like driving an automobile. On Sunday Sid Kuller, Jeff Alexander, Ken and I (Kathy is still in her "I will never set foot on it" mood) took the boat out of King Harbor in Redondo Beach with no mishaps. We got it back into the slip without too much trouble. The twin Chryslers help.

Sunday March 23

Ken and I sailed the boat from Redondo to San Pedro and up the Los Angeles channel. What a feeling! We tied up at the landing stage of the *Princess Louise* and had lunch. In the late afternoon we passed the Los Angeles light and headed back to Redondo. There was an eight-foot swell running and *Valido* stood on her head. We turned back and asked the fellow at the Shell oil dock if we could tie up for the night. He said it was all right with him if we got out at seven a.m. We did.

Saturday April 26

You can fly to Catalina in a big old four-engine Sikorsky amphibian plane. When you get off they hand you a little promotional certificate stating that you have completed an overseas flight. Today, after a last ditch skirmish, Kathy capitulated and we sailed the 22 miles from the Los Angeles light to Catalina, in *Valido*, for the first time. Nothing to it. You keep the compass on 174 and in an hour or so you see Avalon and the Casino dead ahead.

Growing up in Barrow-in-Furness around ships, and my father having been a chief petty officer in the Royal Navy (engine room), I had always had a hankering to go to sea. When we got to Philadelphia I tired of attending Northeast High and before I was 17 took a job as a messman on the S.S. *San Antonio*, a ship running between Philadelphia and Houston. Trips in the *Pueblo*, a tanker chartered to the Humble Oil Company, followed. She made several short runs between Houston and Baton Rouge, then one to Tampico, Mexico and another to Montreal and back to Houston where I was paid off. When my money ran out I got a job as a wiper in the *Tiger*, a flush-deck engine-room amidships Standard Oil Co. of New York tanker. A wiper is the lowest form of life in the engine room but I enjoyed the work more than washing dishes and making up the sailors' bunks. Walking along the shaft tunnel oiling the rotating shaft 27 feet below the waterline is man's work. When we got to New York my mother was on the dock with a man from Standard Oil who fired me because I was underage. Mother hauled me back to Philadelphia in time to celebrate my 18th birthday.

Thursday May 1

Today Norman Corwin, Byron Kane and Sid Kuller joined me and we left King Harbor, Redondo Beach, sailed to San Pedro and put *Valido* into a slip at the California Yacht Anchorage. I bought a camera and started photographing freighters and tankers calling at Los Angeles and Long Beach harbors.

June

My 14-week layoff is over. I'm going back to work.

Ranald MacDougall, writer-producer-gentleman, has a picture at Universal called originally *A Woman for Charlie* then retitled *The Cockeyed Cowboys of Calico County* with Dan Blocker, Nanette Fabray, Jim Backus, Mickey Rooney and assorted comedic folk. It was supposed to be a TV film and that's why we used a smallish orchestra, but then the brass decided to release it theatrically. MacDougall is a joy to work for and his wife, who happens to be Nanette Fabray, plays the musical saw at parties.

July

If you own a boat you have to pay personal property taxes on it. Just sent the State $375.

Metromedia has bought Wolper's operation. They have an hour TV there called "The Time of Man," produced by Marshall Flaum. Needs a very elaborate musical score and when Stanley Wilson called with a Virginian, I had reluctantly to turn it down. I am going to use Paul Beaver's Moog synthesiser, Clark Spangler's fancy, fixed-up Yamaha organ as well as a fairly substantial orchestra. We did the synthesised music first. When I played this very advanced state of the art material for Flaum he said, "It sounds like an organ." I did all this stuff before the picture had been finally cut, but I had to get a jump on the schedule.

Friday August 15

Breaking down the picture. It is rather a monster, purporting to cover the entire history of man.

Friday August 29

Recorded the orchestra at RCA. After the interlock—this is where they put music, effects, dialog and narration together for the first time—I went over to Metromedia to see how it went. Flaum was complimentary with some reservations. For the section on pollution he had asked for music that was "ominous, threatening, with a sense of jeopardy." He thought it too heavy. R.C. Andrews' early exploration of Egypt required music, according to Flaum, that was "light, period, into Lawrence of Arabia mystery." He thought what I came up with "denigrated the scene." The last five minutes of the picture was a review of historical happenings in the 20th century. There was complete coverage of wars, pollution, famine and pestilence, putting a man on the moon. Most of the history of the 20th century is not very nice. The five minutes seemed a compression of catastrophe but Flaum wanted me to ignore what he had up on the screen and have the music sound a note of hope. One comment by Nick Clapp, the picture editor, amused me. He thought I started out too thin. I said, "When you make love do you start with an orgasm?" None of these people know that if you are writing five minutes of climactic music you defeat your purpose if you start with a climax. I got $2,500 for what amounted to five weeks of work with two or three days off to go out on the boat and take pictures. Some of my pictures of freighters got published in *Ships Monthly*, an English magazine. I was prouder of the $35 I got for that than I was of Metromedia's $2,500.

October

Wednesday I met with Warren Sherlock, who has written a play about Ignatius. Going to write some music for it. In the evening to the Beverly Hills High School to start taking the Coast Guard course in small boat navigation.

Sid Kuller and I decided to take all the research we accumulated on Robert Louis Stevenson's life in Samoa and make a two-hour television musical out of it. We took the boat over to Catalina and holed up at 219 Clarissa Street where the phone doesn't ring and the most exciting thing you can do is to go to the Safeway and check the vegetables. On December 11 we finished the first draft of most of the songs we plan to use.

Work done, TV: "Anderson & Co" pilot, "The Time Of Man," 2 "It Takes a Thief," 1 "Bold Ones."

Movie: *The Cockeyed Cowboys of Calico County.*

"Incident at State Beach," band version.

"Tusitala," the Stevenson project. Music for "Ignatius" not yet complete.

1970

January

We are doing a lot of entertaining and Kath is doing a lot of work for the Museum—for free. She's a volunteer. So, at the age of 60, I have arrived at the point where I will do anything for money. The days when I would turn down something I thought beneath me are long gone.

"The Murdochs & the McClays," written by a not untalented man named Bob Wells, is a version of the Hatfields and the McCoys feud. Wells has written a song for the theme and we have decided to score the film using honest to God country musicians. I cleared this approach with Leith Stevens, head of the music department at Paramount, who reluctantly OK'd it.

Monday January 26

Scheduled to record the "Murdoch" theme song nine a.m. at Paramount with the Coleman Boys. They didn't show. Wells called around, found them and re-set the date for 1:30. The duration of this theme song is one minute. We started at 1:45. Five hours later we had it. Country musicians are uncomfortable reading notes. They prefer to read signs. I, IV and V. In the key of C that means C, F and G. If you use any other chords you are dead.

Monday February 9

Today from ten to one and two to five—that's six hours—we recorded ten minutes of music with Lyn Murray and his Southern Fried Down Home Cookin' Band. Stevens and I had a drink after and decided we had made a terrible mistake. Didn't matter. To avoid contamination Paramount probably burned the film.

Monday February 16

To Universal at two p.m. to run a movie with a title they'll never get on a marquee: *Don't Push, I'll Charge When I'm Ready*, produced by a very nice young man who happens to be married to Bob Hope's daughter—Nick Landi. Stanley Wilson thinks it's awful but I like it. You have to like it if you are going to write music for it. It's a World War II prisoner-of-war comedy with Jerry Colonna and Cesar Romero.

Sunday April 19

To a big party at Paul and Georgianna Erskine's. One of the guests was Dennis Stanfill, the new pres of Fox. All the Pasadena folk jumped on him for producing Gore Vidal's *Myra Breckenridge*, a dirty book that is going to be an X-rated movie.

Tuesday April 21

Lionel Newman called and wants me to do a sequence or two for *Myra*. I accepted because I am dying to see the movie that is getting

Dennis Stanfill into such hot water with his Pasadena friends. Unredeemingly nauseating.

Sunday May 3

To the Ahmanson to hear a concert of new music including Berio's Symphonia with the Swingle Singers. Fantastically marvelous. Mehta conducting. In the question-and-answer period after the concert Berio said that the orchestra as we know it is doomed to become a museum piece, and I agree. Before long you will go to hear Beethoven as you go to a museum to see Rembrandt. Mr. Moog and his synthesiser have started a revolution. All of the local composers are beginning to incorporate synthesised sounds with the orchestra.

Wednesday May 27

Joan Harrison, the lady who used to split the producing chores on the Hitchcock TV series with Norman Lloyd, is at Paramount making a Movie of the Week for Aaron Spelling. It is called "Love Hate Love" and, because I have been invited to do the music, I had a very pleasant reunion with her today at the studio. Ryan O'Neal and Leslie Ann Warren are in it. George Duning, a very good composer, is running Mr. Spelling's music department, and we had a little reunion too.

Tuesday June 30

A very pleasant six hours recording the music. Bud Shank on alto a good deal of the time, Artie Kane on a lot of keyboards, plus a dozen other musicians. I wrote some lyrics for the Main Title and hired one of Artie Kane's nine ex-wives to sing them through an echoplex. Nice effect. Everybody, including me, pleased.

Saturday July 4

Oh, it is nice having a boat. Took the Stanley Wilsons and their son Phil, the one who goes to Hawaii and makes surfing films, and Dave Grusin and wife to see the start of the Trans Pac race. Big party in the evening, lots of folk including Jeff Alexander and Lee Cass. He has eyes for her and I think he is closing in.

Dear old Van Cleave, the great orchestrator and arranger with whom I have worked since the days at CBS in the thirties, toppled over this weekend mowing his lawn and is gone. Laid aside the scoring of a Virginian and sadly went to his services on Wednesday.

Sunday July 12

A day edged in black. Stanley Wilson died at 3:30 p.m. at Aspen, Colorado. Harry Garfield has asked me to write a eulogy to be delivered by Benny Carter.

Wednesday July 15

Stanley's brother Mitchell came to our house Monday and I read him what I had to say about Stanley. I cried. He said I should deliver it. After a brass choir played some somber sonorities, I spoke for all the musicians who had loved him:

> At the going down of the sun,
> And in the morning,
> We will remember him.

We speak now for the musicians—the players and the composers who loved him in a light, happy, day-to-day sort of way; who worked with him and played with him. The love was unspoken. In death we speak of the depth of it.

To the young composers—the bright young ones—he opened the doors. Took the chances and set them on their way. To the older, more seasoned among us, he gave new leases on life.

He knew the composer's agony. He had been there.

He understood the players. He had been there.

He knew that men who draw bow over catgut tend to be serious and conservative. He understood them. He knew the woodwinds, fretting and worrying over their reeds. He understood the drummers, who tend to be boisterous. And his brass players, embattled in the long bloody sessions, knew they could count on him to lighten it up and make it easy. He had been there, too.

He wrote a lot of good notes and scored a lot of bad pictures.

Wherever *we* are—he had been there.

Stanley had a soft voice. Not many words. But what there were, were alive with humor. And he had expressions. And we knew them. You asked for too large an orchestra and his brow would go up in little furrows. Tell him something funny and his head would go back in the two-second laugh—caught before it was overstated. Discussing the world, there was a brief sagging expression that told it all. He was aware of the division and discord in the world—but in his own peculiar, understated way, he made a place for us that was untouched by discord and division; a place of love, and respect, and talent.

He invited us all: black and white, red and yellow, Jew and gentile, ASCAP and BMI, foreign and domestic. If a talented Arab had come along, he would have opened the door. He presided over us like a benign Buddha, and protected us. He was aware, and sensitive, and he got around.

We saw him at Donte's, at the Music Pavilion, and at concerts of the *avant garde*. We saw him in London and Paris and Rome. We saw him queasy on a rough Channel crossing. Nervous at the top of Sacre Coeur and happy in Barclay's recording studio.

As time went by he became more rather than less interested. Music is a changing stream and Stanley moved with it. He never got bored. Weary—in mid-season, perhaps. We remember the time he was spotting a Virginian with the producer and Sid Fine. When the lights went up in the projection room they had all fallen asleep. But he never got bored.

We saw him on our stage shaping the sensitive phrase, and whatever happened, he protected us. It was never mentioned but we knew the knocks he took for us. At the end of the day they showed sometimes for a moment in his face—drawn, robbed of its color. But he would go home, rest for awhile with his other family, Gert and the three beautiful people they created.

I guess love is the name of the game.

He had it from his parents, his brother and his sister. He gave it to his own family and he gave it to all of us.

When soft voices die,
Music vibrates in the memory.

Tonight, at home, tomorrow, on the stage, we will remember him.

Thursday July 23

To Universal to run a "Shiloh" and the news that Leith Stevens
had died having lunch at Nickodell's on Melrose.

To wind up this dreadful week Harry Garfield offered me
Stanley's job. I turned it down.

Thursday, Friday August 20, 21

Gil Melle, a composer, has scored an episode of "The Psychiatrist" directed by Steven Spielberg. Melle does not conduct.
Garfield asked me to conduct the score, something Stanley would
have done. I did. At the end of the second day, facing golden hours
overtime, I suggested it would be cheaper to come back tomorrow
and finish it. Both Spielberg and Melle chewed me out. I was a
"company man." Company man or not it didn't make sense to me
to waste the money. We continued and finished it. All it did was
prove to me I was right to turn down the job of department head.
There is no bullshit in my makeup.

Saturday September 12

A memorable weekend on the boat. To Catalina with Bobby
Bain, guitar, Joe Mondragon, bass, and Milton Kestenbaum, also a
bass player. They fished and we went to the Arcade on Catalina and
played skee ball. Memorable.

Did some more work, sans spirit, attended a black tie at the
Museum—one of Kathy's efforts—at which I distinguished myself.
A woman sought me out and said, "You are so lucky to be married
to such a marvelous woman as Kathy." I said, "She's hideous to live
with." Avoid, if possible, telling the truth. Ever.

Work done; TV: 2 "Shilohs," 2 "Matt Lincolns," 1 "Daniel
Boone," 1 "Mannix," 1 "Deadly Game," "Murdochs & McClays"
pilot.

Movies: *Don't Push, I'll Charge, Love Hate Love.*

1971

This year could virtually be dispatched in a sentence or two. A year of death, diminishing work, receding gums, and professional consultations about an exceedingly rocky marriage.

Lenny Adelson, my young lyric writing friend, died. So did Lenny Hayton, a man I idolized. A deep musician and a man who gave up a lot for the love of Lena.

I did four jobs at Universal. "Jamison's Kids," a pilot, an "Owen Marshall," a series about a lawyer, an episode of "The Doctors" and a movie for good friend Randy MacDougall called *Magic Carpet*. For Metromedia I did one of M. Cousteau's films, *Sea Otters*.

The departure of beloved colleagues falls into a sad pattern. You go to the Hollywood Cemetery, where Victor Young is buried, see the musicians and music busines people, some you haven't seen for years and probably won't until the next funeral, and, depending on your character, either celebrate your survival or feel guilty.

April

I have been plugging away at Warren Sherlock's *Ignatius* without much success. The lyrics don't work and are frustrating. Lyric writing is an art requiring first a gift, then if you add a lifetime of singleminded devotion you might become a Hart, a Harburg, an Ira Gershwin or a Hammerstein. I may have to suggest to Warren we call in an expert. If I do, he'll probably be offended. Everyone thinks he can write a song.

On the 15th Dr. Leonard Hural, periodontist, performed some surgery on my gums. He thinks I am five years late getting to him.

Kathy and I went to see our friend Judd Marmor, the psychiatrist, for a little counseling. He saw Kathy alone and then had a session with me. At the end of my session he indicated quite clearly that he thought we had nothing. He ought to know. He is a very distinguished man, well thought of in his profession, and has been divorced. Since booze is one of the problems, I have gone on the wagon. The cocktail hour at our house is six to eight. It is difficult to last until dinner while your partner is getting loaded. It is a matter of contention.

Tuesday May 4

Saw Robert Morley on Dick Cavett's show from London. What a delight he is. He opened by saying, "We are watching the collapse of the capitalistic world. While it is going, there will be a great deal of muddle. But we're emerging slowly into a better world, aren't we? I mean this last ten years has taught the world a great deal about war it never knew before—at a terrible cost. We're not so keen on the soldiers and the drums as we were."

Later he said, "It is one of the great shames of England that I am not Sir Robert or indeed Lord Robert."

And on my current favorite subject, "I was in a Shakespearean company and they all drank and they would have been rather better if they hadn't. I decided not to drink before the show. Some actors act better when they're drunk and *I* might be better. I've known several actors who were wonderful when they were drunk and very boring when they were sober. We've had tragedies in our profession from drink but, my God, there are a lot of drunken surgeons no one's ever heard about. When you're an actor everybody hears about you, but the drunken surgeon—you know—the body's in the lift and away.

"They've just done a film in England to show children the facts of life. They showed it to the grown-ups and of course they were shocked. You must be careful telling old people about sex. It upsets them. It worries the old people very much, you see, when they think what they've missed all their lives."

On kinkiness. "There are certain sexual perversions that used not to be spoken of. People used to dress up in mackintoshes with nothing underneath and show themselves in chemists shops. I don't say it isn't rather tiresome if there's a queue behind you waiting to buy toothpaste. No doubt the sex crime rate goes down as you release people from a sense of guilt for standing in doorways and showing their private parts to the public. There's no harm in sex if it can be indulged openly and jollily. It's very good for you."

Saturday May 15

Went to San Francisco with Sid to have a look at Ed Lester's revival of *Knickerbocker Holiday* with Burt Lancaster playing the Walter Huston part. As usual Ed wants to update the lyrics but Maxwell Anderson's estate says nothing doing. Lancaster can't sing but I think it is very brave of him to strap his leg up and walk around on a stump eight times a week.

Tuesday June 22

Looked at *Sea Otters* with Marshall Flaum, producer, and met old mon capitaine Cousteau himself. A charmer and smart as a whip. If his films were not about animals they would get an X rating—he always manages to get in some footage of the animals he is studying reproducing themselves.

Monday August 2

The Ringling Bros. circus is in town. We went with Jonathan Winters, Louis Nye and wives. The clowns played almost exclusively to our group. In the intermission I said Jonny should go back to see them since they were obviously playing to him, or maybe Louie. When we got back it turned out they were playing to me. Thought I was Jack Benny.

Wednesday October 20

Duane Bogie produces the "Hallmark Hall of Fame" television specials for Foote, Cone & Belding out of Chicago. We met with him and presented *Tusitala* as a possible production. He was most interested and encouraged us to get to work on a story line. We said we'd have it for him in a month or so and sailed to Catalina this day and started. We toiled, off and on, until November 10 when we stopped while Sid had some root canal work done on his teeth. His 17-year-old son has run off with an 18-year-old girl. Between Sid's teeth and comforting his wife, who has gone into a decline, we are temporarily unproductive. I used the time to try to find out about

Stevenson's sex life and discovered something we probably can't use in a script for the Hallmark audience. He lost his virginity at the age of 19 to a great-haunched, two-shilling Edinburgh whore, and it is apparent he and Fanny consummated their love well before they were married. Bogie wants to use Richard Harris as Stevenson. He is a remarkable lookalike. As I said in a letter to Bogie, "These are very interesting pieces of information no doubt unusable in the script but they might put a glint into Harris's playing attitude."

Wednesday December 1

Today the Composers and Lyricists Guild struck the major studios. We are making a stand to get our publication rights and it may be a long strike.

Work done; TV: "Jamison's Kids" pilot, 1 "Owen Marshall," 1 Cousteau, 1 "The Doctors."
Movie: *The Magic Carpet.*

1972

January

A month of meetings about the CLGA strike. We have hired Theodore Kheel, an important labor negotiator, to represent us in dealings with the major studios. Sid and I working on *Tusitala.*

February

Met with Alan Landsburg about a series he is contemplating— "The New Explorers"—and it looks like I'll be immersed in the rain forests of Costa Rica for awhile.

The Atlantic Richfield Company has a new tanker, the Arco

Prudhoe Bay, running between Los Angeles and the new oil fields in Alaska. Fairly big—about 120,000 tons. Norbert, my friend in the chart and chronometer store in San Pedro, introduced me to the Arco shore captain, Captain Winkler. He wants a picture of his new ship. On the 23rd I got into *Valido* and went down to the Long Beach harbor entrance and got some good color shots as she came in, dripping crude oil, alas, down her port side, smearing the Arco logo. I had the negatives processed and took proofs to the Captain. He ordered 140 prints of all sizes provided the smear of crude could be airbrushed out. I guess you could say I am now a professional photographer.

Winkler is interesting about his business. The oil dock at Valdez, due to a snafu on the part of the contractors, sits in a five-knot current at such an angle it is impossible for a large tanker like the *Prudhoe* to tie up and ring down "Finished with Engines." They have to keep turning slow astern throughout the loading procedure. Engines don't like to go astern so the extra wear on equipment built for a life of ten years will be considerable.

March

The composers and the studios have come to an agreement. Our suit against the majors will continue but in the meantime we will work under a "gentleman's agreement." That means the studios will pay the existing scales for composition until the argument on ownership of rights is settled in court.

Recorded the "New Explorers" show using some rented electronic equipment as part of a fairly large orchestra. I have decided to buy some of my own and for a start acquired a Sony 4 track recorder, a mini Moog and an echoplex. I already have a Yamaha EC3. That's an organ.

April

Met with Richard Harris who is keen to play Robert Louis Stevenson and likes the musical material. Things are moving.

Patsy Melchior and Eleanor Forester, a friend of Kathy's, staying with us. Patsy knows the lyrics to every song ever written. Not so Eleanor. One night, gathered round the piano, singing all the goodies, Eleanor sang what I'm sure in her heart she thinks is the right lyric, "Somebody loves me, I wonder why ..." That broke us up then she topped herself on "Body and Soul" as follows: "I spend my days in longing, And wond'ring why it's *you* you're wronging ..."

May

Kathy is doing one of those fancy fashion shows at the Museum. A review of all the great 20th century designers. For the section devoted to Courreges I concocted 12 minutes of swingy stuff on the electronic equipment. Worked fine. Better than the usual piano and bass ad libbing while the models parade. (Didn't stop Kathy bitching about my wasting money on playthings.)

I have arrived at the age when young composers seek me out for advice and help in breaking into the business. Stan Levine is one of them. He has connections at Cal Arts, the university founded with $20,000,000 of Walt Disney's money. They have an electronic music department run by Morton Subotnick and a good young film makers' course. One of the young film makers has asked me to do a score for his little movie. I scored it for string quartet, woodwind quartet, a piano and a percussionist. One morning at 9:30 a student orchestra gathered and we started to record. At 12 they wanted to stop because there was a luncheon concert of music for winds written by a son of Earle Hagen's. I wanted to hear it too. We went to the cafeteria. The atmosphere at this university is, I would say, loose. There were four girls at the next table, none of them wearing shoes. One of them put her feet up on the table and the soles were filthy black. Did I say loose? Walking along a corridor I saw an announcement pinned on a bulletin board. It announced a St. Valentine's Day "Gender Fuck." Walt must be spinning in his grave.

After the concert, which was excellent, we reassembled to continue recording my score. My lady first violin, a very important member of the orchestra, was missing. She had something else to do. No problem. A call went out and shortly another first violin appeared and we finished in an hour or so. And very good they were, too.

One other little anecdote about Cal Arts. At a graduation

ceremony all the candidates wore the regulation mortar boards and black gowns—and sneakers. Roy Disney was handing out the diplomas and got high. The entire front row of students was smoking pot.

Monday June 19

Tusitala was presented to the Hallmark people in Kansas City. Bogie wrote us on the 29th that the reception was favorable and he would be out next month to work out the details.

Thursday July 20

Bullets Durgom, in spite of his fearsome name, is a thoroughly charming agent. We have engaged him to represent us on the *Tusitala* deal.

Monday July 24

Met with Duane Bogie at the Sheraton Universal and he says we have a deal. Did we want a letter of intent? Sid said it wouldn't be necessary—we would meet with Bullets next week and the fine points of the contract would be worked out. On the 28th Bullets and Duane agreed on the outlines of the arrangement—so much up front, so much on completion of the script, etc. Bullets went off to get it all spelled out and Duane went back to Chicago.

Kathy is promoting something called The People's Gallery for the Foster & Kleiser division of Metromedia. The F & K div is run by Ross Barrett. On account of this connection I get to go out in what passes for high society around here. For example: a party at the Bistro (a high class joint) given by Rita and Ross Barrett for John and Yolanda Kluge (Kluge is the pres of Metromedia) attended by folk like Dennis Stanfill, Evelle Younger. We sat with Joni James, her husband Tony Aquaviva and James Wong Howe, the great cameraman, with whom I had lots to talk about. Another time Ross Barrett had to entertain Gina Lollobrigida and I got invited because he thought we would have something in common, and I wouldn't mind having something in common with Gina Loll, but all she wanted to talk about was material for an act she was going to do in Las Vegas. Besides, her off-white evening dress could have stood a visit to the cleaners.

Friday July 28

Byron Kane, onetime dialog director on "Peter Gunn," now the voice of Kathy's People's Gallery project, called and invited himself to dinner. He is going through a crisis.

Betsy, the woman he has been living with for the last three years, who casts horoscopes for a living, has left him. He loves her and she loves him and, as far as Byron can figure out, the only problem they had was premature ejaculation. He suggested they go to the Masters and Johnson clinic at St. Louis where, for $2,500, they could get it fixed. They found two disciples of M & J practicing in Los Angeles and went to them without positive results because they didn't do the homework, whatever that was. (Cunnilingus, fellatio?)

A couple of months ago Betsy came home from her class at the Innate Awareness Center and announced she had fallen in love with the teacher, a 45-year-old defrocked minister of the Universal Church. They were going to run away together and set up housekeeping in Ventura. He had put down $350 for the first month's rent. Anguish. Tears. Byron came right out and said he wanted her to stay. She said, "But he's put down $350 rent." Byron said, "Well, you can give him the $350." Betsy: "Where would I get it?" Byron: "Borrow it. You must know someone who would lend you $350."

Betsy said she was going to leave, taking her bed, lamps, dishes, pots and pans, blankets and sheets, and the dish washer. She would not take the clock because Byron loved it so and could keep it in trust. Nor would she take the refrigerator and stove because the place in Ventura had one of each. Now she's gone and Byron is going to an analyst-hypnotist who is taking notes and running up the bill and so far hasn't got down to hypnotizing him and slowing down the ejaculation.

Wednesday August 16

A lovely breakfast meeting with Duane Bogie at the Sheraton West. All the details are in place and Sid and I, elated, left to put in a final two weeks on the script.

Friday September 22

A letter from Bogie postmarked Rome. He's there working on one of the shows. Our project is all off. Seems one of the Hallmark shows that used music, somewhat in the manner we intend to use it, got a bad rating. Musicals are expensive, much more so than straight dramatic shows, and Hallmark has the heebie jeebies about our $400,000 budget.

Tuesday September 26

Bobby Dolan, here conducting *Sound of Music,* didn't show up yesterday. They found him dead in his hotel room. I've known him since 1936 when he was married to Vilma Ebsen. Come to think of it, I knew both his wives, the other was Nan Martin, a really superb actress, and he has known all four of mine. I remember our time in New York most fondly. When Vilma was pregnant she would wake Bobby up and send him to the Plaza to get some chicken hash. In the summertime we all took houses in Connecticut and visited each other. I played badminton against Vilma's brother Buddy, who is nine feet tall, and lost. Robert Emmett Dolan was a cocky Irishman (his own description) and a first-class theatre conductor. You couldn't get a word in with him. I remember when he was conducting *Louisiana Purchase,* the Irving Berlin show, he got laryngitis and had to write notes. Berlin said, "Now you'll find out what some of your friends think."

Friday October 6

Took the one o'clock plane from Wilmington to Catalina, got to 219 Clarissa Street, turned on the kitchen radio and heard Gary Owens on KMPC reporting a rumor that 15,000 Chinese were massed on the border at Tia Juana, Mexico, ready to invade California. This rumor, said Gary, was untrue. Actually there were only 8,000 and they were swimming toward Catalina wearing wet suits.

It was hot—94 degrees. All the windows in the house were opened. We went to bed early and at six a.m. a fleet of trucks went by. This is a sound you don't sleep through. My first thought was that the wetsuited Chinese had arrived and troops were moving to repel the invasion.

Wednesday November 15

I am going to do a marvelous Cousteau Called "Hippo!" Hippopotami live most of their lives under water. They have a lot of footage in the film of these great creatures performing what appear to me underwater ballets and I am going to score all these sequences on my magic machinery. Everything above water to be scored by a conventional orchestra. I think the lovely electronic sounds will make a nice contrast. Incidentally this film is Cousteau's son Phillippe's baby.

Wednesday December 6

Sixty-three today, feeling all of 43. Or maybe 39.

1973

January

Michael McClure had a play produced a year or two ago called *The Beard*. It did a little business mainly because of the sensational use of four-letter words. A new work of his titled *McClure on Toast* is to be done by a little Equity waiver group calling themselves the Company Theatre, and my young student friend, Stan Levine, has been invited to do some songs for it. He came to me for advice and help. I helped to the extent that I recorded accompaniments for his songs on my electronic equipment and went to the theatre and rehearsed the singers. When I went to the opening they had put my name on the program as musical director. It made me mad. If I had been asked I would not have wanted to have my name associated with such drek but as it happened it did me no harm and considerable good. You never know.

Norman Lloyd, who used to produce the Alfred Hitchcock television series and is now the executive producer of the "Hollywood Television Theatre," saw the play and called me. The "Hollywood Television Theatre" is produced at KCET for the Public Broadcasting System. Norman said, "How would you like to do the music for a play that in all probability will put the Public Broadcasting network out of business?" He was going to produce Bruce J. Friedman's controversial off-Broadway sensation, *Steambath*. I gladly accepted.

The play takes place in a steambath run by a young Puerto Rican who is quite obviously God. The cast, including Valerie Perrine, works virtually naked, towels covering the parts even Norman Lloyd knows the television audience, much as it might like to, may not look at. God gives His orders for small and large miracles to a small robot which acknowledges them with appropriate electronic blips and bleeps. I had a lot of fun concocting these on my mini Moog. When I took the tape in to the rehearsal I also took my camera and got a lot of pictures of the half naked cast before an officious official of KCET warned me off the stage.

Flash. Budgets are a problem on PBS. When Tony Charmoli the choreographer, used as he is to the opulence of commercial TV, came in to stage a dance for the two gay inmates of the steambath and saw our skimpy seven-piece orchestra he had to be brought round with smelling salts. He was brilliant. To me that dance is an historic piece of television.

Steambath aired April 6 with a repeat announced for April 30. After the first broadcast an outraged elderly lady from Orange County drove to KCET for the express purpose of preventing the second showing of this sacrilege. [It went on to become one of the most successful shows ever produced by KCET although it is a matter of record that a large number of member stations refused the first feed.]

Wednesday March 21

My friend Sid Kuller has been made entertainment director of the Hacienda, a second-rate Las Vegas hotel-casino. We are writing several pieces of second-rate material for his opening show, a revue to be called "Turn It On."

Thursday April 12

We have sold the house at 1227 Sunset Plaza Drive and bought a 14-room mansion at 1919 Outpost Drive in Hollywood. Since 1954 it was the French consulate. The six weeks of negotiations with the French Government proved harrowing, since all the offering and counter offering had to be done through Paris. Our final offer of $85,000 was more or less accepted by the local consul but as we moved in today had not been officially approved by Paris. The cultural attaché had been sleeping on a mattress in the otherwise empty house. We overlapped a bit. The first night we slept in our bedrooms and he on his mattress. He wondered what would happen if Paris turned our offer down. We intimated that since we were in, that would be Paris's problem. The house has an aura; Romain Gary was once a resident here. I have a whole wing for myself and we have installed the two grand pianos, back to back, in the great beamed living room. All the oaken, iron-studded doors in the house had for some strange, un-French reason been painted white. We shipped them out to be stripped back to the original wood. Kathy has ordered a pool dug and is putting in a new kitchen.

On April 17 I went up to Vegas for a week to help Sid get his Hacienda show on. I didn't have much say and an orchestrator had been engaged who had never done a show before. Judging by the noises I doubt if he will ever do another one. The costumes were ghastly. Each night, for seven nights, I went to a different Italian restaurant. Each night, for seven nights, I ordered salad and spaghetti. I like spaghetti.

Sunday April 30

The lady from Orange County notwithstanding, *Steambath* aired again to one of the largest audiences in KCET's history. Norman Lloyd called. The next outing on Hollywood Television Theatre will be *Double Solitaire,* the play by Robert Anderson, and I am to do the music.

Tuesday May 22

Double Solitaire was produced by Martin Manulis, a nervous man who gave me the usual instructions about the music, using the usual terms like "lush strings," etc. When I told him the music budget wouldn't run to any lush strings, that we had to do his score with only four players, he was alarmed. "Won't it sound *thin?*" I said, "Not necessarily." The play was directed by Paul Bogart, a bull-bear man who looked a bit like Norman Corwin but didn't behave like him. Two parts were badly miscast. The four instruments I used were bass, guitar, fender piano and Yamaha organ, masterfully recorded by Thorne Nogar, the wizard of the Annex Studios. It was, in my biased opinion, very good. At the dubbing Mr. Manulis paid me what I suppose was a compliment. He said, "It doesn't sound as bad as I expected it to."

Wednesday June 13

To Ensenada for a few days. Not alone. And that is all I am going to say to protect the guilty. Took some nice pictures of gulls, sunsets and an old sailing ship, the *Regis Mare*, 400 tons, 98 feet at the waterline, registered in Valetta. She was in the drydock having the copper on her bottom replaced along with a few planks the worms had got at.

Tuesday July 10

Recorded the music for Norman Lloyd's production for the Hollywood Television Theatre of Albert Hayes' play *The Gondola*. I scored it for harmonica, played by the virtuoso Eddie Manson; guitar, bass and fender piano, an invaluable instrument, always played for me by Artie Kane, who is only the best. (There is a nice story about Artie. On some date or other a conductor was making a boring speech about how he wanted his music played. He looked at Artie, who was yawning, and said, "Am I keeping you awake?" Artie answered, "No.") For the End Credits my friend Roger Hamilton Spotts brought around two black friends, guitar and harmonica, who ad libbed about six minutes of blues which we cut down to the two minutes required. Best thing in the score. Roger, incidentally, is the only friend who called during our first six weeks at 1919 Outpost Drive to see what was going on and showed up every other day to paint.

Tuesday August 21

A strange dream. Outside a New York building. Normal façade, doorman, people going in and out. I am going to see some Mafia people. I go into an area of the building which seems to be an elaborate club. I am taken in charge and conducted to the person I am to see. The way is difficult. There is a swimming pool, suspended in the air, constructed of a see-through plastic material. You could see the enormous downward bulge to the deep end, the slope to the shallow end, and the people swimming in the pool. We go under it—just enough space under the deep end to crawl through, the going getting easier under the upward curve of the shallow end. We emerge at length in a reception area. A uniformed guard allows us to go through a door. We are in a large Union League type room with lots of leather armchairs. A man says, "Friends of Norman Lloyd go in here." I go into another room where there is a four-sided television set mounted on a pedestal showing four different channels. The news is on. They are announcing Norman's death. [1986: The news of Norman's death was premature. At this writing he is alive and well, appearing every Wednesday night on the tube in "St. Elsewhere."]

Tuesday September 25

Jack Kaufman, a producer at Wolper's, has an elaborate four-hour project called "Primal Man." We met and I liked him very much. One of the hours will be done this year. Lots of time. They have barely started shooting. The films will look like the *Planet of the Apes*, all the actors dressed up in ape costumes.

Norman Lloyd is doing *Incident at Vichy*, the Arthur Miller play. He has hired Stacy Keach to direct it.

Thursday October 4

Met with Norman and Keach. It is not going to be as satisfying for me as it usually is because Keach thinks he's a composer and has written a simple little French country tune he wants me to use.

Played by an accordion, yet. Not the sort of thing that would occur to me right off for a story about Nazis and Jews and the holocaust. We recorded the score on the 19th.

One of the most important pieces of music in this play, oddly enough, is the one that is heard during the credits at the end. The music is supposed to say what happened in Act IV if there were an Act IV. One extends oneself. In the dubbing, which I did not attend because I was working on "Primal Man," Keach dropped my end credits music and stuck in his goddam accordion tune. I wrote him a fierce letter.

Wednesday November 14

Recorded the music for the first "Primal Man." On the 20th Mr. Wolper threw a big cocktail party at the Bistro to show the film to the press. The cast in their ape suits were crawling all over the place, scratching themselves. The film was run on a faulty 16mm projector that had such a wow in it I got seasick.

Friday December 14

Today we lost a dear man, Randy MacDougall. Last December 6 I slipped into my 64th year and one does get the feeling they are closing in on one. But I am stubbornly alive and feel full of notes waiting to be written on the manuscript paper.

Work done this year, TV: "Steambath," "Double Solitaire," "The Gondola," "Incident At Vichy," "Primal Man."

1974

Sunday January 20

The Japanese send their kids to the U.S. on a three-year student visa to learn the language. Like many other people we have two of them staying with us. They do some housework and go to school. Our pair are ladies: Mieko and Yasuyo. Delightful. They swim in the pool, go out with me on the boat and on sightseeing trips about Los Angeles, and make entries in notebooks about things that interest them.

Saturday March 9

Dear, sweet, joyous Barbara Ruick, married to Johnny Williams, is dead.

Wednesday March 13

The entire cast and crew of "Primal Man" were killed in a plane crash returning from location. The exposed film in the tail of the plane survived.

Thursday March 14

Met with George Schaefer, the prolific director, who has signed on to do six hours of "Carl Sandburg's Lincoln" for David Wolper.

Sunday April 21

Charles Ives quoted in a piece in *The New York Times* magazine: "Father felt that a man could keep his music interest stronger, cleaner, bigger and freer if he didn't try to make a living out of it. Assuming a man lives by himself, with no dependents, no one to feed but himself and is willing to live simply as Thoreau, he might write music that no one would play prettily, listen to or buy. But if he has a nice wife and some nice children how can he let his children starve on his dissonances? So he has to weaken—and he should weaken for his children—but his music, some of it, more than weakens. It goes 'ta ta' for money. Bad for him, bad for music." Ives was married to Harmony Twitchell and stayed in the insurance business all his composing life.

Tuesday May 7

Working on the music for the footage of "Primal Man" that 36 people lost their lives making.

Monday May 27

Started the Lincolns. Hal Holbrook super. This job, six one hour shows, will consume the better part of the next six months. They want us to bring the music in for $30,000. I have proposed scoring two at a time. This way I think we can manage to stay within the budget. Music isn't all. You have to be an administrative accountant, too. I love writing music for films, so you learn to put on your other hat and deal with the business folk.

Thursday May 30

Ted Cain, the executive director of the Composers Guild, who has guided us through all the unpleasantness of our suit against the major studios, died today. The suit isn't over so I don't know what will happen.

Saturday June 1

Kath is going to Europe for a month. Sid and I poured her on the plane. She still has this inordinate fear of flying.

Monday June 3

Recorded the third "Primal Man" and went back to the peace and quiet of my wing at Outpost to continue writing the Lincoln music.

Tuesday July 9

On the "Today" show this morning a report on the Canadian election. Trudeau vs. a man named Stanfield. Trudeau won. It was no contest. Stanfield lacks charisma, has no sense of occasion and seems uncomfortable and stodgy in the role of vote getter. In one city in Canada, when a political leader is visiting, it is the custom for a band of pipers to march into the hall, the visitor bringing up the rear. The pipers turn right at the stage and exit while the leader mounts the platform to the cheers of the crowd. Stanfield followed the pipers out and had to be brought back in.

August, September and October

Writing and recording the Lincolns.

Friday November 15

The Pacific Pioneers, a society of old radio people, gave a lunch honoring Norman Corwin. I was on the dais and made the following speech:

I have a few words on the subject of Corwin's relations with his composers. With special reference to the summer of 1941.

In those days Corwin was an austere young man down from Boston, with his rumpled tweeds and blue shirts, but with a sense of mission. His vision, which never wavered, was to revolutionize radio drama and if it overthrew the establishment in the process he wouldn't have minded. Given his strict Puritan-Jewish upbringing he had no trouble fending off the beautiful young radio actresses who tried to deflect him from his purpose.

In the summer of 1941 CBS commissioned him to do a series of half hour shows to be called "26 By Corwin." He wanted to do verse plays, dramas, comedies, satires and three operas. To do the music for this series he hired four composers. One was Deems Taylor.

Deems was a distinguished gentleman who lived in a magnificent apartment on Fifth Avenue with 14-foot ceilings, carved mantelpieces and a view of the Plaza Hotel, and he bitched all the time about it costing him $250 a month. He did one of the operas. These three operas were based on stories from the Bible. Norman asked Leith Stevens to do one of them. I thought this peculiar casting for at that time Leith's chief claim to fame was as maestro of the "Saturday Night Swing Session."

When Norman asked *me* to do one I thought that *really* peculiar casting because at that time I was working on the "Hit Parade" making arrangements of things like the "Hut Sut Song," "Mairzie Doats" and "Don't Fence Me In." But, Norman [turning to Corwin], I want you to know I appreciate the honor. And I will tell you something now you never knew. I did it for the money. In those days, for an opera, CBS paid $75. Well, you could get a pound of sugar for 5 cents then.

The other composer on the series was God's last angry man, Bernard Herrmann. Deems and Stevens have gone to their reward and in a way Herrmann has, too. A couple of years ago he got into one of his towering rages and went to live in England. As if they haven't enough trouble there.

In the Spring of 1941 Corwin took a house at Sneden's Landing overlooking Pare Lorentz, Tallulah Bankhead, Katherine Cornell, Clifton Webb and the Hudson River. I went to see him. He told me he wanted me to do seven or eight of his shows. From where we were sitting, through the trees, you could see another house. I was recently divorced from my first wife—free as a bird—and wanting to be near Corwin I rented that house.

The first thing we did was to get to work on the opera. It was based on the story of Esther. I was studying then with a man named Joseph Schillinger, the teacher of Gershwin. (Maybe I thought some of it would come off on me.) Gershwin had just done *Porgy and Bess*. When I finished one of the songs—a song a character named Mordecai sings to Esther—I played it for Norman one night after dinner. There was a little pause and Norman said, "I think we should change the title of the show to *Mordecai and Bess*."

The only trouble with writing music for Corwin is that his production assistant doesn't know how to time a show. To close I'll give you an illustration. In "Radio Primer" he took the alphabet, A to Z, and related each letter to some function of radio. A is for Announcer, B is for Breakfast Food, O is for Orson, D is for Deadline and so forth. V was for *Variety*. This was a big cantata for chorus, orchestra and a bunch of soloists.

Variety, Variety,
All radio society,
Deems it an impropriety,
Not to read
Variety.

The show was going fine and we got into the *Variety* thing. I'm riding herd on the orchestra, the chorus and the soloists when Norman's assistant comes threading his way to the podium with a query, "Can you cut some of it?" I shook my head—how in hell could I cut it?—and we finished it as written. The next thing I knew—instead of W, X and Y, Everett Sloan goes up to the microphone and executes the most brilliant cut I've ever heard. "Z," he said, "Stands for Z end of Z program." Then followed 15 seconds of dead air relieved only by the sound of the orchestra scrambling to find the music for the closing theme.

But Norman I want you to know. I didn't really do it for the money. I did it for love.

Daily Variety in reporting this lunch picked up one line of my speech—the line about Corwin not minding if he overthrew the establishment.

Thursday November 21

Did the last "Primal Man," recording the music as usual at RCA. The saddest part was playing a piece to go under the dedication to the men who had lost their lives making this film.

Saturday November 30

My friend Roger Hamilton Spotts gets me into the damnedest things. His friend Buddy Harper takes a band and some entertainers to prisons in the area to bring a breath of the outside to the inmates. I am not an entertainer but Buddy Harper says the people are grateful to see anyone from "the street." Today I joined an entourage going to the California Institute for Women and spoke. Most of the women are in on drug charges. Walking across the grass to a cafeteria to get a cup of coffee, a woman walking ahead of me dropped her handkerchief. I stopped. She turned and said, "If you were a gentleman you'd pick it up." I did. She said she was getting out in a month and could I get her a job? I asked her what she was in for. She said, "Armed robbery # 1." I gave her Roger's phone number but she never called. Most of these women are back in before they have time to get straight.

Wednesday December 4

Hughes Rudd in his wrap-up at the end of the CBS news this morning said three stories struck him. Annabelle's chain of bordellos in Germany has gone bankrupt to the tune of $1,000,000. A lady in a small mid-western town was serenaded by some early Christmas carollers. After a chorus of "Silent Night" they asked for money. She refused. They set fire to her porch. A man having breakfast in his kitchen. A bomb falls through his roof. He calls the police. They come. It is not a bomb. It is a block of frozen effluent from an airplane. I love Hughes Rudd.

Friday December 27

Bought another plaything. This time a Fender-Rhodes piano.

Monday December 30

Jeff Alexander, Lee Cass (yes, they are getting it on), Kathy and I to Vancouver. The non-stop flight from Los Angeles to Vancouver on Western was fine and comfortable. The casting department at this airline is apparently run by Toulouse-Lautrec. The stewardesses are all 4′ 2″ which makes for easy communication when you are sitting down. Not like on PSA where you are talking into a crotch.

A Hertz car awaited us at the Vancouver airport because I have a card from the Dramatists Guild, and one from the Composers Guild, entitling me to 20 percent off any Hertz car I rent. They had a nice Granada for us at $20 a day plus fringes amounting to $3. To no one's surprise the 20 percent-off cards didn't work. They only apply if you plan to use the car for some purpose other than driving it somewhere.

Between us we have ten pieces of luggage. When the porter got them all stowed in the Granada there was only room for the driver. This turned out to be Jeff because he gets carsick in any other seat unless he takes dramamine. We made it to the Vancouver Hotel in very unusual positions.

Returning on the plane Kathy discovered she was out of cigarettes. Two Beverly Hills ladies wearing Fuhrmann furs were seated behind us—smoking. I asked them for a cigarette for my wife. They refused.

Arriving Los Angeles we were held on the ground for 30 minutes until the plane ahead of us cleared. Customs was par for America. That is, worse than England, France, Italy, the Netherlands,

Denmark and all the Scandinavian countries combined. Yuzo, our houseman, had brought the car to meet us and we were glad to see him. But not the ticket he got for double parking.

Work done. TV: 2 "Primal Man," 6 "Carl Sandberg's Lincoln."

1975

Thursday January 23

Met with Norman Lloyd, his assistant, and a director, at KCET. They are going to do the Dorothy Parker—Arnaud D'Usseau play *Ladies of the Corridor* for the "Hollywood Television Theatre." The director wants to use Gershwin's "Concerto in F" as the basis of the score. Considering the content of the play—a bunch of old ladies living in a New York hotel—it's not a bad idea. We have to get permission from the Gershwin estate and I have to figure out the minimum number of musicians I can get by with to recreate passably a full symphony score. I decided to re-orchestrate the sections of the work we would use, for 18 men.

At this meeting I discovered the musicians union was charging KCET the tape scale, which is correct, because these plays are done on videotape. This scale is much higher than film scale. Carl Fortina, my contractor, and I went to the union and talked them into using the lower film scale for these taped shows on the grounds that this was impecunious public television. This ploy eventually saved KCET thousands of dollars and made it possible for them to let us use the 18 men for this score.

Friday February 14

Recorded the *Ladies of the Corridor* score at RCA. Peter Abbott the mixer gave us a pickup that made our 18 men sound as if they were playing in Carnegie Hall. The men rose to the occasion, particularly Artie Kane, who played the piano part brilliantly. Great sound. (To further lessen the strain on the budget I neglected to send in a bill for the orchestration.) I have always been puzzled that reviews of these shows, and almost all other television shows, never mention the music. I thought surely the reviews of *Ladies of the Corridor* would notice the Gershwin music. I made a point of going in to KCET a few weeks later and reading reviews from all over the country. Not one of them mentioned the music.

Sid Kuller and I are working on a most interesting and artistic project. It is called "Fables of the Green Forest," an animated version of the Peter Rabbit stories. The animation was done in Japan. Jonathan Winters is going to do the character voice-overs. We are writing some songs.

Wednesday March 19

The *Queen Elizabeth II* paid her first call to Los Angeles, arriving this morning at 6:45. I was there in *Valido* and took pictures. It was barely dawn when she came in sight but I persevered and dodged among the fireboats spraying a welcome, and got some good shots.

"Requiem for a Nun," Hollywood TV Theatre opus scored, out of deference for the budget and because I wanted to, for a string quartet.

Wednesday April 23

A long, long session with Jonny Winters recording the songs for "Fables of the Green Forest." He is marvelous playing frogs and rabbits but when it comes to songs—well. We recorded them two or three bars at a time and spent hours cutting the bits together.

Friday May 23

Bought some very fancy electronic equipment today for $7,500. It is called an RMI (that stands for Rocky Mountain Instruments) and consists of a digital synthesizer and an organ operated by inserting IBM cards. I got round the usual objections by using some of my pension money from the musicians union and mortgaging some of my Social Security (I am a senior citizen composer now). [The stuff paid for itself eventually. I charged clients $150 every time I used it on a score and I used it frequently.]

Friday August 8

Saw *Wonderful Town* tonight with Nanette Fabray, my absolutely favorite female performer. Went with George Cates who is still producing the Lawrence Welk shows. He added a pair of items to Welk lore. Lawrence called George a while ago and said, "Tschaikovsky is playing at the Bowl Thursday. Do you want to go?" George said, "Yes. I haven't heard him play for a long time." At the concert, during the Bb Concerto, Welk said, "Couldn't we play a tune like that sometime?" George said, "Yes." Next night, on a re-run of one of their old programs, the fourth number was the Concerto.

Welk and his organization play Lake Tahoe every year. This year he cut a number played by Charlotte, his featured cellist. She pouted all the next day. Before they went on that night, Welk said, "Charlotte, just because we cut your number there's no need to sit around with a sour pussy." The band laughed and Welk thought he had said something funny. Later, playing Madison Square Garden to a large and enthusiastic audience, Welk said, "What a nice audience you are. There's not a sour pussy among you."

October/November

Julie Harris is to do Jimmy Prideaux' play *The Last of Mrs. Lincoln* for the "Hollywood Television Theatre," George Schaefer directing. She had done it on Broadway. At the first reading she was the only person round the table not using the book. Usually first readings are halting and tentative and make the playwright wonder if he has written a playable line. Not this one. A beautiful, touching play and a pleasure to write a score for. Lots of time to do it—it won't record until next year.

Nothing much happened for the rest of the year. Inexorably, I passed the line between 65 and 66 without paying any attention at all.

Work done. TV: "Ladies of the Corridor," "Requiem for a Nun." "Fables of the Green Forest," "The Ashes of Mrs. Reasoner."

1976

February

Harry Lojewsky was my music cutter on the film *Period of Adjustment*, now he is head of the music department at Metro-Goldwyn-Mayer. On the 9th he called me in and gave me an episode of a TV show called "Medical Center." I had a bit of trouble at the recording because of the orchestra set-up. Woodwinds were placed to my right, strings to the left, about 30 or 40 feet apart, to achieve what mixers so dearly love—"separation." I couldn't keep them together in concerted passages. I don't think Toscanini could have. They finally gave in and distributed headsets to the players so that they could hear each other.

On the 11th I attended Percy Faith's funeral. I had known Percy since 1936. On his trips down from Canada with a batch of scores under his arm he would pop into my office at CBS looking for work. His big, stringy arrangements were a great success for years on Columbia Records. He did some picture scores but that wasn't his true métier. At lunch one day at Universal, where he was doing a picture, he told me he had discovered the key to writing for the movies. He said, "You get a good theme and make above twelve different arrangements of it." Sometimes that works but this time it didn't. The producer threw out his score; but Percy's theory was more right than wrong. In *Dr. Zhivago*, David Lean was so enamored of "Lara's Theme" he dumped the last third of Maurice Jarre's score and repeated and repeated the theme until musicians in the audience thought if they heard it one more time they would have to leave the theatre. But Lean was right, the great movie audience loved it, Jarre got an Academy Award and at one point the record album was making more money than the picture. Stanley Kubrick did the same thing to Leonard Rosenman in *Barry Lyndon*. He repeated an idiotic little theme played by a piccolo and a cello so much Rosenman wanted to take his name off the picture. That is, until the score was nominated for and won an Academy Award. So who's right?

March

Bought a Tascam 8-track recorder. I can now score a whole picture in my workroom.

Saturday March 13

To Oakland. The Oakland Museum is staging "A Tribute to California Film Composers." Elmer Bernstein, Fred Steiner, David Raksin and I conducted the New Beginnings Chamber Orchestra in scores we had written for some short films, which were then shown. Bernstein did his "Toccata for Toy Trains," Steiner "The Merry-Go-Round in the Jungle," Raksin his "Unicorn In The Garden," "Giddyap" and Gail Kubik's "Gerald McBoing Boing." I did the Ronald Searle film we made for Standard Oil. The orchestra was prepared by a young woman named Sally Kell and all we had to do was wave at them. It was a good experience. As I said to the lady who organized it, it was nice to get out of the asylum for a few days and mingle with real people.

Sunday April 4

The Los Angeles International Film Exposition (FILMEX), along with its roster of current films from all over the world, resurrects an old silent film each year and presents it with orchestral accompaniment. This year they ran *Rebecca of Sunnybrook Farm*, a Mary Pickford film, and I prepared and conducted the music. I came out of this experience with renewed respect for the conductors who used to do this sort of work. There are problems. The number one difficulty is that these old films do not run at a constant speed. A scene that runs three minutes, depending on the projectionist, can vary as much as 15 seconds or more either way—faster or slower. In the old days the conductor had a film speed indicator on his desk. We didn't have that. Another problem is that the music plays from the first frame to the end of the picture. I was smart and had Gaylord Carter playing the organ for certain sections, not only to give the orchestra a rest, but to protect me in case the variable speed messed up my sync. Another problem was that we never had an orchestra rehearsal with picture because the theatre was not available. This is doing it the hard way. I borrowed a lot of music from the MGM library and painstakingly built the score, with the help of Stan Levine and Roger Hamilton Spotts, xeroxing, cutting and pasting. It took days. One of the rewards was the audience response. They loved it and when we got through the orchestra stood and took bows for ten minutes.

Working on a little six-character musical written by Jerry Devine with lyrics by Ellen Fitzhugh.

Monday May 3

At Capitol recording an album with Bob Hope. Has to do with the bi-centennial. Sid and I wrote some songs, went out to rehearse Bob at his estancia on Moorpark in the Valley. He is a phenomenon still. We told jokes for an hour and rehearsed the songs for at least ten minutes; just like the old days at Paramount when Bob would come in swinging his golf stick and spend more time entertaining the orchestra than he did in the isolation booth recording the tunes. We recorded both Monday and Tuesday and the only one who did not tire was Hope. He paid me sort of a compliment. He said, when it was all over, "You've still got it."

Monday June 21

Nick Noxon has produced a film for the National Geographic Society called *Treasure!* We ran it today. Has to do with a man named Mel Fisher and a group diving for treasure to be found in Spanish galleons lost in hurricanes off the Florida keys in the 16th century. There is a lot of underwater stuff, naturally, and I am going to score all these sequences on my machinery at home.

Thursday June 24

At John and Jane Hesses for dinner. Their friend Dick Dunne told of an incident which occurred during the shooting of the film

Paper Moon at a location somewhere down south. A person had been assigned to cast certain local characters. A mother, black, brought her eight-year-old daughter, who was wearing a shocking pink tutu, to audition. The mother was asked to wait outside while her child went in for the interview. When the little girl emerged she said, "He say they don' need no nigger ballerinas at dis time."

Friday July 9

I took my 8-track Tascam containing the underwater music for *Treasure!* to Capitol where we hooked it up and mixed it down.

Wednesday July 21

To the Burbank Studios to record the orchestral music for the show with a 28-piece orchestra. Danny Wallin, the best mixer in town, gave us such a great sound that Linda Reavely, the delightful lady in charge of post production for National Geographic, exclaimed, "It sounds just like a movie!"

Eddie Constantine here. He has written a book. The publisher gave a cocktail party at Ma Maison, a high class boite, where if you are not driving a Rolls they hide your car in sheer embarrassment.

Doing a "Serpico" at Paramount.

Wednesday December 22

Tom Talbert, a friend of Kathy's, came into town a few weeks ago. He is a band leader and arranger who wants to score pictures. I introduced him around and he wangled himself a TV episode at Paramount. I helped him with the mechanics of scoring for film and today I went to Paramount and conducted it for him.

Work done. TV: "The Last of Mrs. Lincoln," "Medical Center," "Serpico," National Geographic's *Treasure!*

Record album: "Where There's Hope."

1977

Friday January 14

Dominic Frontiere, now head of the music department at Paramount, called me with a strange request. He wanted me to sit in the booth and attend to the balances on two sessions (one on Thursday 6, and this one today) conducted by George Tipton. There is a union scale for this sort of function—$147—and since I wasn't doing anything I thought what the hell, I'll do it. I'll see what kind of music the competition is writing and get to say hello to musicians I haven't seen in a while. I am beginning to have trouble with my hearing, though, and after these two sessions I decided not to do any more.

Tuesday February 8

Everybody knows commercials pay more money than regular television. Example: Larry Orenstein came over to Outpost and in one hour we made some simple music for a Baskin-Robbins commercial. I got $1,000 for the hour's work. (After the commercial had been running awhile I got a further residual payment of $588. Unbelievable.)

Saturday February 19

Recorded songs for Jerry Devine's *Sing We Now of Love* in Les Remsen's church from 1:30 to 4:30 and 7:30 to 1:30. Odd thing about this effort. Jerry's friends love the book and don't think much of the score. My friends like the score and make uncomplimentary remarks about the book.

Wednesday March 2

To the Academy to see the film *Obsession*, scored by Benny Herrmann. I sat with Arthur Morton. The Main Title came on— vintage Herrmann—and Arthur said, "One gets tired of hearing 'Jeepers Creepers' without ever getting to 'Where'd you get those peepers?'" At the end I defended Herrmann's peculiar dramatic vision. He seems to see a movie score whole with all its ramifications and developments and, of course, his orchestration is superb.

Monday March 14

Bill Kronick, a producer at Wolper, has a film called *Mysteries of the Great Pyramid*. We have run it a few times. He has definite ideas about music, most of them cancelling each other out. I took my hand-held recorder and taped all his comments.

Tuesday March 29

Recorded the music which was, according to instructions, bright, dissonant, elegant, entertaining, full, rich and sonorous, historic, spooky, hollow, informational, intellectual, light-hearted, lush, lyric, mocking, mysterious, powerful, questioning, romantic, unorthodox, unsettling and occasionally upbeat. In light of the information above about the $1,588 I was paid for an hour's work on a commercial for Baskin-Robbins, I made a breakdown of what I was paid for the Egypt score, which took over three weeks to write.

Gross pay	3,500
Commission	350
Federal Tax	1,100
FICA	204.75
SDI	35.00
State	312.50
Motion Picture Relief	35.00
Permanent Charities	35.00
Alimony	393.75
Net	1,777.75

It wasn't quite that much, though. I've forgotten what the union gets for Work Dues and Health & Welfare.

Friday April 29

Drove to Santa Barbara with Jerry Devine and his wife Marilyn to take a look at the Lobero Theatre to see if it will do for our *Sing*

We Now show. Jerry had made a reservation for us at the Upham Hotel. When we drove by it and Kathy got a look at the old folks in rocking chairs on the porch she said she wouldn't stay there. Preferred the Santa Barbara Biltmore. Jerry and I went in to look at the accommodations, which were clean and comfortable and furthermore the folks running the hotel "recognized the profession" and made us a rate of $16. We stayed there. Will Geer and family were staying at the Upham and playing the Lobero, a cheerless, uninviting auditorium we didn't like a bit.

Geer was on the blacklist in the fifties. Couldn't get a job acting and worked as a gardener. One of his clients was Sid Kuller.

Thursday June 30

Patsy Melchior arrived for an extended stay. I think all is not well with them and I am sorry but happy to have her here. She is gay company (in the old sense of the word) and her presence cuts the bickering some.

Thursday July 7

Saw *Providence* at the Academy, directed by Alain Resnais, a beautifully designed film with an interesting performance by Elaine Stritch and a strange one from John Gielgud, miscast as a writer who has laid everybody in the world, the part as written calling for him to utter all the dirty words in the language, which sound wrong coming out of his Shakespearean mouth. Ellen Burstyn, too, sounds uncomfortable using such language. Dirk Bogarde plays her husband like someone newly released from the closet. Very stylized sets. Shocking shots of an autopsy being performed on an old man dead of cancer. Rozsa's score was old style, rather poorly recorded, I thought— sounded like it came out of his trunk, but solidly composed as usual.

Thursday July 21

The Composers Guild is suing the Motion Picture Producers. We are represented by Theodore Kheel, and today we had a meeting. The producers' legal team is headed by Louis Nizer, whom I ran into at the foot of the stairs leading to the Association of Motion Picture and TV Producers conference room. I introduced myself and said I was honored to meet him. He said he loved music and was honored to meet me, then went upstairs and beat the bejesus out of us.

August

Saw a startling and stimulating rock version of Ovid's "Metamorphosis" written by a bright 24-year-old named Tony Greco. They are just scraping by at the Callboard Theatre. He came to see me bringing tapes and the scores. The tapes (of a performance) have nothing to do with the scores. He explained he allowed the performers lots of leeway. I wish I knew how to do that.

Edwin Lester's production of *Irma la Douce* is playing at the Music Center as one of his Civic Light Opera offerings and he has asked Sid and me to write a new first act finale. We did it but Michael Kidd says he hasn't time to stage it, so it never went in.

Wednesday October 12

Frank DeVol is writing the music for *The Choirboys,* a dreadful film by Robert Aldrich. He asked me to write and conduct the Main Title. I am getting to be a regular mother's little helper.

Tuesday December 6

May Collins, who pays attention to such things, threw a party for my 68th birthday at her mansion. Three comments: I can't seem to get any work; I feel about 35; I admire May Collins.

1978

Wednesday March 15

A composer I don't know, de Benedictis, called me for help on a television show he can't finish in time. I wrote a sequence for him and recorded it today at the Burbank Studios.

Thursday April 27

Daughter Joyce gave birth to a baby girl, in so doing joining the army of single parents. My first grandchild.

Sid Kuller to dinner. He has written some additional lyrics for Jerry Devine's show, *Sing We Now of Love,* and we discussed going to Carmel to take a look at Alan Gilbert's Barnyard Theatre to see if we might mount a production of *Sing We* there. While we were at it we could go to San Francisco to see Joyce and the baby. The idea of Joyce having a baby out of wedlock is repugnant to Kathy and she vetoed my going to see her. I decided to go anyway and on the 29th Sid and I flew to Carmel and went to see Gilbert's theatre. After the perform-ance we met the musical director, a woman named Joan D. Swarz. On the 30th Sid and I went to San Francisco and visited Joyce in the hospital, saw the baby, and returned the next day to Los Angeles.

May

I had a letter from Joan Swarz saying she had to come to Los Angeles to rent some percussion instruments for the next show and could I help? She came down, as it happened on a day Kathy was out of town, and I took her to Drum City where Roy Hart was able to supply what she needed. I took her to dinner at the Pavilion and later in her motel we went to bed.

I heard from her again. This time she wondered if I would write an overture for *Stop the World.* She has a skimpy little six-piece orchestra which sounds awful playing the orchestrations supplied with the shows, written as they were for much larger orchestras. I wrote back and agreed to do it. We corresponded mostly about her instrumentation but I also learned she has three children aged 16, 18 and 20 by ex-husband Swarz, a doctor. I wrote the overture and mailed it off. She telephoned and wondered if I would like to come up for the rehearsal. When I told Kathy I was going up to Carmel to rehearse the overture she put her foot down. Didn't believe I had written an overture, had noted the correspondence and thought I had a woman up there. I said I *had* written an overture and I was going. I went, rehearsed and had a further pleasant experience with the lady.

Saturday June 10

Sid came to dinner last night. He is not a favorite of Kathy's but he is my closest friend and, even when we are not working on something, he comes to dinner about once a week. After dinner Kathy sounded off about my trips to Carmel saying it was quite obvious to her I was carrying on. Sid and I went to my wing to play Yahtzee, as we usually do. We discussed the situation. He said something about my cooling it. I suppose it is common for a man in my situation to conduct an affair with the subconscious hope that he will be found out. At any rate this morning Kathy came into my bedroom and said she had been listening outside my door last night and made an ultimatum. "Her" she said, "or me." I said, "Well, that'll take a minute to think over." After a few hysterical moments she went into her room, packed a bag and left.

I called May Collins and told her what had happened. While we were talking Kathy arrived at her house, hysterical, wounded. Later in the day Kathy had May call to suggest I leave and find a place to live, on the grounds that Kathy could handle it better if she was staying in our house which meant so much to her, etc. I spent the weekend looking for a furnished apartment—a depressing experience. Thought of the Presnells and their guest house. They gladly welcomed me.

Tuesday June 13

Got some clothes together and moved in.
Someone has bought all the old Laurel and Hardy films and

proposes to chop them up into small segments for sale to television. He wants them all scored and has engaged Fred Steiner to do the job. Fred has invited Jeff and me to help. I figure it will take about seven weeks to write. David Abell sent me a beautiful little Yamaha upright piano and I am working. During this period Joan Swarz came down to spend a night. The Presnells not impressed.

Saturday July 15

May called (all contact with Kathy is through her) saying Kathy has to go to Wyoming for a few days to see about leasing a piece of property there she owns to an oil company for gas exploration. By request I moved into Outpost to cat-and-dog-sit and took my work with me, returning to the Presnells on the 19th.

Communications through May continue. I wanted to take Bob and Marsha out for a fancy dinner and asked her to be my date. She asked Kathy if she would mind. Kathy would mind very much. She didn't want May making my life pleasant and asked her not to go. May thought it was nonsense and came with us.

Finished with the Laurel and Hardy music, I thought I would go up to Monterey for a month to be with Joan, as she suggested. I was receptive because she had brought me to life after about four years of nothing much. I wrote and asked her to get me an apartment.

Tuesday August 1

Left the Presnells at 11. Half an hour up the Ventura Freeway I realized I had forgotten to pack clothes. Went back, corrected the oversight, and set out again. At seven I arrived in Salinas where I decided to have dinner. I pulled off the Freeway and stopped at Cindy's Restaurant and asked if they had a bar. No bar. Nor did they have a bar at Hobo Joe's. Ran into a man with the same problem. We joined forces and wound up at the East of Eden, a very nice restaurant in an old church, where we had a leisurely dinner. My thirsty friend was Leslie Dwyer, a man engaged in the trade book publishing business. He talked a lot about his business but most of the two hours was devoted to the story of the murder of his daughter Marcia.

She was a student at UCLA with a part time job in a restaurant where the maître d' was a 32-year-old Chinese named Lu. One morning Lu appeared at Dwyer's door and asked to see Marcia. Dwyer refused, and after an argument turned to call the police. Lu produced a gun and shot him in the back. Dwyer turned and Lu shot him twice more in the chest. Marcia appeared from her room. Lu shot and killed her. The Chinese escaped to Canada and hid out with a brother, surfacing when the Canadian police arrested him for armed assault. Dwyer was in the hospital for seven months, the length of time it took to extradite Lu. At the trial the Chinese claimed self-defense but the bullet entry in Dwyer's back exploded that. He was convicted of second degree murder and got a minimum of nine years.

Arrived Monterey at 9:45 and went to 256 Watson Street, a newish, jerrybuilt apartment house but clean enough.

There followed three days of pleasure and lovemaking. Also I picked up a rather disturbing piece of information; Joan was living with a man, and had been for the last four years. She had a three-year-old child by him but claimed she had been trying to oust him for some time and he was moving out—slowly. "Trust me," she said, "I can handle him." It was a rather surreal experience visiting old Missions with her, walking that spectacular shoreline and meeting between rehearsals of *Carousel* while what turned out to be a time bomb ticked away around the corner.

Friday August 4

Sid arrived, as planned, to spend a few days with me. *Carousel* opened tonight and we took Joan to the cast party. Someone reported my presence to the live-in ex-lover whose name is Richard Monat. Alan Gilbert described him to me as a large, bearded, mid-thirties, alcoholic carpenter and photographer who has not worked for two years. Over the following weekend this chap ransacked the house, found my letters, read them, learned my name (apparently I had written one of them on my stationery) confronted Joan and made threats. Can't say I blame him.

Monday August 7

Joan called me from a telephone booth. She sounded terrified. She was walking with the three-year-old. Richard was following them in his truck. I told her to either shake him and bring the child to my apartment or go to the police. Sid, upbeat as usual, comforted me, saying that this fellow was probably yellow. I was not especially comforted. The phone rang again. This time is was Joan's 20-year-old daughter April, calling from the police station; Richard had doused himself with gasoline, laid a trail of it into the house, locked himself into his truck and was threatening to set himself afire, and incidentally burn down the house. I told her to have the police send a fire unit and a police car to the scene.

Sid and I were scheduled to take Alan Gilbert, his wife and Joan to dinner at the Whaling Station in Cannery Row. Understandably Joan begged off. We went and had a nice dinner. Before leaving the restaurant we called Joan's house. No answer. Back at the apartment we called again. Joan answered and reported that police and the fire department, after a four-hour standoff, had talked Richard out of the truck. He fought them but was eventually subdued and placed under restraint. At 11 o'clock, strapped in an ambulance, he was taken to a county facility and incarcerated under a law which allows a 72-hour "hold" on people who are a threat to themselves or others. I couldn't help but think that this plot would make a script for one of Presnell's Movies of the Week.

Tuesday August 8

A serious discussion with Joan. I urged her to get a restraining order, to protect herself and the children, and said I would stay until the situation was temporarily resolved, then I thought it best that I leave. She was upset and left without a word. I called her shortly and told her to come back. She did. She felt I was rejecting her. I was supportive and she calmed down.

Wednesday August 9

Joan brought her three-year-old round to meet Sid. When they left I took Sid to the airport to catch his one o'clock plane. At two o'clock I called the house and a man answered. A few minutes later Joan appeared at my door. That was Richard on the phone. He had talked his way out of the hospital nine hours early.

Joan said she had decided against getting a restraining order because poor Richard would have no place to go. He was rational, lucid, sober and repentant. She felt it would be more humane and caring if she allowed him to stay in the house until she could arrange somewhere for him to go and get help. She interpreted his behavior as a cry for help. We were together from five until ten. We made dinner, and love, which was nice if you like playing with fire.

Saturday August 12

Joan came over in the afternoon and we behaved as though nothing untoward was happening. How important can sex be to a 68-year-old idiot? We arranged to meet tomorrow morning and go to her church, and in the afternoon to a jazz concert where Manny Klein was due to appear. She did not show on Sunday morning. At one o'clock two kids appeared at the door—David, 16 and April—with a note from Joan. She said she was outraged, and wouldn't be surprised if I didn't want to see her again, and that I could either send her a note by April or leave a message for her at the theatre. While I was pondering this enigma the phone rang. It was Sid reporting that Kathy had called him. She was, shall I say, upset, because Richard Monat had telephoned her Friday night and read excerpts of my letters to Joan. He quoted a passage saying I had given Joan $1,600 (untrue), that I had said Kathy's friends hated her (untrue), and other such goodies. With this development I sent a note to Joan asking her to call me. When she did I told her I thought she had made a mistake in her handling of the situation and since my presence was, to put it mildly, complicating things, I was leaving that afternoon.

I learned later that this ape had made three or four more midnight calls to Kathy. May listened in on at least one of them and said he sounded drunk, incoherent and not exactly sane.

Driving back to the Presnells I thought the situation over. Kathy has had to deal with an extraordinary series of events following my departure. I feel awful that all this has occurred. A little dalliance *ordinaire* has turned into a bloody nightmare. In spite of all this I still feel that Kathy and I are better off apart, that we were destructive together. She chooses not to believe this. She thinks we had a good marriage, that she devoted her life to me and that I was happy with the way it went. I wasn't, because I was not an equal partner; Kathy ran things her way and no other way, and even now runs the money. I settled for it because I thought I was too old to make a change, but this peccadillo certainly wrought a change and, sad as I am about Kathy, I know it is better for me, if not for her.

Monday August 14

Arrived Presnells at noon after spending the night in Santa Maria. Louise Losey and her husband Peter Huan are in the guest house rendering me temporarily homeless. I called seven motels and got into the Carriage Inn in Van Nuys for one night. The town is full of conventioneers and tourists. Having settled the problem of tonight I called Dick Dunne who is occupying the Hess's house to see if I could stay there for a few days. He said he was expecting a friend named John, would call him and find out when he was coming and would call me back. He didn't.

Tuesday August 15

The Carriage Inn is letting me stay an extra day. I called Tom Talbert, who has a large house and owes me for introducing him around to my contacts in this business, to see if he would let me in for a few days. He hemmed and hawed—he was starting a job, etc.—and finally agreed to take me for a couple of days. I called Jeff Alexander who also owes me. He was leaving town for a week and said his daughter Jill and a friend were coming to stay in his house while he was away. I said I didn't mind sharing his house with Jill—what the hell, I sat up with him the night she was born— but he said he thought she wanted to be alone. I got on the phone and turned up a motel in Canoga Park, a suburb barely on the map, and got a two-week commitment. Jeff called back and said he had called hotels and got space in a Holiday Inn for $42 a day which he said he would pay. Guilty, I guess. Dick Dunne called and said his friend (whose name had now changed to Brian) was coming Thursday—sorry. I called Talbert and let him off the hook, and his guilt prompted him to invite me to dinner. I went and paid for it by listening to a tape of his last show.

Friday August 18

Kathy called me for the first time since we separated. She thinks it is time for us to meet and discuss our future. Doesn't remember much about the ultimatum, thinks my current behavior erratic and referred to a long, carefully wrought communication I had written her, as a Dear John letter. I told her I had found an unfurnished apartment on the beach at Belmont Shores for $600. It was agreed that I would try to manage on $1,000 a month. I asked her to help me organize the apartment—I wanted my bed, some of the things from my workroom, etc.—but she refused. She was against the Belmont Shores apartment because of the expense and the fact that I would be lonely there—away from friends. She seems to want a reconciliation on any terms. She has not told anyone of the separation, now ten weeks old, but a lot of people know. I called John Hess in Bucks County on the day of the confrontation to see if his house here was empty and I had to tell him why I wanted it. His wife Jane was on the extension. I asked her not to say anything, to leave it to Kathy to announce it when she felt like it, and she promptly called Tom Talbert who told Patsy Melchior, so everybody knows.

The Belmont Shores apartment is settled. I will move in September 4.

Wednesday August 23

Moved back into the Presnells' guest house. It seems they are my only friends.

Monday September 4

To the Caillous for dinner. Alan, an English writer and professional character; Alisa his wife, an interesting Russian lady; and Nadia, their daughter. She has a lion cub for a pet that is on a diet of furniture.

Tuesday September 5

Moved to 7001 Seaside Walk, Long Beach. Landlady a very fussy retired Dean of Women at Long Beach State named Fauré Rilliet. Incidentally, when I went to Outpost to supervise the moving of what stuff I needed, Kathy hung around against my wishes and said, "I hope you are as miserable as you have made me." Very sticky.

Got the apartment organized. Called a carpenter to build a cabinet I had carefully designed to hold the Sony, amps, the Teac, the turntable and the patch board. It was supposed to have been made of white pine but he showed up with a dreadful looking thing made of some kind of plywood and he and his helper were drunk to boot. I think I got screwed. It cost $405. I bought carpets, had Mike from Westwood Upholsterers cover the sofa and chairs in dark blue denim, got some dark fabric from Sears and tacked it over the bedroom window to keep out the light, which it did, but did not keep out the sounds of cars revving up at 7:30 a.m. That woke me Mondays through Fridays the entire five months I was there.

Wednesday September 13

My first allowance check came. $600. I called May, who called Kathy, who said she didn't have enough to send the $1,000 this month. (May thinks it ridiculous that I still let Kathy run the money.) She told Kathy not to be silly, and another $400 was forthcoming.

Tuesday September 19

A surprise visit from Joan of Monterey. She drank two bottles of champagne and got stoned. When I drove her to Santa Monica where she was staying with friends, she couldn't remember the address. Another nightmare.

Monday October 23

Had lunch with Linda Reavely, Jack Tillar and Bob Light (my agent) at Musso Franks to discuss the National Geographic's film *The Tigris Expedition*. Linda is in charge of post production at NGS, makes the deals for composers and lives with Barry Nye the head cutter; Tillar is the music cutter and general music mogul on the series. The film is being produced by Dale Bell, who is an utter delight.

Tuesday October 24

Ruby Raksin, David's younger brother, who is in the same boat marriage-wise as I am, came to dinner. Everyone who is separated from his wife, except me, lives in the Marina. Ruby is a mathematics genius. He has written textbooks on the mathematical aspects, and there are many, of scoring films.

Friday October 27

Sid's birthday. His middle son Jeff owns and operates a discotheque on an old Alaska steamer, the *Lady Alexandra*, tied up at King Harbor, Redondo Beach. The three sons gave a dinner party and invited me. Rich, the eldest, never knows where he is and was two hours late. Kenny, the youngest, is a bartender on the boat and was there anyway.

Sunday October 29

Journeyed to the Valley for dinner at Bob and Marsha's. It is a sleeper jump from Long Beach but gas is only 54 cents a gallon at the neighborhood Arco.

Monday November 6

Ken Murray has been making home movies of the famous for years and has spliced all the footage together into a feature-length film. Pete Rugolo recommended me to do the music so today I went to the Burbank Studios to take a look at it. I've known Ken for a long time. I took an old picture of us taken in 1934 at my apartment at 31 Sutton Place South. In this picture we look 44 years younger. I showed it to Ken's wife. She looked at it a long time, then said, "What happened?"

This picture needs a lot of music, and there is the usual lack of time to do it, so I called Fred Steiner to look at it. We figured and came up with a budget which was too high, and we didn't get to do it.

Thursday November 9

Sent flowers to Kathy for our anniversary. When the bill went to Outpost she sent it to me with no comment.

Saturday November 11

Doug Broyles, Marsha Presnell's young nephew whom we saw doing *Hamlet* at the Globe Theatre in Hollywood; his lady friend; Sid and his current (he's married but his wife lives in their house at Arrowhead and he can't go there because it is bad for his pacemaker); and a lady named Myrna Dell here for dinner, at which Doug passed around some perfectly lousy marijuana. Myrna Dell was my date. She is an old movie-star friend of Marsha's who, said Marsha, would "talk me to joy." She didn't.

Wednesday December 6

It is my birthday and I am 69. My landlady, Fauré Rilliet, is the leader of the local chapter of Common Cause. She may be fussy but she is liberal. Tonight they are running an auction to raise money. I contributed an old but unused Mark Cross attaché case, an 8mm projector and some books. Norm and Jackie Brown, my neighbors from across the street, are at the auction to help out. It is a failure. Only 30 people showed up and they are the ones who contributed the stuff. They wind up buying each other's junk.

Thursday December 7

A party at May Collins's. Kathy, Bill Talbott, Tom and Pierette Frieburg, Jeff Alexander and Lee Cass. Jeff sat next to May and (she told me later) discussed each man at the table in terms of strengths and weaknesses. I was weak but he was strong. Everyone left and I stayed behind for a nightcap. May and I sat on the rug before the fire in the library and talked. Eventually I said I would be going and leaned over to give her my usual peck on the cheek. Ever since I have known her, I have given her a peck on the cheek on arrival and departure. This time she didn't turn her cheek and we kissed on the mouth. When we stopped to get our breath there was a long silence full of implication. What vestiges of English reserve that linger in me prevent me from saying more than that. Later we discussed at length the implications.

Since the separation May had, at Kathy's request, played the role of go-between. She was Kathy's only confidante and my only conduit to Kathy. Kath kept the whole thing secret as long as she could. After she returned to Outpost she talked to May daily, progressing from deep depression, through hysteria, to vindictiveness.

I had admired May for years. She is smart and was a survivor in a tough business; she had gone through her husband's long decline and death from cancer with a courage you seldom see in women in that situation. She disciplines her body, dresses elegantly and always treated me with a kind of respect that startled me, being accustomed to Kathy's ball-breaking destructiveness. After her husband's death, when May stayed with us for a few weeks while looking for a house, the obvious thought crossed my mind. As far as I knew she had been alone for over a year but she never sent the slightest intimation in my direction that she might be receptive or available, and every man knows when he gets such a signal from a woman. There was absolutely none from May. I had no trouble dismissing any thoughts I might have had because this disciplined woman would have rejected any kind of liaison with the husband of her old friend even though, having sat through the interminable bickering, there was no marriage there to break up.

So here we were at the start of what we both sensed was something of importance, discussing the impact it would have on Kathy. Kathy who, six months after the separation began, was still given to fits of hysteria and depression and was still wallowing in self-pity. Some time before this it had been arranged that I would celebrate my birthday with Art Lavove and his wife, as we had done for years (since Art and I have the same birthday), with a little dinner at Long Beach. May had accepted the invitation to be my hostess. Kath objected to this arrangement on the grounds that May would be helping me through a boring evening (she is not fond of Lavove) and she did not want anyone helping me through a boring evening or anything else; but May took a stand. We parted rather soberly as we thought of the possibilities.

Saturday December 9

I like Art Lavove and the four of us had a nice jolly evening. I saw the Lavoves to their car and May to hers and when the Lavoves pulled away we went back into the house.

Thursday December 14

I went to May's for dinner, and that night we knew this was serious and irrevocable, and a true commitment. It is a joy and a delight. How easy it is to love a woman who never utters a discouraging or negative word.

Sunday December 24

Christmas Eve party at Kath's. May there, of course. Later we proved that this love affair is a conflagration that cannot be quenched by thoughts of what might happen if—or when.

Tuesday December 26

David Raksin came down to dinner and I went over the choral parts of a piece he has written to be sung at the wedding of one of his students. This meticulously wrought piece amazed me, considering the purpose for which it was written.

Saturday December 30

Wrote the *Tigris* stuff all day Friday and in the daytime Saturday. In the evening, a day too soon, May and I ended the year with fireworks, not the kind you apply a match to.

1979

Monday January 1

I am writing cue twenty one which concerns the building of the *Tigris*, the introduction of Heyerdahl and his crew, involves some tricky mathematical problems—catching the guys pulling on the ropes that bind the reeds—and introduces the Edvardian flavored main theme (Grieg, that is).

I have become very fond of Dale Bell, who produced this film. He walks about in sandals even when it is raining, which it has been doing around here lately, and he, Linda, Barry, May and I have had some nice rollicking dinners. The writer on this show is Theodore Strauss, a spiffy fellow with a nice wife named Ludie. The group on this picture is such a joy, and how bloody rare that is.

Saturday January 6

Went to George Kast's house to meet the new president of the musicians union who came out from New York to meet some of the locals and establish lines of communication that under previous administrations had become rather fogged. This gent grew up in Baltimore where he played the clarinet and got a law degree. He said he played in the pit when I was there conducting *Hollywood Pinafore*. Nice fellow.

Sunday January 21

Saw May Monday, Thursday and Sunday. Our relationship gets better and better and solider and solider. We spend a lot of time discussing the situation with Kathy, whose attitude has hardened. She intends, she tells May, to stay in the Outpost house as long as she can, delaying any settlement of our affairs in the expressed hope that if she drags it out long enough I might die and she will get it all. In letters to me Kath says she still cares for me, thinks we should get back together, but in conversations with May says she is going to show me who is boss. May presents my view, backing it up with her opinion, that it would be best for both of us if we sold the house, now worth about $450,000, and each bought a smaller house with the division of the proceeds and invested the rest for income. This solution Kath rejects out of hand saying she is not emotionally ready to give up the style of living she has become accustomed to.

This week Charlie Blackman, who has been looking, found a house he thinks might be satisfactory for me at 4731 Halbrent in Sherman Oaks for $630 a month. It is owned by a terrible man named Leonard Schneider. I popped up to see it and, for the price,

I thought it might work and be an interim solution until Kath and I get a settlement worked out. I gave Schneider $630 for a security deposit and got Kath to issue a check to him for $1,260 for the first and last month's rent.

Sunday January 28

Finished the score on Wednesday. After dinner Friday I played the score for Linda, Barry, Jack Tillar and Dale Bell. They liked it. I went to the Halbrent house, made measurements and decided it would not work. The rooms are too small to accommodate all my equipment. Schneider doesn't want to give the money back. I got May to talk to him on the phone—one landlord to another—but he was abusive. Tonight May and I together, discussed these mounting problems.

Tuesday January 30

Recorded the *Tigris* score at what used to be RCA, now operated by Wally Heider.

Tuesday February 6

Sid's first wife, whose name is Jinny (for Virginia) is married to a scientist named James Dill. They live in the Marina City Club but are poised to leave for Florida and are trying to sublet their apartment. Sid took me to meet them and I agreed to take it. The only problem is the Dills don't leave until February 22 and I have to vacate Long Beach February 14 because Mme. Rilliet has rented it. Norman and Jackie Brown, my dear, friendly, supportive neighbors, came to my rescue and are going to let me stay in the room over their garage. I will have to put my stuff in one of those self-storage places in the interim.

Friday February 9

Went to Joan Colman's house to have dinner with Alan Gilbert, Yip Harburg, a brace of UCLA people and Jimi Kauffer, a friend of Yip's. They are going to do a show at UCLA, a retrospect of Yip's work, and I have promised to help.

Sunday February 18

Wednesday I packed, moved my stuff into the public storage place and installed myself in Jackie and Norm's garage room. Wednesday night to UCLA for the first rehearsal of the Harburg show. The lady in the parking kiosk had not heard of me and suggested I park off campus. I said, "I'll park *way* off campus," and went to May's instead, which turned out to be much nicer than rehearsing.

Sunday February 25

Last Monday, having received a parking card, rehearsed at UCLA. There are nineteen students in the show, all delightful and many of them talented. I am making the ensemble arrangements.

Saturday rehearsed at UCLA 10:30 to 12:30. Young Fred Weiss, a rather good choreographer from Alan Gilbert's Carmel theatre, is staging the routines. Trouble is he doesn't wait for the arrangements to be finished before he stages the numbers so we are going through the usual problems; someone with an important line to sing is facing upstage, or a group entrusted with a phrase involving a joke are engaged in violent acrobatics making it impossible for them to do justice to the joke etc., etc.

May and Kath leave for China next week for a three-week tour. In anticipation of this terrible long drought, we met Tuesday, Wednesday, Friday and Sunday.

A comparison of what I spent and what Kathy spent in January and February:

	Kath	LM
Jan	5,130	1,480
Feb	3,880	2,109
Totals	9,010	3,589

Looks like I'll have to do something about this sometime.

Sunday March 4

Thursday I moved into Outpost to see that the dogs and Sheba the cat are taken care of during Kathy's absence. Rehearsed from eight to ten at UCLA.

Yesterday we had a disaster of a run-through of the Harburg show at 11 a.m. Disaster because another rehearsal pianist was presiding. He played all the accompaniments from the published copies of the numbers, disregarding all the different keys my arrangements were in, all the different harmonies, extensions, codas, etc. The effect was that the singers were singing what I wrote and the pianist was playing something else. I raised hell at a meeting and it was decided and agreed that I would take a week off, write out rehearsal piano parts and finish up the half a dozen or so arrangements I still had to do.

Sunday March 11

During the preceding week I made vocals and rehearsal piano parts of four more arrangements and sent them to Alan Gilbert so that Joan Coleman could start drilling the kids in the notes.

Yesterday, Saturday March 10, Fred Steiner, Jerry Devine and I were guests of something called SPERDVAC (Society to Preserve and Encourage Radio Drama Variety and Comedy) at a meeting at the First Christian Church at Van Owen and Lindley, far out in the Valley. Present were a bunch of fans who knew everything we had ever done in radio and a lot we had forgotten. The three of us talked and answered questions. They played excerpts from "This is Your FBI" and "The Ford Theatre," but the Ford Theatre excerpt was from *Laura* which of course was Raksin's music, not mine.

Sunday March 18

Postcard from May, mailed in Peking, with a message I treasure: "Vite! Vite! Je t'embrasse." On Sunday 18 they returned and I moved back to the Marina.

Monday March 19

With May, and got the story of the trip. She said she had had great difficulty getting away from Kathy long enough to write and mail the postcard. Outside of that, the story was a re-run of every trip with Kathy, who is one of those unfortunate people who has to be drugged and drunk to get on a plane, who never likes the location of her seat once she is on the plane, and who has never, ever had an edible meal away from home. In China you get started early, frequently having dinner at six in order to be at the Opera or somewhere by 7:30. This cuts into the cocktail hour which, in Kathy's case, starts at six and goes till eight. One item I found amusing. At one of the entertainments they were taken to, a Chinese baritone sang "Old Man River."

Sunday March 25

The Norwegian consul's and his wife gave a reception and cocktail party for Thor Heyerdahl who has arrived in Los Angeles for the broadcast of the *Tigris* show on Sunday April 1. I asked May to go with me.

The consul's wife is a heavy, matronly lady, older than the consul, who is a boyish middle-aged man. He spent most of his time charming the ladies, looking down their dresses and quite obviously trying very hard not to pinch their bottoms. After the reception Linda, Barry, Dale, May, the Strausses, Heyerdahl and I to dinner. Heyerdahl loosened up and talked.

During the war he was a young lieutenant attached to a Norwegian unit training in Scotland. They were to be ferried to Murmansk then dropped into northern Norway to harass the Germans. On the ship to Murmansk Heyerdahl was promoted to captain. Arriving in Murmansk the colonel in charge of the detail handed his personnel list to a Russian officer who checked the passports. The Russian refused to let Heyerdahl land because he was listed as Captain Heyerdahl and the visa'd passport was issued to Lieutenant Heyerdahl. According to Heyerdahl, who is a reconteur par excellence, they sent him back to Scotland to get his passport and visa reissued.

A delightful evening. May meticulously reported that she had accompanied me to this event and Kathy promptly laid down the law. She was not to go out with me because that just makes my life more pleasant and Kath has a vision of me isolated, alone and lonely at the Marina and wants to keep it that way.

Monday March 26

Abe Marcus is my lawyer. His partner is Ed Ezor. Abe is away so I met with Ezor to discuss the divorce. The meeting was devoted to acquainting Ed with details he has to know.

Tuesday March 27

Rehearsed the singers at UCLA and turned in the balance of my orchestrations of the fifteen numbers. The combination in the pit is to be two pianos, a bass player, and a drummer, presided over by Rob Webb, one of the pianists. Webb asked me an extraordinary question. Did I want him to play the arrangements "as written"? He wanted to play the numbers in the sheet music keys (not the keys I had used) because his bass player "couldn't read." I told him to play them as I had written them, and as the singers had learned them.

Thursday March 29

Milton Rosenstock, who is in town conducting *The King and I*, has been after me and Sid to come and see the show. He got us tickets. When we got to the box office the man said, "$36 please." I was stunned, but reached into my pocket for the money. Sid said, "You don't want to pay $36 to hear Brynner sing 'It's a Puzzlement' do you?" I said, "No," and handed the tickets back. We went to the stage door to see Milt before he went into the pit. He was upset, saying he would have to pay for the tickets. I said if he did I would reimburse him, but didn't feel like lining Rodgers' pockets to see something I had seen in the original with Gertie Lawrence. They sold the tickets, so I didn't have to pay.

Saturday March 31

Sid, May and I went to the opening of the Harburg show on Friday night. When we got there we were handed two tickets on row O. Sid, not one to take this sort of thing lying down, got hold of Jimi Kauffer, who took the two tickets for row O and gave us three on row E. It was mostly a good show except where Yip's politics took over. The entertainment parts were good, the self-indulgent political parts embarrassing. The orchestra sounded like two loud cocktail piano players incessantly pounding the melody. Fortunately the bass player, because of the microphone pick-up, couldn't be heard at all.

Addendum: A week or two later Jimi Kauffer called me and asked who owned the arrangements. I asked why, and she said Yip was planning to have Lee Guber produce the show in New York. I said they were welcome to the arrangements; have Lee Gruber call me and I would make a price. (I was not working for money on this show. Just love.)

Sunday April 8

Monday April 2 a meeting with Ed Ezor about the divorce. Kathy has a lawyer, James Foster of Santa Monica. Ezor is in receipt of Kathy's demands: Half my income and the right to live in the house. Her income not to count as a credit against my obligation.

It is income tax time. Kathy and I met on Saturday the 7th with Ephraim Sales, May's accountant, now ours. Sales endeared himself to Kathy by saying our books were the worst he had ever seen, and as a result his bill for preparing our tax return will be twice as high as that of any other client because of the hours consumed straightening them out. (Kathy had fired our business managers and hired a bookkeeper to make out the checks and keep the records.)

Sunday April 22

I am helping Jeff Alexander on the score for a picture *Wild, Wild West Revisited*, produced and directed by his pal Burt Kennedy. On Friday 20 to Temple Beth-El to see Milton Rosenstock and Sally Cook married. Yul Brynner and Maureen Stapleton there. Tonight, Sunday, I gave a little dinner party for the Hesses and the Lloyds. I made the stew which Jane Hess said was good but not as good as hers.

Sunday May 6

This week Ezor got a letter from James Foster stating I must provide living expenses for Kathy not geared to the sale of the house or any other assets, and that she is legally entitled to this. He suggests $2,500 a month.

Monday May 14

Abe Marcus has taken over the divorce negotiations.

Joan Blumofe called and wants an arrangement for the Share party. We all contribute arrangements when asked. Went to the rehearsal and saw the number, a parody by Ray Evans and Jay Livingston of one of my favorite tunes, "I Guess I'll Have to Change My Plan."

Thursday May 17

Went to the UA theatre here in the Marina to see Woody Allen's *Manhattan*. The much touted Gershwin score was ruined for me on two counts: Lousy, but *lousy* sound and a preponderance of dull, unimaginative arrangements of the tunes played by symphony orchestras conducted mostly by Mehta and Tillson-Thomas in a show-off way with no attempt to vary the scoring to fit the cutting of scenes. I mean it's full orchestra in Central Park and full orchestra for two people in bed in a dim-lit room. I went to see it again at the Academy, thinking that the sound at least would be spectacular but it was not good there either. There are for my money only three places in the film where the music thrills you and there is a hell of a lot of music in it.

Friday May 18

Went to the Share rehearsal at the Palladium, Hank Mancini conducting. Five thousand mikes on the orchestra and all you can hear is the drummer. Hank said he knew what was going to happen when he saw the kids setting up the sound equipment. They were rock concert specialists. He said they balance the drums and the 1st trumpet equally, everything else is secondary. (We have 5 trumpets, 4 trombones, 6 saxophone-woodwinds, 6 violins, 2 violas and 1 cello besides the rhythm.) The best arrangement I heard was by Nan Schwartz, daughter of Hymie Schwartz the saxophone player. She is a delightful young girl, very talented and intense. She had written elaborate arpeggiated string parts which went unheard due to the rock pick-up.

Saturday May 19

May and I to the Share party on freebies handed out to the arrangers. As we arrived in the lobby of the Palladium Sammy Davis was just ahead of us and one of the network news teams was filming him. We were concerned that we might be in the picture and Kathy would see us on the evening news and renew her complaints about May going places with me. The tables are furnished with bottles of scotch, gin, vodka, bourbon and wine. When we left we saw security people relieving folks of bottles they were trying to sneak out. They probably figured if they paid $250 they were entitled.

Richard Pryor did a routine that didn't exactly kill the people. The whole routine was built on two words, "Fuck you." He asked the right hand section of the audience to say it after him. They did, rather timidly. He cried, "Louder!" They did it a little louder. Then he got the left section to do the same, then the middle. It was all very half-hearted. Then he got the whole audience to do it together and it was fairly impressive to hear about 800 people shouting "Fuck you" at Richard Pryor. He then said, "Fuck *you*" to the audience and walked off. Danny Thomas climbed up on the stage and said, "In all my experience in show business I have never heard anyone use these words in a comedy routine on the stage." (I guess he missed Lenny Bruce.) He continued, "In all my career I have never used a word stronger than damn in a comedy routine. Maybe I'm behind the times or something." He took a long beat, then said, "Fuck you," and walked off. Danny Thomas, the Lebanese Catholic.

Donna Summers sang. At least I think she did. The band was so loud, particularly the drums, that not much of her came through. Sammy Davis and Steve Lawrence closed by singing the piece of material they did on the Academy show this year, "Not Even Nominated," but not until Sammy ordered the mixers to turn the band mikes off. They did and the balance was perfect.

Tuesday May 22

Ruby Raksin dropped dead. On Friday 25 I went to a funeral

place in Westwood where his brother David and Elmer Bernstein spoke.

Monday May 28

Saw May off for New York.

At four to see Abe Marcus, my lawyer. We are filing a petition for divorce on May 31.

Tuesday June 5

About the divorce petition. The routine is that one's lawyer calls the other lawyer and asks if he will accept service of his copy. Kath's lawyer, Foster, had agreed, but the day before the filing, when Abe called Foster to arrange a time for him to accept service, he was "out of town." In this case it is customary to serve the defendant, and Kathy was so served, complaining later that it was done by two black women who stood outside the front door hollering and alerting the neighborhood.

Monday June 18

Had two kids from the Harburg UCLA show down for dinner with Sid. I love hanging out with starry-eyed, talented 22-year-olds. They know more about current musical theatre than I do.

Sunday June 24

ASMA (the American Society of Music Arrangers) each year gives an award called the Golden Score to a distinguished member of the fraternity. This year they honored Russell Bennett, who asked me to go and accept for him. Ernani Bernardi, an ex-saxophone player member of the Los Angeles City Council, presented Russell with one of their handsome proclamations. Tom Talbert was there and saw me with May. He couldn't resist reporting this item to Kathy, who promptly broke off relations with May. In a telephone call she disinvited May to her annual July 4th party saying it had been canceled. Sort of dumb because she had the party and someone told May.

Friday June 29

Dear friend George Whitsett died. He would have been 90 in August. I learned this in a letter from his daughter Sue, forwarded to me from Outpost—opened.

Saturday July 14

I attended a meeting of the executive committee of the music branch of the Academy to hear Tom Pearson's appeal against our decision that his score for *Manhattan* was not an achievement worthy of an Award for adaptation. He said he had arranged the music exactly as Gershwin would have done, and that his preserving the "Gershwin speech" was an artistic decision that merited consideration for an Academy Award. Woody Allen and the producers have brought pressure to bear on the Board of Governors of the Academy, and they in turn have pressured us to reconsider.

Pearson has long, stringy hair and wears dirty white trousers. He made an impassioned speech about his contribution to the film. I was wrong about there being a lot of music in the film— actually there were only 29 minutes, 7 or 8 minutes of it printed versions of the Rhapsody, etc., 2 minutes of an old Gershwin piano roll, three or four numbers arranged by Don Rose, one number a "head arrangement," the rest, played by Mehta and the New York Philharmonic, arranged by Pearson; and he had the scores with him to prove it. We examined them. Irwin Kostal pointed out that in 18 minutes they played 19 tunes, which did not allow much time for what we call adaptation. To us adaptation is taking 32 bars and making 9 minutes out of it. We decided to stick with our decision and take the heat sure to follow.

Friday July 20

I have received an order to show cause a) why I shouldn't pay Kath $3,500 a month support and b) to appear in the Santa Monica court on August 13. I met with Abe Marcus to see if we could get a court order forcing sale of the house. He is not sure we can get such an order. We will go in and try to prove that $3,500 a month to Kath is exorbitant.

Tuesday July 31

I am reading Ned Rorem's *Critical Affairs*, Braziller, New York 1971. Charles Ives, listening to something he did not understand, "I have my ears on wrong." Rorem's imagery would knock any musician out. Quote: "Billie Holiday didn't need 'meaningful' lyrics to grab your heart; her 'Stange Fruit' came from a basket of familiar corn, much of it rotten but which, on her Midas tongue, turned gold." And on Edith Piaf and Billie Holiday: "Both sank back into publicized poverty then both perished early and accidentally in the icy light of abject stardom."

Saturday August 4

Night thoughts. I always wake up at 4:30 a.m. mad at something or somebody. If we don't go into court soon enough to force the sale of the house I may not qualify for the $100,000 tax exemption. These are the kinds of thoughts that wake me up when the unfairness of the law in divorce cases intrudes on my sleep. The Valium takes hold at six and I sleep until 9:30, undisturbed by the twin engines warming up outside in the slips, and the jets out of LAX heading out to sea before turning for San Francisco or San Diego.

In the market I got in line. There was a man behind me. An Asian woman carrying a pack of cigarettes and a *TV Guide* got behind him. He let her go ahead of him and I let her go ahead of me. She paid for the cigarettes and the *TV Guide* with a check. She did not have a check guarantee card and it took the store 20 minutes to work it out. Moral: never give an Asian a break.

Tuesday August 7

Yesterday to the offices of James Foster, Kathy's lawyer, for her deposition. I like him.

Today Foster took my deposition. When he asked me if I had made any investments since separation, Kathy seethed when I outlined the two investments in condominiums I had made with May. He asked me if I had any bank accounts other than those I had listed. I said there was one other joint account in a bank on Catalina I had not listed, because when I called to get the balance they told me Kath had closed it out. In a discussion of how "her share" of my ASCAP income would be distributed, Foster stated he wanted ASCAP to do the division. I objected. Kathy blew and said, hysterically, that she didn't trust me.

Night thoughts: My lawyers tell me the law is not concerned with music—just the money it produces. The law divides this money among the ex-wives and is not concerned with a composer's state of mind. There is one thing the law cannot divide among the ex-wives and that is the great thrill of filling the inviting blank pages with notes, sharps, flats and clefs, or the great sense of power that fills a composer at two o'clock in the morning when he is writing something for violas, cellos and horns that has never been heard before. And the piece you write for sixteen brass instruments and a double massed choir; the sounds that penetrate human ears and the human heart. That cannot be divided among ex-wives. Only the money it produces. The law is not concerned with providing the composer with the comfort to which he has become accustomed—just that of the ex-wife. Even these practitioners of the law may have heard some strains of melody and counterpoint in some film they may have enjoyed, written by the composer whose substance they are slicing up. Though law proceedings are an insufferable interruption in the composer's life, one thing is sure—a couple of weeks after the turmoil is over, if there is enough money left to rent some space, he will be at his table translating the sounds in his head into notes an orchestra can understand and play for the pleasure and perhaps edification of listeners all over the world. If they haven't divided up his piano and, in my case, his electronic instruments.

Wednesday August 15

To Santa Monica court for the hearing to show cause why I should not pay Kath $3,500 a month interim support. It is not heard before a judge. Under their system a lawyer, in this case a woman, Charlotte somebody, in the presence of the parties and their lawyers, examines the issues and attempts to settle some or all of them before a pro tem judge takes a whack at it. Many interesting things came up. The law apparently examines the wife's requirements to live in the style to which she is accustomed and, if they are not exorbitant, awards her an amount which does not take into account the husband's requirements. In my case there will be a large percentage of my ASCAP income awarded to Kath since most of my catalog was composed during the marriage. An analysis of last year's figures shows that, if I am allowed to deduct some works which may not have been composed during the marriage, Kath would have got something over $22,000.

I was ordered to pay Kath 37½% of ASCAP received since January 1, plus half of my pension income. I sent a check for $5605.45. It begins to appear that the 12½% of the gross Florence gets is my problem. Jeff is being helpful. He has offered to lend me his brand new .38 magnum.

Monday August 27

Abe Marcus is fond of Kathy and, at the Santa Monica hearing, I felt he avoided making a lot of points in my favor. Vic Mizzy has urged me to see the lawyer who handled his own divorce: Manley Freid, a specialist in "family law." I had written a memo covering the case since its inception, including the appearance before Charlotte, the lady referee, at Santa Monica. Freid read it, shaking his head at every paragraph. He said Charlotte is a leading women's libber in Santa Monica but that the pro tem judge, Leonard Alexander, is a fair fellow and that Abe should have avoided the woman and taken Alexander. He is interested in the divorce arrangement with Florence. He thinks that under the 1970 changes in the divorce law, it might be breakable now. I wrote a very-hard-to-write letter to Abe and we have formally changed lawyers. Manley is about 41 and I like him very much. He charges $100 an hour, has two assistants to help on the preparation. One gets $80 an hour, the other $70. I paid a retainer of $3,500 which Manley says should take us to the trial.

Friday August 31

Bill received from Marcus: $4,275.00.

Friday September 14

To the Devines for Marilyn's birthday with Eloise and Pat O'Brien, Jeannie and Dick Widmark, and Roy Ringer and his wife.

Ringer, who writes editorials for the *Times*, told a Meizner-W.C. Fields story. Meizner to Fields, "Will, that 90 proof breath of yours would start the windmill in a Dutch painting."

Having a lot of trouble with Manley Freid, the lawyer. I called Judith Saffer, an ASCAP attorney in New York, and discovered Foster, Kath's attorney, joined ASCAP to the suit on September 4. She said she had called Freid twice and had been unable to reach him. I can't even get Freid's secretary on the phone. Called her three times and she ducked me. Finally, mad, I called again and when told she was busy asked for an assistant and spoke to a Pat de Carolis. With icy, Anglo-Saxon frigidity asked the questions I wanted answered. Freid was graduated from Temple University and displays the Harvard Law Review in his reception room. When I finally got him on the phone I learned he had granted a 60-day continuance to Foster to allow him time to have the two houses re-appraised. I thought this could be accomplished in two weeks, in plenty of time for the scheduled October 9th hearing. I told him Judith Saffer was trying to reach him and that she had said she, Manley and Foster could arrive at a division of the ASCAP income in one meeting.

Sunday October 14

I can't say enough about May's help. On Friday 19, to mend my fences with Abe Marcus—understandably hurt because he is off the divorce—she built a dinner party around him and his wife inviting Jeff Alexander, Bronny Kaper, David Raksin (all friends and clients of Marcus's) and the Norman Lloyds. As a result I am still friends with Marcus, who is still my lawyer in matters other than the divorce.

Tuesday October 30

Mother died Friday 26. I went to Philadelphia to attend the funeral.

Friday November 2

Alan and Ronnie drove me to Bucks County to the Hesses. On the way Ronnie told of a friend of his who was always two hours late for work. He got fired, went on welfare and was sent to a psychiatrist. That didn't work because he was always two hours late for his appointment with the shrink.

Tuesday November 6

Took the train to New York, met May at the airport in a limousine and checked into the Warwick where Russell Bennett had arranged a nice, dark suite for us on the eighth floor.

Monday November 12

I thought it would be nice to have a pied à terre in New York. Went to the Ritz Tower, where John and Jane Hess maintain a small apartment, spoke to the manager, who put me on the waiting list. Russell and Louise took us to dinner at a restaurant in 55th street, a block from the hotel. Russell uses crutches and walks very slowly and painfully. He told me had finished his memoirs. Thinking of his long relationship with Dick Rodgers I asked if he had told the truth. He said, "No." Tuesday we went to Newark to catch a 5:30 flight home. We sat on the ground for two hours while they served drinks. I had far too many and when we got home I threw up for three hours.

Monday November 19

Nick Noxon, a producer at National Geographic, has made a film titled "Superliner: End Of An Era," starring the *Queen Elizabeth* II. Ran it Tuesday with Nick, Linda Reavely and Barry Nye. Right up my alley. Tonight with May to see *A Little Romance* with a score by Delerue based entirely on Vivaldi. On Sunday to see *Kramer vs. Kramer* also with a Vivaldi score. I am getting tired of him although I admit he works rather well. Thursday 29 to the Mark Taper for a memorial service for Eleanor Pinkham, Edwin Lester's executive assistant, a lady we all loved. Luther Davis there. Took me and Sid to lunch in Chinatown. That night at May's a dinner for Jeff Alexander, Lee Cass and the Devines. They got along fine because Jerry likes curmudgeons. He puts me and Jeff in that category.

Tuesday 4 to a Composers & Lyricists dinner where we were seen by Tom Talbert who made his usual report to Kathy. Vic Mizzy did a stand up routine so funny I almost forgave him for introducing me to Manley Freid, the invisible, unavailable master of let's-run-up-the-bill family law. Thursday 6 I ignored my 70th birthday.

Monday December 17

A sad call from Vivian Rennie. Guy Rennie, friend of my Philadelphia days, died December 4. The last time we saw him, a few months ago, I said to Sid, "There goes a dead man." I can always tell the mark of death when I see it.

1980

Wednesday January 2

Linda Reavely splits with Barry Nye after living together for fifteen years.

Tuesday January 15

Recorded the "Superliners" score at Motown with Guy Costa mixing assisted by Glen Jordan. They gave us the best sound I have had on a National Geographic. The score was good and, pardon me, well orchestrated à la Russell Bennett. A good experience. May attended and I took everybody to dinner at the Studio Grill which, as May points out, is deductible. Good thing, too. $232 cuts into the net.

Sunday January 27

Two small items: Jerry Devine's Edinburgh bus driver's remark to a noisy passenger, "If I have any more trouble with you I'll waft you off the bus."

Sid's remark, about someone whose name I have forgotten, "He's got no fucking taste."

Tuesday February 19

I had a call from a woman telling me Jerry Fielding had died in a Toronto hotel room of an apparent heart attack. As I said in a note to his wife Camille, he was our conscience. He wanted us all to live up to his standards, and at meetings of the Executive Committee of the Academy music branch he fought all the materialists to a standstill. He was a much valued friend and, as usual with me, I was shocked, saddened, then filled with a guilty elation that I am still alive at 70, and he was 57.

Wednesday February 20

Had a meeting with Manley Freid. He is finally going to meet with Foster, Kath's lawyer, to work out a settlement. His appraiser has been to Outpost and valued it at $485,000 which, according to all the information I have gathered, is low. This apparently disturbed Manley enough for him to check with his man, who revised his estimate upward to $525,000. Kath wants to buy me out. This will require a down payment of $100,000, the balance in, as far as I am concerned, a maximum of two years. Incidentally, when Freid's appraiser wanted to make a list of the contents of the house, she wouldn't let him, saying it was all hers. I gave Manley copies of my lists of the contents showing what was community property. The other big problem in a settlement is the division of the ASCAP income. I am currently paying her 37½% based on exclusion of material written before marriage and after separation, and also excluding about 20% of unidentified works. If they challenge the unidentifieds, Freid maintains it is their responsibility to determine when the music was written.

I had asked that her share of my ASCAP revert to me at her death. It narks me to think that her heirs might collect on the music I wrote during a marriage that after five years was not a marriage at all but a burden. Come to think of it, if I wasn't trying to escape her leaden presence, I might not have isolated myself in that room and written that much music. If I had been a happily married man—as happy as I am now with May—I might not have spent seven days a week, 14 hours a day, writing all those notes for television. And if you think that seven-day, 14-hour line is an exaggeration ask any working composer. That is one thing we never won from the studios—enough time to do a good job and Sundays off.

Saturday March 1

Sid and I are working on a musical called *Song of Frankenstein*, book by Curt Siodmak and Sid, with a partial score by Lee Wainer. Wainer died before completing it.

Tuesday March 4

Finished a song for *Frankenstein* called "Amo, Amas, Amat." Manley called. Kath is sticking to the 37½% of ASCAP and wants the house for less than the appraised price. The amount not stated. We countered with 30% of ASCAP, $510,000 for the house, $100,000 now, the balance in one year at 15%.

Saw on the tube, quite by accident, a show called "Fantasy Island," a Spelling-Goldberg production. Everybody connected with it ought to be thrown into jail. Then I saw Agnes de Mille's PBS show, "Conversations on the Dance." Milton Rosenstock told me she had had a stroke, but on the show she sounded fine. I've loved her since I worked with her in the thirties.

Monday March 17

My lease at the Marina City Club expires at the end of April. I have a notice from them stating they are willing to renew the lease at a 55% increase to $1,050 a month. I went to see Jim Murray who, as he told me, "runs the joint." I explained I was in a protracted divorce action with the trial set for April 28; that I expected the judge to order my two houses and other assets liquidated but, given the size of the properties, it could be six months before I see any proceeds. I made him an offer. I would stay in the apartment "as is" month to month and pay him $850—an increase of 30%. A day or so later he turned the offer down, and I suppose I will have to look for another place to live until the divorce is settled.

Thursday March 27

May's daughter, her husband, a professor of English, and their six-year-old son here for their annual invasion. May locks up all the available art objects. We had our dinner rather late. The child is served his dinner in the kitchen and it takes a concerted effort to clean up the floor and the walls before poor Chie can begin to prepare ours. On Wednesday we took them to Scandia for dinner and on Friday I had them all, with Sid and Vic Mizzy, to dinner at my place. Show biz characters like Sid and Mizzy don't mix too well with English professors. Thank God Mizzy can do no wrong as far as May is concerned. She understands his humor. On Tuesday April 8 we entertained Linda Reavely, still grieving, and Norman Corwin, one of her heroes, at dinner. Took her out of herself for an evening.

Monday April 11

May and I to San Francisco to see all the people we like to see there. Staying at the Huntington. So is Bill Blass. I know this because he gave the elderly lady elevator operator a $60 box of Godiva chocolates he "designed," although he claims to be a Snickers man himself. We got back in time to have a long session with Freid on the eve of Kath's deposition.

Wednesday April 30

Bill for $3,078.07 received from Freid.

Saturday May 17

To the Share party. June Blumofe had asked me to make an arrangement of "A Pretty Girl Is Like a Melody" for Sammy Davis in the key of Bb. When we got there June told me Sammy was not going to sing it—someone else was. This someone else has to sing it in the key of F and the copyists have transposed the whole thing down a fourth which throws all the instruments out of their effective range. I was sitting with Ralph Burns, Pete Rugolo and Van Alexander, sterling arrangers all. I said the only thing I could do was to find a pretext to leave the room while my number was being played. I stayed, though, and for some reason I cannot explain, it didn't sound bad. Nothing matters.

Friday May 30

Bill from Freid for $5,194.21.
Today I made my seventh move since Kathy and I separated, this time to an apartment at 4250 Via Dolce, Marina Del Rey. It is more spacious than the Marina City Club but costs $890 and I have had to buy a refrigerator. I threw my back out unpacking books and setting up the equipment.

Tuesday June 10

Two items: Jack Lemmon has written a song called, "The Bottom's Dropped Out of Everything But You."
Johnny Carson on longevity: "Never get excited. Only have sex with your wife."

Friday June 13

A few social notes while Mr. Freid is off on his vacation from the rigors of negotiating divorces. Sunday May took me to see the Harlem Ballet which friend Rosenstock conducts with too little rehearsal. How would you like to conduct "Firebird" with 45 minutes to prepare the orchestra? It is not possible but he got away with it. On Tuesday when Carmencita the cleaning lady turned the washer on, it decided to flood the apartment. The carpets had to be sent out. Mr. Altman, my landlord, was mad. Claims I did it on purpose.
At the end of June I got a bill from Freid for $5,776.71, including services during June for $630.

Monday July 21

Returned tonight from New York on TWA Flight 1 scheduled to

depart at six p.m. When we got on line there were about 40 planes ahead of us. We took off at 8:43.

New York was hot. We saw *Ain't Misbehavin'*, *Sugar Babies* and *Barnum*. Sum impression of all three shows: pace and more pace plus volcanic energy. All very stimulating.

Had Hobe Morison, Dave and Elaine Terry and Milton Rosenstock for cocktails. Hobe told of being asked by Oscar Hammerstein to have lunch with him and Richard Rodgers shortly after the opening of *Flower Drum Song*. After lunch Rodgers revealed the reason for the lunch. Brooks Atkinson in his review in the *Times* had characterized the show as "pleasant." They both thought the use of that word might prove damaging at the box office. Hobe, the legit reviewer on *Variety*, didn't know how he could help—*Variety* vs. the *Times* is no contest. Rodgers cited a healthy advance sale, big returns on the cast album and sheet music. Hobe said, "Send me the figures and I'll do a piece on it." The figures came that afternoon and he wrote a page 1 story quoting them.

Hobe lunched regularly with Hammerstein. At a subsequent lunch Oscar told Hobe the story of *Flower Drum Song*. Rodgers was in the hospital having a sort of nervous breakdown brought on, possibly, by not having a project in work. Rodgers read the novel, liked it, sent it to Hammerstein to read. Oscar read it, thought there wasn't a show in it and said so. Rodgers begged him to read it again. He did, felt even more strongly that it wasn't much but, sensing something, called Rodgers and said he liked it and would do it. Rodgers left the hospital the next day. Hammerstein said to Hobe, "You might say that *Flower Drum Song* is the only show I wrote that saved a man's life." He added he thought Atkinson's review was correct—a "pleasant" show. Hobe felt these luncheons were off the record and never used the story. After Hammerstein's death Hobe told this story to a friend who thought it was obvious Oscar told him the story so that he *would* use it. With Oscar gone but Rodgers still alive, Hobe did not run the story feeling that perhaps Rodgers would deny it.

Rosenstock told of being engaged to recreate an album for Rodgers of *I Remember Mama*, with Barbara Cook playing the Liv Ullman role. He asked for an extra musician—an item costing about $100—and Rodgers refused. Rosenstock gave me a piece of rather bad news. Sid and Curt Siodmak and I are working hard on our version of *Frankenstein* and the bad news is a producer named Max Azenburg is doing a play version of the work which will probably knock ours out. [It opened and closed at a total loss for the investors, and that makes it all the worse.]

Met Russell and Louise Bennett for dinner. We walked them home—one block. It took forever with poor Russell's crutches and his bent spine. Sad. His memoirs have been turned down by his publisher. I gather the committee didn't know who he was. Jim and Jayne Beach came in from Tarrytown. They had been to a doctor. Jayne has had a lump on her throat excised, now she is undergoing radiation and later will have chemo. Remarkably upbeat about it.

Sunday we rented a car and drove to Cliff Carpenter's house at Quaker Hill, near Pawling, in blazing heat. Carpenter was an actor who got himself on the blacklist and went into the stockbroking business and did well. When the Committee nailed him, he was appearing in *Sunrise at Campobello*. He was on a lot of radio programs I did; 26 By Corwin, Columbia Workshop, Campbell Playhouse, etc.

Saturday July 26

Wrote to Jack Melchior: "I am supremely happy for a number of reasons. One of them is that we might—just might—get into court in the next three weeks and I will be rid of the albatross finally. The case was filed May 31, 1979. They tell me a year and three months is not bad when the venom and vindictiveness of a contested divorce flows as virulently as it does in this one. It is expensive. She has sat in the house for more than two years. Tying up this asset—my not having the use of the money it represents— is costing me $25,000 a year. Add the $24,000 I paid her last year plus the 12.5% Florence gets, you can believe it when I tell you I am heavily into deficit financing. About $15,000 went out over what came in."

Wednesday July 30

The lawyers decided we should have a two-on-two meeting; Foster and Kath, Freid and the plaintiff, me. They decided to start on items on which there was no disagreement and promptly ran into a disagreement. I receive two pensions: $89.38 monthly from the Motion Picture Fund, $150 a month from the American Federation of Musicians. Foster has asked for, and Kath is going to get, half of these. However, the American Federation pension was $126 a month when we separated, and due to work done since the separation has escalated $24. Foster wants proof that the $24 is indeed the result of work done since separation. He doesn't give up $12 easily.

On the subject of my ASCAP income, Foster insisted on a third party receiving the reports and the checks and distributing accordingly. I objected on the grounds of an emotional attachment to the music, the pleasure of seeing where it was playing and what it was earning; that a third party examining four domestic quarterly distributions and two foreigns, and computing who was entitled to what, could cost about $1,000 (which I was expected to share); that I was an experienced distributor of my income, having paid three previous wives on time and without complaint except for the few times when Kathy was running the books and could not bring herself to remit Florence's 12½% when due. Freid asked Foster if he had any reservations about my responsibility. Foster said, "No. But what if he skips the country, or the *state*?" I said if I left the country I would agree to the principle of the third party. This subject was left for a judge to decide. Kath closed it, saying she did not want me distributing the income from "her copyrights."

After the meeting Freid told me the judge would give them the third party. I said I would spend the rest of my life and the rest of my resources fighting it. He asked for, and got, a letter from me acknowledging he had informed me the judge would order my ASCAP income paid to a third party who would determine the community portion and make the distribution. I suppose this was to indemnify him against a suit for malpractice. Oh, his bill, received today, was for $7,326.91.

Friday August 1

Saw *Airplane*, a funny picture owing a lot to old Hope pictures such as a pair of vultures appearing in the cockpit when the plane is in trouble, and a shot of the pilot's wife in bed at home, the camera panning over to show us she is in bed with a horse. Both bits out of *Son of Paleface*.

It is nice to see funny pictures, and I am having a lot of laughs at

4250 Via Dolce. After the washing machine overflew I had a letter from landlord Altman saying his wife Sue had strained her back taking up the carpet and he was going to send me her doctor bill. May very kindly called Sue—nobody is speaking to Mr. Short Fuse—and explained, as an experienced landlady herself, that there is no such thing as tenant responsibility if something goes wrong. The landlord is stuck.

Tuesday August 5

To see the Roland Petit Ballet de Marseilles at the Pantages. They did "The Bat," but, alas, Jeanmaire did not appear. Nice, showbizzy ballet. The orchestra was out of tune at the outset, warmed up as the evening wore on and played the Fledermaus music very nicely. The leading boy missed a jump on to a table in a cabaret scene and lost his confidence for the rest of the ballet. A sad thing to see.

Friday August 8

Before a mediating judge, areas of disagreement were discussed: the disposition of my ASCAP income and what should happen to the two houses. When Foster got to his line, "What if he skips the country?" the judge suggested I open a blocked savings account to which the enemy would have access if I didn't pay. Freid said if I left the country I would agree to the third party concept.

Saturday August 9

Conversation with landlord Altman, who really is a not unattractive young man, leading up circuitously and with rancor to, "What would it take to get you out of there by September 1?" I said, "You couldn't afford it." He tried again, saying, "You're unhappy, I'm unhappy. I would like to get a 'decent' tenant in there." I gave him a brief rundown on my life in court and said I couldn't think of discussing anything with him until it was over.

Monday August 11

We were all in court at nine a.m. All except Kathy. Foster said she was sick. The judge put it over to the next day. That afternoon Freid called me. Kath has fired Foster.

Tuesday August 12

In court at ten a.m. Freid and I, an ASCAP attorney and Kath, accompanied by a short, swarthy woman who said she was a lawyer but not there officially—just as a friend—appeared before Judge Choate. The judge denied the short lady the right to speak. Kath asked for a continuance to get new counsel. She has spoken to a law firm in Long Beach but the principal is on vacation. Judge Choate asked her why she had fired Foster and when she replied she had "lost confidence" in him, he denied the continuance and ordered us back at 1:45. At that time he took her into chambers. About 20 minutes passed. Manley said, "This is beginning to look very bad." I said, "Don't worry—deduct ten minutes for crying time." They came out. The judge ascended the bench and ordered her to be back Thursday 21 with new counsel. This gives her new attorney six days to learn a case Foster has been on over a year.

So Kathy has fired a well-known Santa Monica attorney, Foster, and explained to a Santa Monica judge, who inquired why, that she had "lost confidence" in him. By what has got to be the oddest coincidence in this whole saga, May saw a picture in this evening's paper. It was a photograph in the society section of Mrs. Judge Choate playing golf with Mrs. Lawyer Foster.

Saturday August 16

Sid and I have been working on *Frankenstein*. Today Curt Siodmak, who wrote the original book, came to visit. He brought along his wife Henrietta and we had a pleasant afternoon. Henrietta is Swiss, Curt German. I can't understand a word either of them speaks.

Thursday August 21

Kathy appeared with a new attorney, an apple-cheeked, mid-thirtyish man named Robert Baker, Jr., who, I gathered, until that week had never heard of ASCAP. Judge Feinerman ordered the two attorneys to draw up an agreement based on what had been worked out between Foster and Freid and to come back with it on

Thursday August 28. Freid, who apparently has more cases than Seagrams, said he would work over the weekend reducing it to writing. I hope, like composers, he does not get double time for working weekends. The document was ready on Wednesday 27. I discovered errors. It had to be retyped.

Wednesday September 17

Baker called Freid and said we had an agreement. It just had to be retyped to include our acceptance of her right to meet any offer. Thursday 18 I delivered five signed copies to Baker's office.

Friday September 19

Baker called Freid requesting another change. If she matches an offer on the Catalina property she wants to delay payment until Outpost is sold and the proceeds received. We refused. In the meantime ASCAP in New York refused to sign the agreement. They do not want to be obliged to pay my money to a third party, as called for, at my death or if I move permanently out of the country. A few hours later this was worked out.

One hates to interrupt the flow of the plot of a soap opera, but there is really wonderful news. Dear Linda Reavely and Dale Bell, the nicest man in this business, are going to get married.

Wednesday September 24

We appeared in Judge Feinerman's court this morning at 8:30 and seven minutes later the divorce was granted. As of tomorrow, September 25, the divorce will be fait accompli. The court order will stipulate that Kathy will turn over keys to Outpost to a real estate person of my choice and to an agent of her choice.

Monday September 29

I have chosen Jeanne Rains of Mimi Styne's office to represent me in the selling of Outpost. Kathy has chosen Bob Crane. Crane does not want to split the commission with another agent. He wants an exclusive. Today Kathy refused to sign the authorization to have Styne/Rains act for me "on advice of counsel."

Thursday October 9

The authorization is signed. On Saturday 11, an associate of Jeanne Rains, Judy Leach, is allowed into Outpost to examine the house. On Sunday 12, Kathy refuses Leach access to the house with a client. On Tuesday 14, Leach is allowed to take members of the Styne organization through the house. Kathy was not there. She left a key under a flower pot outside the front door wrapped in the following note: "Under *no* condition is Lyn to be given a duplicate of the key or to be brought into the house without my consent or permission in advance. I will indeed know if he has been here and my lawyer will step into it. It is a very serious matter." (I can only surmise she thinks I will steal the silver or take one of my books, or something.)

Styne put up a For Sale sign in front of the house which Kathy promptly took down. She has not spoken to Jeanne Rains for 12 days—they used to communicate daily in happier days—and poor Jeanne is having nightmares about it. May and I try to shore her up.

Kathy is buying me out of the Catalina house for $62,500. A payment of $40,000 has arrived.

Altman, my landlord at Via Dolce, has bought me out of my lease and I have to move by October 31.

What is there to learn from this experience so far? The period from June 10, 1978, when I left the comfort of Outpost until September 25, 1980, when Judge Feinerman signed an interlocutory decree of divorce in his court at Santa Monica? I have been surprised by the love some people have expressed and equally surprised by the indifference of others.

Anyone who writes for a living knows the disciplines involved, and if he does it more or less successfully until he is 68 years old, has spent too many hours and years alone in a room, happily filling empty pages, and has written enough words or notes to fill a warehouse or two. I have found refuge in work when suffering, joy in it when feeling fine, I have used it to avoid boring dinner parties and to escape the burden of burdensome marriages.

My first marriage enriched my life and cost nothing but the pain of discovered infidelities. The second, third and fourth produced fleeting happiness and, in the case of the second and fourth, high, continuing and punitive payments—the fees of freedom. Your agent takes 10% for making your life easier, your wives 50% for having made it impossible.

Friday October 31

Moving day. I have an apartment at 11970 Montana Avenue, Brentwood #310 on the top floor. $850. It is billed as a luxury condominium but has only one oven. It is owned by Jerry Drucker. Haven't met him, all business conducted with a short, round, South African woman, Wendy Evans. Most of the owners here seem to be middle-aged or older. Most of them are Jewish and friendly. One, Sid Gould, built the place and knows of me because he once was a song plugger. He must have married money, for this is a big place. On one of our chance meetings in the elevator he told me my owner, Drucker, is known as Jerry the Goniff.

Thursday November 27

May and I off to Paris for six weeks.

1981

Monday January 26

We have an offer of $550,000 on the Outpost house. Freid received a letter from Baker stating that Kathy elects to exercise her right of first refusal as set forth in the interlocutory judgment of dissolution. (This calls for wife to match the offer exactly, including a deposit of $5,000, $7,500 at opening of escrow and $62,500 at closing of escrow. None of these requirements was met, and the offer expired unanswered.) Freid's bill for this month hardly worth mentioning—$2504.67.

Monday February 2

May, Sid, his girl Dolly and I to San Diego to see Buddy Ebsen's musical *Turn to the Right*. All thought it awful. I thought it could be fixed with judicious cutting.

Tuesday February 17

Judge Alexander turned down the offer of $550,000 because it did not conform to the terms spelled out in the interlocutory. He thought it "a terrible offer" and referred constantly to Jeff Hyland, the young real estate man representing the buyer, as "Mr. Expert."

I met next day with the buyer, an elderly writer named Apstein. I suggested (since the first 90-day period has expired) that he lower his offer to $455,000, all cash to a $136,500 Trust Deed. This is a little hard on him because his initial offer and its terms were structured on the sale of his own house. He figured out how to do it, and on Friday the offer was presented in court and accepted. Kathy immediately exercised her right of first refusal, matched the offer, and is buying me out. I feel sorry for the Apsteins because they love the house more than the other 75 they looked at. Now the battle of the division of the community contents of the house begins. I suspect Kathy will fight over every fork and spoon.

Sunday February 22

May, Sid and I to Visalia to confer on the *Frankenstein* script with Siodmak. He and Henrietta live on a 35-acre ranch at "Three Rivers" in the beautiful redwood country. We went in May's expensive new Volvo with the Bertone body. She and I bore gifts of a large salami, a bottle of Lillet and assorted cheeses. Sid stayed with the Siodmaks, May and I went to a motel.

Foodwise the trip for me was a disaster. The first lunch was a salmon mousse. I am not too mad about salmon and Henrietta wouldn't hear of my popping down to the village to get a bite. That was a no-no, so I ate some of the salami and cheese we brought. Dinner was a cold meat salad of chicken, veal and vegetables. I loath cold chicken, cold veal and cold vegetables. Furthermore, there was a television show announced for eight o'clock they wanted to see— "Ballet in America"—which would have made dinner about 9:30. I begged to be allowed to go to the village for a bite. Horreur. Curt would give me a steak at 7:30. At 7:30 he put a steak on a small electric grill they had bought in Sweden, which kept blowing out the fuses. At eight Henrietta started hollering on Curt to come and watch the television show. I said I would watch the steak and put in fuses. I asked, "What comes with the steak?" (I am a charming guest where my north England stomach is concerned.) He said something I translated as, "What would you like?" I said, "A baked potato and a green salad." They had a salad, sliced cucumbers and beets, to which I added some of our cheese and more or less got by, and even saw some of the television show which was dreadful. The American Ballet Theatre, performing on some college campus. If the members of the company weren't gay when they started, they must have been when they finished because everybody wore flesh body stockings and executed a series of tumbling movements in duet, one member of each duo with his nose in the other's crotch.

Sunday March 1

Felt strange. Sid took me to meet my doctor, Michael Pomo, at St. Joseph's hospital in Burbank. I am having an attack of pleurisy.

Tuesday March 24

The escrow has closed on Outpost so I am looking at houses. Legal bite this month: $2,515.57.

Wednesday April 15

A letter from Baker to Abe Marcus says Kathy wants him to receive, compute and disburse my ASCAP income. I sent Abe a copy of the language in the interlocutory, which states he may function in this manner only at my death. He had the grace to decline the honor.

Tuesday April 28

Hearing postponed to Tuesday May 5 at Baker's request.
April's billet doux from Monsieur Freid $2,761.97.

Tuesday May 5

9:30 a.m. in the Santa Monica court before Judge Darlene
Schemp. She ordered the parties and the lawyers to confer and
agree on a division of community property. She said if the parties
were unable to agree, the court would be disposed to order
everything sold. We returned at 1:30 with a rather lop-sided
agreement. The judge examined the lists, ordered Kathy to pay me
$5,204 to balance the distribution, awarded attorney's fees of
$2,500 to Freid for the March 20 hearing and the current hearing,
both items to be paid by June 15. In the discussions the other side
reiterated the idea that my equipment was worth the same as the
furniture and I should keep the equipment and she would keep the
furniture. Judge Schemp ordered the musical equipment sold and
established May 21 as the date I could pick up my share of the
contents of the house.

Baker, the other attorney, brought up the subject of scores. The
judge ruled that half of them were Kathy's property and that she
could keep them. I raised the point that I needed them to refer to
and the judge said that if I needed to refer to any of the scores in
Kathy's possession I could have them microfilmed.

Kathy wanted me to ship all the musical equipment to her at
Outpost. I said I would prefer to send it directly to whomever she
was going to choose to handle the sale.

Thursday May 21

With Sid as observer, to Outpost to divide such items as dishes
and glassware and the scores. Kathy was attended by Polly
Tribolet. There was resistance. The scores are filed, by year, on
shelves in the basement. When we got to the basement I asked if
she would like to divide the years, I taking the first half, she the
second. She said *she* would take the first half except for certain scores

she especially likes, and "I don't want any of the junk you wrote with Sid." After five hours we had not finished and it was agreed I would come back Saturday.

On Saturday 23, Sid not being available, Charles Blackman accompanied me. There was one especially uncomfortable moment. When it came to the six scores for "Sandburg's Lincoln," Kathy said she wanted all of them. I said I needed them to make a suite a publisher had requested. (True.) She was adamant. So was I. I handed them to Blackman and told him to lock them in his car. Kathy and Polly Tribolet tore them from his hands. I retrieved them, told Blackman to get them into his car quick while Polly Tribolet called me a monster. I said, "I thought you liked me, Polly." She said, "Not any more."

Vic Mizzy, my composer friend, when he recommended Freid to me, paid him a rare compliment. He said, "In college he majored in blood." Bill this month: $2,414.37.

Tuesday June 30

To keep the record consistent, with the payments I have made, and deducting the $2,500 paid by wife, I now owe Mr. Freid $21.37. I didn't want to pay this, just to be mean, but May made me. The Grand Total (for once I approve of the use of the word Grand in this context) paid to Marcus and Freid to achieve this divorce was $24,411.44. I suppose the wife's bills were somewhere in that neighborhood, too, so it might not be an overstatement to say that family law is a good branch of the law to go into. (Reminds me of a young medical school graduate I met once who, when asked what branch of medicine he was going into, said, "Women's ailments. It's easy. You only have to learn about five things, and it is *lucrative.*")

Thursday July 9

We have finished recording the numbers for our *Frankenstein* project. We may have a deal to produce this show with a friend of Dax Xenos's named Pat King, who apparently has access to money.

Wednesday July 15

Sid has brought Edwin Lester into the project and we have done one rewrite for him. We are going to Three Rivers for a final polish on the script before we turn it over to Lester next week so he can start his nit-picking.

Thursday July 16

Pat King has taken a year's option on the show. May suggested we open a *Frankenstein* account to pay the expenses we incur. We went to the bank where I have an account. Carol was not at the New Accounts desk and my favorite teller, Roger, was not at a teller's window. A new girl was at Carol's desk. "Where's Carol?" "She's no longer with us." "Where's Roger?" "He's gone to Brentwood Savings." I said, "Carol and Roger were my favorite people at the bank." She said, "My name is Judy. I'll be your banker." I said I wanted to open an account for a show. She didn't know anything about shows and called the manager, who didn't know about shows either. I said it's like opening an account when you buy an apartment house. You call it the "Fawlty Arms Account" or whatever. They said, "If it's an apartment house why didn't you say so?" I said, "It's not an apartment house, it's a show." They didn't think we could open an account for a show. We prevailed and opened a "Frankenstein Account."

In one of our meetings with Ed Lester, he didn't like the Festival scene and wanted it out. We made the point that send-ups of old forms were selling these days, viz: *Raiders of the Lost Ark*, *Pirates of Penzance*, etc. In this Festival number we have an opportunity to dump on every Civic Light Opera show ever done, and make it funny to boot, something Ed does not especially appreciate.

Friday July 31

Our first meeting with Ed Lester to go over the final script (at least final until a director requests a rewrite) and the new music.

We started presenting the script at two. By 5:30 we had got through 24 pages and the first three songs. We had the usual discussion of the blackout line for Scene 1 in the graveyard. It reminded me of the story of George Kaufman and Marc Connelly in New Haven breaking in a show. Their second act curtain line wasn't getting anything. Next morning they were walking the streets trying to get a new line. Kaufman went into a department store and asked a salesperson if they had any second act curtains.

In Scene 2 Ed objected to Eva saying, "Now the Baron's instruments are sterile—like all the men around here." Also he thought it vulgar to establish Turhan as a homosexual. He objected to having the glass jar containing eyeballs shown. We compromised on an opaque jar. He objected again to the length of the first song, "Paean" and raised his old aversion to the number ending on the word "whore."

Ling, one of Frankenstein's servants, uses the word "headstrong" in one of his lines. Ed maintained the word would not be in Ling's vocabulary. Half an hour later a compromise was reached and the word "stubborn" substituted for "headstrong."

Ed likes the page of dialog of the confrontation between Frankenstein and Heidi, changing only the line, "Never enter the east wing without my permission" to "Don't come into the east wing without my permission."

Saturday August 1

Meet #2. Ed didn't like the way the boy on the tape sang "Welcome Love." Too staccato. I said it was the best we could get for $50. After the Monster is made and the brain seems not to function, Frankenstein says, "There appears to be some dyslogia." Objection from Ed. Audiences won't know the word. We argue it doesn't matter if they don't know the word. The next two lines of dialog explain there's something wrong with the brain, and that the Monster speaks but does not rationalize. We lost.

At one point the Monster is taken to the dungeon. Ed doesn't like the word dungeon. Wants the Monster taken to a cell, a cage, or his quarters.

Lester likes our song "Amo, Amas, Amat" but raises a question about the accent of the words. We have A*mo*, A*mas*, A*mat*. Ed thinks *A*mo, *A*mas, *A*mat is correct. We win. Veni, vidi, vici—50%.

Thursday August 6

The air controllers are on strike, so is the chorus of the Munich Opera. They are employing different strategies. In a performance of *Die Meistersinger* the Munich chorus sang the first two acts and just mouthed the words in the third act. Must have been hilarious.

Thursday September 3

To a meeting of the music branch Executive Committee at the Academy to pass on 19 applications for membership. Seven accepted, nine rejected and three tabled.

Willie Nelson was nominated for an Academy Award for the song "On the Road Again" from *Honeysuckle Rose*. We always consider inviting those non-members who are nominated or get an Award. It was decided that Nelson wasn't really a film songwriter, and that it was best to wait to see if he in fact becomes a part of the film community. Rejected. I said we ought to invite him if only because he looks like he has six months to live.

Dolly Parton, nominated for the song "Nine to Five," tabled. She is adding songs to the score of *The Best Little Whorehouse in Texas*. We are going to wait to see how she does.

Carmine Coppola is asking to be considered for an Award for his score for the 1927 silent film *Napoleon*, 4½ hours of music played by a live 60-piece orchestra. John Addison said his was probably a minority opinion, but when he saw the performance, after a couple of hours he prayed for a moment or two of silence. John said he admired Carmine's stamina, being able at his age to conduct for 4½ hours. I suggested that Carmine be given the Jack LaLanne Award.

Wednesday September 30

Moved into 20540 Pacific Coast Highway.

November

Writing the music for another National Geographic called "Egypt: Quest For Eternity" written and produced by Miriam

Birch who, in a previous incarnation, played one of the strippers in *Gypsy.*

Wednesday December 16

Recorded the "Egypt" music at Motown. Four woodwinds, 5 brass, 2 keyboards, 2 percussion, harp, guitar, 6 violas, 6 cellos (no basses). A nice man named Jihad Racy played nays and buzuqs. His stuff gave the score some authenticity.

1982

Wednesday March 10

May and I to Paris via New York.

In New York we stayed for five days at the Excelsior, a soiled, old, overpainted hotel at 45 West 81st Street across from the Museum of Natural History. (Don't unless you must.)

I like New York. The city stimulates me and the people have a special quality. In front of the Hotel the first morning, nippy and clear, an elderly lady is walking a large German Shepherd. An equally elderly man wearing a watch cap and Nikes, walks briskly by and barks at the dog.

Lunch with Nell and Bill Schneider at the Illustrators Club. He's a past-president.

To the office of the French Line in the World Trade Center to get our tickets and instructions. Irene, a very sharp fiftyish French lady, processes us. (We are going on the *Atlantic Champagne*, a container ship carrying five passengers.)

Wednesday May 26

Since returning from Paris I've been busy balancing my check book, going to the grocery store and doing what every out of work composer does. I am writing another musical. This one is a shortened version of Offenbach's *Orpheus in Hell*, inspired by seeing Peter Brooks' truncated version of *Carmen* in Paris. Gene Lees, once an editor of *Downbeat*, now living in Ojai and turning out a monthly called the *Jazzletter*, is going to do the lyrics.

Sunday July 4

A man named Jim Lipscomb has made a film about trains for the National Geographic Society and is coming out next week to interview me about the music. I hope I get it because if I don't I will have to do one about pandas produced by Miriam Birch. She has ideas about the kind of music she wants in the panda show. She does *not* want the Chinese scale used but thinks a *flute* would be nice.

Thursday July 8

Lunch with Lipscomb, to discuss his train film.

Lipscomb worked with Barry Wood on the Telephone Hour. Wood was on the "Hit Parade" when I was. He is a large, uncouth, funny, vulgar fellow. Lipscomb told about being in Paris once with Wood and going to the Mediterranée, a five star restaurant on the left bank. They had finished their entrée. A waiter passed carrying a beautiful dessert. Barry stopped him and asked what it was. The impeccable waiter said it was a mousse. Barry said it looked good—he'd try some. He took a spoon from the table and scooped a large dollop of it onto his plate. Lipscomb looked at the waiter, who was aghast. Lipscomb wondered what he would do. The waiter paused, then placed the rest of the mousse before Lipscomb and said, "Pour vous, m'sieu."

Back at the offices I saw Linda Reavely, who is happily pregnant at the age of 39. I am going to do her show about platectonics to be called "Born of Fire." In the half-awake half-asleep time this morning, I got the idea to score it for a large brass choir in New York at Liederkranz Hall. Probably won't be able to do it, because Linda is not supposed to fly in the last two months of her term.

Thursday July 29

I have finished my version of *Orpheus*. Finally did the lyrics myself and found I really enjoyed writing them.

Saturday August 28

To the Devine's for dinner. We always pick up Eloise and Pat O'Brien on these evenings because they live nearby in upper Brentwood and don't drive at night. Pat has bad arthritis of the knees and I help him into the car and up the walk. He moves slowly and painfully but when he gets up to tell a story he drops the cane, prances about and when it's over limps back to his chair. He is 83 and he and Eloise and their daughter still go out and play *On Golden Pond* in dinner theatres. He gets $3,500, Eloise gets $1,500. Pat says "They don't know I'd do it for nothing."

Tuesday September 7

Last Thursday dear May hauled me over to Cedars Sinai and bright and early Friday morning Dr. Stephen Sacks did a biopsy. Today he told me I have cancer of the prostate. He gave me the options. Do nothing, have it out, have a radium implant. I told him before I did anything I had a couple of shows to do. He was not concerned about the delay.

Thursday September 30

Ran "Born of Fire," the show on platectonics and the coming disaster in southern California. The last great earthquake here was in 1837—we had those in-betweeners at San Francisco and Sylmar. The show warns we are due for a biggie. It will probably be accompanied by a 36-foot tidal wave.

Thursday November 11

Update on the fate of my version of *Orpheus*. I sent it to eleven producers and opera companies. Beverly Sills rejected it, nicely, by return mail, another person called on the telephone from New York and said he didn't know what to do with it. The other nine are silent so far. It is almost as though one sends one's oeuvre out into space never to be heard from again.

Thursday December 16

Linda, Dale Bell, Bob Brubaker and Jack Tillar came down to hear me demonstrate the "Born of Fire" score. Silly, the way the post production phase on these National Geographics is organized: You write the music before the writer has finished concocting the narration, because music recording is scheduled some days before they call in the narrator to do his stuff. You are, however, given a general idea of what he is going to say. Tonight there was a good example of the idiocy of this system. At one point in the film there is a high shot of a tiny speck in the Atlantic ocean, one of the Icelandic islands, and the narrator, according to Linda when she turned the film over to me, was going to say just that: "A tiny speck in the Atlantic ocean." I started the cue with a high violin line, answered in canon by the lower strings in their upper registers, producing a stark and lonely effect. When I described this instrumentation and played the phrase, Linda said, "That won't do." I got a little mad and said, "That's what I hear for a tiny speck in the ocean." Here is the problem of the writer who is off somewhere composing the narration while you are doing the music: I am further along with the music than he is with the narration, because he doesn't have the same deadline I have. However, Linda had received the page referring to the speck that very day, and Ted Strauss had added four words that made my approach wrong. The description now went, "The island of Heimay, a tiny speck in the Atlantic ocean *lashed by wintry gales* ..." The next day I got un-mad and gave the lines to trumpets and horns.

You cannot satisfactorily demonstrate an orchestral score on a piano, especially if you play as badly as I do, but I got through it successfully.

1983

Wednesday January 12

Yesterday we recorded "Born of Fire." Everybody happy except in the last four bars of the end credits, Linda didn't like the ending. When we got through interpreting what she didn't like it turned out she wanted the last note to go down, not up. So we did it that way and she was happy. Kindly explain that to me.

Today we recorded the Panda music and Miriam was ecstatic with the way Bud Shank played the flute parts.

Saturday January 29

This month we have had great storms, high tides and rain. The stairway to the beach was washed away—at least the bottom eight feet of it—and our bulkhead was demolished. The bulkhead is protected on the seaward side by riprap rocks and on the house side by sand piled up to its top. The sea removed the sand, leaving the bulkhead unsupported. Sand was lost around the Malibu Pier and the seaward end collapsed. Pilings were carried along the beach and we got our share of them, attacking the pilings under our houses. The racket was fearsome. Tonight I went down to investigate the noise, forgot about the missing stairway and fell to the rocks below. The sea was breaking under the house to a depth of about three feet. Young Duane from next door threw me a rope and hauled me out. Didn't break anything but mighty stiff and sore. A man up the beach in the same situation was drowned.

Wednesday March 9

Tonight May and I gave a party for Miriam Birch and 40 of her friends to watch the Panda show broadcast. I had not seen the show as dubbed, and was surprised to discover that Birch had made extensive changes in the score. I know the producer has the contractual right to do what he or she will with the music but I object to the fact that I was not told. It's an old story. The show was flawed because they didn't have enough footage of the pandas and devoted a lot of time to people doing scientific things. I very carefully designed some cues to give these areas added interest and wrote a couple of pieces with emotional content, using the strings, for two high points in the film which were replaced with reprints of some of the earlier cues featuring Bud Shank on flute. This music was what you might call surface music, describing scenes of China. The music describing the emotional involvement of the characters was not surface, it delved beneath the surface, leaving the realm of abstract, and became specific.

I questioned Tillar, who was at the party, on what happened at the first run with the music as written. He told me that when the emotional strings came on Barry Nye, the supervising cutter, looked at Birch and said two words, "Lush Life" (an allusion to a lovely, complex tune composed by Billy Strayhorn and widely recorded). Birch replaced the strings with the Bud Shank flute phrases she had fallen in love with. I am one of those unfortunate musicians who, when he sits down to write, has to have confidence in what he writes, the confidence that it will survive. Hitchcock never changed a note of my music (except for the re-do of the fireworks music in *Catch a Thief*, to get him off the hook with the front office). Neither did Norman Lloyd or Joan Harrison or Lawrence Weingarten.

Friday April 8

I am reading William Goldman's book *Adventures in the Screen Trade* in which he says that the single best demonstrated fact of the entire movie industry is:

NOBODY KNOWS ANYTHING.

CODA

I had planned to close this journal as follows:

Lyn Murray, who perished at (time) on (date) attempting to swim the Los Angeles River, had his ashes hauled to the middle of the Santa Catalina Channel and committed to the deep from the stern of an 18' Boston whaler by Bobby Bain, guitar, and Milton Kestenbaum, bass, at an unseemly hour this morning because both had an early call at Fox. (The swimming of the Los Angeles River would have to be carefully timed because it is usually dry.)

This ending has not yet been invoked.

Pacific Palisades
May 19, 1986

INDEX

381

I n d e x